present volume are in many ways typical of Hill. They reflect his remarkably wide reading in secondary and printed primary sources, his fondness for unorthodox topics and relatively neglected figures and movements, and his attempt to combine a broadly sociological approach to history with a keen interest in religious ideas and cultures. The book will undoubtedly be an important contribution to the field." – Malcolm Smuts, *University of Massachusetts, Boston.*

The Author:

CHRISTOPHER HILL was formerly Master of Balliol College, Oxford. He was a fellow of All Souls from 1934 to 1938, Assistant Lecturer in Modern History, University College, Cardiff, from 1936 to 1938, Fellow and Tutor at Balliol College from 1938 to 1965, and Master of Balliol College from 1965 to 1978. He is the author of many books, including *God's Englishman: Oliver Cromwell and the English Revolution, Antichrist in Seventeenth Century England, Change and Continuity in Seventeenth Century England, Milton and the English Revolution, The Experience of Defeat: Milton and Some Contemporaries* and *The Collected Essays, Volume I: Writing and Revolution in Seventeenth-Century England.*

The Collected Essays of
CHRISTOPHER
Hill

The Collected Essays of
CHRISTOPHER
Hill

Volume Two
Religion and Politics in
17th Century England

THE UNIVERSITY OF MASSACHUSETTS PRESS
Amherst

© Christopher Hill 1986

First published in the United States of America
in 1986 by the University of Massachusetts Press
Box 429 Amherst Ma 01004

Printed in Great Britain by Anchor Brendon Ltd, Tiptree, Essex

Library of Congress Cataloging in Publication Data
(Revised for vol. 2)

Hill, Christopher, 1912-
  The collected essays of Christopher Hill.

  Includes bibliographical references and index.
  Contents: 1. Writing and revolution in 17th-century
England — v.   2.   Religion and politics in seventeenth-
century England.
  1. Great Britain — History — Stuarts, 1603-1714 —
Collected works. 2. English literature — 17th century —
History and criticism — Collected works. 3. Literature
and society — Great Britain — Collected works. I. Title.
DA375.H54   1985   941.06   84-16446

ISBN 0-87023-467-6 (v. 1)
ISBN 0-87023-503-6 (v. 2)

Contents

Preface   vii
Acknowledgments   x
Abbreviations   xi

I   Introductory   1
   1.   History and Denominational History   3
   2.   The Necessity of Religion   11

II   The First Century of the Church of England   19
   3.   The Protestant Nation   21
   4.   The Problem of Authority   37
   5.   The State-Ecclesiastical   51
   6.   From Grindal to Laud   63

III   Heresy and Radical Politics   87
   7.   From Lollards to Levellers   89
   8.   Sin and Society   117
   9.   Dr Tobias Crisp (1600-43)   141
   10.   Antinomianism in 17th-century England   162
   11.   The Religion of Gerrard Winstanley   185

IV   The Millennium and After   253
   12.   John Reeve, Laurence Clarkson and
      Lodowick Muggleton   255
   13.   "Till the conversion of the Jews"   269
   14.   Occasional Conformity and the Grindalian
      Tradition   301
   15.   God and the English Revolution   321

Index   343

For Victor Kiernan
— wit, provocateur and
generous friend for
fifty years

Preface

As with a preceding volume, *Writing and Revolution in 17th Century England*, the pieces collected here are based on lectures, articles and reviews written over the past twenty years or so. Some have been substantially rewritten, and I have tried to remove repetitions and contradictions. I hope allowance will be made for the diverse origins of these occasional pieces. I should like to think I have been fairly consistent in my attitude towards the relationship of religion, economics and politics in seventeenth-century England. When I first started working on the period it was necessary, many of us thought, to challenge the then dominant concept of "the Puritan Revolution" and to establish, with the help of Marx, Weber and Tawney, that sixteenth- and seventeenth-century religious beliefs were related to the societies in which they arose.

But in the nineteen-fifties, with the gentry controversy, religion was abruptly thrown out of the window; and it became necessary to recall that those who lived through the Revolution thought religion more important than economics; to recall that Independency and Roman Catholicism were not just beliefs which gentlemen took up when their debts overwhelmed them, that the ecclesiastical patronage of peers was at least as important as their ownership of manors. But now, predictably, hemlines are coming down again. We are told, rightly, that when gentlemen had to choose sides in the civil war which started in 1642, religion was probably more decisive than any other single cause. What happened in the mid-century, Dr Morrill tells us, was not the first of the great revolutions but the last of the wars of religion.[1] Well, yes of course, in a sense; I think German Marxist historians are saying something similar when they call the Peasants' Revolt of 1525 the first bourgeois revolution.

But in stressing the importance of religion in both upheavals we should beware of isolating "religion" as a self-sufficient factor unrelated to this-worldly concerns. In a society in which church and state were one, where many ecclesiastics were great landowners and

vii

all incumbents collected tithes from their unwilling parishioners, where church courts punished "sin" — in such a society "religion" meant something fundamentally different from what it means today. It is important that we should not forget the sociological insights which have helped recent historians to recapture a richer and more all-round understanding of the German Reformation and the English Revolution, an understanding closer to that of contemporaries. Brian Manning has argued (to me convincingly) that the civil war came to look like a religious war only when the middling sort began to play a larger part on the Parliamentarian side. This was both consequence and cause of the deepening of the Revolution.[2] If I appear to labour this point in the present volume, it is because I think it may be forgotten in the excitement of rediscovering that those who lived and strove and suffered in the seventeenth century were not statistical automata. We must not go back to the facile anachronism of "the Puritan Revolution": though at least that phrase did recognize that there was a revolution.

Many people have helped me in preparing this volume. I have tried to acknowledge specific debts in the notes. I am especially grateful for help and encouragement to Norman O. Brown, Leland Carlson, Patrick Collinson, Penelope Corfield, Margot Heinemann, Ann Hughes, James Jacob, Margaret Jacob, Richard Popkin, Barry Reay, Judith Richards, David Taylor, Mayir Vereté and David Zaret. Joyce Appleby very kindly sent me a copy of her *Capitalism and a New Social Order* just in time to make me see (or think I saw) connections between themes in my own book which I hadn't fully appreciated. John Morrill and Geoffrey Nuttall were generous with their time and patience in helping me to avoid repeating errors I have made in previous books. None of these is responsible for what I have obstinately persisted in saying. I am very grateful to the staff of Harvester Press for the courtesy and skill with which they handled a difficult typescript. Bridget encouraged, consoled and stimulated all the time, and crowned everything by helping with the index.

I have modernized spelling, capitalization and punctuation except in titles of books. All books quoted were printed in London unless otherwise stated.

3 January 1985.

NOTES

1. J.S.Morrill, "The Religious Context of the English Civil War", *T.R.H.S.*, fifth series, 34 (1984), p. 178.
2. Manning, "Religion and Politics: the Godly People", in *Politics, Religion and the Civil War* (ed. Manning, 1973), pp. 83-123.

Acknowledgments

Earlier versions of many of the pieces collected in this volume were originally published elsewhere. I am grateful for permission to include them in this collection.

"History and Denominational History" appeared in *The Baptist Quarterly* (XXII, 1967). "From Grindal to Laud" incorporates material from reviews which appeared in *Economic History Review*, New Series, XX (1967), *Journal of Religious History*, 11 (1981), *The Times Literary Supplement*, 18 March 1983, *Journal of Ecclesiastical History*, 35 (1984). "Dr. Tobias Crisp" was originally published in *Balliol Studies* (ed. J. M. Prest, Leopard's Head Press, 1982). "The Religion of Gerrard Winstanley" appeared as *Past and Present Supplement*, No.5 (1978); for "John Reeve, Laurence Clarkson and Lodowick Muggleton" I have drawn on material from a discussion in *Past and Present*, No.104 (1984): these are reprinted with the permission of the Past and Present Society. "From Lollards to Levellers" was originally published in a Festschrift for A.L. Morton, *Rebels and their Causes* (ed. M. Cornforth, Lawrence and Wishart, 1978). "Occasional Conformity" first appeared in a Festschrift for Geoffrey Nuttall, *Reformation, Conformity and Dissent* (ed. R.B. Knox, Epworth Press, 1977). "God and the English Revolution" was printed in *History Workshop Journal*, 17 (1984).

Abbreviations

The following abbreviations have been used in the notes:

C.S.P.D. (Ven.)(Scottish)	*Calendar of State Papers, Domestic (Venetian) (Scottish)*
D.N.B.	*Dictionary of National Biography.*
H.M.C.	Historical Manuscripts Commission
M.E.R.	*C. Hill, Milton and the English Revolution* (1977; Penguin edn., 1979).
M.C.P.W.	Ed. D.M. Wolfe, *Complete Prose Works of John Milton* (Yale U.P., 8 vols., 1953-82).
P. and P.	*Past and Present*
T.R.H.S.	*Transactions of the Royal Historical Society*
U.P.	University Press
V.C.H.	*Victoria County History.*
W.T.U.D.	C. Hill, *The World Turned Upside Down* (Penguin edn., 1975). First published 1972.

I Introductory

1. *History and Denominational History*[1]

"The Church of England hath three main divisions: the Conformist, the Non-Conformist, and the Separatist." *

The principal headache of the historian — at least of the sixteenth and seventeenth century historian — is not too few documents but too many predecessors. Much of his work consists in sifting and criticizing the writings of previous scholars, whose conclusions have often ceased to carry conviction with professional historians by the time they have become commonplace in the school text-books. Now there is, of course, an element of academic show-off here: demonstrating the folly of your elders and betters is always a good way to earn a reputation, even if a transient one. But there is more to it than that. Each generation naturally and necessarily questions the assumptions of its predecessors, assumptions which spring from and change with the society in which historians, like everyone else, live. Fresh questions are asked about the present, and things which one generation took for granted are called in question by its successor. It is difficult, in this healthy process, to avoid the appearance of ingratitude towards the great historians of the past. But we can see further, if we do see further, only because we pygmies are standing on the shoulders of giants. Anything I say here must be premised by this apology.

With that premise, many historians today would I think agree that, especially in the sphere of the religious history of Europe in the sixteenth and seventeenth centuries, there is some criticizing to be done. Considerable confusion was caused by historians, great historians in some cases, writing the history of their own sect, looking for its origins, and so tending to draw dividing lines more sharply

---

*Lord Brooke, *A Discourse opening the Nature of that Episcopacie, which is Exercised in England* (1642), p. 87.

3

than contemporaries would have done. Having assumed that their predecessors held (or ought to have held) the same views as they did, these historians rebuked the men of the sixteenth and seventeenth centuries for failing to live up to nineteenth-century standards.

To the nineteenth-century historian protestants were protestants and Catholics were Catholics; the criteria for distinguishing between them seemed perfectly clear, even if there was some blurring towards the centre. But when we are considering English history between, say, 1530 and 1560, it is much less certain how many English men and women thought of themselves as either "protestants" or "Catholics". If they asked such questions at all, most would probably think of themselves as members of a Church of England whose doctrine and discipline were at times subject to changes from on top, the full import of which would not be obvious in the localities. This was true of clergymen as well as of the laity: it is much the most satisfactory explanation of the fact that the overwhelming majority of the clergy who survived from 1545 to 1560 held on to their livings in a church which (in our modern terminology) was successively Anglo-Catholic, protestant, radical protestant, Roman Catholic, and then again protestant — if that is the word for the Elizabethan settlement! They were not chameleons, nor were most of them any less high-principled than we are: the lines of division were not so clear-cut for most contemporaries as they seem to the historian looking through his end of the telescope. There were of course men who did feel that profound issues of principle were involved, like the Marian martyrs and some of those who condemned them to the flames. But the vast majority of the martyrs were laymen, not clerics: it is arguable that most of them were backward-looking Lollards rather than forward-looking protestants. Many of them would certainly have won Elizabeth's disapproval.

The same consideration applies equally strongly to the next period of rapid development and transformation, the years between 1600 and 1660. Patrick Collinson emphasized that the search for sectarian origins may impose a retrospective strait-jacket on a struggling reality. "To make the problem of denominational history one of simple genealogy is to face difficulties in the period 1604-40, where it is hard to trace much continuity of either leadership or ideas. It is at least equally desirable to conduct the search in the half-formed attitudes and positions adopted in the inchoate groups of the godly-minded which never acquired a label through separation".[2] Environment is more important than heredity in the evolution of ideas. Sectarian lines of division begin to be clearly drawn only when the possibility and the necessity of the co-existence of different religious bodies has been accepted: it certainly had not been accepted by more than a tiny minority of Englishmen before 1640. Most of the small groups of émigrés in Holland and New England, even those who had most self-consciously separated from what they regarded as the corruptions of the Church of England, still hoped for the total reformation of the state church. Robert Browne's slogan, "reformation without tarrying for any", implied that men separated in order to reunite. It is easy for historians looking backwards to think they see sharper lines of division than contemporaries could. Before 1640, as Professor Haller warily pointed out, a congregation was much more likely to be swayed by the personality — often the developing personality — of its preacher than by attachment to any theological "-ism"[3] We should see diversity in a united opposition to Laudian control of the state church rather than an alliance of consciously differing religious communities.

When after 1640 the sectaries emerged from their underground existence in England, or returned from exile, their new freedom kept the situation fluid. Congregations expanded rapidly, and account had to be taken of the views of the newcomers; there were many "sermon-tasters", or "seekers", who went from congregation to congregation, some genuinely questing for truth, others out of curiosity or a desire to make mischief. It was long indeed before clear-cut lines of sectarian division were imposed on this flux. Bunyan's Bedford congregation, looking back to the early sixteen-fifties, said that its members "neither were nor yet desired to be embodied into fellowship according to the order of the Gospel; only they had in some measure separated themselves from the prelatical superstition, and had agreed to search after the nonconformity-men, such as in those days did bear the name of Puritans".[4] The Broadmead Baptist church at Bristol started in the sixteen-thirties as a meeting of "awakened souls and honest-minded people" with no doctrinal allegiances. They were all laymen, who separated "from the worship of the world" but were willing to listen to carefully selected ordained ministers. They so continued for over twenty years.[5] It was such non-sectarian congregations that George Fox found waiting for him all over the north of England when he rode thither in 1651-2.

Presbyterians from Queen Elizabeth's time to 1640, and indeed to

1662, were never willingly sectarian. They hoped for the transformation of the Church of England into a Presbyterian church.
They wanted to change its management, not to abolish it.[6] It is
therefore absurd, as well as anachronistic, to differentiate before
1640 between "Puritans" and "Anglicans". "Puritans" were just as
much Anglicans as the "episcopalians" or "Laudians" or whatever
we choose to call them. To place "Puritans" in opposition to
"Anglicans" suggests that the latter held the "true" tradition and
the former are odd men out: it assumes the hindsight of after 1660.[7]
The early history of the Church of England had been one of
permanent reformation; there was no reason to suppose that this
process had come to an end in 1559. Even if it had, the Elizabethan
settlement contained room for Puritans as well as conformists. The
word "Anglican" is appropriate as a sectarian label only after 1662,
when "dissenters" had withdrawn and "nonconformists" had been
extruded from the national church.

Henry Burton, for instance, whom historians call an Independent,
thought it was the Laudian bishops who were disrupting the unity of
the state church. "They have laboured to bring in a change in
doctrine; in discipline; in the civil government; in the prayer-books
set forth by public authority; in the rule of faith, and in the
customs".[8] Many who were to remain within the church agreed with
him in regarding Laudianism as a brief aberration. Lord Brooke
thought the Laudian prelates had been the true schismatics.[9] So did
two preachers of Fast Sermons in 1644, as well as Francis Cheynell in
1648 and John Milton in 1660.[10] For long after 1640 such men hoped
for a reformed Church of England which would be acceptable to
many of those who had felt forced to separate. Before 1662, at
earliest, most of those whom we call Presbyterians and Independents,
and some of those whom we call Baptists, still believed in a national
church, and their ministers were prepared to accept its livings and its
tithes. A circular signed by Independents among other divines of the
Westminster Assembly, for instance, urged "all ministers and people
...to forbear, for a convenient time, the joining of themselves into
church societies of any kind whatsoever, until they see whether the
right rule will not be commended to them in this orderly way". (The
Five Dissenting Brethren were rebuked by the nineteenth century
historian of Congregationalism as having "much to learn in relation
to religious freedom".)[11] The necessity of a state church was still
being expounded in the Independent Savoy Declaration of 1658;

Yarmouth Independents in 1659 defended tithes against Quaker criticisms, and professed their "utter dislike and abhorrence of a universal toleration, as being contrary to the mind of God in His word". ("It is very evident", commented another nineteenth century historian, "that though they had learned much, they were not already perfect; . . . it was necessary that they should again go into the school of affliction.") [12]

The Cromwellian state church of the sixteen-fifties included men whom we should today, no doubt, label "Anglican", "Presbyterian", "Congregationalist" and "Baptist". But it also included many men, and indeed many leaders, whom it is difficult to pigeonhole in this way at all. The disagreements among historians as to the exact sectarian classification of an individual or a congregation is the best evidence that what they are trying to do is unsatisfactory because anachronistic. Richard Baxter rejected in advance the label "Presbyterian" which historians continue to put upon him during this period. As late as 1672 John Bunyan registered himself and his congregation as Congregationalist; in the sixteen fifties many congregations could be described equally well as Congregationalist or Baptist. They practised intercommunion. Who knows what label to attach to Oliver Cromwell, John Milton, Major-General Fleetwood, John Ireton, Colonel John Hutchinson and Lucy his wife? If we cannot classify such well-documented figures as these, it is absurd to try to be more precise about men who have left fewer traces.

In time those sects whose community of believers was united by covenant or adult baptism lost hope of recapturing the state church from which they had seceded; they accepted the permanent status of sectaries. The unique freedom of the forties and fifties hastened this process by enabling far more national organisation on a sectarian basis than had ever before been possible. The Particular Baptists for instance organized themselves sufficiently to have evolved a Confession by 1644. But in the sixteen-fifties Baptists were still quarrelling among themselves about the lawfulness of taking tithes — which means about the lawfulness of a state church,[13] and some few Baptists actually held livings in, and acted as Triers for, the Cromwellian church. The Quakers I think were the first sect organised on a national scale which rejected any possibility of compromise with the state church. They consistently denounced its "hireling priests" and its "steeple-houses". But the Quakers themselves embraced many trends of thought, bellicose as well as pacifist, political as well as quietist, until George Fox united them into a sect after 1660.

Quaker influence may have helped to harden Baptist attitudes. By the end of the fifties Quakers, General and Particular Baptists were nationally organized as sects. After 1662 they were joined, extremely reluctantly, by Congregationalists and Presbyterians. The latter were deliberately excluded from the restored episcopalian church, which rejected the idea, put forward by Baxter and others, of returning to something like the pre-Laudian state church in which there had been many mansions. In 1672 John Owen spoke of those "who separate, or rather are driven from, the present public worship". He claimed that dissenters were the true Church of England.[14]

Occasional conformity, the habit of going to the services of the Church of England once a year or so, was often practised in the later seventeenth and eighteenth centuries as a means by which nonconformists could qualify themselves for state office. For this reason it has been denounced as a hypocritical practice, and so no doubt it often became in the eighteenth century. But occasional conformity sprang from the logic of John Owen's position, and indeed has a very respectable intellectual ancestry.

Before 1640 only a very small minority were separatists on fixed principle, and they almost certainly hoped that their separation would lead to reunion — either as a consequence of the abolition of bishops, or of the rule of the saints or of the personal appearance of Jesus. Men like Henry Jacob and the New England Independents wished to retain some communion with the national church. Even Robert Browne in 1588 had envisaged something not unlike the Cromwellian state church when he said: "The civil magistrates have their right in all causes to judge and set order, and it is intolerable presumption for particular persons to scan of every magistrate's gifts or authority, or to deny them the power of judging ecclesiastical causes. ...If again it be said that while men might take and refuse their ministers as they list, all factions and heresies might grow, I answer that the civil magistrate must restrain that licentiousness. But the way to restrain it is prescribed of God. ...None be suffered to have their voice or right in choosing church offices and officers but only such as are tried to be sufficiently grounded and tried to be able to give a reason of their faith and religion. And that the civil magistrates may, if they will, be both present and directors of the choice, yet permitting any man to make just exceptions against them which are to be chosen."[15]

Congregationalists and some Baptists participated in Cromwell's state church, side by side with Episcopalians and Presbyterians, and many whose views were indeterminate by our standards. This confusion (as it seems to us) immensely strengthened the hand of the bishops after 1660. Take John Tombes, for instance. Doctrinally he was a Baptist. But he is not usually claimed by Baptist historians because he held a living from 1630 to 1662, and in his licence under the Indulgence of 1672 he described himself as a Presbyterian. On his death-bed he declared that he dared not separate from communion with the Church of England "any farther than by going out of church whilst that office [baptism] was performed, and returning in again when it was ended".[16] Thomas Grantham, who is accepted as a Baptist by Baptist historians, was buried in St. Stephen's Church, Norwich, by the vicar of that church, who was later himself buried in the same grave.[17] The Presbyterian Philip Henry was also buried in his parish church.[18]

When popery threatened again under James II the firm stand of the Seven Bishops no doubt contributed to Presbyterian willingness to consider comprehension once more in 1689. So though the practice of occasional conformity may ultimately have degenerated into a device by which dissenters dishonestly qualified themselves for government office, it was in origin the outward sign, among those forced into separation, of the continuing hope that a church uniting all protestant Englishmen might still be realizable. Oliver Cromwell's state church deserves more attention from those interested in protestant reunion: so too does the maligned practice of occasional conformity.[19]

Above all we need continual vigilance to preserve a historical attitude towards the evolution of bodies of worshippers who after 1662 became dissenters. We must neither attribute to them views which crystallized only later, nor criticize them too severely for not knowing what their successors were going to think. "We are the men of the present age!" cried the Leveller Richard Overton; he and his contemporaries must be studied as they were, warts and all, in relation to the society in which they lived: just as the assumptions and beliefs of our generation will one day be the subject of (one hopes) charitably relativistic historical enquiry.

NOTES

1. A lecture to the Baptist Historical Society, printed in *The Baptist Quarterly*, XXII (1967).
2. Collinson, *The Elizabethan Puritan Movement* (1967), p. 372; *Godly People: Essays on English Protestantism and Puritanism* (1983), p. 14; cf. pp. 15-17 and Chapter 20 *passim*.
3. W. Haller, *The Rise of Puritanism* (1938), pp. 179-80.
4. Ed. G.B. Harrison, *The Church Book of Bunyan Meeting, 1650-1821* (1928), p. 1.
5. Ed. R. Hayden, *The Records of a Church of Christ in Bristol, 1640-1687*, Bristol Record Soc., XXVII (1974), pp. 83-8.
6. See p. 305 below.
7. The title of J.F.H. New's *Anglican and Puritan: the Basis of their Opposition, 1558-1640* (Stanford U.P., 1964) makes my point. But I am sad to see that even Collinson falls into the same error, referring to those whom "we are bound, for want of a less anachronistic label, to call Anglicans" (*Godly People*) p. 1. It seems to me wrong as well as anachronistic, as no one has demonstrated better than Patrick Collinson. Contrast Barbara Lewalski, *Protestant Poetics and the Seventeenth-Century Religious Lyric* (Princeton U.P., 1979) p. 434.
8. Burton's sermon, *God and the King*, is quoted by J. Waddington, *Congregational History, 1567-1700* (1874), p. 338.
9. *A Discourse ... of ... Episcopacie*, pp. 92-5.
10. John Strickland, *Immanuel, or The Church Triumphing in God with Us* (1644), p. 32; Thomas Hill, *The Right Separation Encouraged* (1644), p. 65; Milton, *Brief Notes Upon a late Sermon* (1660), in *M.C.P.W.*, VII, p. 486. For Cheynell see pp. 80, 302 below.
11. Waddington, *op. cit.*, pp. 426, 430.
12. J. Browne, *History of Congregationalism ... in Norfolk and Suffolk* (1877), pp. 167, 225-6.
13. B.R. White, "The Organisation of the Particular Baptists, 1644-1660", *Journal of Ecclesiastical History*, XVII, pp. 211, 223-4.
14. J. Owen, *Discourse on Christian Love and Peace* (1672), in Works (ed. W.H. Goold, 1850-3), XV, p. 102; *The Nature and Causes of Apostacy* (1676), *Works*, VII, p. 74; cf. p. 133, XV, pp. 184-5, 345-58. See Chapter 14 below.
15. Robert Browne, *An Aunswere to Mr. Floweres letter*, in *The Writings of Robert Harrison and Robert Browne* (ed. A. Peel and L.H. Carlson, 1953), pp. 521-2. See Avihu Zakai, *Exile and Kingdom: Reformation, Separation and the Millennial Quest in the Formation of Massachusetts and its Relationship with England* (Ann Arbor, 1984), *passim*, for the continuing acceptance of this principle by New England divines.
16. A.C. Underwood, *A History of the English Baptists* (1947), pp. 69-70.
17. *Ibid.*, p. 111.
18. Ed. M.H. Lee, *Diaries and Letters of Philip Henry* (1882), pp. 379-82.
19. See Chapter 14 below.

2. *The Necessity of Religion*[1]

"Take away kings, princes, rulers, magistrates, judges and such estates of God's order, no man shall ride or go by the way unrobbed, no man shall sleep in his own house or bed unkilled, no man shall keep his wife, children and possessions in quietness, all things shall be common. . . . Wherefore let us subjects do our bounden duties, giving hearty thanks to God, and praying for the preservation of this godly order."*

Whether or not we think of the sixteenth and seventeenth centuries as "an age of faith", there can be no doubt that contemporaries thought of religion as necessary to the maintenance of civil order and of the state power which defended that order. William Thomas, Clerk of the Council in Edward VI's reign, asked the King "whether religion, besides the honour of God, be not also the greatest stay of civil order? And whether the unity thereof ought not to be preserved with the sword and rigour?"[2] "How vile a treason is heresy", declared a pamphlet against Wyatt.[3]

This note runs throughout the *Homilies*. Whitgift told Elizabeth that "religion is the foundation and cement of human societies", a commonplace which he used to urge that ministers should not be "exposed to poverty", lest "religion itself . . . be exposed to scorn and become contemptible".[4] The free-thinking Christopher Marlowe agreed with the Archbishop: "the first beginning of religion was only to keep men in awe".[5] Robert Burton the anatomist, a parson and not an irreligious man, wrote, disapprovingly but realistically, "it hath ever been a principal axiom with them [politicians] to maintain religion or superstition, which they determine of, alter and vary upon all occasions, as to them seems best; they make religion a mere policy, a cloak, a human invention. . . . No way better to curb than superstition, to terrify men's consciences and to keep them in awe: they make new laws, statutes, invent new religions, ceremonies,

---

* *An Exhortation concerning Good Order and Obedience to Rulers and Magistrates,* in *Sermons or Homilies appointed to be read in churches in the time of Queen Elizabeth of famous memory* (Oxford U.P., 1802, p. 88).

11

as so many stalking horses to their ends. . . . What devices, traditions,
ceremonies have they [priests] not invented in all ages to keep men in
obedience, to enrich themselves?"[6]

Helen White noted that "the maintenance of religion and the
maintenance of the existing civil social order were viewed as inter-
dependent by the preachers, both those who were fairly well satisfied
with the existing religious settlement, and those who wished to see
it substantially changed".[7] Neither group, that is to say, envisaged a
society in which inequalities of property did not exist, nor the state
power necessary to maintain them. Crowley with some simplicity
expressed the view that preachers taught the poor:

> "To pay all with patience
>   That their landlords demand;
> For they for their sufferance
>   In such oppression
> Are promised reward
>   In the resurrection".[8]

When the Revolution came, this useful function of religion was
noted on both sides. The Marquis of Newcastle impressed on his
pupil, the future Charles II: "Were there no heaven or hell you shall
see the disadvantage for your government. . . . If no obedience to
God, then none to your Highness". Newcastle disliked sermons; he
much preferred homilies, which should limit themselves to preaching
(1) that Christ is our saviour; (2) the desirability of living a godly life
and (3) instruction to the people in "their obedience to their
superiors and governors, with all the respects that may be".[9] Peace,
thought the gentle Izaak Walton, can "never be expected till God
shall bless the common people of this nation with a belief *that schism
is a sin — and they not fit to judge what is schism*".[10]

There was thus nothing new in the view of the pamphleteer who
expected "those that say in their heart there is no God" nevertheless
to be ready to "allow the political convenience of persuading the
people otherwise".[11] Sir William Petty in his cold scientific way drew
up a balance between the social advantages of religion — making men
behave well even when not under observation, making the poor
cheerful and patient, giving strength to oaths — and its costs and
disadvantages to science. He concluded "civil laws may for the most
part effect what religion pretendeth to do".[12] Charles II, pupil of
both Newcastle and Hobbes, continued to believe that "an implicit-

ness in religion is necessary for the safety of government, and he looks upon all inquisitiveness into those things as mischievous to the state". This, Burnet tells us, was "an odd opinion".[13] How did the commonplaces of the Book of Homilies become "odd opinions" for a Whig bishop? Religion still continues to play a social role; but it is no longer an authoritarian, undiscussable creed. Something has happened to society which makes relatively free discussion even of fundamental philosophical problems possible within the framework of the existing law and order. The wild peasant revolts and communist heresies of the Middle Ages have been tamed. Religion was — or seemed to be — a prime mover in the sixteenth century; it certainly was not in the eighteenth century.

Not only was religion held to be indispensible to society, the church to the state, but before 1640 it was difficult to distinguish between them. Even before he became Head of the English church Henry VIII issued in 1530 a proclamation against "blasphemous and pestiferous English books" which were being sent to England with the dual object of perverting the people from the true Catholic faith and of stirring them to sedition against their prince. The 39 Articles of the Church of England come right down into the political arena, pronouncing on the subject of the civil magistrate, the righteousness of private property and the legitimacy of oaths demanded by the magistrate. John Selden pointed out that many of the 39 Articles "do not contain matter of faith. Is it matter of faith how the Church should be governed? Whether infants should be baptized? Whether we have property in our goods?"[14] But if not articles of faith, all these matters were of key importance to the state as it existed before 1640. The Homilies are even more manifestly political, notably the Homily against Disobedience and Wilful Rebellion, originally aimed at Papists but couched in the most general terms:

"All kings, queens and other governors are specially appointed by the ordinance of God", and therefore should be obeyed, good or bad, just as servants must obey their masters. "What a perilous thing were it to commit unto the subjects the judgment, which prince is wise and godly, and his government good, and which is otherwise; as though the foot must judge of the head". Only "the worst men" even raise such questions. Rebellion is "worse than the government of the worst prince"; since opinions are bound to differ, freedom in this respect would mean that "no realm should ever be without rebellion".[15]

Since it was assumed on all sides that in England there could be only one church, control of this church was a highly political question, a question of power. By the circumstances of England's Reformation, church and monarchy were inextricably linked. Bishop Bancroft believed that Puritan demands for modification of the settlement of the church in 1559 were in effect demands for a change of government in the state.[16] Elizabethan judges regularly accused Puritans who had conscientious scruples about the forms of discipline established in the church of being "rebels", to their extreme indignation.[17]

If religion is necessary to any government, bishops are especially necessary to monarchy. Sir Robert Cecil, for instance, said in 1605 that Puritans "dream of nothing but a new hierarchy, directly opposite to the state of a monarchy". They wish "to break all the bonds of unity to nourish schism in the church and common-wealth".[18] "The discipline of the Church of England by bishops etc.", wrote Bacon, "is fittest for monarchy, of all others. . . . It is most dangerous in a state to give ear to the least alterations in government". The existing government of the church could scarcely be abandoned without "perilous operation upon the kingdom". Reformation was necessary, but it must proceed from the state and not from the people.[19] Sectaries are inconsistent with monarchy, he advised the future Duke of Buckingham.[20] So Cottington was not making a new point when he declared: "The truth is, Mr. Prynne would have a new church, a new government, a new King; for he would make the people altogether offended with all things at present".[21]

Hooker is the most theoretically respectable exponent of the hierarchical view. The title of *The Laws of Ecclesiastical Polity* illustrates the point I am labouring. When Hooker published his first five books few indeed of his opponents would have disputed his starting position, that all who are born in England are automatically members of the English church. Sir John Eliot expressed himself with some vigour: "Religion only it is that fortifies all policy. . . . The strength of all government is religion. . . . Religion it is that keeps the subject in obedience, as being taught by God to honour his vicegerents". Eliot perhaps thought this view more important to be taught to the mass of the people: in the same treatise he spoke of the excitability of the House of Commons on religious matters as a weakness which he did not share; but went on to explain for the benefit of posterity that the security of the state was involved in such questions.[22]

By 1640 Rudyerd on the Parliamentarian side, no less than Laud on the government's, strikes a more urgent note: "If we secure our religion, we shall cut off and defeat many plots that are now on foot. ... They who would introduce another religion into the church must first trouble and disorder the government of the state, that so they may work their ends in a confusion".[23]

This interest, common to both sides in the civil war, in religion as the buttress of a society founded on property, helped to make possible the restoration. Those who defended bishops in 1640-2 defended them for fear lest other institutions, including their own property, might next be attacked. Many who opposed bishops opposed them as the instruments of a political régime: once that régime had been destroyed, this reason for hostility to bishops ceased to exist. Nor should we forget the body of men who frankly recognized the political function of religion. We have no idea of their numbers, since (apart from Marlowe) for the most part they remained prudently silent. Hobbes is the great exemplar; but more typical, and certainly more influential on the Parliamentarian side, was Selden: "When a man has no mind to do something he ought to do by his contract with man, then he gets a text and interprets it as he pleases, and so thinks to get loose". "If men would say they took arms for anything but religion, they might be beaten out of it by reason; out of that they never can, for they will not believe you whatever you say".[24]

Lord Brooke's starting point, according to Haller, was that the clergy owed their authority and their property solely to their ability to secure the obedience of the people to political powers which represented the oppressive weight of vested interests in society.[25] Thomas Taylor put the point more naively: "If Christian religion confirm civil authority, then the way to bring men to become subject to superiors is to plant the gospel. ... It is not power, it is not policy, that will still, subdue and keep under a rebellious people without the power of the Word and their consciences".[26]

An important part of the church's function was to control the people. Once consensus between the court and the bulk of the landed ruling class broke down the question arose, Who controls the church? The early sixteen-forties revealed that the crown could not control it without the gentry: but in the revolutionary conditions which followed it became equally clear that many of the middling and poorer sort no longer accepted gentry control unquestioningly. Under stable circumstances religion could subdue people and keep them under. But it could also be used for rebellious purposes when their superiors were not united in support of a state church. The question, Where was your church before Luther? had focused attention on mediaeval lower-class heresies, to which Foxe looked back with pride: they ran riot in the sixteen-forties and fifties.

Restoration of the church in 1660, complete with bishops and our most religious King Charles II at its head, demonstrated that the natural rulers had learnt their lesson. Robert South, former panegyrist of Oliver Cromwell, reminded the lawyers of Lincoln's Inn early in 1660 that "if there was not a minister in every parish you would quickly find cause to increase the number of constables". Churches would be needed as prisons if they ceased to be places of worship.[27] Winstanley and Bunyan also saw the established clergy as aggressive defenders of the privileged social order.[28] Samuel Parker, former Cromwellian and future bishop, was unsubtle but clear: "Put the case, the clergy were cheats and jugglers, yet it must be allowed they are necessary instruments of state to awe the common people into fear and obedience. Nothing else can so effectively enslave them as the fear of invisible power and the dismal apprehensions of the world to come".[29] It was no doubt with such arguments that the Latitudinarian and Whig Gilbert Burnet convinced the libertine Earl of Rochester that Christianity's social usefulness should stop him attacking it publicly.[30] Jeremy Collier spelt out Parker's point in 1698: "if eternity were out of the case, general advantage and public reason and secular policy would oblige us to be just to the priesthood. For ... religion is the basis of government". Even supposing "a scheme of infidelity" could be demonstrated, "they had much better keep the secret. The divulging it tends only to debauch mankind, and shake the securities of civil life".[31] "General advantage, public reason and secular policy": these are a far cry from Divine Right and the sacred Scriptures. I hope this book may help to illuminate the transition from one set of ideas to the other.

NOTES

1. Chapters 2 to 5 derive from lectures which I gave in the Theological Faculty of University College, Cardiff, in 1966-7. I am grateful to the audience for helpful discussions, and particularly to Dr Archie Cochrane for usefully caustic comments.
2. H.Ellis, *Original Letters Illustrative of English History* (1825-7), second series, II, p. 190.
3. Cf. an edict of Charles IV of Spain, published in 1789: "Everything which tends towards the crime of propagating revolutionary ideas contains the crime of heresy" (H.T.Buckle, *History of Civilization in England*, World's Classics, 1903-4, II, p. 112; cf. pp. 198-9).
4. Izaak Walton, *Lives* (World's Classics, 1927), p. 194.
5. P.H.Kocher, *Christopher Marlowe* (Chapel Hill, 1946), Chapters 2-3.
6. Burton, *Anatomy of Melancholy* (Everyman edn.), III, pp. 328-9, 331.
7. H.C.White, *Social Criticism in Popular Religious Literature of the Sixteenth Century* (New York, 1944), p. 188.
8. R. Crowley, *Select Works* (Early English Text Society, 1872), p. 41.
9. Ellis, *op. cit.*, first series, III, p.289.
10. Walton, *op. cit.*, p. 207. Walton's italics.
11. [Anon.], *A Memento* (n.d., ? early 1660s), p.206.
12. Ed. the Marquis of Lansdowne, *The Petty Papers* (1927), I, pp. 116-18.
13. Ed. H.C.Foxcroft, *A Supplement to Burnet's History of My Own Time* (Oxford U.P., 1902), p.50.
14. Selden, *Table Talk* (1847), p. 4. Selden's point was that the clergy were bound by Act of Parliament to subscribe only to Articles which contained matters of faith: it was Bancroft who had extended this to subscription to all the Articles.
15. *Sermons or Homilies appointed to be read in churches.* pp. 471-3.
16. Ed. A. Peel, *Tracts ascribed to Richard Bancroft* (Cambridge U.P., 1953), pp. 47, 78, 81-3, 90-3, 105. Cf. a Puritan petition of 1585, in *Select Statutes and ... Documents* (ed. G.W.Prothero, Oxford U.P., 3rd. edn., 1906), pp. 219-21.
17. Prothero, *op. cit.*, pp. 442-3; cf. D.Neal, *History of the Puritans* (revised edn., 1837), I, pp. 209-10.
18. Quoted by W.K.Jordan, *The Development of Religious Toleration in England (1603-1640)*, I (1936), p. 28.
19. [Anon.], *Cabala, Mysteries of State* (1654), II, p. 46; Bacon, *Certaine considerations touching the better pacification and edification of the Church of England*, in *Works* (ed. J.Spedding, R.L.Ellis and D.D.Heath, 1857-72), X, pp. 107-9.
20. Bacon, "Matters of religion and the church ... in these times are become so intermixed with considerations of estate" *(Advice to Sir George Villiers)*.
21. H.R.Trevor-Roper, *Archbishop Laud, 1573-1645* (1940), p. 164.
22. Eliot, *Negotium Posterorum* (ed. A.B. Grosart, 1881), I, pp. 70-1; J. Forster, *Sir John Eliot* (1865), I, pp. 11, 213.

23. Forster, *op. cit.*, I, p. 60.
24. Selden, *Table Talk*, pp. 196-7.
25. *Tracts on Liberty in the Puritan Revolution, 1638-1647* (ed. W.Haller, Columbia U.P., 1934), I, p. 20.
26. T.Taylor, *A Commentary Upon the Epistle of St. Paul Written to Titus* (1658), pp. 398-9. Taylor died in 1633, but his writings could not be published because of "the iniquity of those times" (title-page to *Works*, 1653).
27. South, *Sermons Preached Upon Several Occasions* (1737), I, p. 131.
28. See chapter 11 below.
29. Quoted by Marvell, *The Rehearsal Transpros'd* (ed. D.I.B.Smith, Oxford U.P., 1971), p. 139. Marvell's comments are agreeable.
30. G.Burnet, *Some Passages of the Life and Death of the ...Earl of Rochester* (1774), p. 58. First published 1680.
31. J.Collier, *A Short View of the Immorality and Profaneness of the English Stage* (4th edn., 1699), pp. 129, 190.

II *The First Century of the Church of England*

The first century in which England had a separate national church may be taken either from the fifteen-thirties to 1640 or from 1559 to 1660. Such a perspective attaches great importance to the Reformation as the turning point in the history of religion in England. But with a slight shift in perspective we could equally well call the period The last century of the Church of England. In the thousand or so years between the Synod of Whitby and the English Revolution there had been, in theory always, and in practice nearly all the time, a single Christian church in England. But it had always been part of an international organization. During the first century after the Reformation, uniquely, there was a single national church, dependent on nobody. The existence of a large Roman Catholic minority introduced an element of fiction into the legal theory that all English men and women were members of this state church: but it was still a plausible aspiration. But after 1640 it rapidly became obvious that there was no longer a single English protestant church; the restoration of the Anglican Church to a privileged position in 1660 highlighted the fact that it was one church among many. The first century of the Church of England was also the last in which it could claim to be *the* English church.

The absence of international controls meant that this was a century of instability for the church: the rapid changes of direction made under Henry VIII, Mary and Elizabeth encouraged many to see the Reformation as a beginning, not an end. However hard Henry VIII and Elizabeth tried to insist that their church settlements were final, there remained those who called for continuous reformation. Lord Brooke in 1641 referred, provocatively, to "the first reformation".[1] Some even thought that a second reformation should be financed by confiscations of bishops and dean and chapter

19

lands, as Henry's Reformation had been financed by monastic lands. Impropriated tithes in the possession of lay successors of the monasteries tempted reformers to suggest using them to finance preaching.

This church, then, to which all English men and women belonged by virtue of having been born in England, was created in the fifteen-thirties and collapsed in the sixteen-forties. But though the institutions of the hierarchical church collapsed, protestantism did not. Religion, as Sir Lewis Namier used to say, is a sixteenth-century word for nationalism. After as before 1640, any threat, real or imagined, to protestantism at once rallied national unity, as Laud, Charles I and James II all found to their cost. During the Revolution many English men and women showed they were attached to the rhythms and rituals of the prayer book.[2] But no one seems to have expressed much regret for the passing of bishops. Whereas in Scotland and Ireland it was the Kirk and the Roman Catholic church which focused national unity, in England protestantism, not the episcopal church, was associated with patriotism.

This sets us two problems. How do we account for the collapse of the state church in 1640? How do we account for its restoration in 1660?

The occasional pieces that follow manifestly do not deal systematically with these problems. But some of them, approaching from several different angles, may help to suggest the form that answers should take. Over all of them broods the majestic figure of Patrick Collinson, with whom I occasionally venture to disagree, but whose powerful presence can never be forgotten.

NOTES

1. Brooke, *A Discourse... of Episcopacie, passim.*
2. John Morrill, "The Church in England, 1642-9", in *Reactions to the English Civil War* (ed. Morrill, 1982), pp. 89-114.

3. *The Protestant Nation*

King James upon the conference at Hampton Court did absolutely conclude, "No bishops, no king, no nobility"; which as you see, hath lately fallen out according to his prediction. It is the church which supports the state, it is religion which strengthens the government; shake the one, and you overthrow the other. Nothing is so deeply rooted in the hearts of men as religion, nothing so powerful to direct their actions; and if once the hearts of the people be doubtful in religion, all other relations fail, and you shall find nothing but mutinies and sedition. Thus the church and the state do mutually support and give assistance to each other; and if one of them change, the other can have no sure foundation.*

I

The great changes of the sixteenth century — renaissance, new astronomy, consciousness of great non-Christian societies revealed by long-distance trade — were accompanied by the rise of a lay learned intelligentsia. Before the Reformation schools were being founded under the auspices of merchant companies rather than of the church. The monarchy increasingly employed lay civil servants and patronized humanists whose speculations were as much secular as spiritual.

Yet urban civilization produced great insecurity. The obverse of the wealth of urban patriciates was unemployment, vagabondage, crime and disease. The village community, at a very low economic level, had produced some sort of social security, an equality in poverty; it was to the advantage of landlords, to say no more, to keep their tenants and labourers alive in time of famine. But big towns were impersonal: a man could starve there unknown to his neighbours. By the seventeenth century many London parish churches could not possibly have held all their parishioners at one time. Ultimately sectarian congregations were to replace the parish as community centre and social security agency in the towns; but

---

*Bishop Godfrey Goodman, *The Court of King James I* (1839), I, p. 421. Goodman died in 1656.

that was far ahead. Meanwhile masterless men were by definition a menace to order: the Tudor poor law, the protestant emphasis on the wickedness of the mass of mankind and the Hobbist war of every man against every man, all seemed to make sense in this society. So too did the Puritan stress on discipline and hard work for the good of the commonwealth, which saw England through the economic crisis of the sixteenth and seventeenth centuries, performing a social role similar to that of Marxist theories in the Soviet Union and China in our own day.[1] Protestantism lumped idle monks and idle beggars together as reprobates: some radicals threw in idle gentlemen for good measure. Sir Francis Drake was never a better Protestant than when he said he would have the gentleman to haul and draw with the mariner — and executed the highest ranking gentleman on board to reinforce the point. Having done its job, the ideology lost its leading role when political and economic stability were established in the Lockist state after 1688.

Dryden summed up the sociological approach to the Reformation, looking back from a century and a half later:

> "In times o'ergrown with rust and ignorance
> A gainful trade their clergy did advance;
> When want of learning kept the laymen low
> And none but priests were authorized to know:
> When what small knowledge was in them did dwell,
> And he a God that could but read or spell;
> Then Mother Church did mightily prevail;
> She parcelled out the Bible by retail,
> But still expounded what she sold or gave,
> To keep it in her power to damn or save.
> Scripture was scarce, and as the market went,
> Poor laymen took salvation on content,
> As needy men take money, good or bad;
> God's Word they had not, but the priest's they had …"

After the Reformation each man read the Bible for himself, "And saved himself as cheap as e'er he could".[2] (The "cheap church" was a familiar jibe. Sir Thomas Overbury's "devilish usurer" "likes our religion best because 'tis best cheap".[3] Sir Benjamin Rudyerd in the Commons' Committee on Religion in 1628, apropos the need to establish a well-paid preaching ministry, feared lest "this backwardness of ours will give the adversary occasion to say that we choose our religion because it is the cheaper of the two")[4] The appeal to the business classes reached caricature form in verses summarizing the covenant theology prefixed to a volume of sermons printed in 1622:

> "No desperate debts or bankrupts in this trade,
> God is the creditor, Christ surety made,
> And both have bound themselves to pay for us
> The principal, with gracious overplus".[5]

Already the connection between gain and godliness was presenting the problem which was to worry John Wesley. Thomas Adams lamented that "religion gives us riches, and riches forget religion. . . . Poverty makes us religious, religion rich, and riches irreligious".[6]

II

The Reformation left the believer and his conscience alone in the world with no help except from divine grace. Looking back over the centuries, we can see how this theological attitude could be adapted to a society of rugged individualists, wrestling with God and their consciences, recognizing no superiors, whether priests or feudal lords. Church courts making money out of the people's sins would seem to such men as iniquitous as the sale of indulgences. The payment of tithes to non-preaching ministers would seem sacrilege. So would popish vestments, whose object was to differentiate the priest, however ungodly, from any layman, however godly. "Now I can make no more holy water", said Latimer with heavy irony when he was forcibly disrobed as part of his degradation from the priesthood.[7] "Conjuring garments of popery", a separatist called a bishop's cope and surplice in 1567.[8] The *Admonition to Parliament* of 1572 said that in primitive times ministers were "known by voice, learning and doctrine: now they must be discerned from other by popish and antichristian apparel".[9]

Protestants demanded communion in both kinds, for laymen as well as for priests, to emphasize their equality. Holy communion was not a mystery, a miracle in which the priest — and only the priest — actually turned bread and wine into body and blood; through shades of opinion protestants came increasingly to think of communion as a commemoration, a reminder of a miracle that had once taken place. Further consequences followed. Bishop Joseph Hall was to justify kneeling at communion on the analogy of kneeling to kiss the King's hand,[10] and Elias Ashmole bowing to the altar because men bowed in the royal presence.[11] But for Puritans these were not merely polite gestures, but an acknowledgment of the real presence. ("Papists kneel to the corporal presence", said a Newcastle merchant caustically in the late seventeenth century; "but protestants kneel to they know not what").[12] Those who denied transsubstantiation felt it a point of principle to withhold such gestures. "Altar-worship is idolatry", said Pym in the Long Parliament.[13] Railing off the altar at the east end of the church emphasized not only the real presence but also the mediating role of the priest. Puritans wanted the communion table to be in the centre of the church, with the *minister* attending on seated communicants, not the *priest* mediating the miracle of the mass.

So two utterly different conceptions of religion are concealed behind quarrels over vestments, altar rails and the position of the communion table. The protestant approach was at once less sacramental and less materialistic: it stressed the moral state of the worshipper, not the correct performance of ceremonies on his behalf. Again the question of human responsibility, of the equality of laymen with priests, was involved. "The table of communion", said Milton in 1641, "now become a table of separation, stands like an exalted platform, ... fortified with bulwark and barricado to keep off the profane touch of the laics, whilst the obscene and surfeited priest scruples not to paw and mammock the sacramental bread as familiarly as his tavern biscuit". In Milton's eyes, the believer is "more sacred than any dedicated altar or church".[14]

These are commonplaces, but I emphasize them to recall that the issues at stake even in vestiarian disputes were not trivial. As the *Admonition to Parliament* declared, "Neither is the controversy betwixt them and us (as they would bear the world in hand) as for a cap, a tippet or a surplice, but for great matters concerning a true ministry and regiment of the church according to the Word".[15] When the Long Parliament met in November 1640 the House of Commons insisted on receiving communion at a table placed in the middle of the church. It was a political gesture.

Puritans said that they were trying to return to the practice of the primitive church, just as common lawyers and Levellers said they wished to return to the customs of their free Anglo-Saxon ancestors. In both cases one advantage of appealing to earlier, allegedly less corrupt, practices was that the appeal could be highly selective. Texts were applied, with no historical sense, to a context in which they were quite inappropriate. The reformers looked back to a church which owned no lands, which was in no position to persecute or censor, which indeed was out of sympathy with the then existing political order, not part and parcel of it. They found very few of the institutions of mediaeval society mentioned in the Bible. The reformers, like the early Fathers, abhorred the concessions which any established church has to make to the social and political order which maintains it. Hence the attraction of the simplicity of early Christianity as against "the subtleties of the schoolmen", those painful adaptations of the New Testament to the needs and standards of mediaeval society. This society was being transformed by geographical discoveries and industrial developments: forward-looking thinkers were correspondingly impatient with the old ideas. This is one of the points at which Renaissance and Reformation, intellectual criticism and theological protest, met. Erasmus and Luther agreed in their hostility towards scholasticism.

Hence the primary importance for reformers of getting the Bible translated into the vernacular, for which so many of them paid with their lives. The fortunate coincidence (or divine providence, Foxe thought) that the craft of printing had just been discovered made possible the mass circulation of Bibles and pamphlets, so that all who could read were open to the influence of the new ideas (and, in towns especially, many who could not read but listened to discussion). But literacy confined the main impact of the vernacular Bible to the middling classes, not the very poorest. As Thomas Münzer asked of Luther in the fifteen-twenties, "Doesn't he realise that men whose every moment is consumed in the making of a living have no time to read the Word of God?"[16]

Mediaeval heretics had relied on the Bible in opposing the miracle of the mass, confessions, images, church courts and ceremonies. But their Bibles were laboriously copied out by hand or learnt by heart. Printing made protestantism possible because it facilitated the rapid spread of popular theology among the literate, mainly in towns. Where the Lollard Bible had circulated in tens of copies, Tyndale's New Testament circulated in hundreds, and the Geneva Bible in thousands. But printing also ruined protestantism as a single coherent creed, because the reading of books is even harder to control than the reading of manuscripts. The portable Geneva Bible could be privately digested, privately interpreted, and discussed in small clandestine groups. The protestant appeal to the mind through the

Word, rather than the traditional appeal to the eye through symbols and ceremonies, may again have limited the range of its original spread in a society where the peasant majority was not only largely illiterate, but addicted to concrete visual symbols. The Homilies declared that "all images ... set up publicly have been worshipped of the unlearned and simple sort shortly after they have been publicly so set up. ... Images in churches and idolatry go always both together. ... The nature of man is none otherwise bent to the worshipping of images (if he may have them and see them) than it is bent to whoredom and adultery in the company of harlots".[17] Iconoclasm was educational, as Burnet realised.[18]

The Reformation, just because of this return to the primitive sources of Christianity, gave a great impetus to scholarship. It was vital to be sure what the Bible said, to have a certain text: and printing made this possible. The Reformation brought an advance in controversial methods and textual criticism, just because there were two sides (at least), each passionately convinced the other was wrong. Busy attacking papal forgeries and suppressions, men like Jewell, Hooker, William Crashawe, Chillingworth, laid the foundations of a new critical method. Protestants were convinced that Catholics believed ignorance to be the mother of devotion, and this made many wish to act on the opposite principle. In *Areopagitica* Milton could find nothing worse to say of censorship than that it was of popish origin. In fact an important part of Milton's argument for responsible freedom had been anticipated eighty years earlier in the Elizabethan Homily *Exhorting to the reading and knowledge of holy Scripture*: "If you will not know the truth of God ... lest you fall into error; by the same reason you may then lie still and never go, lest, if you go, you fall into the mire; nor eat any meat, lest you take a surfeit; nor sow your corn, nor labour in your occupation, nor use your merchandize, for fear you lose your seed, your labour, your stock".[19] As late as 1691 Richard Baxter tried to make the gentry's flesh creep by suggesting that if monastic lands were recaptured by the church, many landlords would repent that they did not spend more on educating the poor.[20]

The Bible was in the parish church for all to read, and the church was still a real community centre. The early reformers encouraged men not only to read but also to study and discuss the Scriptures. They thought that once the Bible was available in English, all men would agree on what it said. But many of those who in sixteenth-century England were encouraged to study the Bible were poorly educated, had little critical or historical sense, and regarded every word of the Scripture as divinely inspired. Their daily lives were filled with mysterious and inexplicable events which they accounted for in magical or miraculous terms. They tended to take the Bible entirely literally, and to apply its texts as a standard of criticism of the world about them. They found denunciations of the rich and powerful and praise of the poor and lowly, together with threatenings of wrath to come, which fitted well into the mood of rebellious despair that the crisis of their society was producing. In 1643 the Rev. John Jegon, an Essex parson, was accused of saying "'twas pity that ever the Bible was translated into English, for now every woman and beggarly fellow think themselves able to dispute with reverend divines".[21] He has our sympathy.

III

The first century of the Church of England saw the emergence of new loyalties to replace that to one's feudal overlord, which over most of Europe was losing its point. The newly consolidating national states were trying to subsume feudal and religious loyalties: the new Messiah, some said, was the King. But kings do not cut very inspiring figures in the Bible. For all their devotion to the godly prince, early reformers like Calvin, Tyndale and Becon found in the Bible the command "that we ought to obey God more than man".[22] Knox is very quotable on the subject. Preaching in 1559 he recalled "when we were a few number in comparison of our enemies, when we had neither earl nor lord — few excepted — to comfort us, we called upon God and took him for our protector, defence and only refuge".[23] "Who dare enterprise to put silence to the spirit of God, which will not be subject to the appetites of wicked princes?"[24] Even more ominously, he remarked "the prophet of God sometimes may teach treason against kings".[25]

Direct loyalty to God should bypass all mediators and mesne lords. "If earthly lords and masters will defend their servants", argued Bishop Pilkington in 1562, "much more He that [is] King of heaven and earth".[26] Archbishop Grindal warned Elizabeth that, though she was a mighty princess, yet "He that dwelleth in heaven is mightier".[27] The separatist John Penry was even less tactful: "He that hath made you and me", he told Elizabeth, "hath as great authority to send me of his message unto you, as he had to place you over me".[28] "These heretics neither fear God nor obey their betters", observed the Spanish ambassador, apropos the 1566 Parliament.[29]

Such doctrines could be socially as well as politically subversive. "Glory not that thou hast a gentleman to thy father", counselled Silver-Tongued Smith; "glory not that thou hast a knight to thy brother, but glory that thou hast a Lord to thy brother. . . . Seemeth it a light thing to you to be the sons of the King of kings, seeing you are poor men and of small reputation?"[30] "Shall your loyalty towards men excuse your treasons against the Lord?" Joseph Hall asked.[31] Sir Henry Slingsby in 1628 told the Earl of Huntingdon that "he cared not for any lord in England except the Lord of Hosts".[32] If conscience bids us, declared the preacher of an assize sermon in the same year, we should denounce "a neighbour, a kinsman, a landlord".[33]

How such attitudes could affect political action is shown by Oliver Cromwell's preference for a godly yeoman over a gentleman who is "nothing more". When the defenders of Taunton were called on to surrender in October 1644, they declared they would not "prefer the honour and reputation of gentlemen before the goodness and power of the almighty Saviour".[34] At a different social level we may compare the Baptist Henry Denne's answer to a man who felt he could not cease "to hear the priests of England" because "he hired a farm of Mr. Bendich, and if he should know he was baptized he would turn him out". Denne told him "the earth was the Lord's and the fullness thereof, and wished him to trust God, and he would be a better landlord than Mr. Bendich".[35] The Diggers in June 1649 told Fairfax that they had "chosen the Lord God Almighty to be our king and protector".[36] "The whole world", Colonel Daniel assured Monck in 1657, "is governed by superiority and distance in relations, and when that's taken away unavoidably anarchy is ushered in".[37] The future Duke of Albemarle hardly needed the warning.

So personal feudal loyalty was replaced by loyalty to God, to a cause. Treason was in origin a breach of *personal* fealty owed to an overlord; but Martin Marprelate in 1589 spoke of those who were "obedient subjects to the Queen and disobedient traitors to God and the realm".[38] Such distinctions were ominous: sixty years later Charles I was condemned for high treason against the people of England. Loyalty to God was the mediating term between loyalty to the person of the King and loyalty to the abstraction of the state.

Stephen Marshall in 1644 had said "The question in England is, whether Christ or Antichrist shall be lord or king?"[39] By 1649 Milton could write, with enviable simplicity, "the kings of this world have both ever hated and instinctively feared the church of God", since this church's doctrine "seems much to favour two things to them so dreadful, liberty and equality".[40] Loyalty to God came in practice to mean loyalty to conscience, the inner voice. "Greater is *he that is in you*", Margaret Fell assured her husband in 1653, "than he that is in the world".[41]

Loyalty to the king was replaced by loyalty to the commonwealth, to the nation. Dr Firth has argued that neither Bale nor Foxe saw an apocalyptic role for England, and she even suggests that Haller was wrong to see any conception of England as an elect nation before 1640.[42] But J. W. McKenna argues that "God became an Englishman" as early as the fourteenth century.[43] Latimer wrote in 1537 God "hath shown himself God of England, or rather an English God". The dying Edward VI was said to have called on God to "save thy chosen people of England".[44] Haller quoted Bishops Aylmer and Parker proclaiming that "God is English".[45] Richard Fitz's congregation in 1571 assumed a merciful relation of God to England and the English church, like that to Israel — a mercy dependent on the obedience of the people to his revealed will.[46] Philip Stubbe thought that the English were a chosen people.[47] "Passing by many other nations", wrote a Puritan who may have been Thomas Cartwright, "thou hast trusted our nation" with the gospel.[48] John Rolfe in 1616 described England as "a peculiar people marked and chosen by the finger of God" to possess North America.[49] Richard Bernard in 1619, Alexander Leighton in 1628, thought that the English were "the Lord's own people".[50] George Wither between 1625 and 1628 wrote an exceptionally long poem whose object was to call to repentance the land which God had "elected from among the heathen isles".

> "Thou wert as often warned and furnished
> As Judah was ...
> The Jewish commonwealth was never deigned
> More great deliverance than thou hast gained"

in 1588 and 1605.[51]

After 1640 such comments are of course even more frequent — in Fast Sermons[52] and in almanacs, for instance.[53] In 1681 George Hickes said sneeringly that the Puritans "made the common people

of Great Britain consider themselves as the people of Israel and ...
act like enthusiasts and follow their leaders like the Jews of latter
times, to commit such execrable treasons as are not to be mentioned
without horror and tears"; he went on to compare the execution of
Charles I with the crucifixion.[54] But it was not only Puritans: Fuller
in 1655 argued that "England is God's on several titles".[55] Charles II
spoke of the English as "His own chosen people", and throughout
Dryden's *Annus Mirabilis* the parallel between Londoners and Jews
is maintained.[56]

Foxe depicted Englishmen defending the truth throughout the
centuries, now against Antichrist personified by the Pope and the
King of Spain. Catholicism lost Calais, Bishop Pilkington recalled;
the preaching of Jesus Christ, thought Knox, would bring about a
perpetual concord (for the first time in history) between England and
Scotland. [57] So the rather vulgar nationalism which we find among
the Elizabethans was sublimated and idealized. Puritans, as the most
anti-Catholic and anti-Spanish of Englishmen, seemed also to be the
most patriotic, especially during the two great crises of the fifteen-
eighties and the sixteen-twenties.

IV

Calvinism moreover was an *international* movement, like Catholicism. Even if its adherents came to despair of the English church,
they could still hope that our brethren in the Netherlands, France,
Scotland, would help against the common enemy. From the reign of
Edward VI to that of James I connections with continental protestantism were close. Bucer and Peter Martyr, John à Lasco,
Bernardino Ochino and many others played an important part in
establishing the faith of the English church under Edward. Marian
exiles fled to Frankfort, Strasburg, Basle, Geneva, Zürich. Under
Elizabeth epistolary contacts were kept up with leading continental
protestant divines, and Bullinger's *Decades* were compulsory reading
for non-graduate English clergy. Essex ministers in the fifteen-
eighties regarded it as a powerful argument against unqualified
acceptance of the English prayer book that it would put them out of
step with continental reformed churches.[58] English theology was
heavily dependent on the continent, Patrick Collinson reminds us.
Covenant theology "derived from the theological tradition of the
Zwinglian reform in Zürich". Sabbatarianism was not invented by
English Puritans either: it was well-known in Zürich, Geneva,

Heidelberg and the Netherlands.[59] Only after the rise of William Perkins in the last decade of the century was the debt repaid. Over fifty editions of Perkins's works were printed in Switzerland, nearly sixty in Germany, and over a hundred in the Netherlands, as well as smaller numbers in France, Bohemia and Hungary.[60]

The hierarchy came to stress the nationalism of the English church rather than the internationalism which appealed to Puritans and the first generation of bishops.[61] Grindal had friendly relations with the foreign churches, in London and on the continent: the former contributed to the development of prophesyings.[62] But Whitgift challenged the ordinations of non-episcopal churches, and cited in defence of the hierarchy the practice of the fourth and fifth centuries, when the church was fitting itself into the institutional framework of the Roman Empire. The decisive break came with Bancroft and his "Babylonian faction".[63] Bancroft thought French Huguenots as seditious as English Puritans.[64] He was, Andrew Melville thought, "the capital enemy of all the reformed churches of Europe".[65] His sharp distinction between bishops and the other ranks of the clergy made the former a superior order by Divine Right, with the sole power of ordination and of discipline. This justified a graded hierarchical concept of the church, with authority descending from above, thus isolating England from continental Calvinism. It was naturally accompanied by an elevation of the parson over the congregation.

This is reflected in the vicissitudes of the word "minister". It was normally used even in official documents in the later sixteenth century. When in 1606 an M.P. objected that "the old and usual word is clerk", the House of Commons agreed that "the word minister ... hath been used and is now usual and well understood, and an apt and good term".[66] It was ground for complaint against John Cosin in 1628 that "he hath changed the word 'minister' into the word 'priest'".[67] The ultimate compromise was "clergyman".

As James VI restored episcopacy in Scotland, as the Edict of Nantes registered acceptance in 1598 by the French Huguenots of the position of tolerated minority, as the victory of the Dutch struggle for independence created a national church in the Netherlands, the trend towards national isolation was strengthened. At the same time English and Dutch victories over Spain, and the succession of Henri IV of France rather than the Spanish candidate, removed the danger of a restoration of Catholicism in England by

Spanish arms, and so reduced the government's need for Puritan support.

The Synod of Dort in 1618-19 was the first and last international Calvinist council. England was represented at Dort, but the experience did nothing to reassure James I that Calvinism and monarchy were compatible. There followed the disastrous attempt of the Elector Palatine to seize the Bohemian crown. Frederick's defeat, and the failure of England and the Netherlands to combine in support of his cause, showed that the Calvinist international was in ruins. James turned to negotiations for a marriage alliance with Spain; Richelieu seized the opportunity to abolish Huguenot territorial power in France. The fatuous diplomacy of Buckingham and Charles I, intervening first against and then for the Huguenots, showed that English foreign policy had no firm ideological commitment; when the Habsburgs were checked in Germany, it was by Lutheran Sweden and Catholic France. The Calvinist international had failed.

Laud passed over to the offensive against it. He harried foreign protestant churches in England, nearly ruining the Wealden and Norwich clothing industries in the process. The English ambassador in Paris ceased to attend Huguenot worship. Laud tried to bring under his control both the English merchant churches overseas and the chaplains of English regiments in the service of the Netherlands, thus endangering relations with the Dutch republic and driving many English refugees from the Netherlands to a further emigration across the Atlantic. He tried to force conformity on Presbyterian Scots. At all points he seemed to be stressing the insularity of the English church. Small wonder that men suspected his little Englandism of being a cover for schemes to reunite with the Roman church. A papal agent appeared in England in 1636 for the first time since the reign of Mary Tudor. It was reported to Rome, *teste* Bishop Montagu, that Laud and several other bishops "held the opinions of Rome on dogma, and especially on the authority of the Pope".[68] Laud believed in the real presence, turned communion tables into altars, repaired broken images. We know, as contemporaries did not, that Laud refused a cardinal's hat. But the important thing may be that the Pope thought the offer worth making. The theories of monarchical absolutism prevalent in Counter-Reformation countries were entirely congenial to Charles I, Laud and the "Arminian" party. It was not unreasonable to suspect them of favouring the theology of the Counter-Reformation too. We know now that Laud disliked and was embarrassed by the "Popish Plot" carried on by Henrietta Maria and her courtiers, perhaps with the connivance of the King.[69] But the fact that such a plot existed had disastrous consequences for monarchy and episcopacy in England. When Henrietta Maria appealed to Rome for help in February 1641, explaining that her husband could not embrace Catholicism or he would lose his crown, Cardinal Barberini drily replied that Charles had lost his crown already.[70]

NOTES

1. Cf. M.Walzer, "Puritanism as a Revolutionary Ideology", *History and Theory*, III (1963), *passim*.
2. Dryden, *Religio Laici* (1682), in *Poetical Works* (Globe edn.), p. 200.
3. Overbury, *Characters* (1616), in *Miscellaneous Works* (ed. E.F. Rimbault, 1890), p. 135.
4. *Memoirs of Sir Benjamin Rudyerd* (ed. J.A.Manning, 1841), p. 137. Cf. William Chillingworth: "The late slovenly profaneness, (commonly called worshipping in the spirit, but intended to be worship without cost)" (*Works*, Oxford U.P., 1838, III, p.171).
5. John Wing, *The Best Merchandise* (Flushing, 1622), introductory verses.
6. T.Adams, *The Souls Sickness*, in *The Sermons of Thomas Adams* (ed. J.Brown, 1909), p. 215.
7. W.Pierce, *An Historical Introduction to the Marprelate Tracts* (1908), p. 9.
8. J. Strype, *Life... of... Edmund Grindal* (Oxford U.P., 1821), p. 175.
9. In *Puritan Manifestoes: A Study of the Origin of the Puritan Revolt* (ed. W.H.Frere and C.E.Douglas, 1907), p. 11.
10. Hall, *Works* (Oxford U.P., 1837), X, p. 69.
11. Ed. C.H.Josten, *Elias Ashmole (1617-1692)* (Oxford U.P., 1966), III, p. 819.
12. Ed. W.H.D.Longstaffe, *Memoirs of the Life of Mr. Ambrose Barnes* (Surtees Soc., 1867), p. 124.
13. Ed. J.Bruce, *Verney Papers: Notes of Proceedings in the Long Parliament* (Camden Soc., 1845), p. 123.
14. *M.C.P.W.*, I, pp. 547-8.
15. Frere and Douglas, *op.cit.*, p. 36.
16. Quoted by V.H.H.Green, *Luther and the Reformation* (1964), pp.150-1.
17. *Homilies*, pp. 186, 206. Cf. Chapters 8-10 below for "natural man".
18. G.Burnet, *History of the Reformation of the Church of England* (1825), I, pp. 314-17.
19. *Homilies*, p. 5. "Like the man that would keep all wine out of the

country lest men should be drunk" was how Cromwell put the same point to the Governor of Edinburgh Castle in September 1650 (ed. W.C. Abbott, *Writings and Speeches of Oliver Cromwell,* Harvard U.P., 1937-47, II, p.339).

20. Baxter, *The Poor Husbandman's Advocate to Rich Racking Landlords* (ed. F.J.Powicke, Bulletin of the John Rylands Library, X, 1926), pp. 178-9.

21. J.W.Davids, *Annals of Evangelical Nonconformity in ... Essex* (1863), p. 236; Hobbes repeated the point (*English Works*, ed. Sir W.Molesworth, 1839-45), VI, pp.190-1.

22. J.Calvin, *A Commentary on Daniel* (trans. and ed. T.Myers, 1966), I, p. 382 (first published 1561, English translation 1570); W.Tyndale, *The Obedience of a Christian Man* (1527-8), in *Doctrinal Treatises* (Parker Soc., 1848), pp. 202-4; Thomas Becon, *Prayers and other pieces* (Parker Soc., 1844), pp. 302-4.

23. J.Knox, *The History of the Reformation of Religion in Scotland* (ed. W.M'Gavin, Glasgow, 1832), p. 172.

24. *Ibid.*, p. 150; cf. pp. 252-3, 290 and *passim.*

25. Knox, *Works* (ed. D.Laing, 1864), III, p. 184.

26. J. Pilkington, *Works* (Parker Soc., 1842), p. 191.

27. Grindal. *Remains* (Parker Soc., 1843), pp. 376-90; cf. Collinson, *The Elizabethan Puritan Movement*, pp. 29, 94, 107, 135.

28. J. Strype, *Life... of John Whitgift* (Oxford U.P., 1822), II, p. 181. Cf. *Writings of Robert Harrison and Robert Browne* (ed. A. Peel and L.H.Carlson, 1953), p. 413.

29. J.E.Neale, *Elizabeth I and her Parliaments, 1559-1581* (1953), p. 139.

30. H.Smith, *Three Sermons* (1632), p. 34; cf. my *Economic Problems of the Church* (Panther edn., 1971), p. 23; John Goodwin, *God a Good Master* (1641); Richard Sibbes, *The Soules Conflict* (1635), in *Works* (Edinburgh, 1862-4), I. p.123.

31. J.Hall, *Works*, X, p. 66.

32. Quoted by L.Stone, *The Crisis of the Aristocracy* (Oxford U.P., 1965), p.265. Conrad Russell rather oddly suggests that this remark may not show declining respect for the aristocracy but for the militia (*Parliament and English Politics, 1621-1629*, 1979, p. 376). Possibly; but it is not what the words say.

33. Robert Harris, *Two Sermons* (1628), quoted by M.Walzer, *The Revolution of the Saints: A Study in the Origins of Radical Politics* (Harvard U.P., 1965), pp. 233-4.

34. Quoted in C.D.Curtis, *Blake, General-at-Sea* (Taunton, 1934), p. 46.

35. Ed. E.B.Underhill, *Records of the Churches of Christ Gathered at Fenstanton, Warboys and Hexham, 1644-1720* (Hanserd Knollys Soc., 1854), p. 82. Note the reference to "the priests of England" in 1653. The Church of England, like landlords, still existed. See p.6 above.

36. Ed. G.H.Sabine, *The Works of Gerrard Winstanley* (Cornell U.P., 1941), p. 284

37. Ed. C.H.Firth, *Scotland and the Protectorate* (Scottish History Soc., XXXI, 1899), pp. 362-3.

38. M.Marprelate, *The Epitome* (1588), Sig.E iv. An analogous distinction had been drawn by some of the followers of Sir Thomas Wyatt (John Proctor, *The History of Wyatt's Rebellion*, 1555, in *An English Garner*, ed. E. Arber, 1896-7, VIII, p.54).
39. S.Marshall, *A Sacred Panegyric* (1644), p. 21.
40. *M.C.P.W.*, III, p. 509; cf. W.Dell, *Several Sermons and Discourses* (1709), p. 18. First published 1652.
41. Isobel Ross, *Margaret Fell, Mother of Quakerism* (1949), p. 119. My italics.
42. K.R.Firth, *The Apocalyptic Tradition in Reformation Britain, 1530-1645* (Oxford U.P., 1979), pp. 108, 252-3.
43. In *Tudor Rule and Revolution: Essays for G.R.Elton* (ed. D.J.Guth and J.W.McKenna, Cambridge U.P., 1983).
44. D.M.Loades, *The Oxford Martyrs* (1970), p. 26; J.N.King, *English Reformation Literature: The Tudor Origins of the Protestant Tradition* (Princeton U.P., 1982), p. 410.
45. W.Haller, *Foxe's Book of Martyrs and the Elect Nation* (1963), pp.87-8; cf. *Correspondence of Archbishop Parker* (Parker Soc., 1853), pp. 418-19.
46. B.R.White, *The English Separatist Tradition: From the Marian Martyrs to the Pilgrim Fathers* (Oxford U.P., 1971), pp. 30-2.
47. W.T.MacCaffrey, "The Anjou Match and the making of Elizabethan foreign policy", in *The English Commonwealth, 1547-1640: Essays in Politics and Society presented to Joel Hurstfield* (ed. P. Clark, A.G.T. Smith and N.Tyacke, Leicester U.P., 1979), p.66.
48. Ed. A.Peel and L.H.Carlson, *Cartwrightiana* (1951). pp. 143-4.
49. Rolfe, *A True Relation of the State of Virginia Lefte by Sir Thomas Dale Knight in May Last 1616* (ed. H.C. Taylor, New Haven, 1951), pp.33-41.
50. R. Bernard, *A Key of Knowledge* (1619), pp.127-9, 279; Leighton, *Sions Plea against the Prelacie* (Amsterdam, 1628), quoted by S.Foster, *Notes from the Caroline Underground* (Hamden, Conn., 1978), p. 263; B.S.Capp, *The Fifth Monarchy Men: A Study in Seventeenth-Century English Millenarianism* (1972), p. 34.
51. Wither, *Brittans Remembrancer*, 1628 (Spenser Soc.,1880), pp.37-8, 46, 64-5, 314, 325-30, and *passim; cf.* Sibbes, *Works*, VII, pp.396-7. Professor McGiffert collected much evidence on England as chosen nation in "God's Controversy with Jacobean England", *American Historical Review*, 88 (1983), pp.1151-74; *ibid.* 89 (1984), pp.1217-18; cf. Carol Z. Wiener, "The Beleaguered Isle: A Study of Elizabethan and Early Jacobean Anti-Catholicism", *P. and P.*, 51 (1971), esp. p. 124.
52. S.Marshall, *A Peace-Offering to God* (1641), pp. 3, 40, 45-6; J. Burrough, *Sions Joy* (1641), pp. 38-9, 43-4, 49-50.
53. N.Culpeper, *An Ephemeris for the Year 1652*, p. 21.
54. Hickes, *Peculiam Dei* (1681), pp. 21-2.
55. T.Fuller, *Church History of Britain* (1842), I, p. 221.
56. M.McKeon, *Politics and Poetry in Restoration England* (Harvard U.P., 1975), pp. 63, 68, 159, 232.
57. Pilkington, *Works*, pp. 70, 86.

58. W. Hunt, *The Puritan Moment: The Coming of Revolution in an English County* (Harvard U.P., 1983), p. 97.
59. P. Collinson, *Godly People,* pp. 433-7.
60. I. Breward, "The Significance of William Perkins", *Journal of Religious History,* 4 (1966-7), p. 113.
61. See Peter Lake, *Moderate puritans and the Elizabethan church* (Cambridge U.P., 1982), pp. 208-10, 220-1, and *passim.* See pp. 67-9 below.
62. Collinson, *Godly People,* Chapter 9 *passim.*
63. See pp. 76, 80 below.
64. Bancroft, *Dangerous Positions* (1593), Book I, Chapters 3-5, Book II, Chapter 1.
65. N. Sykes, *Old Priest and New Presbyter* (1956), p. 57.
66. Ed. D. H. Willson, *The Parliamentary Diary of Robert Bowyer, 1606-1607* (Minnesota U.P., 1931), p. 149.
67. *The Proceedings and Debates of the House of Commons in ... 1628. ... Taken and Collected by ... Sir Thomas Crewe* (1707), p. 73. I benefited from being able to listen to Wallace Notestein on this subject.
68. S. R. Gardiner, *History of England, 1603-1642* (1883-4), VIII, pp. 138-9.
69. On this see the valuable book by Caroline Hibbard, *Charles I and the Popish Plot* (North Carolina U.P., 1982).
70. Ed. Wallace Notestein, *The Journal of Sir Simonds D'Ewes* (Yale U.P., 1923), p. 321.

4. *The Problem of Authority*

"With God, if we have belief, [there is not] any porter to keep any man out."*

The age-old problem of authority came into sharper prominence with the Reformation. Lollards had challenged the authority of the Pope; if they had won Parliamentary backing, as at one time seemed just possible, the royal supremacy might have been instituted a century and a half before the Reformation Parliament.[1] Henry VIII's Reformation publicly and stridently rejected the Pope's authority, and that of the international church, replacing them by the royal supremacy. There had been mediaeval precedents for the lay power limiting that of the church; in the sixteenth century many Catholic monarchies were to establish a great deal of control over churches within their dominions. But such actions were taken with the agreement of the papacy. This agreement might be reluctantly conceded to *force majeure*; but its existence sharply differentiated Gallicanism from Anglicanism. A great war of words followed England's Reformation, in which fundamental questions were asked about the grounds on which religious authority was justified. The rapid changes in England from Henry to a nine-year-old boy and two women showed that it was difficult merely to replace the authority of the Pope by that of the monarch without raising vast problems about the nature of authority and allegiance. So what authority was there?

Protestants thought that the answer was to be sought in the Bible, now for the first time officially translated into the vernacular and so made available for popular discussion. But the original protestant hope that all men would agree in their interpretation of the Bible proved unfounded. The Bible said different things to different people: who was to decide between rival interpretations? Even if it was agreed that "the church" should decide, who is the church? Civil service bishops appointed by the government? and dependent on it

---

* William Tyndale, *The Obedience of a Christian Man* (1527-8), in *Doctrinal Treatises* (Parker Soc., 1848), p. 291.

for promotion? Bishop Jeremy Taylor in the seventeenth century taught that denial of the Apostolic Succession would be "a plain path and inlet to atheism and irreligion; for by this means it will not only be impossible to agree concerning the meaning of Scripture, but the Scripture itself, and all the records of religion, will become useless, and of no efficacy or persuasion".[2] That sounded like popery to radicals: conversely the extreme position of Milton seemed anarchy to conservatives, yet it was only an extension of Luther's logic: "Every believer is entitled to interpret the Scriptures ... for himself. He has the Spirit who guides truth, and he has the mind of Christ. Indeed, no one else can usefully interpret them for him, unless that person's interpretation coincides with the one he makes for himself and his own conscience".[3] The essence of protestantism — the priesthood of all believers — was logically a doctrine of individualist anarchy. "Here I stand, so help me God, I can no other"; in that cry Luther rejected the authority of Pope, church and secular power.[4]

By proclaiming that the church is composed of all believers, and not a privileged corporation of clerics, protestantism undermined the authority of the church as a self-sufficient institution. By denying the immunity of the priesthood as a separate caste, and by denying the Pope's right to pronounce authoritatively in secular affairs, Luther by implication justified the intervention of the secular power in the internal affairs of the church. Luther had no hesitation in calling on the secular power against Anabaptists, just as Henry VIII martyred Catholics and Anabaptists impartially.[5] By what authority? It was not long before Parliament was determining what was and what was not heresy, and imposing its views on all subjects as a test of political reliability. They have "made laws", Sir Thomas Wilson noted, "that every man that hath voice in the Parliament or any state of possession in the land shall take his corporal oath for the maintenance of the religion now established".[6] The road runs straight from Luther to *Leviathan*.

Thomas Hall illustrated the point vividly in a sermon preached at the election of the Lord Mayor in 1644. Frederick Duke of Saxony "was almost discouraged by the popish doctrine about magistracy". But on reading Luther's *De Magistratu* the Duke "lifts up his hands to heaven, thanking God that at last he was convinced the state of magistracy he lived in to be pleasing to God, and that he might in it do him a great deal of service".[7] Yet the protestant emphasis on conscience, the inner light, leads logically on to anarchism. Once a constraining authority exists, be it state or bishops or presbytery, it is bound at some stage or other to come up against dissenting consciences.

Hobbes faced, and thought he had solved, the problem of authority. The absolute natural rights of individuals necessitate the absolute power of the sovereign; the only alternative is anarchy. This was a wholly protestant solution to a wholly protestant paradox. Tyndale for instance, wrote that "the king is in this world without law; and may at his lust do right or wrong and shall give accounts but to God only". James I had little to add to that: no wonder Henry VIII thought *The Obedience of a Christian Man* a book fit "for him and all kings to read". Tyndale is quite clear about the social functions of the monarchy: it gets rid of the Pope on the one hand; on the other, "it is better to suffer one tyrant than many".[8] The point was hammered home in the *Homily against Disobedience and Wilful Rebellion.* "Perfect submission to kings" is "the glory of the protestant cause", Jeremy Taylor wrote, with some justification.[9]

But though the Mortal God triumphed in the short run, the paradox remained. Protestant doctrine was primarily concerned with the inner man. Luther taught individuals to stand on their own feet and question authority. Yet he (and the English reformers) had to shelter behind the temporal authority both against the power of the international church and against those of the unprivileged who carried the appeal to conscience further than suited their betters. But this was a political necessity, not a logical consequence of the reformers' teaching.

Tyndale, unlike Hobbes, left the paradox wholly unresolved. "The most despised person in his realm is the king's brother and fellow-member with him and equal with him in the church of God and of Christ".[10] John Knox was to address stern words to Mary Queen of Scots on that theme. The same arguments that prevailed against the absolute authority of the Pope could be used against the absolute authority of the King: authority having once been challenged, the logical road to theories of democracy in church and state was clear — and not only with the hindsight of the historian. Whether and when any given community would travel down that road depended less on logic than on the development of social forces within that community.

The point was made by a critic of Henry Barrow, who had written "To our prince we are humble and obedient subjects in all things which are not repugnant to God's laws". His contemporary critic added the marginal comment: "in all things that you fancy".[11] Barrow thought that if "the estate of these prelates, clergymen, ministers and their proceedings ... be found repugnant unto the Testament of Christ, then are they ... for the safety of the state to be abolished", lest they draw down the wrath of God.[12] Barrow found no warrant in the Bible for fasting on ember days, the eve of saints' days or in Lent.[13] Robert Browne told Burghley that "the Word of God doth expressly set down all necessary and general rules of the arts and all learning", and that the universities should be reformed in accordance with these rules.[14] The antinomian separatist John Traske came to require express instructions from the Bible for everything that was done.[15] More subtly, Stephen Marshall in 1646 found social mobility and the career open to the talents justified by the lives of Moses, Issachar, Gideon ("a private gentleman, it may be but a yeoman's son"), Saul ("a private gentleman's son"), David, Amos and the fishermen of the New Testament. So God had taken "gentlemen from following their hawks and hounds, and tradesmen from their shops, and husbandmen from their ploughs" to command the New Model Army.[16] The Marquis of Newcastle was not absurdly exaggerating when he warned the young Charles II that "if any be Bible-men, ... they may think it a service to God to destroy you and say the spirit moved them".[17]

There is thus a tension between any state church and protestant individual consciences. Some consciences some time are likely to feel called upon to obey the God within them rather than the state or its church. Such clashes occur more often, and affect larger numbers of people, at times of social, economic or political crisis than when all is going relatively peacefully and normally: under Edward VI and Charles I rather than under Elizabeth, at least before the fifteen-nineties.

In 1656 Francis Osborne pointed out that "if faith is not allowed to be taken implicitly from the authority of any church, a freedom of choice will result to all. ... And since so considerable a falsehood is thought to be discovered by our governors in the clergy's tenet for the impunity of kings, why may not their poor subjects be unsatisfied about heaven and hell?[18] It was a powerful argument for the restoration of king, bishops and parochial clergy to interpret the Scriptures to their congregations.

Before the Reformation, first-hand knowledge of the Bible was normally confined to those who could read Latin. Lollards produced their own illicit translations into the vernacular, with the democratic intention of allowing all Christians to have access to the sacred text. After the Reformation the Bible was available for popular discussion. Henry VIII's attempt to confine Bible-reading to those of the rank of yeoman and above, and to abolish "diversity of opinions" by statute, were both unsuccessful. The circulation of an English Bible had been authorized in order to fortify Henry VIII's Reformation against Rome, which as all protestants knew preferred ignorance.[19] After 1525 Luther recognized the dangers of unsupervised and uncontrolled Bible-reading by the lower classes and their spokesmen. He tried to replace, or to control, Bible-reading by the use of catechisms. Since the answers were intended to be learnt by rote, catechisms could be used for indoctrinating the illiterate as well as the literate.[20]

In England the protestant emphasis on the importance both of preaching and of a learned clergy testifies to a similar anxiety to have qualified experts ready to undertake the ticklish job of interpreting the Bible. But the ethos of protestantism itself bred resistance to expert (and upper-class) interpreters. The Bible — in part perhaps thanks to Lollardy — proved a time-bomb which humbler protestants used against their betters. Whitgift discouraged Bible-reading in households, where there would be no university-trained divine handy to interpret "difficult" passages.[21] One of the objects of the Authorized Version of 1611 was to produce an approved official version to supplant the Geneva Bible, which was popular with Puritans but which James thought of all translations the worst because of its subversive marginal notes.

William Bradshaw had written in 1605: "The Word of God contained in the writings of the Prophets and Apostles is of absolute perfection, given by Christ the head of the church to be unto the same the sole canon and rule of all matters of religion and the worship and service of God. ... Whatsoever done in the same service and worship cannot be justified by the said Word is unlawful".[22] Nor was this just a separatist emphasis. Thomas Cartwright thought that the Bible called for the elimination of all remnants of popery, and that society could not be properly ordered or stable until this had been done. Until then everything would be topsy-turvy: "the water should go to the stream, the scholar should teach his master, the sheep control their pastor". The possibility of short-term disorder must be faced, in order to establish the right order permanently.[23] Whitgift on the other hand saw Cartwright's approach as permanently disorderly, since it called for aristocratic or democratic government of the church — and so was incompatible with monarchy.[24]

The point was summed up nicely by William Sanderson. If men seek "direct warrant from the written Word of God" for everything they do, "all human authority will soon be despised". The orders of princes no less than of parents and masters "shall be taken into slow deliberation, and the equity of them sifted by those that are bound to obey, though they know no cause why, so long as they know no cause to the contrary".[25]

So the original protestant hope that the conclusions to be drawn from the Bible were self-evident and incontestable proved woefully false. Officialdom assumed that the protestant clergy would continue to be the official interpreters of the Bible, under guidance from above. Hence insistence on a learned clergy, on a university education which would include Latin and theology, and which might include Greek, Hebrew and other languages. But — apart from the fact that most of the clergy fell short of the desired educational standard — if all believers are priests, why should officially ordained clergymen have a special capacity to interpret the Scriptures? The point was made forcefully by the Leveller William Walwyn. "Since the Scriptures are now in English, which at first were in Hebrew, Greek or Syriac or what other language; why may not one that understands English only both understand and declare the true meaning of them as well as an English Hebrician or Grecian or Roman whatsoever? ... I pray you, what are you the better for having the Scripture in your own language? When it was locked up in the Latin tongue by the policy of Rome, you might have had a learned friar at any time to have interpreted the same. ... Now ... you must have a university man to interpret the English, or you are in as bad a case as before — but not in worse; for, for your money, you may have plenty at your service, and to interpret as shall best please your fancy".[26]

This is looking rather far ahead. Under Elizabeth attempts had been made, through prophesyings and classes, to arrive at an agreed consensus of clerical opinion. But these meetings were discouraged, to put it mildly, by Elizabeth, and were suppressed by her bishops. In any case, after the invention of printing, with literacy increasing, not only for economic reasons but also because lay protestants strove to read the Bible for themselves, it was difficult to preserve a clerical monopoly. The protestant and later Puritan emphasis on preaching as necessary for salvation was a way of maintaining clerical supremacy whilst allowing the laity to think for themselves within limits laid down by the clergy. But repetitions of sermons in families and among groups of the godly could easily develop into conventicles in which the laity usurped the authority of priests, some of whom were still dumb dogs. So preaching — and gadding to sermons when one's incumbent was a non-preacher — could lead to conventicles, conventicles to separatism.[27] In separatist congregations the whole body of believers, not merely the minister or the elders, joined in discussions and the administration of discipline.[28]

Professor Collinson has shown how compatible Puritanism was with the interests of the gentry — offering a diminution of episcopal control over the clergy and the substitution of the influence of the propertied laity.[29] It would have been a *via media* between democratic sectarianism and monarchical episcopacy: the example of the Scottish kirk, in which aristocratic lay elders played a prominent part, was always attractive. Hence the failure of attempts by Presbyterian ministers to build up classes of ministers within the state church. Such attempts foundered on the opposition of the secular power, whether Elizabeth working through her civil service bishops or the Long Parliament asserting its supremacy over the classes which it set up.

Separatism was one answer, though a very hazardous choice before 1640, since it involved exile or a risky illegality. Separatism signified among other things a rejection of the specialized, educated priests of the established church as fitting interpreters of the Bible or expounders of God's will. Against them appeal was made to the congregation of believers.[30] But even when separatism became easier after 1640, the ideal of a national church still retained its hold, as was demonstrated by the practice of occasional conformity when dissenters were excluded from the national church after 1660.[31] Tensions remained, between individual consciences and the state church before 1640, between individual consciences and all churches after 1660. For in order to survive after the restoration the sects had to organize, to define their beliefs, to expel or disown those who would not or could not accept what the majority accepted. Splits and schisms among the Quakers in the fifties and sixties show that most anarchical of all the religious groupings having to accommodate itself to the needs of organization and discipline. The sense of the meeting was a more democratic authority than that of bishops; but it was authority, and the Society of Friends became something like a church. The minutes of Baptist meetings in this period would almost suggest that excommunication was the main business of the congregations.[32] Hobbism prevailed.

Different tensions were felt between 1640 and 1660, but they too related to the problem of authority. Free trade in ideas replaced monopoly. Attempts to preserve or restore a group of professional expert interpreters roused intense hostility. Walwyn in his *Prediction of Mr. Edwards His Conversion* (1646) made that great persecutor confess to "base fear that plain unlearned men should seek for knowledge any other way than as they are directed by us that are learned". For "if they should fall to teach one another . . . we should lose our domination in being sole judges of doctrine and discipline, whereby our predecessors have overruled states and kingdoms. Or lastly, that we should lose our profits and plenteous maintenance by tithes".[33]

A state church depended on the clergyman's legal right to collect tithes from his parishioners. If ministers were dependent on the voluntary contributions of their parishioners, Sir Walter Mildmay reflected in 1587, they would have but "a bare and uncertain" living. Abolition of tithes would have meant the end of a national church as it had hitherto existed: here again we can cite Bancroft, in agreement with interregnum radicals.[34] Milton thought abolition of tithes essential to religious liberty; the Master of Gonville and Caius, William Dell, shared Milton's hostility. In Winstanley's ideal commonwealth preaching for hire was one of the few offences which merited the death sentence. For most beneficed clergymen it was a bread and butter question, but there were strong traditional arguments in favour of the national community being organized within a single church.

The radical attack on Oxford and Cambridge must be seen in the context of the problem of authority. The universities trained clergymen with special linguistic skills which were thought to fit them to interpret the Scriptures. Those who believed that any layman could interpret the Bible for himself, and that mechanic preachers gifted with God's grace could interpret it far better than the most learned cleric lacking divine grace, had no use for the universities as they existed in the early seventeenth century. And indeed there is ample evidence that the behaviour of undergraduates and dons was often far from godly. In *An Almond for a Parrot* (1590) Nashe had accused Puritans of wanting to abolish the universities. Winstanley and other reformers hoped to get rid of them as seminaries training the clergy, to get rid of a special clerical caste altogether. "From Oxford and Cambridge come hireling priests", declared Edward Byllynge, speaking for many within and outside the Quaker movement.[35] Some would have been happy to see reformed universities surviving to give a secular education, with greater emphasis on science and modern subjects.[36] Restoration of a single state church and tithes, and preservation of the universities for training a learned clergy, were major achievements of 1660. Bishops lost their political power, but the exclusion of dissenters from the universities ensured a clergy more loyal to the established church than before 1640.

But there was too a long-standing popular hostility to education as a source of privilege, of class distinctions. The most obvious example of this was benefit of clergy, which allowed anyone who could stumble through the neck verse to escape the major penalties of his first criminal conviction. Originally this privilege had been restricted to the clergy; but with the extension of literacy it became a social privilege. Not until 1692 was it extended to women.[37] Jack Cade in *2 Henry VI* complained "because they could not read thou hast hanged them". "Away with him. He speaks Latin" (IV. vii 42-3, 55-6). Henry Barrow made the point rather differently when he spoke of the universities as guardians of Antichrist's throne and Latin as the language of the Beast.[38] "Cobblers and tinkers" in Chelmsford in 1642 were alleged to preach "that learning hath always been an enemy to the Gospel and that it were a happy thing if there were no universities, and all books burnt except the Bible".[39] "The common cry of the multitude", a preacher told the House of Lords in May 1647, was "down with learning": "ye may see what good learning did in the bishops' time".[40]

The Bible of course had to be interpreted. Calvin himself had done a good deal by way of interpreting the letter to mean what he wanted, as Milton was to do later.[41] Calvin developed the useful idea that the Holy Ghost spoke to the capacity of his audience. "Moses wrote in a popular style things which, without instruction, all ordinary persons endued with common sense are able to understand". He did not write for professional astronomers when describing the creation, for example. "Because he was ordained a teacher as well of the unlearned and rude as of the learned, he could not otherwise fulfil his office than by descending to this grosser method of instruction". Similarly Moses "was not ignorant of geometry", but in describing the building of the ark he "spoke in a homely style, to suit the capacity of the people".[42] This idea that God "accommodated" his Scriptural revelation to the capacity of the unlearned vulgar was to prove useful for seventeenth-century scientists like Galileo (under threat from the Inquisition) and a Puritan turned Latitudinarian like John Wilkins.[43]

A further advance was actually to criticize the Biblical text in the process of interpreting it. Ralegh did this frequently in his *History of the World*.[44] So did Milton, and Jeremy Taylor.[45] The profane had long pointed out the Bible's contradictions and inconsistencies. In Ralegh's dashingly advanced circle in the fifteen-nineties men agreed that religion had been invented "to keep the baser sort in fear".[46] Such ideas caused alarm even when limited to this restricted group of intellectuals. But in James's reign ordinary people were expressing scepticism about the Bible.[47] A Lancashire assize sermon of 1632 insisted that a ministry was essential to "keep the consciences of men in awe".[48]

During the Revolution Walwyn and Clement Wrighter were free to discuss publicly the contradictions and inconsistencies of the Bible, treating it as a historical document to which normal scholarly techniques should be applied. Samuel Fisher argued with much learning that a text so corrupt and self-contradictory could not possibly be the Word of God. His book was appropriately named *The Rusticks Alarum to the Rabbies: Or, The Country correcting the University, and Clergy*. It threatened to put interpreters of Scripture out of a job; and the suggestion that it came from the rustics who composed the mass of tithe-payers did not make it any more welcome to the rabbis. But Fisher's book was not published until 1660, and so made its main impact on scholars including, it appears, Spinoza.[49] If it had appeared earlier, when it could have been discussed by rustics and artisans, the undermining effect on the status of the Bible might have been more serious.[50] The restoration came just in time. Characters in restoration comedy made jokes about "faults in the translation" when faced with an inconvenient Biblical prohibition.[51] To the argument that women owed obedience to men because God created Adam before Eve Mary Astell — a serious and pious lady—retorted that God had created animals before Adam: what conclusion should be drawn from that?[52] The whole tone of intellectual discussion had changed.

The important thing for our purposes is not the conclusion reached, or not reached, to the problem of authority, but the process of discussion which the appeal to the Bible unleashed. Matthew Arnold was utterly wrong when he wrote "the one who says that God's Church makes him believe what he believes, and the other who says that God's Word makes him believe what he believes, are for the philosopher perfectly alike in not really and truly knowing, when they say 'God's Church' and 'God's Word', what it is they say or whereof they affirm".[53] They may be alike for the philosopher, but for the historian the one accepts an external and (for him) arbitrary authority, the church, the other an internal authority, whose validity he can test in discussion with other believers. That distinction is what the Reformation had been about. The mere fact of accepting the Bible as ultimate arbiter forced Biblical criticism upon protestants.

Desperate attempts were made to reassert the authority of Scripture by providing a convincing overruling authority, whose dicta would win acceptance. John Reeve's announcement that God had appointed him sole interpreter of the Bible was one such attempt; but Reeve won relatively few adherents. For Quakers the inner light within all men and women was to provide the answer; but new inner light proved to be but old conscience writ more extensively. "The Lamb's War" of the Quakers, Professor Bauman says, "was in one major outward sense a struggle between the charismatic prophets of Quakerism and the upholders of the priestly tradition of established religion, as rival claimants to exclusive religious legitimacy as spokesmen of the divine word".[54]

So all roads lead to Hobbes. His insistence that the sovereign and only the sovereign could interpret the Bible was unpopular among theologians, but it proved more acceptable to ordinary citizens and—in practice if not in theory—to governments. In 1676 Chief Justice Hale ruled that to say religion was a cheat was an offence punishable in the common-law courts.[55] Authority, which in the sixteenth century had belonged to the Pope, or to a divine king, or to the Apostolic Succession of bishops, now rested with the King in Parliament, and with the common law, taking over the functions of the declining ecclesiastical courts. After 1688 even Tories recognized that toleration must be extended to nonconformists. The Church of England kept rural congregations under control, with the aid of the gentry; but the help of dissenters was needed to check urban speculation. The Societies for the Reformation of Manners were one form of co-operation between the state church and nonconformists for social purposes.[56] "If the common people are induced to lay aside religion," wrote Charles Davenant in 1698, "they will quickly cast off all fear of their rulers."[57] It was worth expending time and money to avert that double catastrophy.

NOTES

1. K.B. McFarlane, *John Wyclif and the Origins of Nonconformity* (1952), pp. 51-2, 61, 92.
2. J. Taylor, *The Whole Works* (1836), II, p. 33. See p. 322 below.
3. *M.C.P.W.*, VI, pp. 583-4.
4. Cf. *The Reformation Crisis* (ed. J. Hurtsfield, 1971), p. 1: "in the profoundest sense a crisis of authority".
5. See p. 163 below, and a valuable paper by Robert Weimann, "Shakespeare und Luther", in *Shakespeare Jahrbuch*, Band 120 (1984), esp. pp. 20-4. For the crisis of authority in general see his "Autorität und Gesellschaftliche Erfahrung in Shakespeares Theater", *ibid.*, Band 119 (1983), esp. pp. 92-4. See also A. Sinfield, *Literature in Protestant England, 1560-1660* (1983), pp. 138-9.
6. Ed. F.J. Fisher, Thomas Wilson, *The State of England Anno Dom. 1600*, p. 41, in *Camden Miscellany*, XVI (1936).
7. T. Hall, *The Magistrates Commission from Heaven* (1644), p. 2.
8. Tyndale, *Doctrinal Treatises*, pp. 178-80.
9. Taylor, *The Whole Works*, II, p. 62; cf. p. 47, and III, p. 717.
10. Tyndale, *Doctrinal Treatises*, p. 125.
11. Ed. L.H. Carlson, *The Writings of Henry Barrow, 1587-1590* (1962), p. 125.
12. *Ibid.*, p. 241.
13. Ed. Carlson, *The Writings of Henry Barrow, 1590-1591* (1960) p. 68.
14. Ed. A. Peel and L.H. Carlson, *The Writings of Robert Harrison and Robert Browne*, p. 530.
15. B.R. White, "John Traske (1585-1636) and London Puritanism", *Trans. of the Congregational Historical Soc.*, XX (1968), p. 225.
16. Stephen Marshall, *The Right Understanding of the Times*, a sermon preached to the House of Commons, 30 December 1646 (1647), pp. 4-5.
17. In Ellis, *Original Letters Illustrative of English History*, first series, III, p. 289.

18. F. Osborne, *Advice to a Son*, in *Miscellaneous Works* (11th edn., 1722) I, p. 99. See chapter 8 below.

19. *Homilies*, pp. 501-2, 507-8.

20. R. Gawthrop and R. Strauss, "Protestantism and Literacy in Early Modern Germany", *P. and P.*, No. 104 (1984), pp. 31-55.

21. Ed. H. Gee and W. J. Hardy, *Documents Illustrative of English Church History* (1896), p. 481.

22. W. Bradshaw, *English Puritanism* (1605), p. 1.

23. Lake, *Moderate Puritanism and the Elizabethan Church*, pp. 90-1.

24. Strype, *Life of Whitgift*, I, pp. 114, 504. Cf. I, pp. 72-3 for the even greater subversiveness of Anabaptists.

25. Sanderson, *XXXV Sermons* (7th edn., 1681), pp. 61, 65.

26. [William Walwyn], *The Power of Love* (1643), pp. 46-8, in Haller (ed.), *Tracts on Liberty in the Puritan Revolution*, II. Cf. Brian Manning, "The Levellers and Religion", in *Radical Religion in the English Revolution* (ed. J. F. McGregor and B. Reay, Oxford U.P., 1984), p. 66.

27. D. Zaret, "Ideology and Organization in Puritanism", *Archive for European Sociology*, XXI (1980), pp. 93-5.

28. Cf. M. James, *English Politics and the Concept of Honour* (*P. and P.* Supplement, 83, 1978), pp. 82-3.

29. See pp. 67-9 below.

30. *W.T.U.D.*, pp. 371-3.

31. See Chapter 14 below.

32. *W.T.U.D.*, pp. 373-8; cf. my *The Experience of Defeat* (1984), pp. 290-4.

33. Walwyn, *A Prediction of Mr. Edwards His Conversion and Recantation* (1646), p. 9, in Haller, *Tracts on Liberty*, III. Cf. [Walwyn], *The Compassionate Samaritane* (1644), pp. 2-3, *ibid.*; [Lilburne], *Englands Birth-Right Justified* (1645), pp. 8-9, *ibid.*

34. S. E. Lehmberg, *Sir Walter Mildmay and Tudor Government* (Texas U.P., 1964), p. 289; ed. E. R. Foster, *Proceedings in Parliament, 1610*, I, *The House of Lords* (Yale U.P., 1966), p. 224.

35. E.B., *A Word of Reproof, and Advice to my late Fellow-Soldiers and Officers* (1659), pp. 19-20.

36. See my *Change and Continuity in Seventeenth-Century England* (1974), Chapters 5 and 7.

37. Susan Staves, *Players' Scepters: Fictions of Authority in the Restoration* (Nebraska U.P., 1979), p. 184.

38. Quoted in my *Antichrist in Seventeenth-Century England* (1971), pp. 138-42.

39. [Bruno Ryves], *Angliae Ruina* (1647), p. 27. Cf. Robert South: "Latin was with them a mortal crime, and Greek ... the sin" against the Holy Ghost (*Sermons*, 1692, I, p. 160).

40. William Hussey, *The Magistrates Charge for the Peoples Safetie* (1647), p. 28.

41. See for example Calvin, *A Commentary on Daniel* (trans. and ed. by Thomas Myers, 1966), II, p. 78. First published 1561. Cf. Milton's divorce pamphlets.

42. Calvin, *A Commentary on Genesis* (trans. and ed. John King, 1965), I, pp. 85-7, 256; cf. pp. 141, 177. First published 1534.

43. B.J. Shapiro, *John Wilkins, 1614-1672: An Intellectual Biography* (California U.P., 1969), pp. 51, 268-9.

44. Cf. for example *The History of the World* (Edinburgh, 1820), I, pp. 63, 75-9, 87-9, 158, 237, 257; II, pp. 130, 222-3, 278-82, 369; III, pp. 214, 266-7; IV, pp. 572-3, and *passim*.

45. J. Taylor, *The Whole Works*, I, pp. 218-21.

46. See p. 131 below. Cf. George Chapman, *Bussy D'Ambois*, in *Comedies and Tragedies* (1873), II, p. 39; *W.T.U.D.*, p. 163.

47. M.J. Ingram, *Ecclesiastical Justice in Wiltshire, 1600-1640, with especial reference to cases concerning sex and marriage* (Oxford D. Phil. thesis, 1976), pp. 81, 91, 104.

48. R. Richardson, *Puritanism in north-western England: A Regional Study of the Diocese of Chester to 1642* (Manchester U.P., 1972), p. 145.

49. R.H. Popkin, "Spinoza and the Conversion of the Jews", in *Spinoza's Political and Theological Thought* (ed. C. De Deugd, Amsterdam, 1984), p. 174.

50. *W.T.U.D.*, Chapter 11.

51. E.g. Sir John Vanbrugh, *The Provok'd Wife* (1697), I, i.

52. M. Astell, *Reflections upon Marriage* (3rd edn., 1706), Sig. a2. I am grateful to Bridget Hill for drawing my attention to this point.

53. Arnold, *Culture and Anarchy* (Nelson, n.d.), p. 256.

54. R. Bauman, *Let your words be few: Symbolism of speaking and silence among seventeenth-century Quakers* (Cambridge U.P., 1983), p. 41. Cf. B. Reay, "Quakerism and Society", in McGregor and Reay, *op. cit.*, pp. 145-7.

55. See p. 338 below.

56. See p. 335 below.

57. *The Political and Commercial Works of Charles Davenant* (1967), pp. 45-7.

5. *The State-Ecclesiastical*

"These differences ... arose originally solely from the constitution of an authoritative national church-state, consisting solely in the power and interest of the clergy – wherein the people, either as Christians, protestants or subjects of the kingdom, are not concerned. ...

"It is no less glorious in the sight of God ... to suffer in giving testimony against the abominations of the apostate, antichristian church-state, than to suffer for the Gospel itself in opposition to idolatrous paganism".*

The idea of the English nation was bound up with protestantism. The state-ecclesiastical, as Owen makes clear, was something distinct from the nation and from the civil state. The clergy formed an estate of the realm, yet although bishops sat in the House of Lords, the lower clergy were not represented in the House of Commons. The Convocations of Canterbury and York legislated for the clergy; but unless the canons passed by them were confirmed by Parliament their authority over the laity was uncertain. Bishops thus occupied a curious constitutional position; the only members of the clerical estate who sat in Parliament.

A besetting problem for historians is the survival of names describing things which have totally changed their nature. It took several reform bills to convince historians that Parliaments in the seventeenth century did not represent the people of England. It is difficult for historians even today to appreciate that seventeenth century radicals often use the word "people" whilst, consciously or unconsciously, excluding "the poor". Similarly with the word "bishop". To us the word conjures up genial rosy-faced old gentlemen patting children on the head; or learned scholars. It comes as a salutory shock to find Milton concluding his first prose pamphlet, *Of Reformation Touching Church-Discipline in England*, by consigning all bishops, apparently *ex officio* and regardless of their

---

*John Owen, *Some considerations about union among protestants* (1680), and *A brief and impartial account of the nature of the protestant religion* (1682), both in *Works* (1850-3), XIV, pp. 520, 555.

individual merits, to "the deepest and darkest gulf of hell", there to remain to all eternity. This is an attitude repugnant to twentieth-century liberal ideas. But before we get too one-sidedly self-righteous, let us recall another judgment of Milton's more congenial to twentieth-century liberalism: "It is disgraceful and disgusting that the Christian religion should be supported by violence".[1] And let us remember that Archbishop Laud normally favoured imposing the most severe corporal sentences on his enemies; when others suggested a flogging, he would add branding or loss of ears. Bishops aroused intense passions because they were vigorous partisans, wielding political power in an age of revolutionary crisis.

Patrick Collinson's splendid Ford Lectures depict conscientious and hard-working Jacobean and Caroline bishops presiding over a broadly-based church which won general acceptance.[2] One problem with this is the volume of literary evidence attesting to the unpopularity of bishops and the clergy. My object in this chapter is to collect evidence on attitudes towards bishops and the church in the two generations before 1640. This was an age of fierce Puritan and separatist attacks on bishops. These are of course biassed and not to be used in isolation. Instead of quoting them, I shall cite almost exclusively defenders of the hierarchy. Whatever allowances we make, it is quite clear from their evidence that "episcopacy had few defenders", as Collinson himself writes.[3] Statements by bishops themselves cannot be lightly brushed aside.

The opening words of the future Bishop Cooper's *Admonition to the People of England* (1589) speak of "the loathesome contempt, hatred and disdain that *the most part* of men in these days bear ... toward the ministers of the church of God. ... He who can most bitterly inveigh against bishops and preachers ... thinketh of himself, *and is esteemed of other*, as the most zealous and earnest furtherer of the gospel".[4]

Cooper put a hypothetical case against the hierarchy, that God has shown judgment against them for their wickedness, "because he hath made them so contemptible, so vile and despised before all the people: for (say they) we may see how all men loathe and disdain them". Cooper's answer is not to deny the contempt, but to deny that it is "always an unfallible token of evil priests and ministers, or a certain sign of God's displeasure toward them, when the people do hate, disdain and contemn them. ... It may be surely, and indeed I think it to be very true, that God hath touched our bishops and preachers with the scourge of ignominy and reproach for their slackness and negligence in their office". "The whole state ecclesiastical ... is grown into hatred and contempt, and all inferior subjects disdain in any point to be ruled by them". "The people ... have conceived an heathenish contempt of religion, and a disdainful loathing of the ministers thereof".[5] That is no doubt hyperbole; but Archbishop Sandys said something very similar: "the ministers of the word, the messengers of Christ, ...are esteemed *tamquam excrementa mundi*".[6] "Our estimation is little", Aylmer confirmed, "our authority is less; so that we are become contemptible in the eyes of the people".[7] The clergy themselves, in a formal document of 1586, remarked "with how great hatred the common sort of men are influenced against the ministers of the church";[8] and the Puritan Richard Greenham spoke of the "great hatred" which had "sprung up from the people" against the clergy because they were more diligent in collecting tithes than in dispensing hospitality.[9] Bancroft was sure that if congregational elections were allowed, candidates favoured by the hierarchy would be rejected because of "the sinister affections of the people".[10] In the Parliament of 1628 Sir Humphrey May argued that "juries of poor freeholders" could not be trusted to be fair to the clergy".[11] Cooper had been alarmed by the dangerous argument that bishops should be deposed and their lands confiscated merely because "our bishops and ministers are evil men". He did not deny the allegation, but suggested that the same argument could be turned against princes and magistrates.[12]

Francis Godwin, in his *Catalogue of the Bishops of England* (1601), admitted that "in the vulgar sort ... is bred a conceit not only that the men [he is speaking of pre-Reformation clergy] were wicked, and so their doctrines corrupt, but also their functions and callings to be utterly unlawful and antichristian".[13] Even Burghley was shocked to see "such worldliness in many that were otherwise affected before they came to cathedral chairs."[14]

Now many of these statements are to be discounted: they were propagandist special pleading by men on the defensive. But their cumulative effect is remarkable; and special pleading pleads in vain if it is recognizably incorrect. The social argument in favour of episcopacy, used by Cooper, had already become familiar. Archbishop Parker had observed that "how secure soever the nobility were of these Puritans, and countenanced them against the bishops, they themselves might rue it at last". Puritans "tended towards a popularity".[15] "If you had once made an equality ... among the clergy", Whitgift told Puritans, "it would not be long or you attempted the like among the laity".[16] "Men", he declared in 1583, "are naturally prone to speak ill of two kinds of persons, viz. of bishops and magistrates". The original cause of this, he thought, was the devil.[17] Hooker pointed out that the title of bishops to their livings was as good as any lay title to property.[18] When in the Long Parliament Oliver Cromwell attacked the great properties of bishops, the answer came pat: parity in the church will lead to parity in the state.[19]

The judicious Hooker was on the defensive about the ecclesiastical establishment. "If we maintain things that are established, we have ... to strive with a number of heavy prejudices deeply rooted in the hearts of men, who think that herein we serve the time and speak in favour of the present state because thereby we either hold or seek preferment".[20] Brightman in 1615 confirmed the unpopularity of bishops with "the people and multitude", and the popularity of Marprelate's attack on them twenty-six years earlier.[21]

This evidence appears to confict with Collinson's scholarly reconstruction of the virtues of many Jacobean bishops. Perhaps there had been a rapid improvement? Perhaps bishops, then as now, varied in their tastes and performance? But we cannot ignore the views I have quoted, however exaggerated. Hostility towards bishops seems to be more prominent under the primacies of Whitgift, Bancroft and Laud. Yet the clergy were not immune from criticism even under James. In 1610 the Bishop of Lincoln said in the House of Lords that the lower House "loved not bishops" — a charge which Lord Saye and Sele sharply denied.[22] Marten in the same year attacked parsons for preaching up a prerogative right to taxation, and both he and Sir Roger Owen in 1614 accused the clergy of supporting absolutism. Bishop Neile was said to have committed a greater treason than killing a judge when he attacked the House of Commons:[23] and there was "murmuring against the bishops" for urging payment of a benevolence after the dissolution of Parliament and then contributing inadequately themselves.[24] The sordid scandal of the Essex divorce, in which the saintly Lancelot Andrewes was involved as well as Laud,[25] also brought discredit on the hierarchy. There were allegations that money was offered for bishoprics.[26] There was the Archbishop of Dublin who, Bishop Bedell's biographer reports, had only one sermon, on the text "Touch not mine Anointed", which he preached every year upon the King's accession day. It was in 1640 that Bishop Atherton was "condemned for iniquities far above all that is kept upon record concerning Sodom".[27]

In the anecdote of James I admitting that he made bad men bishops, his explanation was that "no good men would take the office on them".[28] Hooker had anticipated the point: "Herod and Archelaus are noted to have sought out purposely the dullest and most ignoble that could be found amongst the people, preferring such to the High Priest's office" in order to discredit it. "It may be there hath been partly some show and just suspicion of like practice in some" in England.[29] Weighty words from the church's most distinguished defender. Even a loyal church and king man like Ralph Knevet wrote, probably in the sixteen-forties:

> Now the English crown
> And mitre must go down;
> Forth of his temple Christ will throw
> Those greedy money-changers now.

> A clergy proud and too licentious,
> Ever more ready tithes to gather
> Than to preach truths, and rather
> Conformable than conscientious,
> Neglecting for to give
> Bread truly nutritive
> To hungry souls, may chiefly own
> The troubles of this realm and crown.[30]

The necessity of a hierarchical state church to monarchy was admitted on all sides. Cooper claimed to be afraid that the Presbyterian platform would "bring the government of the church to a democracy or aristocracy", and this would spread "to the government of the common weal".[31] "No monarchy being able to stand when the church is in anarchy", as the Earl of Salisbury put it in 1607.[32] Parity amongst ministers cannot agree with monarchy, James said. "Whensoever the ecclesiastical dignity shall be turned in contempt", he told Salisbury, "and begin to evanish in this kingdom, the kings thereof shall not long prosper in their government and the monarchy shall fall in ruin". "Revolt in the Low Countries ... began first by a petition for matter of religion; and so did all the troubles in Scotland".[33] Innumerable statements could be cited of the necessity of the church to the state, and of episcopacy to monarchy — by Laud, Charles I and the Canons of 1640.[34] But they were not alone.

In the Parliament of 1628 Sir Walter Earle declared "Never was there ... a more near conjunction between matter of religion and matter of state, in any kingdom in the world, than there is in this kingdom at this day".[35] "It is necessary to have a religion to preserve the commonwealth", said Calibute Downing in the early thirties. Aristocracy is more convenient for this state at this time than democracy: the nobility and clergy are the main pillars of a monarchy.[36] "The civil magistrate is a church officer in every Christian commonwealth", added Sir Benjamin Rudyerd.[37]

If episcopacy was necessary to monarchy, presbytery was necessary to aristocracy. Richard Overton observed that "without a powerful compulsive presbytery in the church, a compulsive mastery or aristocratical government over the people in the state could never long be maintained".[38] But links are also suggested between parsons and the ruling class in general. Cobbler How declared that the clergy must be dressed and maintained like "men of honour, and such as be distinct from others"; "reproach and nakedness and living on mere alms they cannot brook".[39] There were to be many such denunciations from radicals during the revolutionary decades. The church's social links are confirmed by Richard Baxter: "If any would raise an army to extirpate knowledge and religion, the tinkers and sowgawters and crate-carriers and beggars and bargemen and all the rabble that cannot read, nor ever use the Bible, will be the forwardest to come into such a militia".[40] Clergymen were "the black guard of Satan", said Buckinghamshire Levellers in 1648;[41] "redcoats and blackcoats" maintained order for Diabolus in Bunyan's Mansoul.

Not unexpectedly, hostility to bishops and the clergy generally was expressed with renewed vigour after the breakdown of ecclesiastical controls in 1640-1. In *The World Turned Upside Down* I gave a good deal of evidence for popular hostility towards bishops and clergy during and immediately after the Laudian régime.[42] "So generally peevish and fanaticized were the people that not any particular discontent or personal quarrel with any private clergyman but 'these bishops, these parsons' (the whole coat)". Chestlin stressed the political connection. Just as Elizabeth's Bishop Aylmer defended the surplice as "the Queen's livery", so Chestlin referred to "episcopal government in England being indeed the King's spiritual militia, and the most powerful as commanding the consciences of subjects".[43] Charles himself had said in 1646 "I am most confident that religion will much sooner regain the militia than the militia will religion".[44] I might have quoted Bishop Warner of Rochester,[45] or Peter Barwick's *Life of Dr. John Barwick,*[46] or Bruno Ryves[47], all defenders of episcopacy.

Those who attacked bishops did so on what were (or what they said were) religious grounds. Those who defended them often defended them as necessary parts of the social order, or of the constitution of the kingdom. Thus a petition in defence of bishops in 1641 declared that "government of the church by episcopacy is most suitable to the form and frame of the civil government here in this kingdom. ... We conceive it may be of dangerous consequence for men of settled fortunes to hazard their estates by making so great an alteration and overturning upon a new form of government." "Every great alteration in church or state must needs be dangerous". The petitioners claimed the support of "many, and those of the better sort, of the inhabitants" of London.[48] Falkland echoed these words. "Since all great changes in government are dangerous, I am for trying if we cannot take away the inconveniences of bishops and the inconveniences of no bishops".[49] Strangeways and Waller expressed the same anxiety more robustly.[50]

In a valuable recent book Dr Joyce Malcolm wrote of the civil war "to the Parliamentarians it was a religious as well as a political war, to the royalists essentially a political and socio-economic conflict".[51] This simple observation clears up some of the confusion caused by an either/or attitude towards the causes of the war. Why should we assume that both sides had the same motivation? Some might be thinking of the dangers of international popery whilst others were concerned with social stability. "Putting religion first" might mean many things which are not "religious" in the modern sense — questions of foreign policy, social grievances, the right of self-expression for those normally denied it.

The conservative position was summed up with all the wisdom of hindsight by Clarendon. Of Laud's activities in Scotland his protégé wrote that it was "almost impossible that any new discipline could be introduced into the church which would not much concern the government of the state. ... It was now easy ... to suggest to men of all conditions that here was an entire new model of government in church and state".[52] "The ecclesiastical and civil state was so wrought and interwoven together ... [that it was unlikely that] the law itself would have the same respect and veneration from the people when the well-disposed fabric of the church should be rent asunder". "Many ... cordially and constantly opposed that [clerical disabilities] act, as friends rather to monarchy than religion", who however after Charles's acceptance of the act "never considered or resisted any attempt or further alteration in the church, looking upon the bishops as useless to sovereignty".[53] Digby said "I do not think that a king can put down bishops totally with safety to monarchy",[54] a point which Clarendon later elaborated in his *History of the Rebellion:* removing the bishops out of the House of Lords was "removing landmarks, and not a shaking ... but dissolving foundations".[55] Clarendon contrasted his own conscientious position on these questions with that of Sir John Colpeper, who "in matters of religion ... was in his judgment very indifferent; but more inclined to what was established, to avoid the accidents which commonly attend a change, without any motives from his conscience".[56] The distinction between Clarendon's conscience and Colpeper's lack of it is perhaps of greater importance to the recording angel than to the historian trying to disentangle the causes of the civil war.

Sir Henry Slingsby, who wanted to curb the political power of bishops, nevertheless feared lest "the common people ... would think themselves loose and absolved from all government when they should see that which they so much venerated so easily subverted".[57] "Episcopacy", said Charles I in 1648, who by that time had learnt Hyde's lesson, "was so interwoven in the laws of the land, that we apprehended the pulling out of this thread was like to make the whole garment ravel".[58] "They that hate bishops have destroyed monarchy" was Jeremy Taylor's brief summing up.[59] But James I had said it long ago: "No bishops, no King, no nobility".[60]

Bishops came back in 1660 primarily for the social reasons that had led middle-of-the-road Anglicans to defend them in 1641.[61] Isaac Barrow noted that the Church of England enjoys "the favour of the almost whole nobility and gentry".[62] But in November 1663 Robert Blackburne, Secretary to the Admiralty Committee, observed to Pepys that "the present clergy ... are hated and laughed at by everybody." Pepys agreed that they "will never heartily go down with the generality of the commons of England, they have been so used to liberty and freedom and they are so acquainted with the pride and debauchery of the present clergy".[63] Samuel Butler likewise spoke of the "general ill will and hatred they have contracted from the people of all sorts ... These officers and commanders of the

Church Militant are like soldiers of fortune that are free to serve on any side that gives the best pay".[64] Barrow, Blackburne and Butler could all be right: that was what the national church had come to. Archbishop Sheldon, Burnet wrote, spoke of religion "most commonly as of an engine of government and matter of policy". This led Charles II "to look on him as a wise and honest clergyman that had little virtue and less religion".[65]

But experience of the scorpions of Presbyterian discipline had perhaps made some of the lower orders less hostile to the whips of the Anglican establishment. Add to this the failure of the sects to sink their differences sufficiently to unite against a restoration. 1660 saw the end of hopes of a broad protestant church, the beginning of the two nations. But protestant patriotism remained. When the second Popish Plot revived fears of foreign-backed absolutism, protestant Englishmen united to bring about 1688,[66] and toleration of a limited sort in 1689. The Non-Jurors were isolated as effectively as the Laudians had been between 1640 and 1660, and this time they had to accept the changes. The Act of Settlement of 1701 finally guaranteed security from a Catholic succession. Attempts to recreate a broad Grindalian church failed after 1688, despite efforts; a limited toleration was established, which survived Tory attempts to repeal it. Protestant England was saved, despite the failure of the protestant international: Catholic allies proved useful in the wars of William and Anne against Louis XIV. The chosen nation became the England whose manifest destiny it was to rule lesser breeds.[67]

NOTES

1. *M.C.P.W.*, I, pp.616-17, VI, p.123. The tolerant Lord Brooke was almost equally virulent about bishops in his *Discourse . . . of Episcopacie.*
2. Collinson, *The Religion of Protestants, passim.*
3. Collinson, *Godly People*, p.346; cf. p.148.
4. *Op. cit.*, p.9. My italics.
5. *Ibid.*, pp.102-5, 175; cf. pp.118-19, 139, 144-5, 148, 159.
6. Quoted by Stone, *The Crisis of the Aristocracy*, p.406.
7. Quoted by Waddington, *Congregational History, 1567-1700*, p.8.
8. Petition of the clergy, in Strype, *Life of Whitgift*, p.500.
9. R. Greenham, *Works* (1612), p.698.
10. *Tracts Ascribed to Richard Bancroft.*, p.83.

11. *Commons Debates, 1628* (ed. R.C. Johnson, M.J. Cole and others, Yale U.P., 1977), III, p.432.

12. Cooper, *op. cit.*, pp.168-9.

13. Godwin, *op. cit.*, Sig. A3 v. The common people came to believe bishops to be Antichrist, Izaak Walton confirmed (*Lives*, p.185).

14. W.T. MacCaffrey, *Queen Elizabeth and the Making of Policy, 1572-1588* (Princeton U.P., 1981), p.107.

15. Strype, *Life of Parker* (Oxford U.P., 1821), II, p.323.

16. Whitgift, *Works* (Parker Soc., 1851-3), II, p.398.

17. Strype, *Life of Whitgift*, III, p.78.

18. Hooker, *Works* (1836), III, p.402.

19. The point had been made by Laud in a sermon to the Parliament of 1626 (Laud, *Works*, Oxford U.P., 1847-60, I, pp.82-3); cf. J.L. Malcolm, *Caesar's Due: Loyalty and King Charles, 1642-1646* (1983), pp.139-48.

20. Hooker, *Of the Laws of Ecclesiastical Polity* (Everyman edn.), I, p.148; cf. II, p.7. Cf. Bowyer's *Parliamentary Diary*, p.169. For parity cf. T. Case, *Gods Rising, His Enemies Scattering*, a sermon preached to the House of Commons, 26 October 1642 (1644), p.12; Francis Woodcock, *Christs Warning-piece*, preached before the House of Commons, 30 October 1644 (1644), p.2.

21. T. Brightman, *The Revelation of St. John Illustrated* (4th edn., 1644), pp. 139, 149: "Yea, and the nobility hath of a long time smelt out this rub".

22. Foster, *Proceedings in Parliament, 1610*, I, p.102.

23. *Ibid.*, II, p.328; T.L. Moir, *The Addled Parliament of 1614* (Oxford U.P., 1958), pp.116-17.

24. *Letters of John Chamberlain* (ed. N.E. McClure, Philadelphia, 1939), I, pp.542, 546.

25. Laud had already blotted his copybook by marrying (illegally) the divorced Penelope Rich to his patron, the Earl of Devonshire. See p.75 below.

26. Chamberlain, *Letters*, II, pp.154, 157.

27. Ed. E.S. Shuckburgh, *Two Biographies of William Bedell* (Cambridge U.P., 1902), pp.146, 149.

28. Lord Brooke, *A Discourse opening the Nature of . . . Episcopacie*, p.138. "Shall I make a man a prelate . . . who hath a flagrant crime upon him?" asked James, referring to Laud's illegally marrying Lady Rich to his patron. The answer was "yes" (Sylvia Freedman, *Poor Penelope: Lady Penelope Rich*, 1983, p.168).

29. Hooker, *Works*, III, p.389; cf. my *Economic Problems of the Church*, pp.308-10, for further examples of reprehensible behaviour by Jacobean and Caroline bishops.

30. Ed. A.M. Charles, *The Shorter Poems of Ralph Knevet* (Ohio State U.P., 1966), p.80.

31. L.H. Carlson, *Martin Marprelate, Gentleman: Master Job Throkmorton laid open in his Colors* (San Marino, 1981), p.14.

32. R.G. Usher, *The Reconstruction of the English Church* (1910), II, p.142 — letter of 7 July to Secretary Lake.

33. D.H. Willson, *King James VI and I* (1956), pp.259, 209.

34. See C. Hill and E. Dell (eds.), *The Good Old Cause* (1949), pp. 167-8, 171-3, 178, 181-2.
35. Crewe, *Proceedings and Debates of the House of Commons in . . . 1628*, p. 31.
36. Calibute Downing, *A Discourse of the State-Ecclesiasticall of this Kingdome, in relation to the Civill* (2nd edn., revised and enlarged, 1634), pp. 2, 63.
37. Quoted by H. Hensley Henson, *Studies in English Religion in the 17th century* (1903), p. 107.
38. R. Overton, *A Remonstrance of Many Thousand Citizens* (1646), p. 12, in Haller, *Tracts on Liberty*, III.
39. S. How, *The Sufficiency of the Spirits Teaching* (1639), pp. 26-7; Walwyn, *A Prediction of Mr. Edwards his Conversion and Recantation* (1646), in Haller, *op. cit.*, III.
40. Baxter, *The Poor Husbandman's Advocate to Rich Racking Landlords*, p. 182.
41. [Anon.], *Light Shining in Buckinghamshire*, in Sabine, *op. cit.*, p. 622.
42. *W.T.U.D.*, pp. 29-34.
43. Pierce, *Historical Introduction to the Marprelate Tracts*, p. 78; [R. Chestlin], *Persecutio Undecima* (1681), pp. 4, 7. First published 1648.
44. Ed. Sir C. Petrie, *The Letters . . . of King Charles I* (1935), pp. 200-6.
45. E. Lee Warner, *The Life of John Warner, Bishop of Rochester* (1901), p. 33.
46. P. Barwick, *Life of Dr. John Barwick* (ed. and abridged by G.F. Barwick, 1903), p. 177.
47. [Bruno Ryves], *Angliae Ruina* (1647), *passim*.
48. Quoted in [Anon.], *The Petition for the Prelates Briefly Examined* (1641), pp. 1v, 4.
49. Quoted by Neal, *History of the Puritans*, II, p. 45.
50. See p. 313 below.
51. Joyce L. Malcolm, *op cit.*, p. 163. Cf. J. Morrill, "The Religious Context of the English Civil War", *T.R.H.S.* (1985), pp. 176-7, though he seems to me to employ a very narrow definition of "religion". I am very grateful to Dr Morrill for allowing me to read this article in advance of publication.
52. Edward Hyde, Earl of Clarendon, *History of the Rebellion and Civil Wars in England* (ed. W.D. Macray, Oxford U.P., 1888), I, pp. 138-9, 142.
53. Clarendon, *op. cit.*, I, pp. 406-7, 568.
54. J. Nalson, *An Impartial Collection of the Great Affairs of State* (1682), I, p. 752.
55. Clarendon, *op. cit.*, I, p. 407; cf. Hyde's letter to Hopton of 2 May 1648 about bishops and aristocracy in Scotland (*Calendar of Clarendon State Papers*, II, p. 403).
56. Clarendon, *The Life* (Oxford U.P., 1759), I, p. 94.
57. *Diary of Sir Henry Slingsby* (ed. D. Parsons, 1886), pp. 67-9.
58. R.W. Harris, *Clarendon and the English Revolution* (1983), p. 179.
59. J. Taylor, *The Golden Grove* (1655), in *The Whole Works*, III, p. 717.
60. G. Goodman, *The Court of King James I* (1839), I, p. 421. On "parity

in the church" leading to "parity in the state", see Joyce Malcolm, *op. cit.*, pp.139-48.
61. See *W.T.U.D.*, p.347.
62. P.H. Osmond, *Isaac Barrow: His Life and Times* (1944), p.77. See also p.318 below.
63. S. Pepys, *Diary*, 9 November 1663.
64. S. Butler, *Characters and Passages from Note-Books* (ed. A.R. Waller, Cambridge U.P., 1908), p.318.
65. Burnet, *History of My Own Time*, I, pp.313-14.
66. See p.316 below.
67. See my *Experience of Defeat*, Chapters 6(4) and 10(5).

6. *From Grindal to Laud* [1]

The personal independency of kings
Is mere state-popery in several things;
That kings have absolute command of fate
Is transsubstantiation in the state;
The senses this new doctrine can't receive,
But what we cannot see we must believe. . . .

That kings can be accountable to none,
And he can do no wrong that wears the crown,
Makes monarchs popes, and civil tyranny
Be furnished with infallibility.*

I

The Reformation gave birth to a new vested interest in protestantism which henceforth forced a *via media* upon successive governments, simply because a return to Catholicism was politically impossible. The Reformation also contributed to the enhancement of royal authority, the centralization and concentration of political power. This again was a long-term process, necessary (among other things) for defence of the landed class against peasant revolt, as well as against the great monarchies forming on the continent. The Commons and the temporal peers were calling for a royal supremacy before Luther produced his 95 *Theses*.[2]

The Reformation and the royal supremacy broke the bonds of Rome, supplied the cash needed for building a substantial fleet, provided windfalls for a large number of courtiers and other government supporters at a time of economic difficulty, and enabled the revolts of 1536 and 1549 to be suppressed (the latter with foreign mercenaries). Henry VIII's French war was a failure, as was Somerset's attempt to conquer Scotland; but land-grabbing in Ireland was to keep a section of the aristocracy happily occupied for years to come. After Mary's reign had tested and proved the strength of the

*Daniel Defoe, *Jure Divino: A Satyr* (1706), Book VI, pp. 6-7.

vested interest, Elizabeth continued her father's and brother's policy, though with sadly diminished assets: the plunder of bishops', deans' and chapter lands was all she had to offer the growing army of hungry courtiers.

The royal supremacy, then, was a necessary price to pay for the economic and other advantages which lay property owners secured from the Reformation, and for the reduction of clerical privileges and immunities. It was a price worth paying, just as the Tudor peace was worth the "Tudor despotism". But the royal supremacy as a fact, and the Divine Right of Kings as an idea, were as riddled with contradictions as was the protestant cause. First, the elevation of the king to headship of the church, as the conduit through which the landed class tapped the church's wealth, in fact gave the monarch a certain independence. The machinery of the church, now entirely at the disposal of the crown, offered itself as an instrument of government independent of Parliamentary control, and with a long tradition of prestige and authority behind it. Conversely it became the interest of the upper ranks of the clergy to cry up the crown's independent power, and with it their own independence of Parliament. The king was the new Pope rather than the new Messiah.[3]

The royal supremacy appealed to many interests — parson and King, spoliators and Puritans anxious to use church property for educational reform or augmentation of parish livings, Catholics needing protection.[4] A paper offered to Elizabeth, and later to James, asking for representation of the lower clergy in the House of Commons, said that "it concerneth the clergy most of all men in England that the present state be continued ... without any alteration".[5]

Secondly, the royal supremacy originally involved the humiliating submission of the clergy, the reduction of ecclesiastical wealth: and yet if the church was to be of any use to the crown as an instrument of government its prestige must be restored and maintained. Plunder of the church created the royal supremacy: but this supremacy was ultimately used to halt the plunder of the church. The Reformation degraded the priesthood and exalted the Supreme Head; yet the Supreme Governor in her own interest wished always to maintain the dignity of the clergy, and especially of the hierarchy. Created by the Reformation, the Head of the Church was always trying to deny his maker. Sir Francis Knollys stated the dilemma neatly when he said that from the Divine Right of bishops preached by Bancroft it would follow that the Queen was not Supreme Governor over the clergy: bishops, he thought, must be under-governors to the Queen, not claim to be superior governors over their brethren by God's ordinance.[6]

Thirdly, the royal supremacy itself contradicted the logical principles of the Reformation. Even Elizabeth, certainly her two successors, always found the Counter-Reformation ideal of monarchy more attractive than did even their greatest subjects, lumbered as they were with monastic lands. This contradiction was felt in its acutest form just before and during the civil war, when Charles I would gladly have employed Irish or foreign Catholic military force, but most of his supporters feared them almost as much as they feared the Parliamentarian revolutionaries.[7] The *via media* turned out to be a *cul de sac*.

The same illogicality appeared when the royal supremacy was looked at from below. Every argument used against the authority of the Pope could be used against the Defender of the Pope's Faith. (The retention of the title conferred before the Pope's authority was repudiated is itself an example of the crown's contradictory position). The Tudor theory of Divine Right was a Divine Right of government: it was powerful so long as the governing class was united.[8] James I's personal theory of divine hereditary right, though it had its uses as an additional justification of the Stuart succession, was a poor makeshift as soon as it no longer expressed this solidarity, as soon as it came up against divine right of the gentry which, according to Fuller, John Ball had denied.[9]

On the one hand, then, the Reformation encouraged discussion and criticism — the Bible in English in every church, denunciations of the Pope and of the miracle of the mass; on the other hand the government tried to limit this criticism to specific objectives. This contradiction led to a division in the ranks of the clergy; as the hierarchy and the government tried to call a halt, to set the clock back to before the Reformation, so a section of the preachers turned increasingly to "the people", to educated and self-confident gentry, yeomen, merchants and artisans who valued the independence which the Reformation had conferred on laymen of status.

A final contradiction derives from the great divide in the landed classes which our period sees. Some become involved in commercial activities, whether in privateering or trade, in the conquest of Ireland, or in industrial or agricultural production. Others remain rentiers and look mainly to the court for economic favours. A growing minority patronizes Puritan ministers, associating through them with the middling sort of laymen to whom they appeal; others flirt dangerously with Catholicism and Arminianism, and wish to see discussion of religious matters suppressed. For the first group the royal supremacy has served its turn. For the conservative group the royal supremacy has come to occupy the position of papal supremacy in the early sixteenth century: a bulwark against change, an ally against movements from below. Protestantism and the royal supremacy were twin births in England. Yet a century later the Parliamentarians attacked the royal supremacy in the interests of advanced protestantism; Laudians and their lay supporters defending the royal supremacy come near to rejecting the principles of the Reformation, and would no doubt have gone further had not most of them been receivers of stolen goods.

These contradictions are reflected in the 39 Articles. But we can see them most clearly in the relations of Parliament to the crown. In the Elizabethan Acts of Supremacy and Uniformity the royal supremacy is affirmed as a defence against "foreign power and bondage", but at the same time attempts are made to subordinate the church to the crown in Parliament rather than to the crown alone. Elizabeth was not opposed to Parliamentary action on religious questions, any more than Henry VIII had been. Her objection was to losing the initiative, to having the running made by Puritan laymen rather than by the bishops.[10]

Nevertheless, and naturally enough, the attitude of members of the hierarchy, because of their office, was different from that of MPs. "I have heard from old Parliament-men", said Peter Wentworth in 1572, "that the banishment of the Pope and the reforming true religion had its beginning from this House, but not from the bishops; few laws for religion had their foundation from them".[11] Peter Wentworth looked back; but the full significance of the activities of the Wentworths and their group can be grasped only if we also look forward, to the period when the House of Commons took command. The divisions were only accidentally constitutional: they were in origin political. They concerned policy for the church, by whom the church was to be controlled. They became constitutional conflicts only as two parties slowly polarized, one grouped around the crown and the bishops, the other entrenched in the House of Commons.

II

The dilemma of the monarchy was manifested during the Archbishopric of Edmund Grindal (1576-83), which Patrick Collinson sees as a climacteric. The crucial issue was preaching, which "godly Maşter Dering" called an essential mark of the church. "If ye will be saved", he told the gentry of Norfolk, "get you preachers into your parishes". The "prophesyings" — day schools for preachers — "were probably the most effective means that had been found for propagating the reformed religion in the rural areas of Elizabethan England".[12]

But they were more than that. "The kind of ecclesiastical reform to which the prophesyings and exercises were a pointer was much to the liking of the protestant nobility and gentry". The effect of these and other Puritan reforms would have been "to reduce still further both the powers of the unpopular ecclesiastical courts and the social status of the higher clergy"; their tendency was "to make the shire rather than the diocese the working unit of church administration and to bring into close harmony, if not to unify, the spiritual discipline of the ecclesiastical courts and the government of the magistrates".[13] The church would have been subordinated more effectively to the "county communities" of the gentry. "A partnership of ministry and magistracy . . . was a real alternative to clericalism on the one hand and naked erastianism on the other". It might well have been a first step to the gentry domination of the church which was established after 1660.[14]

In Elizabethan market towns there was a "firm alliance between 'magistracy and ministry'", and between both and the neighbouring gentry. "The superstructure of the presbyterian movement had been erected on a foundation of market-town exercises, fasts and informal conferences". Bishops were tolerable if their powers were small and if they never "set themselves against the gentry". Grindal's successor Whitgift was accused of being the first Archbishop to do this. The Parliament of 1584-5, which wanted prophesyings restored, proposed to make a commission of laymen the arbiters of the fitness of the clergy. "The essence of the problem was social — the bishop against the gentry".[15] Work published since *The Elizabethan Puritan Movement* has reinforced Collinson's case by emphasizing the appeal of Puritanism not only to magistrates drawn from the gentry but also to parish élites — constables, churchwardens, overseers of the poor, drawn from yeomen and craftsmen — who had to administer the villages, looking after the poor law, vagabonds, squatters on commons and wastes, etc. They might well find the Puritan ethic congenial to their ideals of social discipline.[16]

Many early Elizabethan bishops had been exiles under Mary, sharing the aims of those who came to be called Puritans. For the first two decades of Elizabeth's reign Puritans were relatively leniently treated by bishops, and might reasonably hope that the Reformation would still be pushed further in the direction they desired. They had strong support from gentlemen and towns, expressed in the House of Commons. In Leicester and Walsingham they had powerful patrons at court. Through prophesyings and lectureships, and through the universities, Puritan influence was steadily extending. In Grindal they had an Archbishop who (unlike his predecessor and successor at Canterbury) had been an exile himself and was more sympathetic to their cause than Parker had been. Grindal represents a suppressed tradition in the history of the Church of England, but one that might have preserved a truer *via media*. John Milton, no friend to bishops in general, thought Grindal "the best of them".[17] The Mayor of Bridgewater in 1685 confirmed this from the opposite point of view by describing those who electioneered against James II's government as "Grindallizing self-willed humourists".[18] Until Collinson published his biography Grindal was consistently under-rated by historians, either because they succumbed to the post-humous charms of the Queen who suspended him from office, or because the fact that nonconformists were ultimately ejected from the church led to the hindsight assumption that attempts to create a broad protestant church could never have succeeded.

The immediate cause of Grindal's downfall was the "prophesyings" Many of the clergy badly needed the training in preaching which the prophesyings offered. The north and west of England, and still more Wales, were not yet securely protestantized; in the south and east hundreds of the clergy fell short of the exacting standards of the educated laity. Puritan preachers were needed if the "rustic Pelagianism"[19] of the mass of the population was to be overcome. The prophesyings were held under a moderator, often in the presence of the laity. They were indeed often lay-sponsored, out of the control of the bishops.[20] This last fact rendered them particularly obnoxious to the Queen.[21] She, like Archbishops Parker and Whitgift, deplored any activities that allowed "the people to be orderers of things". She ordered Grindal to suppress the prophesy-ings. Imprudently, he made no attempt to find a compromise formula, but bluntly refused to obey. "I cannot marvel enough", he wrote to the Queen, "how this strange opinion should once enter into your mind, that it should be good for the church to have few preachers". He added, in a very conventional protestant sentiment, "public and continual preaching of God's word is the ordinary mean and instrument of the salvation of mankind". It was also a means of holding subjects in obedience: London, where there was "continual preaching", overflowed with loving loyalty. The ignorant north had risen in rebellion in 1569; but Halifax, a centre of preaching, had rallied to the Queen.[22]

Grindal concluded "I am forced, with all humility, and yet plainly, to profess that I cannot give my assent to the suppressing of the said exercises. . . . Bear with me, I beseech you, Madam, if I choose rather to offend your earthly majesty than to offend the heavenly majesty of God". It was magnificent; but it was not the way to handle Elizabeth. There was no doubt at court of the popularity of Grindal's stand, "the people addicted to that matter as they were", in the words of Sir Walter Mildmay.[23]

But, as Collinson shows, there were wider considerations. Prophesyings, household religion, repetition of sermons, "were a solvent of the ecclesiastical parish, and ultimately of the national church grounded on the parochial principle". They were part of the lay initiative which Collinson saw as essential to Puritanism. They brought the godly into closer voluntary union with one another — "a religion tending towards Independency". "The religious exercises which filled the leisure hours of godly professors literally took the place of what Baxter called 'the old feastings and gossipings'. . . . The godly supplied one another with the love and mutual support which they might otherwise have looked for among kindred and neigh-bours".[24] They came near to forming Independent congregations within the state church of a sort which the Cromwellian church was later to embrace. "Non-separating congregationalism" had deep roots.[25] It helped to forge the godly party of the sixteen-forties.

"Grindal was the victim not simply of a specific issue of conscience but of courtly intrigue. His fall was recognized to be a portent of reaction against the progressive protestantism which he symbolized, at a time when protestant and conservative, even crypto-catholic, forces were in contention for the mastery, at Court and in the direction of domestic and foreign policy". Contemporaries were aware of the relation of the Grindal affair to "the great issues of the day".[26] In the late fifteen-seventies a series of new appointments to bishoprics "led to a rift between the episcopate and the protestant nobility and gentry which was scarcely more marked in the years of Archbishop Laud's ascendancy".[27] In the dangerous international situation many protestants thought the safety of the country depended on support for the Netherlands in their revolt against Spain, close understanding with protestant Scotland, and (as Sir Francis Knollys put it) "the timely preventing of the contemptuous growing of the disobedient papists here in England". "If the Bishop of Canterbury shall be deprived", he added, "then up starts the pride and practice of the papists". Grindal was a symbol of a protestant policy, at home and abroad.[28] The conservatives, under Sir Christopher Hatton's influence, were not strong enough to get Grindal deprived; but he was kept suspended from his duties till his death in 1583. He was succeeded by John Whitgift, "the first Archbishop to set himself against the gentry of Kent"[29] and far more hostile to Puritans than Grindal.

Elizabeth had come to regard Grindal as a thoroughly unsatisfactory primate, whom she by-passed and sequestrated. But after the first year of her reign she never went further than threatening to unfrock a prelate. The prestige of the hierarchy was necessary to the independence of the crown. Elizabeth wanted both to elevate the authority of bishops as against the mass of the clergy and to maintain the prestige of the church and its hierarchy, in their own sphere, as against her lay councillors, some of whom, she may have thought, were aspiring to interfere in an area of administration which was none of their business. An independent *jure divino* episcopacy was a prop of an independent *jure divino* crown. A Puritan councillor like Knollys positively wanted the bishops to be forced to admit that their authority over other clergy derived from royal grant and had nothing divine about it. The deposition of Grindal would have made the bishops' lay dependency clear. Elizabeth therefore was torn. Personally, no doubt, she would have deposed Grindal as cheerfully as she would have had Mary Queen of Scots put to death. But as a politician she had to think of the consequences of her actions. So Grindal remained nominal primate, and Mary's execution was delayed and finally extorted greatly against the Queen's will.

In both these matters Elizabeth had a majority of her councillors against her. Grindal had been Burghley's nominee for the primacy. Councillors did not share the Queen's inhibitions about anointed monarchs. Between 1567 and 1586 there were no churchmen on the Council. We may contrast either the reign of Henry VIII, or the Laudian régime. In between the ecclesiastical hierarchy reached its nadir; and bishops made their way back to positions of political influence not as great magnates but as servants devoted to and dependent on the crown.

During this period many councillors appear normally to have sympathized with Puritans more than with bishops. The Council often reversed its own instructions once the Queen's back was turned, and protected Puritan ministers.[30] Leicester, Walsingham and Essex were well-known patrons of Puritans; but Penry thought it worth while also to make a personal appeal from the bishops to Burghley:[31] and the Lord Treasurer exercised a curious protection over his kinsman Robert Browne. When Whitgift had succeeded Grindal and began to suspend nonconforming ministers, it was to Burghley that Sir Francis Knollys wrote a letter of protest in June 1584: "I do think it to be a dangerous matter to her Majesty's safety that the politic government of matters of state, as well concerning forms and accidents of and to religion as otherwise, should be taken from all Councillors of her Majesty's estate and only to be given over to the rule of bishops that are not always indifferent in their own cases of sovereignty".[32] Within a month Burghley wrote his famous letter to Whitgift comparing the Court of High Commission to the Spanish Inquisition. Yet only two years later the Archbishop himself was made a Councillor at Burghley's instance in order to counteract the influence of Leicester. Divisions inside the ruling group were sharpening; and the conservatives were henceforth to feel the need for support from the ecclesiastical hierarchy.

III

Social consequences followed from this reversal of Elizabethan policy. Edmund Freke, Bishop of Norwich, "found the only course open to him in making common cause with conservative and crypto-catholic elements who for one reason or another opposed the ascendancy of Puritan teachers and justices". The High Commission was used to counteract Privy Council support for the Puritan gentry. "The decline of Puritan influence at court and its steady progress in the country were developments full of portent for the political as well as the religious history of the coming half-century".[33]

The regrouping took place mainly over questions of foreign policy but it was accelerated by Martin Marprelate's appeal to popular opinion against the bishops, encouraging rank-and-file laymen to discuss religious matters, to scoff at their superiors and the government by law established.[34] The proclamation of 13 February 1588-9 against seditious and schismatical books said that they aimed at "the abridging or rather the overthrow of her Highness's lawful prerogative", and at dissolving "the estate of the prelacy, being one of the ancient estates under her Highness".[35] The Marprelate Tracts, Elizabeth thought, tended to the subversion of all government under her charge, both in church and state. Bancroft, in his sermon at Paul's Cross, also in February 1589, echoed these sentiments: "Her majesty is depraved, her authority is impugned". "The interest of the people in kingdoms is greatly advanced".[36]

Bishop Cooper followed up loyally: "If this outrageous spirit of boldness be not stopped speedily, I fear he will prove himself to be not only Mar-prelate but Mar-prince, Mar-state, Mar-law, Mar-magistrate and all together until he bring it to an Anabaptistical equality and community. ...Their whole drift, as it may seem, is to bring the government of the church to a democracy or aristocracy. The principles and reasons whereof, if they be once by experience familiar in the minds of the common people, and that they have the sense and feeling of them: it is greatly to be feared that they will very easily transfer the same to the government of the commonweal".[37] Nashe (or some other propagandist for the hierarchy) pretended to fear that Marprelate would provoke a rising of the masses, who needed no help from him "to increase their giddiness".

> Yes, he that now saith Why should bishops be?
> Will next cry out: Why kings? The saints are free.[38]

In 1590 another pamphleteer accused Martin of betraying the gentry by encouraging "the commons to cast off the yoke of obedience".[39] Some aristocrats at least took the point. "As they shoot at bishops now", wrote the Earl of Hertford, "so will they do at the nobility also if they be suffered".[40] To scare the "Puritan" nobility was perhaps one of the most serious long-term consequences of the Marprelate Tracts.

Puritan ministers too were alarmed by Marprelate's success. Cartwright wrote to Burghley disowning him. Martin himself said: "The Puritans are angry with me; I mean the Puritan preachers. And why? Because I am too open; because I jest. ... I am plain; I must needs call a spade a spade, a Pope a Pope".[41] The hierarchy's defenders were quick to seize their opportunity. Bancroft's police work stopped the tracts. Numbers of separatists were arrested. Cooper published a lengthy and reasoned exposition of the social dangers of popular Puritanism. The defeat of the Armada came opportunely for the government's prestige. The deaths of Leicester and Walsingham weakened resistance to Whitgift's policies on the Council. Field's death deprived the Puritans of a leader who had not been afraid to appeal to "the multitude and people".[42] The absurd plot of Hacket and Coppinger in 1590 was heavily written up, and every effort was made to associate Cartwright and his coadjutors with the plotters.[43] Bancroft's *Dangerous Positions* (1593) reinforced Cooper's social criticism, and advanced into a general attack on Calvinism as an international revolutionary movement.[44] The judicious Hooker completed the work of consolidation for his generation. The reprinting of Marprelate's works after 1640 showed both how timely the government's suppression and campaign of counter-propaganda had been, and that it had failed to achieve its ultimate objective.

Elizabeth and Hatton wrecked the chance of an all-embracing protestant national church. James I at the Hampton Court Conference was only confirming decisions taken by his predecessor. Hatton, who was Whitgift's patron as Leicester had been Grindal's, tried in the House of Commons to "appeal to the self-interest of the property-owning laity", arguing that "the Presbyterian revolution would be at their expense. It would deprive them of their ecclesiastical patronage, while the cost of maintaining the fourfold [Presbyterian] ministry in every parish would require the resumption of secularized church property, impropriate tithes and perhaps even abbey lands. ... 'It toucheth us all in our inheritances'".[45]

The combination of government successes against Marprelate and social panic temporarily frightened off most of the Puritans' influential patrons. But Puritanism was not destroyed by being driven underground and losing support from peers and councillors. When John of Gaunt and his like deserted the Wycliffites, Lollardy found a refuge among humbler people. But now there was a very different social basis for the reforming movement. The agitation for reform through Parliament having failed, many of its supporters turned to establishing independent congregations, inside or outside the church. The Marprelate Tracts were Puritan, not separatist. Yet Penry, who was closely associated with their production, died a Brownist.

Presbyterianism was primarily a clerical movement, with some support from Parliament and gentry. There was however a tension between the land-grabbers, always prepared to work the episcopal system provided they got enough spoil from it, and doctrinaire Presbyterians. Presbyterianism was, in Collinson's words, "strong medicine, impossible to contemplate apart from a general institutional and social revolution from which all but the strongest stomachs shrank".[46] Clerical Presbyterianism was routed. But its lay backers, less committed to the "ism", preserved what Collinson calls "presbytery in episcopacy", or congregational independency in episcopacy. Gentlemen and corporations used patronage or the creation of lectureships to continue the provision of Puritan preaching (and bishops winked at it in the papist north of England).[47] When Presbyterianism revived in England in the sixteen-forties it was again primarily a clerical movement, looking for support from Scotland against the English House of Commons — though by then it had also won some conservative support as a lesser evil than sectarianism.[48]

Increasing government reliance on conservative elements, crypto-papist peers and gentlemen, had consequences both for home and foreign policy. Under James it led to the rise of the Howards, appeasement of Spain, the execution of Ralegh, strained relations with the House of Commons. Bancroft revived theories of the Divine Right of bishops. All these developments made their contribution to the atmosphere in which the breakdown of 1640 became possible.

Bancroft rose to influence, Collinson tells us, in a way "which may recall for the modern reader the methods of Senator Joseph McCarthy in our own time".[49] We may recall the list of qualities which, in Whitgift's view, qualified Bancroft for appointment as Bishop of London. His conduct had never been the subject of complaint; he had the usual academic degrees; he was a resolute opponent of popery and of all "sects and innovations"; he had held various governmental and ecclesiastical posts, and had served for twelve years on the High Commission; he did useful detective work against the Marprelate printing press and in organizing counter-propaganda; he took the lead against Cartwright, Penry and the classis movement; he had been engaged for fifteen or sixteen years in the public service, during which period "seventeen or eighteen of his juniors (few or none of them being of his experience) have been preferred — eleven to deaneries and the rest to bishoprics".[50] It was an unanswerable case for civil service promotion. As a commentary upon it we may recall that Archbishop Bancroft, adjudicating in the Rich divorce in 1605, "chid my Lord Rich very much" for his Puritanism, "and gave my Lady great commendations for her noble birth", observing that her error (adultery) was *"error venialis"* by comparison with Rich's Puritanism.[51]

But pressures for a Grindalian policy continued. When James appointed the Calvinist George Abbott (1610-33) to succeed Bancroft, a revival of Grindal's "first hundred days" even seemed possible. Abbott became one of the main advocates of a protestant foreign policy. Under his genial tolerance bishops like Montague, Lake and Morton allowed prophesyings again, though now they were prudently called "exercises".[52] But with Abbott's disgrace (over foreign policy, in effect) and the succession of Laud, historical tragedy repeated itself as farce. The Kentish gentry loved Abbott and hated Laud, as they had loved Grindal and hated Whitgift.[53] John Chamberlain in 1616 distinguished between Abbott and "the court bishops and other courtiers", whose views "commonly prevail".[54] In 1633 a Puritan — soon to be deprived — was recalling the days when an Archbishop of York — Grindal — had actually favoured preaching.[55] "Such bishops [as Grindal] would have prevented our contentions and wars", declared Richard Baxter in 1656. One argument for supposing that the English Revolution had long-term causes is the fact that Abbott failed no less than Grindal: the victim, like Grindal, of court intrigue. He was effectively succeeded by William Laud long before the latter was appointed Archbishop in 1633. "It was the Laudian successors of such [Grindalian] bishops who believed, with how much justification is a matter to be discussed rather than assumed, that by making itself beholden to the laity and by working with the grain of provincial society the church placed itself at risk".[56] So Collinson sums up.

IV

Whitgift's promotion had marked a turn away from spoliation and towards greater care for the prestige of the hierarchy. The steady move towards conservatism began with economics under Whitgift, tackled organization under Bancroft, and ended with doctrine under Laud. But there was no lasting reconstruction. Each success brought new problems. The church's revenues could be recovered or expanded only at the expense of the politically decisive landed class, far too many of whom were themselves in economic difficulties to be prepared to make sacrifices on behalf of the church, however much their appreciation of its services to their social order may have been growing. Usher's two large volumes on Bancroft's *Reconstruction of the English Church* show how little reconstruction there could be without a frontal attack on the protestant vested interest.[57]

The economic and political retreat from the Reformation led to a theological retreat. Whitgift himself was a sound Erastian Calvinist; but his proceedings against advocates of a Presbyterian discipline, together with the hardening of Genevan positions under Béza's influence, no doubt stimulated a reconsideration of Calvinism in general. Hooker's work of consolidation proved no more final than Whitgift's and Bancroft's. Liberal Calvinism, reasonableness, the attempt to marry protestantism with Catholic tradition: within less than a generation the leading Anglican figures had rejected all this, and had been won for "Arminianism". Laud was trying to get rid of the Lambeth Decrees on predestination which Whitgift promoted and Hooker approved.[58] Calvinism, essential to promotion in the last decade of Elizabeth's reign, was the way to Ireland or a country vicarage under Charles I. In 1595 the University of Cambridge demanded public recantation from a preacher of anti-Calvinist views.[59] Thirty-one years later it was the House of Commons, not the university, which took the offensive against Mr Adams of Cambridge who asserted the expediency of confession.[60] Hooker's reputation was not continuous: it was recreated (by Locke, among others) in the very different social context of the late seventeenth century.

A change in attitudes towards Catholics was harbinger of changes in Anglican theology. Already Sir Christopher Hatton, Whitgift's ally against the Puritans, was advocating lenience towards Catholics. His mother's family adhered to the old religion, and he himself was probably brought up a Catholic. Bancroft was Hatton's chaplain. His leniency towards Catholics is no doubt to be explained by anxiety to preserve their loyalty whilst England was at war with Spain; but it points forward to the days when a papal agent was received by Charles I at Whitehall, when conversion was fashionable at court, and when it was all that £1500 a year could do to prevent Bishop Goodman declaring himself a Catholic.[61]

Bancroft's major achievement was the canons of 1604. Previously no serious attempt had been made to resolve the contradictions of the Elizabethan settlement and of the royal supremacy. But the canons of 1604 codified and excluded ambiguities. They proclaimed the autonomy of the church under the crown, its independence of Parliament. They also represent the culminating point in the campaign against Puritans in insisting on a doctrinal test before admission to any eccesiastical office. Explicit penalties were prescribed for separatists and non-communicants, and for church-wardens who failed to present them. The sacraments were not to be refused if offered by a non-preaching minister. The hands of the ecclesiastical courts were strengthened. The canons make an interesting parallel to James I's attempt to give precision to the theory of the royal prerogative. In each case ambiguous or conflicting precedents were being sharply defined.[62]

The canons were passed by Convocation only, and ratified by letters patent under the Great Seal. Parliament was not asked to ratify them. So in attacking the canons the Commons found themselves attacking one conception of the royal supremacy. "Your Majesty should be misinformed", the Commons kindly explained to James, "if any man should deliver that the kings of England have any absolute power in themselves to alter religion (which God defend should be in the power of any mortal man whatseover) or to make any laws concerning the same otherwise than as in temporal causes, by consent of Parliament".[63] The Commons tried to invalidate all canons affecting the life, liberty or property of laymen which had not received the consent of Parliament. Twenty-three canons were singled out as fit to be voided.[64] But their bill was rejected, thanks to the bishops' vote in the Lords. Only after 1640 did the judges accept the Commons' view that ecclesiastical canons were not binding on the laity unless confirmed by Parliament. That one decision prevented the restoration in 1660 of "the church as Bancroft had left it".[65]

Collinson's main strength as a historian lies in his judicious (and unusual) combination of a theological with a sociological approach. "No form of church polity can be considered apart from the structures of the secular society in which it is set, or from its values", he wrote in 1965. "The policies and actions of Archbishops Whitgift and Bancroft, as later of Laud, seem to have been based on the assumption that ... the Church must defend itself against lay interference by the reinforcement of its ancient claims of spiritual government. ... It is not the historian's place to condemn the ends pursued by Whitgift or Laud, but he may feel bound to declare them unattainable".[66] Such an appraisal should help us to avoid a recent tendency to blame Laud exclusively for the Revolution of 1640.

All conscientious members of the church hierarchy worked under severe restraints. They lived in a rapidly changing society. They had to take account of the wishes, policies and whims of the sovereign. They were subject to ever-present pressures from the gentry. They were conscious of the threat to their church, at home and abroad, from popery; and at home from Puritans and sectaries. Like the crown, they could not rule without the co-operation of parish élites: parishes may not have been able to choose their parsons, but they did elect their churchwardens. The co-operation of the latter was essential to the proper functioning of church courts, and it was unlikely to be willingly given when their communities resented episcopal policies. Collinson used to emphasise, more perhaps than in his later books, lay initiatives in Puritanism — objections to "the surplice, the cross in baptism, and other celebrated dregs of Antichrist still entertained in the English church".[67] This was one approach to "independency within the church." In Grindleton Roger Brearley's congregation seems to have pressed further towards antinomianism than their minister.[68] Collinson's insight helps us to understand such a phenomenon; it received confirmation from a number of subsequent researchers,[69] and helps to account for the transition from non-separating Puritanism to sectarianism in which the laity predominated.[70] It may even help us better to understand the New England way.[71]

Collinson's sociological approach will also help us to keep theological questions in perspective. Naturally his enemies pilloried Laud's "Arminianism", and equated it with popery. Whether Laud actually was an Arminian has exercised historians recently, but it matters not much. The real enemy for Parliamentarians (as opposed perhaps to Puritans) was not Laud's theology but the defence by him and his supporters of what were held to be absolutist tendencies. Most of Laud's theological "innovations", Usher argued, can be found in the canons of 1604.[72] James I's sympathy for Arminians after the Synod of Dort seems to have sprung from a belief that the Calvinist position could lead to rebellion against the higher powers. More important for our purposes, Laud seemed to be putting into effect claims for the royal prerogative which had got Harsnett into trouble in 1610, Neile in 1614.[73] Sibthorpe, Manwaring and Montagu may have been theological innocents; but there was no mistaking their support for Divine Right monarchy. Abbott on the other hand is said to have told James I that he could grant toleration to papists only through Parliament "unless he was prepared to throw down the law of the land".[74] The Grand Remonstrance said that the bishops and the corrupt part of the clergy had tried to subvert the fundamental laws and principles of government of the kingdom.[75]

Just as it has been said that the trouble with Charles I was that he lacked his father's saving laziness, so the trouble with Laud was his seriousness and conscientiousness in carrying out the traditional policies of Whitgift and Bancroft, and the fact that he had Charles's ear as they never had the full confidence of their wiser sovereigns. Laud remembered Udall and Penry when dealing with Prynne, Burton and Bastwick.[76] John Cook in 1652 thought the execution of Charles I was God's revenge for the blood of Prynne and Bastwick.[77] Laud's theological position was however far more provocative than Whitgift's had ever been. He was driven to a fiercer onslaught on Puritans, to a break with international Calvinism and to a total breach with Parliaments. He was met by a concerted opposition of gentlemen and townsmen which brought down the monarchy as well as bishops. Again the roots of the civil war are to be found in Elizabeth's reign.

Church and crown faced similar economic and political problems in the century before 1640. In each case the only possible solutions appeared to threaten the gentry and Parliament — Divine Right of Kings, Divine Right of bishops, Divine Right to tithes, recovering impropriations.[78] The Laudian clergy "have claimed their calling immediately from the Lord Jesus Christ, which is against the laws of this kingdom": the Root and Branch Petition made the point succinctly.[79] The options of both church and crown steadily narrowed and so forced new problems on Parliament and gentry. The fall of Grindal led to enhanced Catholic influences; the fall of Abbott much more so. The York House Conference in 1626 removed the last hope that Buckingham might play the role of a new Northumberland, Leicester or Essex. In 1643 Cheynell looked back to "Bishop Bancroft and the Babylonian faction" in the church.[80] Laud carried much further Bancroft's policy of severing relations with continental protestants; and so he was wide open to accusations of popery, although he seems to have been no party to the court Popish Plot which Professor Hibbard has revealed.[81]

There are many ways in which Laudian policies had been anticipated under Whitgift and Bancroft. The rift between the episcopate and the protestant nobility after the fall of Grindal recalled for Collinson that of the sixteen-thirties.[82] It was James I who first issued the Book of Sports and forbade preachers to discuss predestination and reprobation. James commended bishops for suppressing "popular lecturers", and approved of the "beauty of holiness". The ideological polarization which derived from anxieties about foreign policy dates from the fall of Grindal, and intensified from James's reign.[83] James first promoted Arminians, who were to be virtually the only proponents of a theory of absolutism, derived from French Catholic thinkers.[84] Hooker's synthesis, as Usher pointed out, was based on Bancroft.[85] Hooker's dedication of Book V of *The Laws of Ecclesiastical Polity* to Whitgift reads almost like a prophecy of the Long Parliament: the threat of Presbyterianism "to erect a popular authority of elders, and to take away episcopal jurisdiction" has gained "many helping hands, ... contented (for what intent God doth know) to uphold opposition against bishops" to the disadvantage of Her Majesty's service.[86]

Collinson's picture is of ex-émigré radical protestant bishops settling under Elizabeth for a possibilist second best, less than they had hoped for, better than they had feared. They heroically squeezed as much as they could — prophesyings, lectureships, itinerant preachers in the North — out of the immobile social structure, in the hope of slowly converting the pagan-Catholic mass of the population. So they spurned the radical Lollard-Anabaptist-Familist trend, which for a moment it seemed they might have headed, and drove the radicals into separation and exile.[87] It was not the virulent Laud who forced extremism on the sects; that had been done earlier by the worthiest middle-of-the-road Elizabethan and Jacobean bishops.

Laud reaped the whirlwind they had sown. The case against Laud is not so much innovation, still less "revolution", but that he presided over the upsetting of a balance which had long been becoming more and more precarious. It was his use of his powerful position to monopolize ecclesiastical patronage that was the real innovation, plus the savagery with which he silenced his enemies. I find myself in agreement here with Avihu Zakai, who emphasizes the equally provocative stance of the minority of convinced Puritans.[88]

After Grindal and Abbott one more Archbishop found himself out on a limb. John Williams was a successful courtier and civil servant under James. He was among the first to demand Abbott's suspension and the forfeiture of his estate. A pluralist, whose religion sat lightly on him, he regarded Bohemian protestant refugees as rebels deserving no sympathy. Despite all these well-timed views, he found himself out-manoeuvred by Laud, beaten to the bishopric of London,[89] not for lack of any theological suppleness, but simply because he was late in realizing how important theological politics could be to a court churchman. In disgrace he attached himself to opponents of the court, confident that he could win their sympathy as Abbott had done, and that the next turn of the tide would bring the great territorial magnates back to their proper positions of influence, and himself, in alliance with them, to a dominant position in the church.[90]

It was indeed evidence of the weakness in the position of those who defended "moderate episcopacy" in 1640-1 (and who proposed to solve the King's financial problems by a reorganization of taxation) that Williams became their candidate for high ecclesiastical office. Whatever one may think of Laud, no one has ever challenged his adherence to a principled Christian position. But Williams? As Professor Trevor-Roper pointed out, he was never in the cathedral of which he was bishop for twenty years; during three years in the Tower he never took the sacrament, never indeed attended church service.[91] He was a secularist of the secularists: not even King Log to Laud's King Stork. He would no doubt have made a successful eighteenth-century primate. But in between lay a revolution with which he was temperamentally unfitted to cope. He was neither a De Retz nor a Talleyrand. He could play the game of politics within the old restricted circle well enough, but he was twice defeated — first by Laud's passionate and unscrupulous pursuit of principle, then by a new phenomenon even further outside Williams's range of vision:

effective political action by humble laymen such as those whom Marprelate had addressed fifty years earlier.

NOTES

1. This chapter incorporates material from reviews of four books by Patrick Collinson — *The Elizabethan Puritan Movement* (1967); *Archbishop Grindal, 1519-1583: The Struggle for a Reformed Church* (1979); *The Religion of Protestants: The Church in English Society, 1559-1625* (Oxford U.P., 1982); *Godly People: Essays on English Protestantism* (1983). They appeared respectively in *Economic History Review*, N.S., XX (1967); *Journal of Religious History*, II, (1981); *Times Literary Supplement*, 18 March, 1983; *Journal of Ecclesiastical History*, 35 (1984).

2. A. Ogle, *The Tragedy of the Lollards' Tower* (Oxford, 1949), pp. 144-54.

3. Cf. Defoe, cited as epigraph to this Chapter.

4. Cf. H. White, *op. cit.*, pp. 132-7, 150-5, 169.

5. Burnet, *History of the Reformation of the Church of England*, IV, p. 145.

6. Strype, *Life of Whitgift*, I, pp. 559-65.

7. Cf. royalists cited in John Adair's *By the Sword Divided: Eyewitnesses of the English Civil War* (1983), pp. 37-8, 131.

8. Cf. David Mathew, *The Celtic Peoples and Renaissance Europe* (1933), pp. 53, 75.

9. Fuller, *Church History of Britain*, I, p. 451.

10. M. M. Knappen, *Tudor Puritanism: A Chapter in the History of Idealism* (Chicago U.P., 1939), p. 227.

11. Strype, *Annals of the Reformation ... during Queen Elizabeth's Happy Reign*, (Oxford U.P., 1824), II, p. 12.

12. Collinson, *Godly People*, pp. 297-9, 59-60.

13. Collinson, *The Elizabethan Puritan Movement*, p. 187.

14. *Godly People*, pp. 78-9, 175-80, 187.

15. *The Elizabethan Puritan Movement*, pp. 188-9, 203, 259, 285, 437.

16. K. Wrightson, *English Society, 1580-1680* (1982), *passim*; William Hunt, *op. cit.*, *passim*.

17. M.C.P.W., I., pp. 539-40.

18. R. Clifton, *The Last Popular Rebellion* (1984), pp. 71, 157; cf. p. 302 below.

19. *The Elizabethan Puritan Movement*, p. 37; cf. W.T. MacCaffrey, *Queen Elizabeth and the Making of Policy, 1572-1588* (Princeton U.P., 1981), pp. 38, 83.

20. *Ibid.*, Part Four, Chapters 2, 4 and 5 *passim*; *Godly People*, pp. 59-60.

21. Elizabeth may have been more right than Collinson admits. In Scotland in the fifteen-seventies an easy transition was made from "exercises"

to presbyteries. "The exercise may be judgit a presbytery" (Duncan Shaw, *The General Assemblies of the Church of Scotland, 1560-1600,* Edinburgh, 1964, pp. 176-7). Cf. Aylmer on the "boldness in the meaner sort" that exercises bred in Leicestershire (quoted by Claire Cross, *The Puritan Earl: The Life of Henry Hastings, Third Earl of Huntingdon,* 1966, pp. 137-8).

22. *Grindal,* pp. 247-8, 289, 240.
23. *Grindal,* pp. 242, 260.
24. *Godly People,* pp. 8-9, 11-15, 422, 446, 539-40, 547-8; *The Elizabethan Puritan Movement,* pp. 92-7, 173, 202, 223, 375-82, and *passim*; *Grindal,* pp. 177-8. I use the word "saw" as Collinson has shifted his position on this point. See p. 78 below.
25. *The Elizabethan Puritan Movement,* pp. 82-91, 229-31, 334-5, 343-4, and *passim.* Cf. Strype, *Life of Whitgift,* I, p. 229; B. R. White, *The English Separatist Tradition,* pp. 84-6, 90, 94; T. H. Breen, *Puritans and Adventurers* (Oxford U.P., 1980), p. 198; R. Richardson, *op. cit.,* pp. 37, 86-97; cf. L. Ziff, *Puritanism in America* (New York, 1973), p. 50.
26. *Grindal,* pp. 256-7.
27. *The Elizabethan Puritan Movement,* p. 201.
28. *Grindal,* pp. 257-8.
29. *Ibid.,* p. 286; *The Elizabethan Puritan Movement,* Part 4, Chapter 4; Part 8, Chapter 1. Peter Clark suggests that in the short run Grindal's suspension actually helped the radicals (*English Provincial Society from the Reformation to the Revolution: Religion, Politics and Society in Kent, 1500-1640,* (Hassocks, Sussex, 1977, pp. 167-9).
30. Knappen, pp. 261-2, 275.
31. Ed. A. Peel, *The Notebook of John Penry, 1593* (Camden third series, 1944), pp. 53-77.
32. Knappen, *op. cit.,* p. 275.
33. *The Elizabethan Puritan Movement,* pp. 202-5, 444.
34. One of the charges that led to the condemnation of Protector Somerset had been that he encouraged the common people to have ideas of their own about politics.
35. A. Sparrow, *A Collection of Articles* (1684), p. 173.
36. Pierce, *An Historical Introduction to the Marprelate Tracts,* p. 161, 175.
37. Cooper, *Admonition,* pp. 31, 70.
38. *The Returne of the Renowned Cavaliero Pasquill* (1589), Sig. B i-iii; *A Whip for an Ape.* The attribution to Nashe is in each case uncertain. Field, it will be remembered, had said "seeing we cannot compass these things by suit nor dispute, it is the multitude and people that must bring the discipline to pass which we desire" (Collinson, *Godly People,* p. 370).
39. L. Wright, *A Friendly Admonition to Martine Marprelate and his Mates* (1590), p. 2, quoted in Pierce, *op. cit.,* p. 236.
40. Ed. E. Arber, *An Introductory Sketch to the Martin Marprelate Controversy* (1895), p. 114.
41. *An Epitome* (1588), To all the Cleargie masters.
42. *Grindal,* pp. 314, 397.

43. Cf. Hooker, *Of the Laws of Ecclesiastical Polity*, Dedication to Book V (Everyman edn., II, pp. 5-7), and R. Cosin, *Conspiracy for pretended Reformation* (1591), *passim*.

44. Knappen, *op. cit.*, p. 497. Recalling Marprelate's description of the activities of government *agents provocateurs* among members of underground congregations, and their attempts to snare them into compromising statements or actions (Pierce, *op. cit.*, p. 192), it is perhaps legitimate to wonder whether there may not have been something of the sort behind Hacket's "plot".

45. *The Elizabethan Puritan Movement*, p. 314.

46. *Godly People*, p. 168.

47. *The Elizabethan Puritan Movement*, pp. 405-7; *Godly People*, p. 348. Richardson and Haigh confirm the continuance of prophesyings in Lancashire (Richardson, *op. cit.*, pp. 65-9; Haigh, *Reformation and Resistance in Tudor Lancashire*, Cambridge U.P., 1975, pp. 301-4). Cf. Cross, *op. cit.*, pp. 259-60 (Yorkshire); R.O'Day, "Thomas Bentham: A Case Study in the Problems of the Early Elizabethan Episcopate", *Journal of Ecclesiastical History*, XXIII (1972), p. 153 (Staffordshire).

48. I have benefited from discussing this point with David Zaret.

49. *The Elizabethan Puritan Movement*, p. 397.

50. Pierce, *op. cit.*, pp. 118-19; C. Burrage, *The Early English Dissenters* (Cambridge U.P., 1912), II, pp. 132-3.

51. Freedman, *Poor Penelope*, p. 164.

52. *Grindal*, pp. 291-2.

53. *Ibid*, p. 286, Cf. Clark, *English Provincial Society*, pp. 306-366.

54. Chamberlain, *Letters*, II, p. 44.

55. See p. 302 below.

56. *Grindal*, p. 292.

57. Bancroft was less impressed by the stability of his work than Usher. He cancelled a will leaving his library to Lambeth Palace and left it to Cambridge University, "suspecting an impression of popular violence on cathedrals" (Fuller, *The History of the Worthies of England*, 1840, II, p. 200). If Fuller's account of Bancroft's motives is correct, his was an interestingly exact forecast. In the sixteen-forties the property of bishops' sees was confiscated, but not that of the universities. But learning did not, as forecast, fall together with bishops.

58. P. Heylyn, *Cyprianus Anglicus* (1671), p. 256; Hooker *op. cit.*, II, pp. 542-3.

59. Fuller, *History of the University of Cambridge* (1655), pp. 150-1.

60. Neal, *op. cit.*, I, p. 598.

61. S.R.Gardiner, *History of England, 1603-1640*, IX, p. 279.

62. J.W. Allen, *English Political Thought, 1603-1644* (1938), pp. 123-4.

63. The Apology of the House of Commons, 1604, in Prothero, *op. cit.*, pp. 290-1.

64. Faith Thompson, *Magna Carta: Its role in the making of the English Constitution, 1300-1629* (Massachusetts U.P., 1948), p. 248.

65. Usher, *op. cit.*, II, p. 266.

66. *Godly People*, pp. 187-8; contrast pp. 433-7.

67. *Godly People* p. 541; cf. pp. 11-15, 422, 446, and *English Puritanism* (Historical Association Pamphlet, 1983), pp. 30-1.
68. See pp.149, 163 below.
69. See for instance R.W.Ketton-Cremer, *Norfolk in the Civil War* (1969), p. 72 and *passim*; F.G.Emmison, *Early Essex Town Meetings* (1970), p. vii; B.R.White, *The English Separatist Tradition*, pp. 76-9; R. Richardson, *op. cit.*, pp. 16-17, 27, 97-108; E.J.I.Allen, *The State of the Church in the Diocese of Peterborough, 1601-1642* (Oxford B.Litt. Thesis, 1972), esp. pp. 118-20, 134-42, 153-4; C.Haigh, *op. cit.*, p. 298; A.Fletcher, *A County Community in Peace and War: Sussex 1600-1660* (1975), pp. 74, 90-3, 108; P. Clark, *English Provincial Society*, pp. 170, 174-8, 326-7, 335, 370-2, 389, 440; W.J.Sheils, *The Puritans in the Diocese of Peterborough, 1558-1610* (Northants Record Soc., 1979), *passim*; K.Wrightson and D.Levine, *Poverty and Piety in an English Village: Terling 1525-1700* (1979), p. 161; D. Zaret, *The Heavenly Contract* (Chicago U.P., 1985), *passim*, fully documents his view that lay initiative was central to Puritanism. Cf. J.W. Martin, "The Protestant Underground Congregations of Mary's Reign," *Journal of Ecclesiastical History*, 35 (1984), *passim; Barrington Family Letters*, p. 70; Lake, *op. cit.*, 89-90, 132; Hunt, *op. cit.*, pp. 92, 255-7, 296 and *passim*; Helena Hajzyk, "Household, Divinity and Covenant Theology in Lincolnshire, c. 1595-c. 1640", *Lincolnshire History and Archeology*, 17 (1982), pp. 45-9; J.Y. Cliffe, *The Puritan Gentry*, p. 188; P. Gura, *A Glimpse of Sion's Glory: Puritan Radicalism in New England, 1620-1660* (Wesleyan U.P., 1984), pp. 8, 238. The exodus to New England was primarily a lay initiative.
70. Adam Martindale's experience of the sixteen-forties is relevant: "the enslaving of the ministers" by congregations "to the will of the people", to such an extent that sometimes ministers "have been forced with disgrace to retract" (*The Life of Adam Martindale*, ed. R. Parkinson, Chetham Soc., 1845, pp. 66-7).
71. Zakai, *Exile and Kingdom, passim.*
72. Usher, *op. cit.*, I, p. 382; cf. New, *Anglican and Puritan*, pp. 70, 74.
73. See p.54 above; cf. Foster, *Notes from the Caroline Underground*, p. 108.
74. Lambeth MS 943 f. 79. This document's authenticity has been questioned.
75. Ed. S.R.Gardiner, *Constitutional Documents of the Puritan Revolution, 1625-1660* (Oxford U.P., 3rd edn., 1906), pp. 206-7.
76. Laud, *Works*, VII, p. 329.
77. Cook, *Monarchy no Creature of Gods making* (1652), Sig b.
78. See my *Economic Problems of the Church, passim.*
79. Gardiner, *Constitutional Documents*, p. 137.
80. Francis Cheynell, *Sions Memento and Gods Alarum* (1643), p. 30.
81. C. Hibbard, *Charles I and the Popish Plot, passim.*
82. See pp.69-70 above.
83. See pp.70-5 above.
84. Hunt, *op. cit.*, pp. 175-80, 214; cf. P. White, "The Rise of Arminianism

Reconsidered", *P. and P.*, No. 101 (1983), *passim*.

85. Usher, *op. cit.*, I, pp. 73-4.
86. Hooker, *op. cit.*, II, p. 7.
87. Cf. chapter 7 below.
88. Zakai, *Exile and Kingdom*, pp. 67-8 and *passim*. Dr Zakai stresses that Brightman had the same sense that Winthrop and his colleagues had — that England was a doomed nation; and suggests that this witnesses to a long-term crisis in England *(ibid.*, p. 131).
89. *Cabala, Mysteries of State*, I, pp. 45, 85; Heylyn, *Cyprianus Anglicus*, p. 324. Cf. Zachary Catlin, *Dr Sibbs his Life* (1652), p. 263, and *The Knyvett Letters* (ed. B.Schofield, 1949), p. 30.
90. Lambeth MS. 1030 ff. 38, 94-106.
91. Trevor-Roper, *Archbishop Laud*, p. 137.

III   *Heresy and Radical Politics*

7. *From Lollards to Levellers* [1]

"Heresies are like leaden pipes in the ground. They run on still, though we do not see them, in a commonwealth where they are restrained. Where liberty is they will discover themselves, and come to punishment." *

"If God be a Father, and we are brethren, it is a levelling word. . . . If they be great in the world, brethren of high degree; yet 'brother' levelleth them." †

In the sixteen-forties, when the censorship broke down and church courts ceased to function, a whole host of radical ideas popped up and were freely expressed. The question I want to ask is how far these ideas had had an underground existence before 1640, so that the novelty is only in the freedom to express them: or were they novel ideas, the product of novel circumstances? I shall do no more than throw out a few suggestions: I have no completed thesis to put forward, only a few working hypotheses, a list of questions I am asking myself.

My point of departure was a book that I wrote called *The World Turned Upside Down*, in which I tried to analyse some of the more extreme ideas of the radical minority of the sixteen-forties and sixteen-fifties. I sent a copy of this book to G.R.Elton, with an apologetic remark that I knew it was not his sort of book, but it was what I had written. Professor Elton replied, courteously but trenchantly: "the ideas you find put forward are awfully old hat — commonplaces of radical and heretical thinking since well before the Reformation". I had already noticed some parallels between late Lollard ideas, as described by J.A.F.Thomson and A.G.Dickens, and my seventeenth-century radicals. What began to interest me was the possibility of continuity, and its mechanisms.

* Lord Strickland, 9 December 1656 (*Parliamentary Diary of Thomas Burton*, ed. J.T.Rutt, 1828, I, p. 88).

† Richard Sibbes, *A Heavenly Conference* (1656), in *Works*, VI, p. 458. Sibbes died in 1635.

Now of course there are very special problems in attempting to trace continuities of underground ideas. A successful underground leaves no traces. Before the nineteenth century we rarely hear the lower orders speaking for themselves in a natural tone of voice. We hear instead what JPs in Quarter Sessions, judges in ecclesiastical courts, heresy-hunting pamphleteers, thought their inferiors were thinking, with all the dangers of distortion by such sources. ("Who writ the history of the Anabaptists but their enemies?" asked the Leveller Richard Overton; and the Leveller William Walwyn spoke of "that lying story of that injured people ... the Anabaptists of Münster".)[2] Alternatively, we have to rely on inference, from the survival of particular doctrines in particular areas. In putting together scraps of evidence, which have survived by chance, we are unlikely to arrive at decisive conclusions. The problems are perennial whenever we try to reconstruct the history of the common man, still more of the common woman. Nearly all our history is upper-class and male. One of the delights of the English Revolution is the exceptional nature of the surviving evidence, thanks to the exceptional political liberty and the relative cheapness of printing.

Let us remind ourselves how very radical some of the ideas were which surfaced in the sixteen-forties and sixteen-fifties. Levellers advocated political democracy, a republic with a widely extended franchise, abolition of the House of Lords, election of magistrates and judges, drastic legal and economic reforms. Diggers and others carried the Leveller emphasis on natural rights to advocacy of a communist society. Sectaries and Milton extended the Puritan attack on bishops to rejection of the whole idea of a state church — its courts, its tithes, its fees, its control of education and the censorship, the very distinction between clergy and laity. They carried anti-sacramentalism to the point of regarding worship as discussion. Spiritual equality and the doctrine of the inner light were extended to rejection of the idea of "sin", to a belief in human perfectibility on earth. Many denied the divinity of Christ, the immortality of the soul. Some ceased to believe in a local heaven or hell; the gospel story was treated as an allegory. Winstanley found the word Reason preferable to God. The protestant ethic, the dignity of labour, monogamous marriage, all came under attack.

Many of the proponents of these ideas looked back to Lollards and Marian martyrs as their ancestors. Foxe had of course accustomed

Englishmen to this pedigree, to this answer to the question "Where was your church before Luther?" England differed from most continental countries in having a "respectable" pre-reformation heresy to appeal to. But Foxe, we know, often played down the radicalism of his heretics.[3] Many of the views of Lollards and Marian martyrs would have been punishable under Elizabeth — which did not stop her making political capital out of Foxe's book. In the seventeenth century Levellers like Lilburne, Overton, Walwyn, a reformer like William Dell, emphasized the more radical elements in the heretical heritage. The point was regularly made from the other side. John Cleveland spoke of "Presbyter Wyclif" and "Tyler's toleration"; the sneer was repeated by other poets, Abraham Cowley and John Collop. Charles I, in his answer of 18 June 1642 to the Parliament's 19 Propositions, warned that, if opposition to him continued, "at last the common people ... [will] set up for themselves, call parity and independence liberty, ... destroy all rights and properties, all distinctions of families and merit, and by this means this splendid and excellently distinguished form of government end in a dark, equal chaos of confusion, ... in a Jack Cade or a Wat Tyler"[4] This Answer of Charles's became the classic royal statement of "mixed monarchy", the King's acceptance of a Parliamentary share in government. Charles did not hold consistently to this doctrine, but he repeated it at his trial in 1649, and it played its part in preparing for the restoration of 1660.

Continuities certainly exist between fifteenth- and seventeenth-century radicals. Some are doctrinal, some geographical. I shall try to look at both. Joan Thirsk and Alan Everitt have distinguished between champaign arable areas of the country, with stable docile communities subordinated to parson and squire, on the one hand, and pastoral, forest, moorland and fen areas on the other. In the latter, parishes were often very large, so that ecclesiastical control was less tight, there were fewer lords of manors, and vagrants could squat in relative security ("out of sight or out of slavery", as Gerrard Winstanley put it). In the seventeenth century these forest cottagers formed a pool of labour for the new industries that were developing. Both Lollardy and later heresy are found especially in clothing counties, and in pastoral, forest, moorland and fen areas.

Let us look at some areas where continuities can be seen. The Weald of Kent and Sussex was a region of forests, with few gentlemen and few manors. Parishes were large, and many families rarely attended church. It was a heavily populated and industrialized area (clothing and iron); the population was mobile and wayfaring, with "multitudes of rogues and beggars", since there were many opportunities for casual labour.[5] Masterless men abounded who were fodder for conscription in time of war. The Lollard areas can be roughly correlated with those that produced the most Marian martyrs, and with later Baptist and Quaker regions. Heresy was widespread in Kent in the fifteen-thirties, not only in the Weald; Peter Clark speaks of protestant pressure coming from below in Kentish towns. There were anti-Trinitarians in the fifteen-thirties and among the many Marian martyrs. Rye was especially Puritan, or worse. Its poorer townsmen, their pastor said in 1537, "reeked of Lollardy and ribaldry". There were "free-willers" under Edward VI, and what Patrick Collinson calls "rustic Pelagianism" under Elizabeth.[6]

Radical heresy continued later in the century. Robert Master of Woodchurch denied the resurrection. Another man "maintains . . . usury and says there is no hell". In the sixteen-twenties there were Brownists. There were political rebels in Kent in 1381, 1450, 1549 and 1554. There were food riots in 1630, and the Weald produced the largest single contingent of emigrants to Massachusetts later in the decade. Both John Taylor the Water-Poet, a man of conservative sympathies, and the radical George Wither thought it necessary to distinguish between Christendom and Kent. This tribute to the county's heretical reputation goes back at least to Sir Thomas Wyatt's time.[7]

In 1638 ten labourers from the old Lollard centre of Tenterden were up before the church court for refusing to pay tithe on wages. "What care we for his Majesty's laws and statutes?" the church-wardens of Little Horsted in the Sussex Weald were asking. The Kent and Sussex Weald was firm in support of Parliament during the civil war, unlike the western area of Sussex. A host of sectaries appeared in the forties, at Tenterden among other centres. Kent was one of the earliest areas to have women preachers.[8] The county looms large in Thomas Edwards's *Gangraena* of 1646. Kentish radicalism produced a strong Leveller movement, culminating in a Digger colony and a near-Digger pamphlet. It was a General Baptist and Muggletonian centre of some significance. Samuel Fisher, who evolved from a Baptist into a Quaker, and who argued in a scholarly folio that the Bible was not the Word of God, operated around

Ashford. After the restoration the Weald was "a receptacle for distressed and running parsons."[9]

Essex, my next county, was another woodland region, especially in the north, the traditional radical area. Itinerants and squatters abounded. The cottage clothing industry of this region was described as a breeding ground for Lollardy; John Ball had preached in Colchester. Essex participated in the Lollard revolt of 1414, and heresy survived into the sixteenth century.[10] There were major disturbances in the county in 1549, the year of Kett's rebellion. There were more Marian martyrs from Essex than from any other county except Kent (and London). In 1566 there was an abortive rising in the clothing towns of the north-east of the county. Under Edward VI there had been groups of "free-willers", under Mary lower-class conventicles, and under Elizabeth Familists, in Essex just as in Kent. The Legate brothers, one of whom was burned in 1612, the other dying in prison, came from Essex: they denied the existence of any true church on earth. In 1581 there was an illegal preaching place in the woods at Ramsey, with straw and moss for seating, "and the ground trodden bare with much treading".[11]

Essex was also a county in which there was an unusually large number of indictments for witchcraft in the sixteenth and seventeenth centuries. Here I can only hint at the possible connections which caused Lollards, Anabaptists and early Quakers to be denounced as witches.[12] When the famous Puritan William Ames was expelled from Christ's College, Cambridge, in 1610, he was promptly offered a city lectureship at Colchester. But the bishop ensured that he was not allowed to accept it.[13] Men spoke of "Colchester the Zealous", "the city upon a hill." The Puritan Thomas Shepard thought Essex the best county in England, John Hampden agreed that it was the place of most religion in the land. The Familist John Everard held a living at Fairstead in Essex.[14]

Essex is a county in which economic developments to the disadvantage of the poor are particularly well documented. Parish vestries and élites are busy imposing social discipline. There was an enormous increase after 1600 both in poor rates and in presentation of cottagers and lodgers. In the fifteen-eighties and nineties revolt was being foretold there. Some would even have welcomed a Spanish invasion. "What can rich men do against poor men if poor men rise and hold together?" artisans were asking in 1594. Next year there were threats to hang sellers of victuals — a simple popular remedy

against inflationary price increases. In 1629 there were two riots in
Maldon, led by Anne Carter, a butcher's wife. She was hanged, with
two others.[15] Charles I's enforcement of forest laws in the sixteen-
thirties hit small and large cultivators in Essex particularly hard. The
Venetian ambassador said that the total composition fines to be
levied on the county's forest lands would have amounted to at least
£300,000 — more than ten times the total collected in Ship Money.
So it did not need the Earl of Warwick's encouragement for Essex to
be the earliest and most outstanding of the counties defaulting on
Ship Money payments. When "intelligencers' news" was read in
Colchester streets on market days, "zealants" flocked to hear "as
people use when ballads are sung". In 1637 a parson at Maldon, where
Anne Carter had been hanged eight years earlier, was said to have
preached that the King's sins were being visited upon the kingdom.
He prayed for Charles's conversion, and urged the people to arm
themselves if all else failed. Next year he prayed that God would
"utterly destroy those that are enemies to the plantations" because
these offered a refuge in America to the godly.[16]

After 1638 Essex was the scene of violent anti-clericalism. The
common people pulled down altar rails and images. In 1640 Laudian
clergy were rabbled. Much popular iconoclasm was *social*, directed
against the coats of arms of noble families depicted in churches. At
the county elections in 1640 "rude vulgar people", "fellows without
shirts" (the English equivalent of sans-culottes?) threatened to "tear
the gentlemen to pieces" if the popular candidate were not elected.[17]
"Many thousands" turned out to sack the papist Countess of
Rivers's house. When manorial documents and evidences were
destroyed at Colchester in 1641 the jury gave an ignoramus verdict
against the plunderers. They were indicted again at the assizes, but
the sheriff could not get a jury to convict. At Milford, "no man
appeared like a gentleman but was made a prey to that ravenous
crew". "The rude people are come to such at head", said a Colchester
gentleman, "that we know not how to quiet them". There were
enclosure and other riots in 1641-2. They "must take advantage of
these times", said an Essex enclosure rioter in 1642, "lest they
never have the like again". "There was no law settled at this time
that he knew", declared a poacher in the same county in the same
year.[18]

Essex men "were with the first ... for recovering of liberty". In
January 1642 6,000 Essex freeholders signed a petition against

bishops. Thousands from Essex marched on London after the arrest of the Five Members. Bruno Ryves's account of the principles held by the lower classes of Chelmsford around 1642 is prophetic of much that was to be developed later: but it also recalls much that had gone before. Kings are burdens. The relation of master and servant has no ground in the New Testament; in Christ there is neither bond nor free. Ranks such as those of the peerage and gentry are "ethnical and heathenish distinctions". There is no ground in nature or Scripture why one man should have £1000 per annum, another not £1. The common people have long been kept under blindness and ignorance, and have remained servants and slaves to the nobility and gentry. "But God hath now opened their eyes and discovered them their Christian liberty". Gentlemen should be made to work for their living, or else should not eat. Learning has always been an enemy to the Gospel; it would be better if there were no universities, and all books except the Bible were burned. Any gifted man may be chosen by the congregation as its minister. Essex plays almost as big a part in Edward's *Gangraena* as does Kent. Baptists, Ranters and Muggletonians were all to be found there in the forties and fifties. The main Quaker strength was in North Essex, the new drapery region, an area of arable small holdings. After 1660 Essex was the third county in numbers of ejected ministers.[19]

The Chiltern hills of Buckinghamshire formed another Lollard area, where there was a revolt in 1413-14. Again heresy survived. In 1521 more were persecuted for heresy in Buckinghamshire than in all the rest of England. A century later Isaac Penington, the Long Parliament's Lord Mayor of London, came of a family resident in Buckinghamshire since the fifteen-fifties. There were many refusals to pay Ship Money in the county, including John Hampden's. In 1640 payment of coat and conduct money was almost universally refused, and the elections of High Wycombe and Great Marlow provided classic examples of class conflict. County freeholders elected John Hampden, and rode up to London in their thousands to defend the Five Members against Charles I's attempt to impeach them in January 1642. Buckinghamshire Levellers sponsored anti-enclosure riots, and produced two pamphlets — *Light shining in Buckinghamshire* and *More Light Shining in Buckinghamshire* — which are close to the Diggers in sentiment, though both were published before digging started at St George's Hill. Winstanley's colony was endorsed by a third pamphlet from the Chiltern

Hundreds, *A Declaration of the Well-Affected in the County of Buckinghamshire* (May 1649). Like Kent, Buckinghamshire had a Digger colony, at the old Lollard centre of Iver, with its own pamphlet (May 1650). There had been Baptists in Buckinghamshire in the sixteen-twenties, and Mr Watts sees General Baptist strength in the county (and in Kent) as a Lollard legacy.[20] Quakers found an early welcome in the county of Pennington and Penn: High Wycombe was one of the centres of the near-Ranter Story-Wilkinson separation.

Readers of Dickens's admirable *Lollards and Protestants in the Diocese of York* will remember that many of the most savoury Lollard remarks came from the moorland and clothing areas of the West Riding of Yorkshire, another remote region of huge and uncontrolled parishes. Christopher Shuter, vicar of Giggleswick, a nominee of Archbishop Grindal, opened up or revived a radical tradition in the area. In the sixteen-twenties the Pennine valleys produced Grindletonians, who put the spirit before the letter of the Bible, and thought that heaven was attainable in this life; in the sixteen-forties the lower classes in the West Riding forced the gentry to take up arms for Parliament. John Webster, religious radical and would-be reformer of the universities, came from the Grindleton region; George Fox found his first congregations there in 1651, including James Nayler and many other subsequent Quaker leaders. The Grindletonians were to be associated retrospectively with Coppinger (who had Kentish connections) and the Yorkshire gentleman Arthington, disciples of William Hacket who in the fifteen-nineties believed he was the Messiah. Giles Wigginton, Marprelate suspect and disciple of Hacket, founded a separatist congregation at Sedbergh when he was suspended from his living there. There were Familists in Bradford in the sixteen-thirties, Ranters later.[21]

From another Lollard area, Gloucestershire, the reformers William Tyndale and Robert Crowley came in the sixteenth century, the anti-Trinitarians John Bidle and John Knowles a century later. John Rogers of Colesbourn in 1636 told an audience of young people that women had no souls and therefore could commit any sin without fear of damnation; men could live as wickedly as they wished, confident that they could repent at leisure. The Forest of Dean was an area in which "people of very lewd lives and conversations" found greater freedom for "their villanies" than elsewhere; and this too was a heretical region. "Those tried notorious foresters of Dean" were "constant friends of the Parliament", "ever ready to rise against his Majesty's forces".[22] Levellers and Quakers found their greatest support in south-western England in Bristol. There were antinomians, Brownists and enclosure riots in Gloucestershire in the sixteen-thirties, forties and fifties. There was a Digger colony: later there were Ranters.

The clothing towns of Berkshire (Newbury, Reading) nourished heresy from the fifteenth to the seventeenth century. There had been Lollards in Salisbury in 1443, Brownists and Barrowists in Salisbury and elsewhere in Wiltshire in the late sixteenth century. Mr Watts believed he could trace continuity in Somerset between late fifteenth-century Lollards and seventeenth-century Baptists. Mr Evans saw similar continuity between Lollardy and nonconformity in Norwich. East Anglia generally was a Lollard area. There were Lollards in Ely in 1457, Familists under Elizabeth and Quakers in the mid-seventeenth century. Ely was well known as a haunt of sectaries in the forties, and a recruiting ground for Oliver Cromwell. In the Isle of Axholme there were Anabaptists in the sixteen-twenties, Levellers in the fifties, Fifth Monarchists, Quakers and republicans in the sixties. There had been East Anglian anti-Trinitarians in the fifteen-seventies and eighties. There were Quakers in the sixteen-fifties in parts of Cambridgeshire where there had been Familists eighty years earlier.[23]

In Lincolnshire, Leicestershire and Warwickshire Professor Jordan suggested continuities between Lollards and Baptists. The Midlands industrial region around Coventry produced Lollards in the fifteenth century, heretics in the early sixteenth and again in the early seventeenth centuries, Ranters in the sixteen-forties and fifties. Celia Fiennes at the end of the century noted Coventry as a dissenting town. In London the parish of St Stephen's, Coleman St., harboured heretics from Lollards to Foxe's martyrs and beyond. It had close links with Buckinghamshire and Essex heretics in the fifteen-thirties; in 1628 it produced libels on the Duke of Buckingham; after 1629 many emigrated thence to New England, and in the forties it was London's most notorious radical centre, housing its own secret printing press. Venner's Fifth Monarchist revolt started from there in 1661. Ayrshire, traditionally radical in religion in the seventeenth century, had been one of the few Lollard areas in Scotland. There were "Lollards" in Kyle in 1494; there were anti-clerical demonstrations in the county in 1511; heretics were being hunted there in 1637.[24]

I do not want to impose too much organizational coherence upon those who transmitted the ideas I have been discussing: that is one of the dangers of historical hindsight. In the fifteenth and early sixteenth centuries the orthodox spoke of "Lollards"; under Elizabeth of "Anabaptists" or "Familists". There were indeed Lollard and Anabaptist groups, and the Family of Love also had some sort of organization. We do not know much about any of them yet: more research is needed. But I suspect that clerical inquisitors imposed classifications, "-isms", for their own convenience. They started with some idea of what "Lollards", "Anabaptists" or "Familists" ought to believe, just as they started with assumptions about what "witches" believed. Leading questions would then encourage suspects to conform to the expected type.

So though there were "Lollard", "Anabaptist" and "Familist" trends in popular thought, we should not necessarily postulate the existence of an organized underground. But there are tantalizing hints. A heretical meeting in Colchester in 1555 was so widely advertised that a servant attended from Cambridgeshire. If there was underground organization, itinerants necessarily played a considerable part in it. The clothier Thomas White, involved in Dudley's conspiracy in 1556, carried on treasonable activities under cover of "collecting the wool". Humphrey Newman, a cobbler at one time attached to the household of Sir Richard Knightley, was the principal distributor of the Marprelate Tracts in the Midlands and London. A travelling clothier from Berkshire was alleged to be spreading sedition in Chichester in the late sixteen-thirties. Elizabethan Familists are said to have been linked by itinerant weavers, basket-makers, bottle-makers, musicians, joiners. In 1622 Thomas Shepard in Essex knew about the Grindletonian Familists, lurking in the obscurity of a Yorkshire Pennine valley. The clothing industry linked Essex and the West Riding.[25]

Familists — like Lollards before them — tended when challenged to recant, but to remain of the same opinion still. This unheroic attitude was related to their dislike of all established churches, whether protestant or Catholic. Their refusal of martyrdom no doubt helped their beliefs to survive, but it increases the historian's difficulty in identifying heretical groups with confidence. Only after the excitement of the reign of Edward VI were lower-class heretics for a brief period prepared to court martyrdom: after 1660 one suspects that many former Ranters and Baptists reverted to the ways of their Familist predecessors and returned formally and unbelievingly to the national church. The Ranters "would have said as we said and done as we commanded, and yet have kept their own principle still", said Durant Hotham, stressing this Lollard and Familist way of acting as the main difference between Ranters and Quakers.[26]

Before 1640 the traditions I have been describing circulated verbally. Historians, themselves the products of a literary culture, relying so much on written or printed evidence, are always in danger of underestimating verbal transmission of ideas. Men did not need to read books to become acquainted with heresy: indeed censored books were the last place in which they would expect to find it. Again and again the great heresiarchs deny being influenced by their predecessors. Luther was astonished to find that he was reproducing Hus's heresies: Milton was astonished and delighted to find that many protestant divines had anticipated his views on divorce.

With all these reservations, let me now suggest some continuing lower-class traditions which burst into the open in the sixteen-forties. There is no need to produce further evidence of the point I have already stressed, class hatred, since this has been fully documented in Mr Brian Manning's magnificent *The English People and the English Revolution*. Illustrations of more generalized hostility to social subordination are refusal to remove the hat in the presence of magistrates or social superiors, and addressing them as "thou" in symbolic assertion of equality. (Compare Coke's insult to Ralegh at his trial: "Lo! I thou thee, thou traitor!" Treason demoted a gentleman from his own class to equality with the lower orders: "thouing" a social superior marked an attempt to escape from the social and political contempt to which "thou" condemned those to whom it was addressed). The Quakers inherited a long-standing lower-class rejection of deference here. The fifteenth-century Lollard William Thorpe kept his hat on in presence of authority. So did Marian martyrs, Essex heretics in 1584, William Hacket in 1591, John Traske in 1618, an oatmeal-maker up before the High Commission in 1630, the future Leveller John Lilburne in 1638, John Saltmarsh in 1647, and very many others. John Lewis, burnt at Norwich in 1583 for anti-Trinitarianism, "did thou each wight".[27]

Refusal to take an oath is also a rejection of political authority: we find it among Norwich and Essex Lollards, some Anabaptists,

Barrowists, Lilburne. Some Lollards rejected all judicial proceedings, and any form of deliberate killing, whether in warfare or by execution of criminals. Again these positions were inherited by Quakers. The myth of the Norman Yoke enshrines a similar anti-authoritarian and anti-aristocratic attitude, rejection of the ruling class and its law. So does the 1381 question, "When Adam delved and Eve span/Who was then the gentleman?" quoted in the reign of Edward VI, in 1593, and often after 1640 — "this levelling lewd text", Cleveland called it. Sneers about Jack Straw, Wat Tyler and Jack Cade were frequent. Fuller said the rebels of 1381 were "pure Levellers". Sir Thomas Aston referred in 1641 to "the old seditious argument, that we are all the sons of Adam, born free; some of them say, the Gospel hath made them free.... They will plead Scripture for it, that we should all live by the sweat of our brows". Nor was it only via Scripture that human equality was asserted. In 1310 a peasant pleaded (through his lawyer) that "in the beginning every man in the world was free".[28]

The Digger community at St George's Hill, we now know, was only one of ten or more such experiments; communist ideas are found in writers not directly associated with the Diggers — the Ranters Abiezer Coppe and George Foster, and the author of *Tyanipocrit Discovered;* they were attributed to the Leveller Walwyn. John Ball, and Essex, Norwich and Worcestershire Lollards were alleged to have said that property should be common. Similar charges were made against participants in Cade's rebellion in 1450.[29] Such accusations may be the product of the alarmed imagination of the rich; but since community of property is commended in the New Testament it is unlikely that no lower-class Bible-reader would take the point. An Essex man did, late in Henry VIII's reign: Chelmsford radicals a century later were said to have done so. Tyndale came dangerously near to justifying community of property, and such ideas occurred in the mid-sixteenth century often enough for one of the 42 Articles of 1552 and of the 39 Articles of 1562 to be directed against them. The Presbyterian John Field found it necessary in 1572 to denounce communist theories.[30]

Turning to more specifically religious matters, Essex Lollards said that priests should marry and work, and attacked non-preachers. Pluralism was as bad as bigamy, asserted an Essex Lollard burnt in 1440. Another in the same county seventeen years later said that the best man was the best priest, and that confession should be made only to God — anticipating the lay initiative in Puritanism and the sects. John Ball taught that tithes should be paid only by men richer than the priest. Many Lollards opposed tithes. Ministers should not be paid, said Augustine Draper of Essex in 1587; he also denied the immortality of the soul. Opposition to tithes and church courts became standard among the radicals of the revolutionary decades. Wyclif had thought that the exercise of civil jurisdiction by ecclesiastics, and in particular the use of force, was antichristian. So did many seventeenth-century radicals, including John Milton.[31]

The seventeenth-century view that a layman is as good as a parson, that the whole ecclesiastical hierarchy is antichristian, that tithes and a state church should be abolished, together with universities as training centres for the clergy; advocacy of "mechanic preachers" who enjoy the spirit of God, so much more important than academic education: all these ideas are so familiar from Wyclif and the Lollards through Anabaptists and Familists to Levellers and sectaries that documentation would be superfluous. Some Lollards seem to have accepted that all believers were priests. Familist ministers were itinerant craftsmen, and indeed the conditions of underground sectarianism forced the emergence of mechanic preachers. Anti-sacerdotalism was a necessity as well as an ideology. Some Lollards, and the reformer William Tyndale, even thought that women might preach.[32]

Secondly comes a strong emphasis on study of the Bible, and use of its texts — as interpreted by the individual conscience — to criticize the ceremonies and sacraments of the church. Worship of images, for instance, was denounced as idolatry. Sacredness was denied to church buildings: worship and prayer could take place anywhere. Lollards as well as Edwardian radicals anticipated the iconclasm of the mid-seventeenth century. Essex and Norwich Lollards were accused of scorning infant baptism; so did Francis Kett and Edward Wightman. This looks forward to Samuel Oates, weaver and button-maker, dipping in Essex in 1645 as well as begetting Titus. Millenarianism, familiar in lower-class underground movements, was found among the later Lollards.[33] Around 1580 Familists were alleged to believe that the saints were to judge the world, doctrine repeated by Thomas Collier, Gerrard Winstanley, George Fox, Fifth Monarchists. Ludlow, like John Cook and John Milton, saw regicide as an anticipation by the saints of the Last Judgment.[34]

Arminianism, the doctrine that men may save themselves by their own efforts, does not seem a particularly dangerous heresy to us today. But it did to orthodox sixteenth- and seventeenth-century Puritans. (We must distinguish between radical Arminianism, rejecting the sacraments of the church as aids to salvation, and Laudian Arminianism). Many sixteenth-century English heretics rejected predestination, attached greater value to works than to faith, emphasized human freedom and effort — a sort of pre-Arminianism, which can be found among Familists as well as among continental Anabaptists, from one or other of whom it was taken over by the English General Baptists. A Kentish heretic, Henry Hart, a "froward freewill man", who wrote a treatise against predestination in 1554, anticipated Milton in saying that human freedom to choose between good and evil was essential if God was to be absolved of responsibility for evil. There were "free-will men" in London in 1560. An Essex heretic in 1592 thought that "all the world shall be saved"; Thomas Edwards in 1646 attributed the idea of universal salvation to Familists and other radicals. It was certainly held by Winstanley, and under the 1648 Blasphemy Ordinance was made an offence carrying the penalty of life imprisonment. Thomas Shepard's interest in the Yorkshire Grindletonians led him in 1622 to ask "whether that glorious state of perfection might not be the truth?" The belief that perfection could be attained in this life had been held by London tradesmen in 1549 and 1631, and by many Familists in between. In the sixteen-forties Saltmarsh, Everard and Winstanley believed that Christ would not appear in the flesh but in the saints. Mrs Attaway and William Jenny did not think it could stand with the goodness of God to damn his creatures eternally: Walwyn was to say that eternal punishment was too great for "a little sinning".[35]

Another recurrent heresy is anti-Trinitarianism. Some Lollards denied the divinity of Christ and the Holy Spirit. The rapid spread of anti-Trinitarianism both in the liberty of Edward VI's reign and in prisons under Mary gave rise to great alarm among orthodox protestants — so much so that the godly John Philpot had to apologize for "spitting upon an Arian". In 1549 an Arian said Christ was a prophet, the Son of God, but only the first-begotten amongst many brothers.[36] This gives rise to thoughts about the connection of anti-Trinitarianism with attacks on primogeniture, familiar later among the Levellers.

In 1555 denial of the divinity of Christ by an itinerant joiner, later a well-known Familist, was the subject of illegal discussions in a Colchester tavern, to which servants and husbandmen travelled long distances from outside the county. Some of the Marian martyrs were probably anti-Trinitarians, and between 1548 and 1612 at least eight persons were burnt in England for heresies concerning the Trinity. Among them was Marlowe's friend Francis Kett, grandson of the leader of the Norfolk rebels in 1549, who was also a mortalist, an opponent of infant baptism and of the death penalty for heresy; he rejected the authority of ministers to excommunicate. Marlowe, himself from Kent, was said to have called Christ a bastard; in 1560 a Kentish man had said that those who believed Christ sat on the right hand of the Father were fools.[37] The Legate brothers from Essex, one of whom was burnt in 1612, were anti-Trinitarians: so was Wightman, the last Englishman to be burnt for heresy, also in 1612. Their courage made the common people, Fuller tells us, "ready to entertain good thoughts even of [their] opinions". When Archbishop Neile in 1639 wished to revive the practice of burning heretics his chosen victim would have been John Trendall, anti-Trinitarian stonemason of Dover.[38]

Anti-Trinitarianism was associated especially with Familists, who rejected the whole theology of the Atonement, Christ's vicarious sacrifice: some abandoned belief in the historical existence of Christ. For them the word Christ was a metaphor for the divine spark which exists in every man. William Pynchon of Essex carried anti-Trinitarianism to Massachusetts in the sixteen-thirties; John Bidle of Gloucestershire, John Milton and very many others proclaimed it in England in the forties and fifties. Quakers and Muggletonians were accused of the heresy.[39] The humanity of Christ enhanced the dignity of man.

Another heresy which recurs among underground groups was mortalism, the doctrine that the soul either sleeps from death until the general resurrection or dies with the body. Professor N.T. Burns has so thoroughly demonstrated the continuous existence of *Christian Mortalism from Tyndale to Milton* that I refer to him for evidence, though with a caution that mortalism existed in England well before the Reformation — among Essex Lollards, for example. Tyndale was a mortalist.[40] The 42 Articles of 1552 condemned mortalism, though the condemnation was omitted in the 39 Articles of 1562. Elizabethan Familists were alleged to be mortalists, believing that the resurrection occurred in this life. In the fifteen-sixties in Surrey and in the fifteen-eighties in Wisbech and Wiltshire there were those who believed that the soul was annihilated at death, with no ultimate resurrection. Among mortalists was Augustine Draper of Essex, who also thought the clergy should not be paid, and the anti-Trinitarians Francis Kett and Edward Wightman. Christopher Marlowe was said to be a mortalist; Donne — like Sir Thomas Browne — appears to have toyed with the heresy in his younger days. Mortalism too travelled to New England, where Mrs Anne Hutchinson and Samuel Gorton were accused in the sixteen-thirties of being mortalists as well as Familists. In the forties and fifties William Bowling of Kent, Richard Overton, Clement Wrighter, Henry Marten, Lodowick Muggleton and John Milton were some of a large number of adherents to the belief. The Quakers and Henry Stubbe were also accused of the heresy.[41]

Mortalism was often accompanied by, or led to, a species of materialism. Wyclif, like some troubadours, was said to believe in the eternity of matter. In 1428 the Lollard Margery Backster anticipated Milton in a crude reference to the ultimate physical fate of bread eaten in the eucharist, in order to show that it could hardly be the body of Christ. Dickens quotes many similar remarks. A man from north-west Kent in 1538 denied that God had created him,[42] and many early heretics believed — like Ranters in the sixteen-fifties and the rebel angels in *Paradise Lost* — that "all comes by nature". Ranters, like Milton, held that matter is good in itself. Such doctrines can by a natural progression lead to anti-asceticism, glorification of the body, a belief that life is to be enjoyed here and now. This may be expressed as an antinomian libertinism: the elect are exempt from the moral law since God is in them; they partake of God's nature. A Lollard lay "priest" in 1389 was said to believe himself free from the possibility of sin. Such doctrines in England were denounced by Thomas Rogers in 1607. They surfaced in the sixteen-forties. Baxter said in 1649 and 1654 that all men were naturally antinomians, especially the vulgar. Arminianism on the other hand was a heresy of the learned.[43] John Milton is an example of a learned antinomian.

If at death the body returns to its elements, as a drop of water taken out of the ocean returns to it again, mortalism can also lead to scepticism about heaven and hell, which become states of mind rather than geographical locations. Some Lollards denied their existence, and placed purgatory in this world. The devil too was internalized. This could combine with allegorical interpretations of the Bible to make the whole Christian myth describe conflicts which take place only within the believer. Familists were said to hold that Christ and Antichrist were not real persons, heaven and hell not real places. Francis Kett the mortalist thought there would be no hell before the Last Judgment. In Wiltshire and in Somerset in the early seventeenth century men were denying the existence of a local heaven or hell. A preacher in Lancashire appointed by the Bishop of Chester early in James I's reign thought hell a mere delusion, invented to oppress and torment the consciences of men. In 1619 a Wiltshire heretic was accused of doubting whether the writings of the apostles and prophets were true. Saltmarsh and Everard treated the Scriptures as an allegory, though Everard added "I deny not the history". For Winstanley "it matters not much" whether the Bible was true or not; from his earliest pamphlets he concentrated on their allegorical meaning. James Nayler more cautiously said "there is no knowledge of heaven or hell". In the sixteen-twenties the Grindletonians, like Thomas Müntzer before them and Gerrard Winstanley after them, emphasized the spirit as against the letter of Scripture, a doctrine not unknown to Milton. A Norfolk anti-Trinitarian in 1579 anticipated the Ranters by saying that the New Testament was "a mere fable".[44]

The poet Gower in the fourteenth century described labourers who were not satisfied with the bread and water on which they had been brought up but demanded good food and drink — and did not believe in God. There were "libertines" in Essex in 1551, and later men who denied the existence of "sin" and criticized the Bible in a way that looks forward to Clement Wrighter and Samuel Fisher in the sixteen-fifties. One described himself as an atheist.[45] Antinomianism led to sexual heresies. Whenever suspected Lollards were up before the Norwich church courts in 1428-31 they were asked, in a standard formula, if they believed in church marriage. Clearly the answer expected was No. Miss Hudson confirms this from other regions. Some Norwich suspects were accused of advocating community of women — a recurrent charge long before Münster. "Marriage is superfluous", the Venetian ambassador reported heretics as saying in 1499. "A lewd fellow out of Essex" in 1457 thought marriage should be a civil ceremony; Buckinghamshire heretics taught this in the first decades of Henry VIII's reign, Barebone's Parliament enacted it in 1653. In 1548 it was thought necessary to issue a royal proclamation attacking seditious preachers who advocated divorce. Sixteenth-century Familists married and divorced by a simple declaration before the congregation. The Yorkshire custom of "handfast marriages" was taken up by Ranters and Quakers. Some Lollards may have advocated polygamy, though the evidence is doubtful. It was defended in 1548, in Kent in 1572, and by Milton. In 1592 Nashe referred to "adulterous Familists". Drunken Barnabee repeated the slander against Bradford Familists in the sixteen-thirties. It was entirely in keeping that James Nayler should be accused of saying that "he might lie with any woman that was of his judgment". Similar accusations were more plausibly made against Abiezer Coppe and Laurence Clarkson, who in the sixteen-forties advocated free love. Underlying these radical theories of marriage and divorce was the widely attested fact that lower-class attitudes towards matrimony were much more casual and fluid than the ethic which middle-class Puritans wished to impose. Evidence for *de facto* marriage and easy divorce is overwhelming, especially — but by no means exclusively — among vagrants.[46]

We isolate heresies for the purpose of analysis, but they normally came in combination. Sir Thomas More linked anti-Trinitarianism with advocacy of common ownership of property.[47] Edmund Leach has suggested that anti-Trinitarianism, millenarianism and social revolt go together, among the early Christians and in seventeenth-century England. Radical Arminianism, rejection of infant baptism, antinomianism, mortalism and materialism were frequently linked with Leach's heresies in England, as Thomas Edwards noted in *Gangraena* in 1646. In the same year the respectable inhabitants of Great Burstead, Essex, saw similar connections. They petitioned against "a dangerous sect" which had arisen in their parish, admitting and rebaptizing all comers, "setting up mechanics for their preachers, denouncing the order and ministry of the Church of England as antichristian". They taught "unsound opinions" like universal grace, the abrogation of the law, the sinfulness of repentance. Their name was legion, and they had a long pedigree.[48]

Looking back to Lollards and Familists helps to emphasize that, if there was a continuing heretical underground, it was essentially composed of laymen. This fits in with what we are coming to know about the initiative in Puritanism of lay members of congregations in refusing to allow their minister to wear the surplice or to conform to other ceremonies. The Puritan clergy were moderate reformers, safely educated at Oxford or Cambridge. They naturally had not much use for lay mechanic preaching. There were initially some

Lollard hedge priests, but they counted for less and less with time. Familist ministers seem normally to have been craftsmen.

The church was the official meeting place; and it belonged to the official clergy. The meeting place of the unorthodox was the tavern or ale-house, from Lollards to Familists and on to Baptists, Levellers and Ranters. The only other popular meeting place was the open air; Quakers preached there. Laurence Clarkson said that a tavern was the house of God.[49] The popularity of the ale-house, apart from the obvious reason, was partly due to the evolution of a new itinerant working-class, which sought social intercourse and information about jobs in ale-houses. JPs deeply resented any attempt to remove control of ale-houses from their hands, whether by Buckingham's protégés Mitchell and Mompesson or by Oliver Cromwell's Major-Generals.

So I suggest as a hypothesis for further investigation that there may have been a continuing underground tradition — not necessarily organization — in which we can identify certain heretical and seditious beliefs. Professor Elton's notorious statement that there was no connection between Lollardy and the Reformation is true only if we interpret the Reformation in the narrowest sense as Henry VIII's act of state. But if we ask why England became a protestant country we cannot leave Lollardy out of account, though it was the more radical protestants who looked back to the Lollards. Bruce McFarlane was right to call his book *John Wyclif and the Origins of Nonconformity*. We may be able to trace direct links in ideas from Lollards through Familists and Anabaptists to the radical sectaries, the Levellers, Diggers, Ranters and Quakers of the mid-seventeenth century. The author of *Semper Iidem: Or, a Parallel betwixt the Ancient and Modern Fanaticks* (1661) certainly thought so.[50]

This leads to a final question. What happened after 1660? It took some time to realise that defeat was final, that the above-ground decades had been a mere interlude. In 1678-81 something surfaced again in London. But the defeat of the radicals in 1685 facilitated the coup of 1688, when Whigs and Tories united against the radicals no less than against James II. Some emigrated to the West Indies, New England and the continent. There were Ranters on Long Island and Rhode Island in the sixteen-eighties and nineties.[51] Some of those who remained in England no doubt lapsed into silent bloody-mindedness. Some became sectaries; the Quakers cast off their radical wing and became pacifists. All sects were purged by the fierce

persecution of the three decades after 1660. They had to recognize
that Christ's kingdom was not to be built on earth, but was to be
expected in heaven at a date later to be announced.

But the Levellers were never wholly forgotten. Goldsmith praised
them. Jefferson quoted William Rumbold, who had been para-
phrased by Defoe and cited in an almanac of 1708. There were men
who called themselves Levellers in revolt in Worcestershire in 1670,
in anti-enclosure riots in 1724, in Ledbury in 1735, in the Lowlands
of Scotland in the seventeen-twenties, in the Hudson valley in 1760,
other American rebels under William Prendergast in 1765.[52] Beau
Nash, rather unexpectedly, spoke of Levellers in Bath in 1742.[53] The
Leveller sea-green colours had reappeared on the streets of London
in 1681; the Whig Green Ribbon Club took its name from them.
London weavers in 1675 had rioted in green aprons, and green aprons
soon came to be "almost regarded as a badge of Quakerism".[54] The
French prophets in London in Anne's reign were accused of "levelling" and "Ranterism"; they wore long green ribbons. The fact that
the Chartist flag was green is usually attributed to Irish influence;
but why did Irish protestants adopt the colour in the first place? In
1690 William III's troops in Ireland wore green, and some are said to
have chosen the Leveller sea-green, so there may be continuity here
from Levellers through Whigs to United Irishmen and Chartists. At
all events the Levellers were still remembered in the Chartist movement.[55] Was it only because of Robespierre's complexion that
Carlyle dubbed him "sea-green?" Pamphlets by Winstanley were in
the library of Benjamin Furly, who linked radical Quakers with deist
free-thinkers like Anthony Collins — who also possessed pamphlets
by Winstanley. In the mid-eighteenth century the radical Thomas
Hollis gave a copy of *The Law of Freedom* to Henry Fielding.[56]

Nor is it only a matter of politics. A.L. Morton showed that Blake
was aware of the Ranter past, and Burns may have been.[57] How the
ideas were transmitted is more difficult to document. A lay clerk of
Norwich cathedral about 1700 was alleged to think that "there is no
heaven but a quiet mind, and no hell but the grave" — almost a literal
quotation from many Ranters. There were people called Ranters in
the Midlands, Nottingham, Cumberland, near Inverness and elsewhere at the turn of the century. Wesley in the seventeen-forties met
antinomian preachers in the Black Country — an old Lollard/Ranter
area — who believed in community of property and did not believe in
monogamy.[58] The future bishop George Horne also knew Ranters in

the mid-century, as well as anti-monarchist Presbyterians.[59] The linked doctrines of mortalism, millenarianism and the perfectibility of man on earth were still being discussed in a Kentish General Baptist congregation in the middle of the eighteenth century.[60] In 1756 the Robin Hood Society met every Monday night at a pub in Butchers' Row, London. Here deists, Arians, Socinians, papists and Jews aired their doubts about the resurrection, the incarnation, the Trinity ("their everlasting butt"), the authenticity of the Scriptures, of the gospel miracles. They were a set of mechanics — tailors, barbers, butchers and shoemakers.[61] Where did the millenarian revivalism come from which accompanied the American as it had accompanied the English Revolution? What about the New England antinomians of the eighteen-twenties and eighteen-thirties, whose belief that perfection was attainable on earth led to sexual eccentricities and experiments as it had done in old England nearly two centuries earlier? If we look for them, I think we can find other traces, before 1640 and after 1660. One of the objects of this chapter is to encourage others to look. With that in mind I have documented it pretty fully.

NOTES

1. Originally published in *Rebels and their Causes: Essays in honour of A.L. Morton* (ed. M. Cornforth, 1978); reprinted, slightly revised, in Bulletin Nos. 12 and 13 of *Documenta Anabaptistica Neerlandica* (Amsterdam, 1980-1), and in abbreviated form in *Religion and Rural Revolt* (ed. J.M. Bak and G. Benecke, Manchester U.P., 1984).
2. *W.T.U.D.*, p. 120; G.F. Nuttall, "The Lollard Movement after 1384, its Characteristics and Continuity", *Transactions of the Congregational Historical Soc.*, XII (1935), pp. 243-50.
3. I.B. Horst, *The Radical Brethren* (Nieuwkoop, 1972), pp. 146-8.
4. J. Cleveland, *The Rustic Rampant*, in *Works* (1687), p. 506; A. Cowley, *The Civil War* (ed. A. Pritchard, Toronto U.P., 1973), pp. 88, 103; J. Collop, *Poems* (ed. C. Hilberry, Wisconsin U.P., 1962), p. 48; J. Rushworth, *Historical Collections* (1659-1701), V, p. 732.
5. A. Fletcher, *op. cit.*, pp. 3, 21, 61, 165-6, 193, 200.
6. J. Foxe, *Acts and Monuments* (ed. J. Pratt, n.d.), IV, pp. 123, 181, 619; V, pp. 16, 647-52, 841; VII, pp. 287-321, 383, 604, 750-2; VIII, pp. 130-1, 151-6, 243-7, 253-5, 300-3, 320-77, 394, 430-3, 504-6, 549-50, 566-8, 576, 695, 729-30, appendix VI; Collinson, *The Elizabethan Puritan Movement*, p. 37; cf. pp. 96-7; *Godly People*, p. 12, Chapter 15 *passim*;

Horst, *op. cit.*, pp. 122-40; Fletcher, *op. cit.*, pp. 62, 91, 124; J.W. Martin, "English Protestant Separatism at its Beginnings: Henry Hart and the Free-Will Men", *Sixteenth Century Journal*, VII (1976), pp. 58, 66-7; Claire Cross, *Church and People, 1450-1660* (1976), pp. 25, 28, 37-9, 73-4, 98-9, 112, 114, 170; P. Clark, *English Provincial Society*, pp. 23, 30-1, 56, 60, 63, 67, 77, 101, 156, 399, 401-2, 444 and *passim*; "Reformation and Radicalism in Kentish Towns, c. 1500-1553", in *The Urban Classes, the Nobility and the Reformation* (ed. W.J. Mommsen, Stuttgart, 1979), p. 124; M.R. Watts, *The Dissenters from the Reformation to the French Revolution* (Oxford U.P., 1978), pp. 283-4, 354-5; B. Reay, "Quaker Opposition to Tithes, 1652-1660", *P. and P.*, No. 86 (1980), p. 102. For the geography of surviving Lollardy see J.F. Davis, *Heresy and Reformation in the South-East of England, 1520-1559* (1983), pp. 2, 58, 102, 141 and *passim*.

7. J. Walter and K. Wrightson, "Dearth and Social Order in Early Modern England", *P. and P.*, No. 71 (1976), p. 27; P. Clark, "Popular Protest and Disturbance in Kent, 1558-1640", *Economic History Review*, XXIX (1976), pp. 365-82; *English Provincial Society*, pp. 156, 335, 381, 389, 393; C. Burrage, *Early English Dissenters*, II, pp. 202-3; J. Taylor, *All the Works* (1973 reprint), II, p. 114 (rightly 124); G. Wither, *Fragmenta Prophetica* (1669), p. 130, in *Miscellaneous Works* (Spenser Soc., 6th collection, 1878); Sir T. Wyatt, *Complete Poems* (ed. R.A. Rebholz, Penguin), p. 189.

8. Fletcher, *op. cit.*, p. 22; Manning, *The English People and the English Revolution* (1976), p. 41; my *Society and Puritanism in Pre-Revolutionary England* (Panther edn., 1969), p. 298; D. Underdown, "Clubmen in the Civil War" *P. and P.*, No. 85 (1979), p. 42. Peter Clark helped me with Tenterden.

9. Edwards, *Gangraena* (1646), I, p. 75 and *passim*; *W.T.U.D.*, pp. 46-7, 124-7, 239; *V.C.H.*, *Kent*, II (1926), p. 100; J.F. McGregor, "The Baptists: Fount of All Heresy", in *Radical Religion in the English Revolution*, p. 35.

10. Foxe, *op. cit.*, IV, pp. 214-17, 584-6, 695, 706-7; V, pp. 29-34, 38-42, 251; VI, pp. 729-40; VII, pp. 86-90, 97-123, 139-42, 329, 370, 605, 718-30; VIII, pp. 107-21, 138-41, 303-10, 381-94, 420-3, 433-6, 467-8, 525-6, appendix VI; Horst, *op. cit.*, pp. 122-3; Collinson, *The Elizabethan Puritan Movement*, p. 223; Collinson, "The Godly: Aspects of Popular Protestantism in Elizabethan England", *Papers Presented to the Past and Present Conference on Popular Religion* (1966), p. 16; Martin, *op. cit.*, p. 66; Cross, *op. cit.*, pp. 25, 37-9, 73-4, 77, 98-9, 112.

11. A. Gordon, *Heads of English Unitarian History* (1895), pp. 16-17; D.D. Wallace, "From Eschatology to Arian Heresy: the Case of Francis Kett", *Harvard Theological Review*, No. 67 (1974), p. 467. A.G. Dickens, "Heresy and the Origins of English Protestantism", in *Britain and the Netherlands*, II (Ed. J.S. Bromley and E.H. Kossmann, Groningen, 1964), pp. 53-5, 60; Cross, *op. cit.*, pp. 28-32.

12. C.L.E. Ewen, *Witch Hunting and Witch Trials* (1929), pp. 100, 302; A. Macfarlane, *Witchcraft in Tudor and Stuart England* (1970), *passim*;

W. Hunt, *Bath and Wells* (Diocesan Histories, 1885), pp. 140, 146.

13. K.L. Sprunger, *The Learned Doctor William Ames* (Illinois U.P., 1972), pp. 24-5.

14. *Rump; or an Exact Collection of the Choycest Poems and Songs relating to the Late Times* (1662), I, p. 354; T. Shepard, *God's Plot* (ed. M. McGiffert, Massachusetts U.P., 1972), p. 47; Hunt, *The Puritan Moment*, pp. 87-90 and *passim*.

15. Walter and Wrightson, *op. cit.*, p. 36, and *passim*; K.V. Thomas, *Religion and the Decline of Magic* (1971), pp. 406, 422; Hunt, *The Puritan Moment*, pp. 60-1, 147-8 and *passim*.

16. *C.S.P.D., 1634-5*, pp. 216, 227; *1636-7*, pp. 223, 483; *C.S.P. Ven., 1632-6*, pp. 299-300; *1636-8*, p. 269; *V.C.H., Essex*, II, p. 228. I owe these references and much of this and the following paragraphs to Hunt, *The Puritan Movement*, esp. Chapters 10 and 11.

17. J. Gruenfeld, "The Election for Knights of the Shire for Essex, Spring 1640", *Essex Archaeological Soc. Trans.*, II (3rd series, 1967), pp. 145-6; J.A. Sharpe, "Crime and Delinquency in an Essex Parish, 1600-1640", in *Crime in England, 1500-1800* (ed. J.S. Cockburn, 1977), pp. 90-109.

18. C. Holmes, *The Eastern Association in the English Civil War* (Cambridge U.P., 1974), pp. 33-6, 43-4.

19. [Anon.], *A New Found Stratagem* (1647), p. 4; Marie Gimelfarb-Brack attributes this pamphlet to Richard Overton (*Liberté, Egalité, Fraternité, Justice! La Vie et l'Oeuvre de Richard Overton, Niveleur*, Berne, 1979, pp. 402-3); *W.T.U.D.*, pp. 37, 263; Watts, *op. cit.*, p. 277. I owe North Essex to Barry Reay's Oxford D. Phil. thesis, *Early Quaker Activity and Reactions to it, 1652-1664* (1980).

20. Foxe, *op. cit.*, IV, pp. 123-6, 211-43, 580-6; V, p. 434; P. Gregg, *King Charles I* (1981), pp. 302, 313; K.V. Thomas, "Another Digger Broadside", *P. and P.*, No. 42 (1969), pp. 57-68; *W.T.U.D.*, pp. 21, 117, 126; A.G. Dickens, "Heresy and the Origins of English Protestantism", pp. 53-6; Cross, *Church and People*, pp. 28-32, 35, 42, 73, 98; Edwards, *Gangraena*, I, p. 64; Burrage, *op. cit.*, I, p. 274; Watts, *op. cit.*, pp. 283-4; McGregor, *op. cit.*, p. 35.

21. Dickens, *Lollards and Protestants in the Diocese of York, 1509-1558* (Oxford U.P., 1959), *passim*; Collinson, *Grindal*, pp. 205-12; R. Braithwait, *Barnabae Itinerarium or Barnabees Journal* (ed. W.C. Hazlitt, 1876), Sig. C.

22. C.E. Hart, *The Free Miners of the Royal Forest of Dean* (Gloucester, 1953), pp. 174-5; Buchanan Sharp, *In Contempt of All Authority: Rural Artisans and Riot in the West of England, 1586-1660* (California U.P., 1980), *passim*; B.L. Beer, *Rebellion and Riot: Popular Disorder in England during the Reign of Edward VI* (Kent State U.P., 1982), Chapter 6; B.S. Capp, *The Fifth Monarchy Men*, p. 35, for millenarianism in fifteenth-century Gloucestershire. I owe John Rogers to the kindness of Dr Andrew Foster, citing Gloucester Diocesan Register.

23. A. Hudson, "A Lollard Compilation and the Dissemination of Wycliffite Thought", *Journal of Theological Studies*, No. 23 (1972), pp. 79-80;

"A Lollard Mass", *ibid.*, p.410; M.J. Ingram, *Ecclesiastical Justice in Wiltshire, 1600-1640, with Special Reference to Cases Concerning Sex and Marriage* (Oxford University D. Phil. thesis, 1976), p.70; Watts, *op. cit.*, p.355; J.T. Evans, *Seventeenth-Century Norwich: Politics, Religion and Government, 1620-1690* (Oxford U.P., 1979), p. 84; Claire Cross, "'Great Reasoners in Scripture': the Activities of Women Lollards, 1380-1530", in *Medieval Women* (ed. D. Baker, Studies in Church History Subsidium, I, 1978), pp. 373-5; Reay, Thesis, Chapter 2; Wallace, *op. cit.*, p. 464; W.K. Jordan, *The Development of Religious Toleration in England, 1603-1640* (1936), p. 267; M. Spufford, *Contrasting Communities; English Villages in the Sixteenth and Seventeenth Centuries* (Cambridge U.P., 1974), p. 351. For Newbury I am indebted to an unpublished paper by Mr C.G. Durston. See also Capp, *op. cit.*, p. 35, for millenarianism in fifteenth- and early sixteenth-century Newbury and Wiltshire; K. Lindley, *Fenland Riots and the English Revolution* (1982), pp. 195-6, 234; C. Holmes, *Seventeenth-Century Lincolnshire* (Lincoln, 1980), pp.45, 112, 205. For Wiltshire see also pp.141-2, 151-3 below.

24. *W.T.U.D.*, pp.83, 121, 124-5, 218, 226-8, 234, 239; Manning, *op. cit.*, pp.210-16; A. Hassell Smith, *County and Court: Government and Politics in Norfolk, 1558-1603* (Oxford U.P., 1974), p. 203; Foxe, *op. cit.*, IV, pp.133-5, 243, 557-8; VI, p.612; VII, pp.384-402, 799 sqq.; VIII, pp.163-202, 256, 401-5, appendix VI; Cross, *Church and People*, pp.27-8, 35-7, 73, 75, 112; I. Laxton, "The Reformation and Popular Culture", in *Church and Society in England, Henry VIII to James I* (ed. F. Heal and R. O'Day, 1977), pp.66-7; Cross, "'Great Reasoners'", pp.365-8; J.F. Davis, "Lollard Survival and the Textile Industry in the South-East of England"', *Studies in Church History*, II (ed. C.J. Cumming, Leiden, 1966), p.194; A. Hudson, "A Lollard Compilation", pp.79-80; *The Journeys of Celia Fiennes* (ed. C. Morris, 1947), p.113; D.A. Kirby, "The Radicals of St. Stephen's, Coleman St., London, 1624-1642", *Guildhall Miscellany*, III (1970), pp.98-119; J.N. King, *English Reformation Literature*, p.253; I.B. Cowan, *Regional Aspects of the Scottish Reformation* (Historical Association Pamphlet, 1978), pp. 7-8, 25.

25. Spufford, *op. cit.*, pp.247, 351; *W.T.U.D.*, pp.26-7, 45, 83-4; G.F. Nuttall, *The Holy Spirit in Puritan Faith and Experience* (Oxford, 1946), pp.178-9; L.H. Carlson, *Martin Marprelate*, pp.9, 23, 32-5, 214; K.V. Thomas, *op. cit.*, pp.134-6; D.M. Loades, *Two Tudor Conspiracies* (Cambridge U.P., 1965), pp.206-7; Leona Rostenberg, *The Minority Press and the English Crown (1558-1625)* (Nieuwkoop, 1971), p.181. I am grateful to Peter Clark for information about Coppinger. See also p.73 above.

26. *W.T.U.D.*, p.257; A. Hamilton, *The Family of Love* (Cambridge, 1981), Chapter 6.

27. Foxe, *op. cit.*, VIII, p.314; J. Strype, *Annals of the Reformation* (Oxford U.P., 1824), IV, p.97; F.G. Emmison, *Elizabethan Life: Morals and Church Courts* (Chelmsford, 1973), pp.309-10; *W.T.U.D.*, p.29. For

Traske see p. 164 below; ed. H.E. Rollins, *Old English Ballads, 1552-1625*, (Cambridge U.P., 1920), p. 56.

28. Emmison, *op. cit.*, p. 126; J. Cleveland, *Works* (1687), p. 402; Fuller, *Church History of Britain*, I, p. 451; Sir T. Aston, *A Remonstrance Against Presbytery* (1641), Sig. I 4v; O. Lutaud, *Winstanley: socialisme et Christianisme* (Paris, 1960), p. 10; *Selections from English Wycliffite Writings* (ed. A. Hudson, Cambridge U.P., 1978), pp. 20, 28, 161; R.H. Hilton, *The Decline of Serfdom in Medieval England* (Studies in Economic and Social History, 2nd edn., 1983), pp. 28-9. For the Norman Yoke see my *Puritanism and Revolution* (Panther edn., 1968), pp. 58-125.

29. Hudson, "The Examination of Lollards", in *Bulletin of the Institute of Historical Research*, No. 46 (1973), pp. 146, 154-5. I owe Cade to Mr Robin Jeffs.

30. L.B. Smith, *Henry VIII* (Panther edn., 1973), pp. 144, 149; W. Tyndale, *Doctrinal Treatises*, pp. 97-9; Horst, *op. cit.*, p. 147; *Heresy Trials in the Diocese of Norwich, 1428-31* (ed. N.P. Tanner, Camden 4th series, No. 20, 1977), *passim*; ed. A. Peel, *The Seconde Parte of a Register* (1915), I, p. 87. See Chapter 11 below.

31. Emmison, *op. cit.*, p. 110; cf. my *Economic Problems of the Church* (Panther edn., 1971), pp. 121, 133; Foxe, *op. cit.*, IV, p. 178; Hudson, "The Examination of Lollards", pp. 153, 155.

32. Foxe, *op. cit.*, IV, pp. 213, 234, 580; Tanner, *op. cit.*, *passim*; Hudson, "The Examination of Lollards", p. 151.

33. Ed. H.E. Rollins, *Cavalier and Puritan* (New York 1923), pp. 171-8; J.A.F. Thomson, *The Later Lollards, 1414-1520* (Oxford U.P., 1965), pp. 240-1; Thomas, *op. cit.*, p. 144; Tanner, *op. cit.*, pp. 10-13 and *passim*; Cross, *Church and People*, pp. 76-8; Wallace, *op. cit.*, *passim*.

34. Jean Moss, "Variations on a Theme: The Family of Love in Renaissance England", *Renaissance Quarterly*, XXX: (1976), p. 190; ed. A.S.P. Woodhouse, *Puritanism and Liberty* (1938), p. 390; G. Winstanley, *The Breaking of the Day of God* (2nd edn., 1649), p. 30; J. Nayler, *Sauls Errand to Damascus* (1654), pp. 2-6, 10-11; E. Ludlow, *A Voice from the Watch Tower* (ed. B. Worden, Camden Soc., 4th series, No. 21, 1978), p. 235.

35. Martin, *op. cit.*, pp. 55-74, and *passim*; Horst, *op. cit.*, pp. 122-40; Emmison, *op. cit.*, p. 101; *W.T.U.D.*, pp. 83-4, 147-8, 184; Thomas, *op. cit.*, pp. 133-4; Cross, *Church and People*, pp. 98-9, 114, 170; Collinson, *The Elizabethan Puritan Movement*, pp. 238-9; Winstanley, *The Mysterie of God* (2nd edn., 1649), p. 15. I am indebted to discussions with Professors Joseph Martin and Jean Moss about sixteenth-century Familism. For Grindleton see pp. 149, 163 below.

36. I owe the last point to Mr John Fines of the West Sussex Institute of Higher Education. I am also grateful to Professor Martin for drawing my attention to Philpot. Cf Clark, *English Provincial Society*, p. 101; Tanner, *op. cit.*, p. 91.

37. Thomson, *op. cit.*, pp. 36, 82, 106, 196, 248; J. Jewell, *An Apology for the Church of England* (Parker Soc., 1848-50), II, p. 1241; Spufford, *op.*

cit., p. 247; Wallace, *op. cit.*, pp. 461-2. The last point I owe to Mr Peter Clark.

38. T. Fuller, *op. cit.* (1842), III, pp. 252-6; *C.S.P.D., 1639*, pp. 455-6. I owe this reference to the kindness of Dr Andrew Foster.
39. H.J. McLachlan, *Socinianism in Seventeenth-Century England* (Oxford U.P., 1951), p. 234; Nayler, *op. cit.*, p. 5.
40. N.T. Burns, *Christian Mortalism from Tyndale to Milton* (Harvard U.P., 1972), *passim;* cf. Cross, *Church and People*, p. 95.
41. Burns, *op. cit.*, pp. 57-8, 69-72, 133-4; Moss, *op. cit.*, pp. 191, 194; Emmison, *op. cit.*, p. 110; Wallace, *op. cit.*, pp. 461-2, 473; J. Carey, "Donne and Coins", in *English Renaissance Studies Presented to Dame Helen Gardner* (ed. Carey, Oxford U.P., 1980), p. 162; J.R. Jacob, *Robert Boyle and the English Revolution* (New York, 1977), pp. 171-2.
42. Tanner, *op. cit.*, p. 45; J. Lindsay, *The Troubadours and Their World* (1976), p. 225; Fuller, *op. cit.*, I, p. 445; Foxe, *op. cit.*, III, pp. 594-5. I owe the last point to Mr Peter Clark. Cf Thomas, *op. cit.*, p. 170.
43. T. Rogers, *The Faith, Doctrine and Religion Professed and Protected in. . . England* (Cambridge U.P., 1681), p. 39: first published 1607; Hudson, "A Lollard Mass", p. 409; W. Lamont, *Richard Baxter and the Millennium* (1979), pp. 128, 143. For antinomianism, see Chapter 10 below.
44. My *Antichrist in Seventeenth-Century England* (Oxford U.P., 1971), pp. 142-3; *W.T.U.D.*, p. 66; Thomson, *op. cit.*, pp. 36, 184; Thomas, *op. cit.*, p. 169; Wallace, *op. cit.*, pp. 461, 465; Clark, *English Provincial Society*, pp. 56, 156, 178, 199; J. Everard, *The Gospel-Treasury Opened* (2nd edn., 1659), I, pp. 355-6; G.R. Quaife, *Wanton Wenches and Wayward Wives* (1979), p. 64; Ingram, Thesis, pp. 81, 104; my *Change and Continuity in Seventeenth-Century England*, p. 15; Nayler, *op. cit.*, p. 14; cf. Chapter 11 below, *passim*.
45. R.H. Hilton, *The English Peasantry in the Later Middle Ages* (Oxford U.P., 1975), p. 24; Horst, *op. cit.*, p. 134.
46. Ed. G.L. and M.A. Harriss, *John Benet's Chronicle for the Years 1450 to 1462* (Camden Miscellany, XXIV), p. 166; Foxe, *op. cit.*, IV, p. 243; D.M. Loades, *The Oxford Martyrs* (1970), p. 95; *Politics and the Nation, 1450-1660* (1974), p. 147; Dickens, *op. cit.*, p. 19; Thomson, *op. cit.*, pp. 64-6, 78, 127, 130, 159, 177; Tanner, *op. cit.*, *passim;* Cross, "Great Reasoners in Scripture", p. 363; Hudson, "The Examination of Lollards", p. 151; 'A Lollard Mass', pp. 409-10; Thomas Nashe, *The Unfortunate Traveller and Other Works* (Penguin, 1972), p. 68; Richard Brathwait, *Barnabees Journal*, Sig. C.; Thomas Harman, *A Caveat for Common Cursetors* (1567), in *Coney-Catchers and Bawdy-Baskets* (ed. G. Salgado, Penguin), pp. 101, 121; W. Saltonstall, *Picturae Loquentes* (1635), p. 39; R. Younge, *The Poores Advocate* (1655), pp. 10-11; J.A. Sharpe, *op. cit.*, pp. 99-100; K. Wrightson and D. Levine, *Poverty and Piety in an Essex Village*, p. 133; Ingram, Thesis, pp. 152-3, 216, 370.
47. More, *Refutation of Tyndale* (1532), quoted by G.R. Elton, *Reform and Reformation* (1977), p. 44; *W.T.U.D.*, Chapter 25.
48. E. Leach, "Melchisedech and the Emperor: Icons of Subversion and Orthodoxy", *Proceedings of the Royal Anthropological Institute*, 1972,

pp. 5-14; A.C. Edwards, *English History from Essex Sources* (Chelmsford, 1957), pp. 77-8.

49. M.H. Keen, *England in the Later Middle Ages* (1973), p. 243; L.B. Smith, *Henry VII*, p. 150; *W.T.U.D.*, p. 200; Cross, *Church and People*, pp. 21, 73, 79; Clark, *English Provincial Society*, pp. 63, 156, 181, 405; Hudson, "A Lollard Mass", p. 411. For ale-houses as centres of sedition, see *Mercurius Politicus*, No. 305 (1656), pp. 6899-901; No. 315 (1656), pp. 7053-5; P. Clark, *The Alehouse: A Social History, 1200-1850* (1983), esp. Chapters 6 and 7; D. Underdown, "The Problem of Popular Allegiance in the English Civil War", *T.R.H.S.* (1981), esp. p. 90; J.F. Davis, *Heresy and Reformation*, pp. 58, 76.

50. In *Harleian Miscellany* (1744-6), VII, pp. 376-85.

51. For Long Island see D.S. Lovejoy, "'Desperate Enthusiasm': Early Signs of American Radicalism", in *The Origins of Anglo-American Radicalism* (ed. M. Jacob and J. Jacob, 1984), pp. 235, 240; John Whiting, *Persecution Exposed* (1714), a reference I owe to the kindness of Peter Linebaugh.

52. D.M. Wolfe, *The Image of Man in America* (Dallas, 1957), p. 19; *V.C.H.*, *Worcestershire*, IV, p. 192; G.P. Gooch, *The History of English Democratic Ideas in the Seventeenth Century* (Cambridge U.P., 1898), p. 359; E.P. Thompson, *Whigs and Hunters* (1975), p. 256; W.A. Speck, *Stability and Strife: England 1714-1760* (1977), p. 181; J.H. Lawson, "Parrington and the Search for Tradition", *Mainstream* (Winter, 1947), p. 395; *A Journal of the Life of Thomas Story* (Newcastle upon Tyne, 1747), p. 192; B.S. Capp, *Astrology and the Popular Press, p. 249. See ibid.*, pp. 96, 266-7 for almanacs and radical ideas. For Joyce, Cromwell and other English republicans in the folklore of the American Revolution see A.F. Young, "English Plebeian Culture and Eighteenth-Century American Radicalism", in *Origins of Anglo-American Radicalism*, pp. 194-204.

53. Quoted by P.J. Corfield, *The Impact of English Towns, 1700-1800* (1982), p. 65.

54. E.M. Dunn, "The London Weavers' Riot of 1675", *Guildhall Studies*, I, p. 17; ed. N. Penney, *The Short Journal and Itinerary Journals of George Fox* (Cambridge U.P., 1925), pp. 350-1, where many examples are given; Hillel Schwartz, *The French Prophets: The History of a Millenarian Group in Eighteenth-Century England* (California U.P., 1980), pp. 128, 131, 143. For the Green Ribbon Club see J.R. Jones's article in *Durham University Journal*, December 1956. M.C. Jacob suggests that the Green Ribbon Club had links with early freemasonry (*The Radical Enlightenment: Pantheists, Freemasons and Republicans*, 1981, p. 117).

55. T.A. Jackson, *Ireland Her Own* (1946), p. 63. Penelope Corfield has drawn my attention to a broadsheet of 1795 addressed *To the Poor of Norwich* by "a Leveller, Jacobin and Revolutioner". Dr Morrill points out to me that later use of the name does not necessarily demonstrate continuity of aims: it may have been merely a convenient smear-word. This may be true of some of the instances I cite — notably Beau Nash. But the Levellers were remembered down to the nineteenth century, and, in many of my examples, remembered with approval.

56. *Biblioteca Furliana* (Rotterdam, 1714); T. Bullard, *Biblioteca Antonij Collins, Arm.* (1731); C. Robbins, "Library of Liberty", *Harvard Library Bulletin*, 5 (1951), p.17; see p.339 below. I am grateful to Margaret Jacob for this reference.

57. A.L. Morton, "The Everlasting Gospel", in *The Matter of Britain* (1966), pp.85-121; cf. *W.T.U.D.*, p.382; J. Kensley, "Burns and the Peasantry, 1785", *Proceedings of the British Academy*, LII (1968), p.136. Professor Pocock thinks "there is much to be done with the notion" of an occultist scientific underground from the restoration to the late eighteenth century ("Authority and Property: The Question of Liberal Origins", in *After the Reformation: essays in honor of J.H. Hexter*, ed. B.C. Malament, Manchester U.P., 1980, p.343). See also J.R. Jacob, *Henry Stubbe*, p.213.

58. *W.T.U.D.*, pp.380-1; *Life of Thomas Story*, pp.70-2, 676-7; G.F.S. Ellen, "The Ranters Ranting: Reflections on a Ranting Counter Culture", *Church History*, XL (1971), p.92.

59. Quoted by M.C. Jacob, *op. cit.*, p.98.

60. Burns, *op. cit.*, p.121.

61. Richard Lewis, *The Robin Hood Society, A Satire by Peter Pounce* (1756), pp.v-vi, 19, 79. I owe this reference to the kindness of Dr Vincent Caretta.

8. *Sin and Society*[1]

"The belief in heaven and the fiery pit makes the simple folk give obedience to their governors, and behave with great care, so that they may avoid torment after death and enjoy bliss".

"Continually preaching to the rest their duty towards God ... is the most effectual way to dispose them to obedience to man. For he that truly fears God cannot despise the magistrate. ... There is nothing more apt to induce men to a suspicion of any religion than frequent innovation and change".†

I

In seventeenth-century England there were revolutionary changes in politics, economics and science. Almost as important a turning-point was the emergence of new ideas of sin and hell, of man's fate in the after life and consequently of the way in which he should behave in this life. At the beginning of the century the conviction prevailed among the articulate that a minority was predestined to eternal life, the vast majority to an eternity of torture. By the end of the century we are on the verge of the Enlightenment, of deism, of rationalism. Human effort and morality, based on the demands of the individual conscience, now appear more important than the arbitrary decisions of an omnipotent God. How did this transition come about?

We should not assume that it just happened, that it was a slow triumph for reason, for sensible, middle-of-the-road moderation. Nor do I think that the apparently new ideas were in fact new. They were often traditional ideas which had been submerged by the imposition from on top of what we call "the protestant ethic", though it existed in Catholic countries too: a theology emphasizing the duty of hard and regular work in one's calling, labour discipline, austerity, thrift, monogamy: the bourgeois virtues. It was imposed

---

*Thomas Hariot, *A Brief and True Relation of the New Found Land of Virginia* (1588), in *The New World* (ed. S. Lorant, 1954), p. 268.

†Robert South, *Sermons Preached Upon Several Occasions* (1737), pp. 132, 140. Preached at Lincoln's Inn in 1660.

on populations accustomed to spasmodic bouts of labour punc-
tuated by saints' days, populations accustomed to consume rather
than to accumulate their meagre surplus and regarding marriage as a
much less binding contract than it became in an economy dominated
by the working household partnership.

Throughout human history sin has been associated with scarcity.
The legend of the Fall of Man reflects this. Adam and Eve were
expelled from a Paradise of abundance, and Adam was condemned to
hard agricultural labour: "in the sweat of thy face shalt thou eat
bread", just as women were to perform their productive functions in
labour and sorrow. The existence of a landed ruling class was for long
justified by its duty of alleviating hardship in time of dearth, of
dispensing hospitality to the poor, of remitting rent to the victims of
natural disasters. No doubt these functions had not always been
performed, and by the sixteenth century they were slipping badly as
monasteries were abolished, big households disbanded, and the
hospitality of aristocracy and clergy proved incapable of coping with
growing mass poverty. But the idea of a paternalistic landed élite
presiding over a moral economy and exercising some control over the
production and distribution of food — this idea still made some sort
of sense. It was the basis for hierarchical doctrines of society and
claims to obedience and deference on religious grounds. Such doctrines assume a community with shared needs in face of the constant
danger of scarcity which threatened fallen humanity.

But the consequences of human sinfulness could only be mitigated,
not cured. Too often rulers tended to succumb to sin themselves —
greed, luxury, callousness when the poor were in want, failing to
relieve their necessities from the superfluities which came to them by
virtue of their presiding and organizing role. This role could be
fundamentally challenged only when the possibility of abundance
appeared, when the whole unprivileged population was no longer
trapped in a poverty from which there seemed no escape.

The two generations before the civil war saw a great economic
divide. The mass of the people was getting relatively and probably
absolutely poorer; the poor were becoming a permanent part of the
population. The fortunate few who were conveniently placed for the
market, and who were skilful, industrious and lucky enough to seize
their chances, might prosper by taking advantage of rapidly rising
prices. So new and sharper class divisions were arising — no longer
setting gentry against the rest, but gentry, some yeomen, some

merchants, some artisans, against the poor. As Dr Morrill points out, this situation was so new that contemporaries had no word to describe the emerging new rich as a social group:[2] the term parish élites is an invention of historians. Artisans who had mastered more advanced techniques had greater confidence in their ability to stand on their own feet. The Calvinist preachers' covenant theology looks like an attempt to adapt traditional protestant doctrines to the assumptions of men who worked in a world of bargains and agreements enforceable by law.

The fact that some could better themselves whilst others sank into permanent rightless poverty seemed to justify belief in the wickedness of the poor, the righteousness of those who prospered, often through no merits of their own.[3] Responsibility for such poor relief as there was, and for labour discipline, was increasingly handed over to parish élites, those who by and large were themselves prospering. So the whole system began to seem less natural, less inevitable. If new techniques allowed some to prosper, why not all? Some bold spirits came to envisage prosperity not only for the elect, not only for lucky individuals, but for society as a whole.

Bacon glimpsed this possibility: so did Adolphus Speed and other agricultural improvers of the seventeenth century. Gerrard Winstanley made it the basis for his claim that the poor should have access to uncultivated land: "true religion and undefiled" is "to let every one quietly have earth to manure, that they may live in freedom by their labours". For now they were "kept poor by their brethren in a land where there is so much plenty for everyone". There is "land enough in England to maintain ten times as many people as are in it".[4]

Winstanley rejected the doctrine of original sin, as did many of the radicals. Men could be saved by their own efforts just as they could feed themselves by their own labour — provided the obstacles could be removed. For Winstanley these obstacles were the gentry who monopolized more land than they needed to feed their own families, the law and lawyers who protected this inequality, and "the subtle clergy" who charmed the people "to look after riches, heaven and glory when they are dead"; and so "their eyes are put out, that they see not what is their birthright, and what is to be done by them here on earth while they are living".[5]

Winstanley's was an extreme position. But conservatives were right to see radical Arminianism in general, and antinomianism, as containing a challenge to the whole social order.[6] Sin seemed to be essential to social cohesion. Winstanley, Ranters and early Quakers grasped the obverse — that those who preached up sin were in effect keeping the poor down.[7]

Beneath the veneer of official protestantism in England, the old beliefs continued: of this there is plenty of evidence. The ignorance of the common sort was agreed on all sides, by Whitgift and Lancelot Andrewes[8] no less than by George Giffard and Samuel Hieron.[9] Many Calvinist preachers in the early seventeenth century cried out that the common people are virtually pagans. By this I suspect they meant that they did not accept the Calvinist world outlook, that their attitudes were dominated by traditional magic mediated through Catholicism. For our purposes the important thing is rejection of the comfortable doctrines of original sin and of the predestination of a favoured few to salvation.

Perhaps one in a thousand is saved, thought Thomas Shepard, New England Puritan divine.[10] More generously, John Donne estimated it at one in three, the Fifth Monarchist John Spittlehouse at one in four.[11] John Bunyan varied between one in twenty and one in 5000.[12] The assumption that a merciful God fore-ordained the mass of mankind to hell was challenged in the seventeenth century, initially by religious and political radicals: it is the counterpart of their aspirations on earth.[13]

Calvinist preachers in Elizabethan and Jacobean England believed that most men, women and children were damned, and if they were honest they had to say so to their congregations. The doctrine was not always popular. The "ignorant rout" of Kidderminster did not appreciate being told, even by the saintly Richard Baxter, that their children before regeneration were loathesome in the eyes of God, and that if they died they would almost certainly go to hell.[14]

The doctrine of original sin, however, makes sense to the beneficiaries of a society in which inheritance is the rule. Heaven is not "the hire of servants or the booty of purchasers", explained Hieron; "it is the reward of sons, of inheritance". We receive it only as heirs, with no colour of desert.[15] Sir John Davies demonstrated God's justice from its congruence with human practice:

> Is it then just with us, to disinherit
> The unborn nephews for the father's fault?
> And to advance again for one man's merit
> A thousand heirs that have deserved naught?
>
> And is not God's decree as just as ours?[16]

Thomas Goodwin made a similar point: "It is a strange thing that you will not allow God that which kings and princes have the prerogative of. . . . They will have favourites whom they will love, and will not love others; and yet men will not allow God that liberty", but accuse him of cruelty and injustice.[17]

Original sin is the converse of divine hereditary right, as Dryden made very clear in *Absalom and Achitophel*:

> How then could Adam bind his future race . . .
> If those who gave the sceptre could not tie
> By their own deed their own posterity?[18]

Inheritance of sin may first have begun to lose its immediately obvious inevitability among those living in the contract society which grew up within the world of inherited landed property. Seventeenth-century political theorists still assumed that men are to all eternity bound by contracts which may have been made (though not recorded) by their remote ancestors. This seems odd to us, but Hobbes and Locke were an advance on Filmer: their contracts are tacitly renewed as generation succeeds generation.

Protestant theology not only emphasizes the predestination of the elect. Even more important, it stresses the *freedom* of the elect. By divine grace they are singled out from the mass of humanity. Most men, like animals and the inanimate creation, are subject to and helpless before the forces of nature and society — famine, pestilence, war and death. They are sunk in sin. The elect alone are free, since to them the forces which govern the world are not blind. The elect understand and co-operate with God's purposes, and this sense of intimacy with the source of law gives them a confidence, an inner assurance, which helps them to prosper in this world as well as to inherit the next. Justification by works, by conformity with the ceremonies and sacraments of the church, is fitted to a relatively static civilization: rewards are to be attained not on earth but in the after life, merit is acquired by passive acquiescence. Justification by faith, paradoxically, is an active doctrine, active in this world. It rejected attempts to propitiate an angry God by ceremonies mediated by a priesthood. It preached the supremacy of elect individual consciences, boosting the morale of those who could believe that, against such heavy odds, they were of the number of the saved.[19]

Protestantism established democracy within the élite, as against the traditional hierarchies of mediaeval society and the mediaeval church. Since the elect were in direct communication with God they had no need for mediators; nor was the law for them. But protestantism never solved the problem of the relationship of the elect to the unregenerate. Even the identity of the elect could not be established on earth. At the same time that protestant churches emphasized the freedom of the elect, the protestant state had to keep the unregenerate under control. All protestant state churches experience this dilemma. The elect, who in one sense are the only true members of the church, do not really need its laws and its discipline at all. The ungodly must be controlled and disciplined by church and state, but they were never fully members at least of the former.

So Calvinism stimulated an individualism in behaviour and thought against which it had no external, visible objective checks: it had only the individual conscience itself, and once it had been discovered that men were prepared to die for different truths, Calvinism could ultimately maintain itself only by violence. The burning of the heretic Servetus in mid-sixteenth-century Geneva was a portentous event.[20] Hence the tensions of the Elizabethan church, whose articles were drawn widely so as to include the maximum possible number of English men and women. Puritans called for further reformation, dividing between those who accepted the necessity of tarrying for the magistrate and those who separated in order to secure immediate reform.

From the time of the Lollards, at least, the dogma of original sin had been challenged. Theological distinctions should be drawn between Collinson's "rustic Pelagianism"[21] — the belief that men could be saved by their good works — and the Familist doctrine that men and women could attain to pre-lapsarian perfection in this life. But what matters for our purposes is that both rejected the division of mankind into an elect minority of sheep and the mass of reprobate goats. A husbandman in 1395 had suggested that "sinners and lay persons and simple souls" could understand the "mysteries and ... secrets of the Scriptures" better than the learned.[22] Mid-sixteenth-century London tradesmen claimed that "a man regenerate could not sin"; there were "free will men" in the capital. Henry Hart wrote a treatise denouncing predestination.[23] Bishop Ponet under Mary reported English Anabaptists who denied the doctrine of original sin, with the expected social consequences: they thought that "as when there was no sin, all things were common, so they ought now to be".[24] This conclusion would often be drawn later. In 1592 an Essex heretic held that "all the world shall be saved". John Smyth in James's reign called original sin "an idle term", and said that children dying in infancy are undoubtedly saved.[25] That these were more than isolated individuals is suggested by the fact that the English delegates to the Synod of Dort in 1618, on the insistence of the King, drew the attention of their Dutch brethren to the need for "great wariness and discretion in propounding to the common people the doctrine of predestination, and especially reprobation". John Hales, who was at Dort, thought that "the meaner sort may by no means be admitted" to "disputations and controversies concerning the profounder points of faith and religious mysteries"[26] — sound advice if it could have been followed. But in the free discussion of the sixteen-forties it became clear that there was no way of knowing on earth who were elect and who were reprobate,[27] and that those whom their social betters regarded as unregenerate might have views of their own on the subject.

For the orthodox, a coercive state was a consequence of the Fall too. "The nature of man", wrote Calvin, "is such that every man would be lord and master over his neighbours, and no man by good will be subject". "For we know that men are of so perverse and crooked a nature that everyone would scratch his neighbour's eyes out if there were no bridle to hold him in".[28] In England the *Homily against Disobedience and Wilful Rebellion* taught that after the Fall God "did constitute and ordain ... governors and rulers ... for the avoiding of all confusion which else would be in the world". Without the state "there must needs follow all mischiefs and utter destruction ... of souls, bodies, goods ...".[29] This was a doctrine which Henry Parker and Hobbes took over, together with so much else, from Calvinism. The masses must be held in subordination.

Such doctrines, so comfortable to the lucky few, were less acceptable to the many when they had the opportunity to think about them. And they led some Puritans to adopt a dual standard, together with a rather unpleasing contempt for the mass of mankind. William Perkins, high priest of English Puritanism, thought that the church exists for the elect.[30] He attributed to "the common sort of ignorant people, and all natural men" Collinson's "rustic Pelagianism". "Though in show they profess reformed religion, ... they look to be saved by their good serving of God, and by their good deeds".[31] They "conceive God made all of mercy, without his justice". They reason, "If I be chosen to salvation, I shall be saved;

therefore I may live as I list". "Our common people ... say they ever kept God's law, and loved him with all their heart, and their neighbours as themselves, and think hence all is well".[32] Even worse, they "think, because they deal truly and justly before men, that they are in as good a case as they that hear all the sermons in the world".[33] The common people "hope well, because God is merciful, but to be certain they think it impossible".[34] Perkins always associated ignorance of this kind with popery. It was much more culpable in his day, he thought, than it had been at the beginning of Elizabeth's reign.[35] "The doctrine and opinion of merit", Samuel Hieron confirmed in the sixteen-twenties, "is graven in the tables of every natural heart". He too was speaking of "the common people".[36] "The multitude of our people", Perkins observed, "are justly blamed as enemies of Christ".[37] "The common sort" found even Sabbath observance difficult, claiming that "we shall not be able to maintain ourselves and our families".[38]

The opinion of "the universal redemption of all and every man", Perkins thought, "is a witless conceit, ... no better than a forgery of man's brain": the Bible refutes it immediately. It "may fitly be termed the school of universal atheism". For it "pulls down the pale of the church, and lays it waste as every common field". "When as men shall be persuaded that grace shall be offered to every one effectually, whether he be of the church or not, ... wheresoever and howsoever he live; as in the like case, if men should be told that whether they live in the market town or not, there shall be sufficient provision brought them, if he will but receive it and accept of it, who would then come to market?"[39] The metaphors — the comparison of grace to enclosure which shuts out the poor, or to a market — define the audience for which Perkins is writing. Perkins concluded that the very poor were wicked. "Rogues, beggars, vagabonds ... are (for the most part) a cursed generation", because "they join not themselves to any settled congregation".[40] (They did not join settled congregations, it may be added parenthetically, because when they attempted to settle in any parish not that of their birth the poor law provided that they should be flogged to the next one. Heads I win, tails the poor lose. Perkins thought that the poor law of 1597 was "an excellent statute, and being in substance the very law of God, is never to be repealed". He only regretted that it was not more severely enforced).[41]

The idea that most of the poor were wicked was self-validating:

the lower classes could not spare the labour of their children to give them the education without which they had no hope of bettering themselves; and their family life was inevitably less stable than that of godly householders.[42]

A generation after Perkins wrote, his disciple Richard Sibbes reiterated that many men and women "live miserable poor, ... without laws, without church and without commonwealth, irregular persons that have no order taken for them. ... They live as beasts or worse".[43] Another twenty-five years later, with the experience of the revolutionary decades behind him, Richard Baxter drew political conclusions. "The major part are not only likely but certain to be bad. ... It is in almost all places the smaller number that are converted to loyalty and subjection to God, ... so that ordinarily to plead for a democracy is to plead that the sovereignty may be put into the hands of rebels. ... That the major vote of the people should ordinarily be just and good is next to an impossibility".[44]

The future Bishop Gilbert Burnet, writing to the Marquis of Halifax in 1680, said charitably "For the herd, they are of so little consequence, that if their folly bring on them the punishment due for their sins, a man cannot lament it much".[45] John Winthrop in Massachusetts agreed that too many men "stand for your natural corrupt liberties, and will do what is good in your own eyes, you will not endure the least weight of authority; ... but if you will be satisfied to enjoy such civil and lawful liberties, such as Christ allows you, then will you quietly and cheerfully submit unto that authority which is set over you".[46] Fortunately in New England the godly were the authority. Perhaps that is why the power of sin seemed greater there, as it did in Geneva and Scotland.

II

The Fall then was central to seventeenth-century debates about the nature of the state and its laws, as well as about the justification of private property, social inequality and the subordination of women. "Had all been virtuous men", as George Chapman put it, "There never had been prince upon the earth".[47] The judicious Hooker declared that laws "are never framed as they should be ... unless presuming man to be in regard of his depraved mind little better than a wild beast".[48] In August 1632 the Recorder of King's Lynn told the grand inquest of his borough that "the sins we have are the causes of the laws we have. Sin is a transgression of the law of God, and whoever is a transgressor of the laws of God is also a transgressor of the laws of man".[49] John Pym repeated Hooker's point: "if you take away the law, all things will fall into a confusion, every man will become a law unto himself, which in the depraved condition of human nature must needs produce many great enormities".[50] The Independent divine John Owen in 1655 agreed that the majority of men must be "overpowered by the terror of the Lord" and "threats of the wrath to come", if mankind is to be preserved from "the outrageousness and immeasureableness of iniquity which would utterly ruin all human society".[51]

The sinfulness of the majority was regularly used — by mediaeval Catholics and seventeenth-century bishops as well as by Calvinists — as an argument against social reform, against any change in the direction of a less unequal society. In 1649 the Leveller William Walwyn was told that "a natural and complete freedom from all sorrows and troubles was fit for man only before he had sinned, and not since; let them look for their portion in this life that know no better, and their kingdom in this world that believe no other".[52] Bishop Godfrey Goodman put it more succinctly: "If Paradise were to be replanted on earth, God had never expelled man [from] Paradise".[53] It was the seventeenth-century equivalent of "you can't change human nature", not extinct today.

The tacit assumption, never clearly stated, still less theoretically justified, was that the elect roughly coincided with the ruling class. Once such matters could be freely discussed, the identity of the elect became a crucial question. How many are they? How do we recognize them? The coincidence of the spread of printing with the Reformation, and new translations of the Bible into the vernacular, let loose forces which challenged traditional assumptions on this as on so many other subjects. Supporters of the magisterial Reformation, some German princes and town oligarchies, the bourgeoisie of Swiss and Dutch cities, La Rochelle, London, found no difficulty in accepting that the elect were a minority. But things seemed different to peasants in revolt in Germany in the fifteen-twenties, to lower-class Anabaptists in Flemish towns in the fifteen-thirties, to English Lollards, Familists and Anabaptists throughout the sixteenth century, and to radical sectaries in the seventeenth century. The doctrine of the priesthood of all believers, of the sovereignty of informed consciences, became subversive when taken over by groups normally excluded from political life.[54]

The stark predestinarian theology of the early reformers presented difficulties for conscientious preachers. How could they undertake the pastoral care of congregations of whom they believed 99% to be damned? What was the point of preaching moral virtue to the reprobate, since nothing could change their fate? Calvinism drove many worried men and women to despair and suicide because of their statistically plausible doubts about their eternal state. The covenant theology offered a way out. God covenants with the elect to give them eternal salvation in return for faith. Although it is difficult to be certain that I am one of the believing minority, there are certain plausible signs, notably leading a pious and moral life. The elect are not saved because of their good works — perish the thought — but good works and a moral life offer presumptive evidence that I am in a state of grace. Serious concern about my soul's condition in itself suggests that divine grace is at work. God, in Perkins's famous phrase, accepts the will for the deed.[55] It was a doctrine particularly apt to appeal to parish élites, self-confident men accustomed to a relatively prosperous world of contracts and bargains.

The Laudians went even further, back to a theology of works and ceremonies. But as fear of popery intensified in England during the Thirty Years War, Laudian Arminianism seemed to many protestants a half-way house back to the old religion. A group of clerics whom we call antinomians began to point out that the covenant theology itself led to "works-mongering". The true covenant of faith must surely be unconditional? The gap between the omnipotence of God and the filthiness of fallen men can be bridged only by divine intervention. God saves some men and women of his own mere volition. But since God is omniscient and all-powerful, he must know his elect from all eternity: they are chosen, in Tobias Crisp's vivid phrase, from the womb.[56] But how can they be known on earth, to themselves and to others? One man's conviction of grace may be another man's evidence of total damnation. So long as a punitive state church existed, those who carried antinomian convictions to their logical conclusion could be punished and silenced. But not after 1640.

Crucial was the breakdown of censorship. Lower-class sects emerged from underground and rapidly expanded in numbers; liberty could no longer be restricted to those whom respectable Puritans regarded as the elect. The great deterrent, sin, no longer controlled the lower classes. A ferment of religious discussion ensued

in the forties, which Milton and the radicals hailed enthusiastically as
the way to truth and the establishment of Christ's kingdom on earth,
and which Thomas Edwards and London oligarchs deplored. Religious toleration is the greatest of evils, said Edwards. It disrupts the
family, and deference generally.[57]

Popular rejection of the oligarchy of the elect, and a common-sense
suspicion that perhaps all morally good men might be saved, could
now be discussed freely, side by side with the writings of more
intellectual antinomian theologians who concentrated on demanding
complete moral freedom for the elect without troubling to ask how
they were to be known. This opened a door to a sort of *de facto*
universalism. If all believers were prophets as well as priests, and all
men might be saved, where were we?

Universalism, as we would expect, was widespread among the
middling and poorer sort. A bricklayer at Hackney "maintained that
all men should be saved". So did Mrs Attaway, a woman preacher
who earned notoriety by practising the divorce for incompatibility
which Milton had preached.[58] "One Lamb, a soap boiler", preached
universal grace; so did a trooper in Northamptonshire, and very
many others.[59] The Socinian John Bidle held that "there is no such
thing as original sin"; he was defended by Sir Henry Vane and
Levellers.[60] For Samuel Oates, father of Titus, predestination was
"damnable doctrine".[61] One preacher, addressing a crowd of what he
called "Levellers", deliberately emphasized absolute reprobation
"because this is a doctrine not often insisted upon and at this time
denied".[62]

In 1648-9 Gerrard Winstanley and Richard Coppin independently
proclaimed, for the first time in print, that all mankind would be
saved. Winstanley set up a communist colony, and rejected the state
and its laws. "They were the laws of a conqueror", he wrote, "to hold
the people in subjection". "All laws that are not grounded upon
equity and reason, not giving a universal feedom but respecting
persons", should have been "cut off with the King's head".[63] Coppin
declared that "to deny that there is a full end of sin for all men" is
"damnable heresy".[64] Such doctrines proved popular. Coppin, we are
told, wound "himself into the bosoms of (a many-headed monster),
the rude multitude" in Kent.[65] John Saltmarsh and Clarkson also
preached free grace; many radicals announced that sin was abolished.[66] The anonymous author of *Tyranipocrit Discovered* (1649)
believed that all men had the grace to be saved if they only looked for

God within them. Teachers of absolute predestination were defenders of inequality: "he that teacheth a partial God, loveth partiality".[67] Even so respectable a preacher as Peter Sterry believed in universal salvation.[68]

What did Milton think? In *Paradise Lost* Sin sprang fully born from Satan's head, as Athene from Zeus's. This is one way of exonerating God from responsibility for evil, but it raises a host of other problems. Sin was born in heaven. If Sin is Satan's brainchild, does this mean that Sin does not really exist, that it is a figment of Satan's imagination? That is what Clarkson had said. But it is not what Milton's *Of Christian Doctrine* says.[69]

The radical Arminianism of John Goodwin led in the same direction. George Fox thought that God's light was in everyone, without exception.[70] He knew that his inner voice was from God, as clearly as he knew that his opponents were agents of the devil: an impasse was reached, from which there was no escape on the assumptions of either side. The homogeneity of Calvinism in normally tranquil times stems from its discipline and from fundamental agreement among those who administer that discipline, drawn from propertied social groups. Calvinist leadership in opposition can focus attention upon those aspects of the old régime to which all save the narrow ruling group are opposed. But in times of social crisis and revolution the propertied lost their grip. As was discovered in the French Revolution, the third estate is not a homogeneous class. In the English Revolution those who were least satisfied with the condemnation of the mass of mankind to eternal torment were able to preach what God had said to them, to cast out Calvinism by the inner light. They found an audience in the social groups whom respectable Calvinists regarded as unregenerate, because their standards and outlook on life were different. Samuel Fisher in his Baptist days confirmed that there was much popular hostility to the doctrine of original sin, though the gentry accepted it.[71]

Strong evidence of the contempt in which "the looser sort" held the religion of their betters came when the Long Parliament instituted monthly fasts to deplore the sins of the nation and to urge God to continue his favour towards England. "God punisheth national sins with national punishments", John Downame had written.[72] National fasts and days of national humiliation were attempts to appease God. For month after month from November 1640 the two Houses duly listened to denunciations of idolatry, profanation of the Sabbath, contempt for ministers, sectarian preaching, etc.; and to prayers to God to continue his favour to England. But it soon became clear that outside Parliament the fasts were not taken as seriously as might have been wished. Already in 1642 Cornelius Burges was complaining that they were not observed by the populace.[73] "Are there not multitudes of people", Edmund Calamy asked in October 1644, "even in the City of London, ... carried away with grace-destroying and land-destroying opinions", such as "that God sees no sin in his elect children?... and that God is never displeased with his people, though they fall into adultery or any other sin?"[74] It was "the looser sort", Cheynell and others argued in the same year, who "refuse to observe the monthly fast".[75]

Perhaps Calamy was right. In New England John Wheelwright, accused of antinomianism, outraged his fellow-ministers by using the occasion of a fast-day sermon to say "If he [Christ] be present with his people, then they have no cause to fast; ... when he is taken away, then they must fast". "Those that do not know the Lord Jesus", he added provocatively, "they are usually most given to fasting".[76]

The Act of 23 April 1649 repealing the Act for monthly Fasts admitted that they had been wholly neglected for divers years in most parts of the Commonwealth. One last fast day was held in May to ask God to pardon "the iniquities of the former monthly fast days".[77] Yet still in 1666 Dryden could make Charles II say to God "we all have sinned, and thou hast laid us low."[78] It was more convenient to blame the sins of the nation than the incompetence and corruption of court and government. It was also not illogical, since the merrie monarch had attributed his unexpectedly easy restoration to "his own chosen people" in 1660 to "divine providence."[79]

III

Parliament's Blasphemy Ordinance of May 1648 picked out the doctrine that all men should be saved as an offence carrying the penalty of life imprisonment.[80] Throughout the sixteen-fifties conservative preachers tried to restore some sort of ecclesiastical control over obstreperous parishioners and visiting prophets, either by pressurizing Parliament for legislation or by forming organizations like Baxter's Worcestershire Association.[81] The debates on the Nayler case in Parliament in 1656 show how panic-stricken conservatives were.[82] But as long as the Army remained united and regularly paid nothing could be done. Success was achieved only after

1660, when the Army was disbanded and church courts returned in order to restore social discipline, to restore sin.

In the forties and fifties it had been possible for innumerable English men and women to think of themselves as members of the elect, enjoying the moral liberty hitherto reserved for the predestined minority. Democracy of salvation went hand in hand with the political democracy of the Levellers, the economic democracy of the Diggers. It was a remarkable turning-point. Which came first in men's thinking, the democracy of grace or political democracy, is perhaps a meaningless question. The critique of sin and hell accompanied the criticism of oligarchy; the restoration of oligarchy after 1660 was cause and consequence of a revived acceptance of sin.

In Sir Walter Ralegh's circle in the fifteen-nineties men had said that hell was only a bugbear, and religion invented "to keep the baser sort in fear" in order to protect private property, the family and the state: sin was "a monster / Kept only to show men for servile money".[83] For a brief moment in the sixteen-forties and fifties such ideas were proclaimed more widely. "Many thousands in these three nations", wrote John Reeve disapprovingly in 1656, "count the Scriptures mere inventions of wise men, to keep the simple in awe under their rulers".[84] But once the censorship had been with difficulty restored in the early fifties such ideas could no longer be expressed in print. After 1660 we hear no more of them, though this does not necessarily mean that they ceased to be held. Already the dissidence of dissent was working against the radicals. No unity could be found among the individual consciences which had agreed in rejecting a state church. Milton deplored this:

> O shame to men! Devil with devil damned
> Firm concord holds, men only disagree
> Of creatures rational, though under hope
> Of heavenly grace (*Paradise Lost*, II. 496-9).

The other side learnt unity from their interregnum experience.[85] By 1660 consensus had been restored on this issue.

Robert Boyle in the sixteen-fifties, and the Royal Society after 1660, saw it as the task of scientists to combat "enthusiasm" and what they saw as a tendency towards atheism in the sects; to insist that science demonstrated the existence of God and so contributed to his glory. The quintessential aristocratic rake, the Earl of Rochester, was convinced of the social usefulness of Christianity, and therefore that he should not attack it publicly, well before his death-bed "conversion".[86]

1660 saw a return to what some historians call "normality", by which I think they mean restoration of censorship. But nothing was ever quite the same again. The Latitudinarians who came to pro-minence in the restored Church of England after 1660, and who dominated it after 1688, quietly shed both the Calvinism of their Puritan predecessors and the Laudian ceremonial which had split the Church in the thirties. Just as Daniel Scargill in 1668 was expelled from his Fellowship at Corpus Christi College, Cambridge, for Hobbism, and was only restored after he had recanted, so in 1670 John Edwards was forced to resign from St John's College, Cam-bridge, for preaching too predestinarian a Calvinism. He did not recant, but by the end of the century he was a unique and isolated figure in the state church.[87]

Latitudinarians were closely associated with the scientists of the Royal Society. They evolved a broad Anglicanism with the minimum of theology, which performed useful social functions in the villages. Sin still remained the great deterrent, but the rigours of predesti-narianism were abated, and a non-ceremonial Arminianism led imperceptibly on to rational religion, Socinianism, deism. At the opposite end of the spectrum, the defeated sectaries re-introduced sin as they abandoned politics. George Fox had written of ministers of the state church that they "roar up for sin in their pulpits": "it was all their works to plead for it".[88] But after the restoration, when Robert Barclay systematized Quaker theology, sin returned.[89] Per-fectibility had been a dream of the heady forties and fifties.

Yet although sin returned and church courts were restored in 1660, the High Commission was not, and so there was no power behind ecclesiastical censures. By the end of the century church courts had virtually ceased to function. The only 'sins" now prosecuted were those which led to charges on rate-payers: J.Ps. punished those who bore bastards, and the societies for reformation of manners strove to carry on some of the supervision which church courts had formerly exercised. The later seventeenth century saw a progressive decline of belief in hell, in magic whether black or religious.[90] But the sinfulness of the mass of humanity was no longer a subject for discussion: it seemed somehow irrelevant to the problems of the Age of Reason. Less than a century after the English Revolution so unoriginal a thinker as Bolingbroke, speaking of predestination to damnation, refused to "impute such cruel injustice to the all-perfect Being. Let Austin and Calvin and all those who teach it be answerable for it alone. You may bring Fathers and Councils as evidences ...but reason must be the judge ... in the breast of every Christian that can appeal to her tribunal".[91] So yesterday's persecuted heresy becomes today's self-evident orthodoxy. We are all Pelagians now.

Bolingbroke seems to me to be right, but he is profoundly unhistorical. When his great-grandfathers looked into their breasts they found nothing there about universal grace. Bolingbroke's "reason" has taken into itself the results of two centuries of bitter struggle. And even so, was he quite as liberal as he sounds to us today? What does he mean by "every Christian that *can* appeal to reason's tribunal"? Whom does he exclude? Has he not his own category of those who are outside the pale? Exclusion based on differential rationality, which itself derives from educational opportunity, or lack of it, is not so very different from predestination to damnation.

Rustic Pelagianism leading on to Arminianism — Socinianism — deism was one route into the modern world. Another was from Luther to antinomianism and beyond, to the doctrine that God does not intervene in the day-to-day running of individual lives. If the elect are known from all eternity, then their relationship to God is fixed, and cannot be changed for the worse by their sins nor for the better by their prayers. This led to a new, self-sufficient morality.[92]

Hobbes pushed miracles back into the age of the Apostles; Thomas Mun, writing in the sixteen-twenties but not published till 1664, envisaged a market society in which the hidden hand of supply and demand preserved order; economists began to think that to act according to self-interest was rational, not sinful.[93] Newtonian scientists saw God as the supervisor of a mechanical universe. Socinians, deists and some antinomians virtually abolished a personal God to be propitiated. They based human morality neither on expectation of reward nor on fear of punishment in the after life, but on purely human laws of reason and of nature.[94] Supernatural sanctions were in effect abolished. Man is the measure of all things, and has to solve his moral problems in the light of God's Word but with no more divine guidance than he finds in his own conscience. The saints, the Virgin and priestly mediators had disappeared in protestant countries at the Reformation: now the belief that God exists in all of us undermined belief in divine or Satanic intervention in everyday human affairs.[95]

Hence concern about "atheism", which led Swift in 1708 to say "I look upon the ... body of our people ... as free-thinkers, that is to say, as staunch unbelievers as any of the highest rank".[96] "Atheism" of course was not dangerous because of one man, even so great a man as Hobbes. Nor was it dangerous because aristocratic wits made sceptical jokes about the Bible and the clergy: they had been doing that since Ralegh's time and no doubt earlier. The dangerous atheism was "mechanic atheism", the philosophy of the rude mechanicals, who had learnt about it in the no-holds-barred discussions of the sixteen-forties and fifties. Some of the sects, as we have seen, appear to be driven by a kind of inner logic to denial of the external, personal God of orthodox Christianity.

Saint Evremond, who knew his post-restoration England, noted this tendency in protestantism. "The Catholic might, indeed, spare some ceremonies; yet that hinders not, but that men of understanding may see well enough through them. The Reformed use too little, and their ordinary worship is not sufficiently distinguished from the common functions of life. ... Where it rules, it produces only an exact compliance with duty, such as either the civil government or any other obligation might do. ... The danger is lest after having retrenched all that appears superfluous, religion itself should be cut off".[97]

That was indeed the danger. This illuminating passage helps to explain why "men of understanding" in 1660 welcomed the Church of England back again with its authorized interpreter of the Scriptures in every parish, and why the great Calvinist theologies, Presbyterianism and Independency, which played such a leading role in the Revolution, retained relatively so little hold, losing ground first to non-Calvinist Baptists and Quakers, later to Unitarianism and Wesleyanism. The danger here was that sin, which the Ranters and early Quakers had failed to abolish, might die a natural death. Hence the almost hysterical concern of Boyle and the early Royal Society, Newton and Newtonians, to preserve rewards and punishments in the after life, God and the devil (and perhaps witches too).[98] How else could the enormity of natural man be restrained?

"The great business of religion", said John Fell in a sermon preached before Charles II in 1675, "is to oblige its votaries to present duty by the awe and expectation of future retribution".[99] A die-hard like Henry Sacheverell clung on to sin and hell. "The great sanction of the gospel", he declared in a notorious sermon preached before the Lord Mayor of London in 1709, is "the eternity of hell torments".[100] More sophisticated was Dr John North. An Arminian by conviction, he thought Calvinism, "with respect to ignorant men, to be more politic, and thereby in some respects fitter to maintain religion in them, because more suited to their capacity. But that is referred to art, and not to truth, and ought to be ranked with the *piae fraudes* or holy cheats".[101]

Calvinism, with its stress on God's power and justice, was always more acceptable to the middling sort, concerned about maintaining law, order and property against an unpredictable multitude. A theology of good works, emphasizing God's love and mercy, appealed more to those who had no power and did not expect justice. They looked to the after life to redress the injustice of this. That the number of the elect should be very small made less sense to them than to the ruling minority of their betters. But theirs was *radical* Arminianism, not related to the ceremonies and sacraments of a church which was also a great property owner, and a collector of tithes at their expense.[102]

The rulers of society acted on the assumption that the mass of mankind was sinful; they did not really want the lower orders to discuss the subject at all. It may not have been the object of the censorship and of the discipline both of church courts and of presbyteries to frighten off ordinary people from having ideas above their station, but this seems to have been the effect. The sects' demand for the democratization of salvation offered the possibility of self-respect to the middling and some of the lower sort: salvation was potentially accessible to all, perhaps even especially accessible to the poor and humble. This emerges very clearly in the teaching even of the Calvinist John Bunyan, who was not deferential to ungodly gentlemen.[103] Such a comfortable community religion survived political defeat, and after 1660 helped to create a sense of purpose for like-minded men and women below the privileged classes.[104]

During the revolutionary decades men had dreamt that the world could be turned upside down — by the establishment of Leveller political democracy and of the same security of tenure for copyholders as the gentry had won in their holdings; by the abolition of sin and recognition that all men were sons of God: a move towards secularization. Wildman looked forward to deist freethinking: "If a man consider that there is a will of the Supreme Cause, it is an hard thing for him by the light of nature to conceive how there can be any sin committed; and therefore the magistrate cannot easily determine what sins are against the light of nature and what not".[105] But the radical political and social revolutions failed. In the last resort the middling sort of people followed Oliver Cromwell rather than Levellers or True Levellers. A few yeomen prospered, the majority of husbandmen ultimately sank to the position of wage labourers. Such men had to accommodate themselves to the market society, just as the restored Church of England did: the sects abandoned radical political ideas, and agreed that the millennium was not imminent, indeed that Christ's kingdom was not of this world. When the Licensing Act lapsed in 1695 "normality" had re-established itself; the censor had been internalized by members of the political nation; sectaries were excluded from participation in public life. Prophets were honoured, if at all, only within the enclosed world of their own sects. It was not what Milton or Dell had hoped for, still less Walwyn or Clarkson. Their objectives still had to be fought for a century and a half later when Blake proclaimed that "every honest man is a prophet".[106] But then Blake remembered the seventeenth-century radicals as few did by the early nineteenth century. By his time most democrats talked in secular terms. Religion continued to defend the *status quo*, even when the attack was no longer mounted in religious idiom. Methodism, declared Jabez Bunting, was opposed to democracy because Methodism was opposed to sin.

NOTES

1. An earlier version of this paper was delivered at a Conference on Religion and Revolution held at the University of Minnesota in November 1981. The papers of this conference are to be published in 1985.
2. J.S. Morrill, *Seventeenth-Century Britain, 1603-1714* (1980), pp. 108-9.
3. See p. 123-5 above.
4. Sabine, *op. cit.*, pp. 428, 507, 558; cf. pp. 414, 428. For Speed see *Biographical Dictionary of British Radicals*, III (1984), p. 194. Cf. *Petty Papers* (ed. the Marquis of Lansdowne, 1927), II, p. 232. I have drawn heavily for these paragraphs on Joyce Appleby's *Capitalism and a New Social Order*, esp. pp. 26-9.
5. Sabine, *op. cit.*, pp. 523-4.
6. Not of course Laudian "Arminianism", whose doctrine of justification by works did not reverse the Fall, and whose "works" were associated with the ceremonies and sacraments of the church.
7. *W.T.U.D.*, p. 169.

8. Strype, *Life of Whitgift, III*, p. 268; Andrewes, *XVI Sermons* (2nd edn., 1631), p. 459, contrasting "the common sort" with "true Christians".

9. G. Giffard, *The Country Divinity*, quoted by Hunt, *The Puritan Moment*, p. 87; cf. pp. 151-2; S. Hieron, *Sermons* (1624), pp. 122, 132, 297, 536. Cf. G.B. Harrison, *The Elizabethan Journals* (New York, 1965), I, pp. 184-5: ignorance and anti-clericalism in Devon in 1600.

10. C.M. Andrews, *The Colonial Period of American History* (Yale U.P., 1964), I, p. 48; cf. Walker, *The Decline of Hell*, pp. 35-40, for a general assumption that the majority are damned. Cf. L. Andrews, *Works* (Oxford U.P., 1841), VI, p. 191.

11. Donne, *Sermons* (ed. G.R. Potter amd E.M. Simpson, Berkeley, 1953-62), VIII, p. 372; Capp, *Fifth Monarchy Men*, p. 173.

12. Bunyan, *Works* (ed. G. Offor, 1860), I, pp. 105, III, pp. 20-1.

13. Walker, *op. cit., passim*.

14. Ed. M. Sylvester, *Reliquae Baxterianae* (1696), p. 24.

15. S. Hieron, *Sermons*, p. 373.

16. Sir John Davies, *Nosce Teipsum* (1599), in *Silver Poets of the Sixteenth century* (Everyman edn.), pp. 369-9; cf. John Davies of Hereford, *Complete Works* (ed. A.B. Grosart, 1878), I. p. 471.

17. T. Goodwin, *An Exposition of the Second Chapter of the Epistle to the Ephesians, Verses 1-11*, in *Works* (Edinburgh, 1861-3), II, p. 163.

18. *Op. cit.*, lines 769-71. Cf. William Chillingworth, *Works*, II, p. 426.

19. W. Perkins, *Works* (1609-13), I, p. 563; II, pp. 19-24; III, pp. 270-3. See also my *Puritanism and Revolution*, p. 214.

20. Cf. pp. 37-8 above.

21. Collinson, *The Elizabethan Puritan Movement*, p. 37.

22. C. Cross, *Church and People, 1450-1640* p. 23.

23. Burnet, *History of the Reformation*, III, p. 146; cf. p. 102 above.

24. J. Ponet, *A Shorte Treatise of Politike Power* (1556), Sig. E 8, quoted by H.C. White, *Social Criticism in Popular Religious Literature in the Sixteenth Century*, p. 125.

25. R. Barclay, *The Inner Life of the Religious Societies of the Commonwealth* (1876), Appendix to Chapter 6, p. viii; cf. Burrage, *The Early English Dissenters*, II, p. 188, and pp. 101-2 above.

26. J. Hales, *Golden Remains* (1659), I, p. 32; *Letters from the Synod of Dort, ibid.*, III, pp. 18, 31.

27. Cf. Henry Robinson, *Liberty of Conscience* (1644), pp. 37-8, in Haller, *Tracts on Liberty*, III, pp. 153-4.

28. Calvin, *Sermons Upon the Book of Job* (English translation, 1574), p. 718; *Sermons Upon the Fifth Book of Moses* (English translation, 1583), p. 872, both quoted by J. DiSalvo, *War of Titans: Blake's Critique of Milton and the Politics of Religion* (Pittsburgh U.P., 1983), p. 256; cf. Calvin, *Institutes of the Christian Religion* (trans. H. Beveridge, 1949), I, p. 518; and p. 178: the poor must endure patiently.

29. *Homilies*, pp. 468-9; cf. pp. 87-8, *An Exhortation concerning Good Order and Obedience to Rulers and Magistrates*.

30. Perkins, *Works*, I, p. 298.

31. *Ibid.*, II, p. 300; III, p. 500.

32. *Ibid.*, III, pp. 493-5.
33. *Ibid.*, II, p. 290.
34. *Ibid.*, III, p. 498; cf. I, pp. 537, 631; III, pp. 583, 595.
35. *Ibid.*, III, p. 585.
36. Hieron, *op. cit.*, p. 122. Cf. p. 174-5 below for natural man's confidence in good works.
37. Perkins, *op. cit.*, III, p. 595.
38. *Ibid.*, II, p. 109, cf. Alan Sinfield, *Literature in Protestant England* (1983), pp. 151-2.
39. Perkins, *op. cit.*, I, pp. 295-6.
40. *Ibid.*, III, p. 191 (second pagination); cf. I, p. 755; III, pp. 92 (second pagination), 539; cf. my *Puritanism and Revolution*, pp. 223-4.
41. Perkins, *Works*, I, p. 755.
42. Jackie DiSalvo, *op. cit.*, Chapter 9.
43. R. Sibbes, *Works* (Edinburgh, 1862-4), III, pp. 40-1; cf. *Puritanism and Revolution*, p. 224.
44. Baxter, *The Holy Commonwealth* (1659), pp. 92-4.
45. Ed. H. C. Foxcroft, *Some Unpublished Letters of Gilbert Burnet* (Camden Miscellany, XI, 1907), p. 21.
46. Quoted in Perry Miller, *The New England Mind: the Seventeenth Century* (New York, 1939), pp. 426-7, 455-6.
47. Chapman, *Dramatic Works* (1873), I, p. 331.
48. R. Hooker, *Of the Laws of Ecclesiastical Polity*, I, p. 188.
49. Quoted by W. R. Prest, *Professors of the Law: A social history of the English Bar, 1590-1640* (forthcoming).
50. Pym, speech at the trial of Strafford, in J. Rushworth, *Trial of Strafford* (1680), p. 662.
51. J. Owen, *Works*, XII, p. 587.
52. [Anon], *Walwins Wiles* (1649), in *The Leveller Tracts, 1647-1653* (ed. W. Haller and G. Davies, Columbia U.P., 1944), p. 312.
53. G. Goodman, *The Two Great Mysteries of Christian Religion* (1653), p. 90.
54. See Chapter 10 below.
55. Perkins, *Works*, II, pp. 19-24, 44-5, 629; cf. I, p. 43, and M. McGiffert, "God's Controversy with Jacobean England", *American Historical Review*, 88 (1983), pp. 1161-7, and pp. 143-5 below.
56. See p. 146 below.
57. Edwards, *Gangraena*, I, pp. 121-2, 156; III, pp. 268-70. See pp. 174-5 below.
58. *Ibid.*, I, pp. 80, 87. There is much more evidence to be found here.
59. *Ibid.*, I, p. 92, III, pp. 9-10, 107, 173.
60. Quoted by John Owen, *Works*, XII, p. 164; *The Second Part of Englands New-Chains Discovered* (1649), in Haller and Davies, *op. cit.*, p. 175.
61. Edwards, *Gangraena*, I, p. 94.
62. H. Schultz, *Milton and Forbidden Knowledge* (New York, 1955), p. 128.
63. Winstanley, *The Mysterie of God* (1648), pp. 17, 35-6, 56-8; *The Breaking of the Day of God* (1648), p. 15; *The Law of Freedom* (1652),

Dedication to Oliver Cromwell; Sabine, *op. cit.*, p. 286. See Chapter 11 below.

64. Coppin, *Man's Righteousness Examined* (1652), pp. 9-10, 16. See pp. 146-8, 170 below.
65. Coppin, *Truths Testimony* (1655), pp. 21, 31; Walter Rosewell, *The Serpents Subtilty Discovered* (1656), Sig. A 3; *W.T.U.D.*, p. 222.
66. J. Saltmarsh, *Free Grace* (10th edn., 1700), esp. pp. 47, 67, 86, 104, 111 (first published 1645; by 1649 it had reached its sixth edition); Clarkson, *A Single Eye* (1650), pp. 8-12, 16; P. Gura, *A Glimpse of Sion's Glory: Puritan Radicalism in New England, 1620-1660* (Wesleyan U.P., 1984), p. 85. For Clarkson see *W.T.U.D.*, esp. pp. 213-17.
67. *Tyranipocrit Discovered*, in *British Pamphleteers*, I (ed. G. Orwell and R. Reynolds, 1948), esp. pp. 110-12.
68. Walker, *The Decline of Hell*, p. 108.
69. See esp. Book I, Chapters xi-xii.
70. Fox, *Journal* (1902), I, pp. 28, 34; cf. *M.C.P.W.*, VI, *passim*.
71. S. Fisher, *Baby-Baptism meer Babism* (1653), pp. 27-9, 34-8, 44, 105-6.
72. Downame, *Lectures upon the Four First Chapters of the Prophecy of Hosea* (1608), quoted by M. McGiffert, "God's Controversy with Jacobean England", p. 1161.
73. Burges, *Two Sermons Preached to the House of Commons* (30 March 1642 and 30 April 1645) (1645), p. 33.
74. Calamy, *Englands Antidote, Against the Plague of Civil Warre*, 22 October 1644, pp. 18-19.
75. Quoted by A. Fletcher, *A County Community in Peace and War: Sussex, 1600-1660*, p. 113.
76. Ed. D.D. Hall, *The Antinomian Controversy, 1636-1638* (Wesleyan U.P., 1968), pp. 154, 157.
77. Trevor-Roper, *Religion, the Reformation and Social Change*, p. 140.
78. Dryden, *Annus Mirabilis*, lines 265-6.
79. Quoted by McKeon, *Politics and Poetry in Restoration England*, p. 232.
80. Ed. C. H. Firth and R. S. Rait, *Acts and Ordinances of the Interregnum* (1911), I, pp. 133-6.
81. See R.B. Schlatter, *Richard Baxter and Puritan Politics* (Rutgers U.P., 1957), esp. pp. 45-67.
82. Burton, *Parliamentary Diary*, I, *passim*.
83. *W.T.U.D.*, pp. 163, 175, quoting Marlowe and Chapman among others.
84. J. Reeve, *A Divine Looking-Glass* (1719), p. 94. First published 1656: cf. p. 165.
85. Cf. pp. 57-9 above.
86. Gilbert Burnet, *Life of the Earl of Rochester* (1774), pp. 47, 58. First published 1680.
87. S. I. Mintz, *The Hunting of Leviathan: Seventeenth-Century Reactions to the Materialism and Moral Philosophy of Thomas Hobbes* (Cambridge U.P., 1962), pp. 50-2; R. Stromberg, *Religious Liberalism in Eighteenth-Century England* (Oxford U.P., 1954), p. 11.
88. G. F. Nuttall, *The Welsh Saints, 1640-1660* (Cardiff, 1957), p. 59; R. B.

Schlatter, *The Social Ideas of Religious Leaders, 1660-1688* (Oxford U.P., 1940), p. 242.

89. R. M. Jones, Introduction to W. C. Braithwaite, *The Second Period of Quakerism* (1919), esp. pp. xliv-vii.

90. Walker, *op. cit., passim*; K.V. Thomas, *op. cit., passim*. See pp. 330, 333-4 below.

91. Lord Bolingbroke, *Letters to Sir William Windham and Mr. Pope* (1894), pp. 178-9.

92. See pp. 146, 170-1 below.

93. Joyce Appleby, *Economic Thought and Ideology in Seventeenth-Century England* (Princeton U.P., 1978), Chapters 2-4, 8-9, pp. 115-17, 198 and *passim*. The point had been made by Tawney (*Religion and the Rise of Capitalism*, Penguin edn., p. 152.

94. Cf. Boyle: "Piety was to be embraced not so much to gain heaven, as to serve God with" (quoted by J. R. Jacob, *Robert Boyle and the English Revolution: A Study in Social and Intellectual Change*, New York, 1977, p. 39).

95. I have benefited here by reading in advance of publication an article by Peter Elmer on John Webster's *The Displaying of Supposed Witchcraft* (1677).

96. Swift, *An Argument to prove that the Abolishing of Christianity in England may . . . be attended with some inconveniences*, in *Works* (1814), VIII, p. 194.

97. Ed. John Hayward, *The Letters of Saint Evremond* (1930), p. 140. Sir William Petty made a similar observation, though with more pleasure and less apprehension (*Petty Papers*, II, pp. 116-18, 190-1).

98. J. R. Jacob, *Robert Boyle and the English Revolution, passim*; M. C. Jacob, *The Newtonians and the English Revolution, passim*.

99. J. Fell, *The Character of the last Daies* (1675), p. 1.

100. Sacheverell, *The Perils of False Brethren* (1709), p. 9.

101. D. North, *Lives of the Norths* (1826), III, p. 344. First published 1740-2.

102. See Sinfield, *op. cit.*, esp. p. 108 and Chapter 7 *passim*.

103. E.g. Bunyan, *Works*, I, pp. 88-102; cf. p. 606, III, p. 130 and *W. T. U.D.*, pp. 405-6.

104. I have discussed this point at greater length in my *Society and Puritanism in Pre-Revolutionary England*, Chapter 14.

105. Woodhouse, *op. cit.*, p. 161. Wildman however still believed in fairies (K. V. Thomas, *op. cit.*, pp. 236-7).

106. W. Blake, *Poetry and Prose* (Nonesuch edn., 1927), p. 961.

9. *Dr Tobias Crisp, 1600-43* [1]

"He that fears God is free from all other fears." *

I

Tobias Crisp was born in 1600 in Bread St., London, a prosperous area where Milton was born eight years later. Tobias was the third son of "one of the richest families in the City". His merchant father had been sheriff of London. Tobias's elder brother was Sir Nicholas Crisp (1598-1666), who was "the driving force behind the [West African gold] trade for most of the period 1625-44", and who was also engaged in the slave trade between West Africa and the West Indies. He too became sheriff of London, was a trained band captain and M.P. in both the Short and the Long Parliaments of 1640. He had imprudently become a customs farmer in that year, that is to say one of the very unpopular government financiers. He was also a monopolist, and for this he was expelled from the House of Commons in February 1641. He was perforce a royalist during the civil war, equipping a privateering vessel for the King. He survived to become a baronet in 1665. [2]

Tobias's connections and outlook seem to have been very different from his brother's. He was educated at Eton, which did not then mean quite what it means now. In 1624 he took his B.A. at Christ's College, Cambridge, the year before Milton entered the College as an undergraduate. Crisp incorporated at Balliol to take his M.A. in 1626. [3] His D.D. followed much later. He married the daughter of Rowland Wilson of the Vintners' Company, another prominent London merchant. Wilson commanded a City regiment for Parliament during the civil war, was alderman and sheriff of London and a Trustee for crown lands when they were sold in 1649. He was a recruiter M.P. for Calne, Wiltshire, and a member of the Commonwealth's Council of State. He became a friend of Bulstrode White-

* William Dell, *Sermons*, p.18.

locke, who married his widow after Wilson died in 1650.[4] From the start Tobias seems to have had Puritan leanings. In 1627 he was deprived of his first living, the rectory of Newington Butts, on a charge of having entered into a simoniacal contract. This may be less reprehensible than it sounds: Crisp had been presented to the rectory only a few months earlier by a group which had leased the presentation from the Bishop of Worcester. They may have incurred the wrath of the hierarchy as a Puritan group trying to present Puritan ministers, like the Feoffees for Impropriations, who flourished between 1625 and 1633 before being suppressed by Archbishop Laud.[5]

In the same year, 1627, Crisp was presented to the vicarage of Brinkworth, Wiltshire — the county with which his father-in-law was associated. Here Crisp became famous for his lavish hospitality: "a hundred persons, yea and many more, have been received and entertained at his house at one and the same time, and ample provision made for man and horse". His substantial fortune enabled him to refuse "preferment or advancement", and Crisp stayed at Brinkworth until in 1642 persecution by royalist soldiers drove him back to London, where he died a year later.[6] His preaching appears however to have left memories behind him in Wiltshire.[7]

In the year before his death Crisp preached in London. Among others Laurence Clarkson the future Ranter heard him hold forth against all existing churches — Anglican, Presbyterian, Independent, Baptist (the last three of which had appeared publicly only since 1640). "Be in society or no, though walked all alone, yet if he believed that Christ Jesus died for him, God beheld no iniquity in him". The prose style is Clarkson's but the sentiments are unmistakably Crisp's. Clarkson read all his books as they came out.[8] He was to carry Crisp's antinomian doctrines well beyond anything Crisp advocated.

Crisp's sermons were published posthumously in 1643 and later: it is unlikely that they could have been published before 1640. "Taken in short writing and compared with his notes", their genuineness is attested by his son.[9] But we must recall that they were delivered at a time of rigid ecclesiastical censorship and control, so he had to be careful what he said.

II

Crisp is primarily concerned with the problem of reconciling predestination and free will, God's omnipotence and human freedom — not a new problem. His starting point seems to have been dissatisfaction with traditional Calvinist predestination which — he thought — led many to despair because they could not believe in their election. His initial reaction in the sixteen-twenties was towards Arminianism, then becoming fashionable at court and soon to win control of the Church of England through the Laudians. But Crisp had been brought up to have a strong gut-hatred of popery, and as the Thirty Years War progressed the danger of Roman Catholic domination on the continent (and then in England) alarmed him as it did many other English protestants. Laudian Arminianism revived sacramental emphases which Crisp disliked and which he — again like many others — saw as a reversion to popery.

He expresses himself cautiously, but he makes pretty clear his anxiety about both the foreign and the domestic situation. "Look upon the present time, now you may see what sadness fills the hearts and faces of men, yea even of God's own people. . . . They look every hour when they shall be cut off by the sword". There is no certainty "that our lives and estates shall be spared".[10] "How many among you, yea and of the uppermost form (bishops) have warped of later times and have turned their faces to return back to the fleshpots of Egypt".[11] Thomas Goodwin expressed similar anxieties in 1639 — more openly because he was writing in exile. He foresaw the subjugation of protestantism in its last refuge in Europe, Britain, because of the connivance with popery of men like the Laudian bishops. "It were happy for other states professing the Calvin[ist] religion if they could wash their hands of the blood of the churches not only not assisted but betrayed by them".[12] Because we know that nothing came of such fears, we perhaps underestimate their strength in forging the near-unanimity with which in 1640-1 the Long Parliament set about destroying the power of the Laudian clergy, and of royal ministers in whom they had no confidence. Events in Germany in the sixteen-twenties had created a real and lasting fear of popery; the sixteen-thirties bred suspicions that members of Charles I's government were its accomplices.[13]

Crisp's aversion from justification by works spills over into anxiety about the covenant theology which, thanks to preachers like William Perkins, John Preston and Richard Sibbes, had become almost orthodox among Anglican protestants until the Laudian challenge of the sixteen-twenties. The covenant theology attempted to smuggle works back into Calvinism by arguing that God contracted to save those who kept his covenant. Their good works would not earn the elect salvation, but would testify to their state of grace. It was an understandable attempt by harassed clergymen to preserve their flocks from the despair to which Calvinism was apt to lead. Perkins argued that a sincere and strong desire for grace is presumptive evidence that grace is at work in the soul: God accepts the will for the deed. Crisp thought that sincerity and good intentions were not enough,[14] and that the covenant theology led to presumption. Those who looked for assurance of salvation in the good works that they performed came to rely on their own merits rather than on Christ.

Crisp's own solution was to go back to pristine Calvinist theology before Theodore Béza and the covenant theologians had watered it down.[15] In Crisp's view the elect are ordained to salvation from all eternity; they cannot fall from grace. This, as we shall see, seemed to his critics to run the risk of antinomianism, of encouraging those who believed that their election was secure to indulge in all manner of licentious practices. Crisp's answer was that *no* person is capable of works pleasing to God; all — elect and reprobate alike — are sinful and filthy. We are saved only because "the Lord hath laid on him [Christ] the iniquity of us all" (Isaiah 53.6). This was the text for sermons III to XVII of the 1643 volume. (The association of this passage with the Messiah was commonly accepted by seventeenth-century theologians.)

Crisp's onslaught on the covenant theology arose from his dislike of its legalism, its implied bargaining with God: "you give me salvation, and I will give you faith, and works too". "Even true faith", Crisp wrote, "is no condition of the covenant".[16] "The new covenant is without any conditions whatsoever on man's part". Man "is first justified before he believes, then he believes that he is justified".[17] Crisp was anxious to emphasize that the elect were saved before they were born. Christ himself "is not so completely righteous but we are as righteous as he was; ...Christ became ...as completely sinful as we". Crisp insists with almost monotonous repetition that "as soon as ever [a believer] hath committed this sin, ... the Lamb of God ... hath already taken away this very sin".[18] To restrict justifica-ion until after a man believes in Christ is to bring to life again the covenant of works, to trouble the consciences of those who are convinced that they are under the hatred of God.[19]

The source of all this is Crisp's determination to relieve believers of "horror in their consciences", of the superstition of scarecrow sins which Milton deplored. Stand "fast in the liberty wherein Christ hath made you free, and do not again entangle yourselves with such yokes of bondage that neither you nor your fathers were able to bear".[20] He was against preaching the terrors of the law, the wrath of God, damnation and hell-fire. The object of such sermons, if preached at all, should be not to terrify but to reassure believers that they are secure from damnation.[21] Crisp strongly disapproved of preachers who "fetch blood at the hearts of children with their causeless cautions, and then rejoice to see them in their spiritual afflictions, which methinks is an inhuman cruelty ... Children must not want their food for fear of dogs".[22] In 1643, the year when Crisp's sermons were first published, the future Leveller William Walwyn was also concerned lest "fears and terrors may abound" in those who have been terrified by the fear of sin. Like Crisp, Walwyn attacked the doctrine that God accepts "our wills for our performance".[23]

Crisp was worried about those who "are apt to think their peace depends on this subduing of sin" which they find impossible. "Fetch peace where it is to be had", was his advice. "Let subduing alone for peace".[24] "Sadness in any believer whatsoever ... in respect of his jealousy of his present and future estate", shows that he is "out of the way of Christ". "I believe many poor souls have been held under hatches the longer because some have withheld Christ from them, or themselves have not dared to think Christ belongs to them". "Christ doth not look for your pains; he came to save those that could not tell which way to turn themselves". Believers "must not fear their own sins". "The Father forces open the spirit of the man, and pours in his Son, in spite of the receiver".[25] "This grace of the Lord's laying of iniquities upon Christ is applicable to persons even ... before they have mended their ways", Crisp insisted again and again, though he recognized that it is a view which "will find great opposition in the world", because it gives "way to looseness".[26]

Crisp's continuing concern was to escape from the formal self-righteousness of those who believed that their election was demonstrated by their good works. "Even the most blameless walking according to God's law, not only before but also after conversion, is truly counted but loss and dung".[27] "Righteousness is that which puts a man away from Christ".[28] Good works should be performed only because they are profitable to others, not with any idea that they confer merit on the doer. Loving mankind anyway "is no evidence of our being in Christ. For publicans and harlots love one another".[29] "When we labour by our fasting and prayer and seeking the Lord ...

to take away his displeasure, ... do you serve God or no? Do you not serve yourselves?" "Is there not much self mixed in your performances?"[30] Men must be taken off "from performing duties to corrupt ends", from "idolizing their own righteousness".[31]

Since the elect are saved from the womb, Crisp logically concludes that neither prayers, tears, fasting, mournings, reluctancy and fighting against our corruptions have "the least prevalency with the Lord". "They move God not a jot. ... God is moved only from himself".[32] God hears only Christ's prayers.[33] It was a doctrine later adopted by the Muggletonians. I have argued elsewhere that they derived it from Clarkson, who joined the sect in the late fifties. Clarkson was preaching the doctrine in 1650; so was another Ranter, Jacob Bauthumley. Clarkson almost certainly derived the doctrine from Crisp, whom he had heard preach, and all of whose books he read as they came out.[34]

For all Crisp's hostility to the covenant theologians, he could be as unpleasantly legalistic as any of them. "The Lord's justice", he wrote, must "be satisfied to the full"; "reparation must be had".[35] This recalls Milton concerning Christ's sacrifice on the cross: "Die he or justice must".[36] But Crisp dwells quite unnecessarily on the pleasure which Christ's sufferings give God. "It is Christ's personal bearing of iniquity upon the cross once for all that gives unto the Lord the full pleasure and content to his own heart's desire". Nor does this pleasure and content derive from the salvation of mankind. "Christ's main aim is at the giving his Father content"; that "poor sinners are saved ... is a subordinate thing".[37] Crisp's use of the word "purchase" to describe Christ's sacrifice caused uneasiness to his nineteenth-century editor.[38]

III

I think we should assume that Crisp did not believe that all men were saved. But his rhetoric in insisting that God applies "the laying of iniquities upon Christ" to the ungodly, to the worst of sinners, long before they repent, exposed him to accusations of preaching universal grace. However ungodly a sinner may be, "what hinders but that thou mayst have as good a portion in him as thy heart can wish?"[39] It is rash to speak of those who are still unconverted as damned: their names may be in the Book of Life though they do not yet know it.[40] "There is no man under heaven ..., if he do but come to Christ, ... shall be rejected of him". "There is no better way to know your portion in Christ than upon the general tender of the gospel to conclude absolutely he is yours; and so without any more ado to take him as tendered to you, on his word; and this taking of him, upon a general tender, is the greatest security in the world that Christ is yours".[41] Crisp is anxious here to assure the worst sinner that there is still hope: he may have a better chance of salvation than the formally righteous. But his way of expressing it laid him open in the seventeenth-century to the charge of preaching universal redemption: even his nineteenth-century editor annotates such passages uneasily.

To contemplate the possibility that divine grace might be offered to all does not seem terribly shocking in our liberal age: but to the orthodox in the seventeenth century it seemed horrific. Private property, social inequality, and the state which protected both, were all accepted as the consequence of the wickedness of the mass of fallen mankind, of the fact that God's grace was limited to the few whom he had chosen. Reject the comfortable doctrine of original sin, and the floodgates might be opened — to ideas of human equality such as the Quakers were to preach, to democratic theories such as the Leveller Walwyn advocated, to the communism of the Diggers.[42]

Above all, it seemed to Crisp's contemporaries that licentious and immoral conclusions might be drawn from his theology. The orthodox had always known that the heresy "they can commit no sin offensive to God" appealed especially to "some of the meaner ignorant sort of people"[43] But with the breakdown of ecclesiastical control and of censorship in the revolutionary sixteen-forties such creatures were able to express themselves freely. As a horrified poet put it:

> No teaching now contents us the old way;
> The layman is inspired every day,
> Can pray and preach *ex tempore*; the priest
> With all his learning is despis'd and hiss'd
> Out of the church ...
> The world is a great Bedlam, where men talk
> Distractedly, and on their heads do walk,
> Treading antipodes to all the sages
> And sober-minded of the former ages.[44]

In the forties and fifties the world was temporarily turned upside down: ideas previously unthinkable were freely expressed. Coppe and Clarkson, whom their contemporaries called Ranters, preached against monogamy and in favour of free love. ("Polygamy's no sin/In a free state", Washbourne growled.)[45] And Clarkson at least had listened to Crisp.

Crisp died too early to see the full and scandalous development of popular antinomianism in England, but he certainly contributed to it, however innocent his intentions may have been. It is easy to pick out sentences in his sermons which might reasonably alarm the orthodox. "To be called a libertine is the most glorious title under heaven; take it for one that is truly free by Christ."[46] Sin, Crisp declared, is finished. To the question "Is thy conscience Christ?" he replied in the affirmative.[47] "Suppose a believer commit adultery and murder?" Crisp asked himself. And he replied that before he even confesses his sin "he may be as certain of the pardon of it as after confession". "I know the enemies of the gospel will make an evil construction of it", Crisp admitted.[48] He had earlier recognized that some believed "this kind of doctrine opens a gap to all manner of licentiousness and presumption". His answer was "only such as are rejected and given up of God" would so abuse the doctrine.[49] "Nothing doth more establish a restraint from sin", he asserted. "The children must not want their bread because dogs abuse it".[50] Like Milton, Crisp was so concerned with the freedom of the elect that he virtually ignored the existence of the unregenerate.

It was to the elect that Crisp addressed himself when he declared "If you be freemen of Christ, you may esteem all the curses of the law as no more concerning you than the laws of England concern Spain or the laws of Turkey an Englishman". "I am far from imagining any believer is freed from acts of sin," Crisp expostulated; "he is freed only from the charge of sin. ... God doth never punish any believer, after he is a believer, for sin". "You are in as true a state of salvation, you that are believers, as they that are now already in heaven".[51]

Crisp regarded it as "a gross, notorious and groundless slander that I should affirm that an elect person should live and die a whoremonger and an adulterer ... and be saved." But it was hardly enough in the sixteen-forties merely to assert that the elect "person is changed in conversation."[52] "Good works or inherent righteousness are necessary attendants on free grace."[53] No one can "out-sin the death of Christ."[54]

Crisp counter-attacked. "People are afraid to speak out of things that are Christ's, for fear of giving liberty." Milton might have echoed the phrase. "And in the mean while other things shall be set up above Christ", Crisp continued with growing irony; "the divine rhetoric of repentance and humiliation, the prevalency of tears to wash away sin, and our conscionable walking, will commend us to God at the last day. Here must be a magnifying of man's righteousness; and when these come to be examined they are but rhetorical expressions."[55] By Crisp's theology "the freeman of Christ is let loose to enjoy the free spirit."[56]

If Crisp had survived to see what some who thought themselves Christ's freemen did with the free spirit, he might have realized the inadequacy of his perfunctory assurances that it could not be used to undermine traditional morality.

IV

Crisp's views were not unprecedented. Roger Brearley, curate first of Grindleton, then of Kilwick, in the West Riding of Yorkshire, taught not dissimilar doctrines from 1615 to 1631. His hearers, as often happened, carried his doctrines further than he did.[57] The collapse of censorship in the early forties, which allowed Crisp's sermons to be printed, also led to the printing of writings by other antinomians — John Eaton, Robert Towne, Henry Denne, William Walwyn. Eaton died in 1641. His *The Discovery of the most dangerous dead Faith* was published in that year, "set forth ... (as they say) by Dr. Crisp".[58] Eaton's *The Honey-comb of Free Justification by Christ alone* was also published posthumously, in 1642, edited by Robert Lancaster, who was to edit Crisp's sermons. Eaton's, Denne's and Crisp's books were all condemned by the Westminster Assembly of Divines in August 1643.[59] The Assembly had "an eminent Christian ... secured in gaol for promoting the publishing of Dr. Crisp his works",[60] though the Prolocutor of the Assembly, Dr Twisse, was said to have remarked that opposition to Crisp's sermons arose from the fact that "so many were converted by his preaching and (said he) so few by ours".[61]

In 1643 Abraham Cowley listed antinomians together with libertines and Arians among the most enthusiastic supporters of Parliament in London.[62] The Scots Presbyterian Robert Baillie reported that the number of antinomians was growing even faster than the number of Independents and Anabaptists.[63] By 1643 the House of Commons, egged on by the Assembly, was becoming worried about antinomianism. A succession of sermons preached to the House on the occasion of its monthly fast kept the subject before the attention of M.Ps. In January the Scots Presbyterian Samuel Rutherford denounced antinomianism: he named Crisp in the margin when he printed the sermon.[64] Rutherford's Scottish colleague Robert Baillie took up the cry a month later, followed by Herbert Palmer in August.[65] In October Edmund Calamy attacked those who preached against days of national humiliation on the ground that "God is never displeased with his people", and that "the very being of their sins is abolished out of God's sight".[66] He did not name Crisp, but the allusion seems fairly clear. "National sins", Crisp had preached, "bring about national judgments, yet all the sins of the times cannot do a member of Christ a jot of hurt (even though you have had some hand in them)".[67]

In 1643 John Sedgwick published *Antinomianisme Anatomized*. Thomas Bakewell in 1643-4 directed a series of pamphlets against antinomianism, attacking especially Crisp but also naming Lancaster and Giles Randall. Baillie followed up his sermon by *A Disswasive from the Errours of the Time* (1645). Three fat volumes of Thomas Edward's *Gangraena* appeared in 1646. In one of them he reported an apparently antinomian lady who told a minister that "to kill a man, to commit adultery, or steal a man's goods" were no sins.[68] Thomas Bedford's *An Examination of the chief points of Antinomianism* (1647) devoted two chapters to Crisp.[69] Samuel Rutherford too returned to the fray in *A Survey of the Spirituall Antichrist* (1648), naming Crisp among others on his title-page; and there were many others.[70] In 1644 Stephen Geree, elder brother of the better-known John Geree, had directed *The Doctrine of the Antinomians ... Confuted* specifically against Crisp, "so magnified of many".[71] Antinomianism, Geree observed, was "most plausible and pleasing to flesh and blood": and he referred to Crisp in this connection.[72] He paid tribute to the popular appeal of Crisp's theology in the new circumstances of the forties. Crisp's "strains of rhetoric ... do marvellously allure and ensnare the minds of many simple and unsettled souls". His doctrine "will most abundantly please the carnal palates of the worst men in the world, even atheists, drunkards, rioters and rankest rebels that can be". Geree associated Crisp with Brearley and Eaton, and accused him of preaching universal grace and election: for him Christ belongs "to all sinners without exception of any particulars".[73]

Others were contributing to what Geree called these "sweet

poisons".[74] Clarkson later wrote that Giles Randall ("a great anti-nomian", Edwards called him)[75] and Paul Hobson taught "such a doctrine as Dr Crisp, only higher and clearer".[76] Edwards quoted Hobson as saying "I am persuaded when I used all these duties" — prayer, penitence — "I had not one jot of God in me" — a phrase of Crisp's which his critics had made notorious.[77] John Saltmarsh, William Dell, early Quakers and many others popularized the heresy. William Erbery praised Crisp.[78] But the full libertine consequences of antinomianism remained to be drawn by the Ranters.[79]

Robert Towne, from the Grindleton area, wrote an answer to John Sedgwick in 1644. In this he declared "They that believe on Christ are no sinners".[80] Abiezer Coppe in 1649 repeated Crisp's and Towne's announcement that sin was finished. God's service, Coppe said, is "perfect freedom and pure libertinism", a word that Crisp had used. Coppe claimed that God was "that mighty Leveller".[81] Laurence Clarkson systematized the ideas which Edwards's antinomian lady had so shamelessly put forward, and in sexual matters at least Clarkson practised what he preached. Jacob Bauthumley proclaimed that God is "glorified in sin"; many others alarmingly suggested that sin had been invented by the ruling classes to keep the lower orders in place.[82]

V

In 1655 Richard Baxter introduced a tract against antinomianism by Thomas Hotchkis, "minister at Stanton-by-Highworth, Wilt-shire", who "liveth not far from the place where Dr Crisp did exercise his ministry". After naming Eaton, Towne, Randall, John Simpson and Saltmarsh, Baxter concluded "but the man that most credited and strengthened their party was Dr Crisp". In consequence antinomianism was stronger in Wiltshire than elsewhere.[83] Hotchkis had written (but not published) an *Examen* of Crisp's Third Volume (1648).[84] Henry Pinnell, who wrote a preface to the 1648 volume, knew Crisp personally. "Upon mine own experience and more than twelve years' knowledge" he vindicated the author "from all vicious licentiousness of life, and scandalous aspersions cast upon him".[85] Pinnell's antinomianism was more plebeian than Dr Crisp's. "All the learning I had at Oxford", he observed, "I laid out and improved in opposing the truth". He was no "whit the fitter to be a minister because of the repute and notion of scholarship". "I got more from simple country people, husbandmen, weavers, etc., about Brinkworth, Southwick and those parts in Wiltshire, than ever I did or got here by books and preachers".[86] Brinkworth, where Pinnell was born in 1613, was the living held by Crisp from 1627 to 1642.

Pinnell, formerly chaplain in Colonel John Pickering's regiment, became a separatist preacher at Brinkworth after leaving the Army.[87] This he did in two stages. In December 1646, disillusioned with Parliament's policy, he resigned, but he rejoined in the summer of 1647 after the rank-and-file revolt led by the Leveller-influenced Agitators. But by the end of the year, when the generals had routed the Agitators, "the Army, which was once so beautiful and lovely in mine eye, is now become most black and ugly, God having made me ashamed of my fleshy confidence therein." After expostulating with Cromwell, who listened politely and thanked him for his plain dealing, Pinnell finally abandoned the Army.[88] In the fifties he published alchemical treatises and made an important translation of works by Croll and Paracelsus.[89]

The "cheese" area of north-western Wiltshire, which embraces Brinkworth, Highworth and Southwick, was an area of poorly-paid part-time cloth-workers, which in the early seventeenth century saw weavers' riots and religious heresy. It was strongly Parliamentarian at the beginning of the civil war; from it Clubmen favourable to Parliament later came.[90] There were antinomians there in the fifties, though it is not clear — in spite of Baxter — how far Crisp's teaching had influenced them. Richard Coppin preached "frequently in those parts", collecting "sundry disciples" from "the profane sort of people ... who do hold that there is no resurrection, no day of judgment, no salvation, no damnation, no heaven nor no hell but what it is in this life". ("I do less wonder", Hotchkis commented, "that the antinomian preachers are accounted by the ignorant and profane multitude the only comfortable preachers".)[91]

In the sixteen-fifties Ranters were said to be "building up their Babel of profaneness and community" in Wiltshire, though the writer cited only Thomas Webbe. Webbe, of an old Wiltshire clothing family, was rector of Langley Burhill. He was alleged to be "one of Lilburne's faction" (i.e. a Leveller), was friendly with Joseph Salmon and praised Abiezer Coppe. Webbe allegedly claimed to "live above ordinances, and that it was lawful for him to lie with any woman". His epigram, "there's no heaven but women, nor no hell save marriage" suggests a certain light-heartedness. It was in a letter to Webbe that Salmon wrote "the Lord grant we may know the worth of hell, that we may for ever scorn heaven".[92] William Eyre, minister of a gathered congregation in Salisbury, another son of an old Wiltshire family, published in 1654 a defence of antinomianism, *Justification without Conditions*, which Hotchkis, Baxter and others attacked.[93] In 1656 there was an antinomian group in Lacock, one of whose members echoed Coppin to say "there was neither heaven nor hell except in a man's conscience"; another thought "whatever sin he did commit, God was the author of them all and acted them in him".[94] Langley Burhill and Lacock are both in the "cheese" area of the county.

VI

The most interesting seventeenth-century antinomian, another undergraduate of Christ's College, was John Milton. Milton was in London during the last year of Crisp's life, when he was attracting a good deal of attention. Milton may or may not have heard him preach: it is very unlikely that he did not read the sermons when they were published. In 1645 Milton defended "the maids of Aldgate" who claimed to be incapable of sin because they were "godded with God". Milton believed, like Crisp, that "the entire Mosaic Law is abolished". "We are released from the decalogue". "Everyone born of God cannot sin". "The practice of the saints interprets the commandments". "The greatest burden in the world is superstition . . . of imaginary and scarecrow sins", which "enslave the dignity of man". Apart from the last clause, all the above sentences might have been written by Crisp. Milton was careful, like Crisp, to stress that such ideas gave no authority for licence; but he too was denounced by his contemporaries as a libertine. Like Crisp, he was so concerned with the liberty of the elect that he hardly bothered about the consequences which the unregenerate might draw from his writings. The same is true of his doctrine of divorce, where he gave very great liberty to the husband to put away his wife in cases of incompatibility of temperament, oblivious apparently of the possibilities of abuse. And *The Doctrine and Discipline of Divorce* created scandal because it — like Crisp's sermons — was published in the vernacular. Most of Milton's antinomian ideas — like his acceptance of polygamy — were too dangerous to be published even veiled in the decent obscurity of a learned language.[95]

Crisp anticipates both Gerrard Winstanley and Milton in his interesting belief that "Christ is to be considered collectively: that is, he is not only Christ as he is one person of himself; but he is Christ as he himself in that one person is united to the persons of all the elect in the world. We and they make up but one collective body". To the union of the Father and the Son, and of the two natures in Christ, we must add the mystical union which makes "Christ the Mediator ... one with all the members of Christ jointly".[96] The Godhead is too remote for man to approach, but when Christ's humanity is united to it, it becomes more accessible.[97] Winstanley associated a version of this doctrine with belief in the advent of a communist society, brought about by Christ rising in all men and women.[98] The evidence for the idea in Milton is less clear-cut: it is stronger in *Paradise Lost* than in Milton's theological treatise, the *De Doctrina Christiana*. I had set out the evidence for Milton holding some such doctrine before the possibility that he might have derived it from Crisp occured to me.[99] Some scholars have expressed scepticism of Empson's theory that at the end of time Milton's God will abdicate his power to this collective Christ, to all the saints.[100] The clear exposition of the "collective body of Christ" in Crisp — a more respectable source than Winstanley, and one which Milton is more likely to have read — perhaps reinforces the case for accepting some such doctrine in Milton.

VII

In 1690, when the press was again freer, Crisp's sermons were reprinted by his son. They caused a great scandal. Crisp's main critics now were Presbyterians, anxious to disavow antinomianism lest it bring discredit on the reputation of dissent. Daniel Williams's *Gospel-Truth Stated and Vindicated: Wherein some of Dr. Crisp's Opinions Are Considered and the Opposite Truths are Plainly Stated and Confirmed* (1692)[101] led to fierce controversies with Congregationalists. The furore ultimately broke up the recently-formed union between Congregationalists and Presbyterians. Isaac Chauncy, one of the first to withdraw from the union, declared that "according to the opinion of our modern divines", Luther "was an antinomian himself, and Calvin but a little better".[102] Richard Baxter now thought Crisp's views antichristian, and that opposition to them was a cause which "will endure no indifferency or neutrality".[103] An anonymous tract published in 1693, *Crispianism Unmask'd*, reverts to the social threat implied in Crisp's doctrine, with a dark reference to "Mr. Saltmarsh and such like men ... in those days". If only the learned read Crisp, no harm will be done. "But when I saw that the book was bought up, and read, and (which is more) applauded by the common readers, I thought it was time" to protest. Crisp's doctrine "cuts the sinews of all the duties and exercises of Christianity". Why should we bother to be good if nothing we do is acceptable to God?[104] "By means of Crisp's book", we are told by the pious biographer of Bishop Bull, "the poison of antinomianism soon spread, not only in the country but infected London too".[105]

Congregationalists rallied to the defence of freedom of expression. Crisp's son Samuel wrote on behalf of his father in 1691 and 1693, pointing out that the Presbyterian attitude recalled the Westminster Assembly's attempt to suppress Crisp's sermons in 1643.[106] These sermons were again reprinted in 1791: perhaps a significant date if we recall that they were first published in the revolutionary sixteen-forties, and reprinted after the revolution of 1688. There was a further republication in 1832: the editor was still nervously aware that controversial conclusions could be drawn from Crisp's doctrine.

VIII

A final question, to which I have no clear answer, is Was Tobias Crisp as simply innocent as he appears? When it was suggested to him that libertine conclusions could be drawn from his doctrine he protested with outraged incredulity; and so far I have assumed that he erred on the side of naiveté rather than of duplicity. Yet this raises worrying questions too. Crisp was no unsophisticated provincial; he was the son, brother and son-in-law of highly-powered London business men, all of them deeply involved in City and national politics. The circumstances in which Tobias was deprived of his first living suggest either that he committed the sin of simony or that he was deceiving the ecclesiastical authorities in the interests of what he thought a good cause — neither the act of a political innocent.

Crisp was certainly aware of the accusation that his doctrine opened a door to all licentiousness. But his answer was alarmingly inadequate for so clever a man. He said, in effect, the elect could by definition not indulge in licentious practices (as we may be pretty sure that he himself did not: he and his wife had thirteen children). He gave no indication at all of how we know who the elect are, how we differentiate between elect and unregenerate, how we distinguish those who wrongly believe themselves to be elect. He must have known that this was one of the crucial questions of seventeenth-century protestant theology. The covenant theologians answered it by saying that the visible elect could be known by their good works: they were not saved by their works but their works demonstrated that they were saved. Crisp utterly rejected works as evidence of salvation at the same time that he widely extended the freedom of the elect. Like Milton, Crisp appears to regard the unregenerate as totally unimportant; he says nothing about them at all. Curious for a man with fifteen years pastoral experience in Wiltshire.

The further question then arises, Who are the unregenerate? How many people are we talking about? If you believed that they were the vast majority of the population, could you just ignore them? Did Crisp believe that all men and women would be saved, as some Ranters did? Did he believe that salvation was offered to all who threw themselves on Christ, as Milton perhaps did, and as many were to suggest in the sixteen-forties? Did he believe in hell? Many came to regard hell as an inner state rather than a geographical location.[107] Crisp once wrote rather testily of those who were not satisfied with his doctrine: "for aught I know they may have their deserved portion in the lowest part of hell".[108] It is an ambiguous remark, committing him to nothing: could the ambiguity be deliberate?

I think it unlikely that Crisp was as unorthodox as Milton became: but the evidence does not exclude the possibility that he was moving in that direction. Men had to be very careful how they expressed themselves on such questions. The possibility of universal salvation was not raised in print in England till 1648, by Winstanley and Coppin: though almost certainly it had been discussed verbally much earlier. Most of Crisp's sermons were presumably delivered under the Laudian régime, when it would have been foolhardy in the extreme to commit oneself on paper to unorthodox opinions.

So the question must remain open. We just do not know what Crisp's attitude to Ranters and suchlike would have been if he had lived to see them. All we can say is that some of them looked back to him with respect. Crisp's ideas excited the lower orders in the sixteen-forties and again in the sixteen-nineties; they still caused discomfort to the orthodox two hundred years after his death. We all try to provoke: but which of us can hope to enjoy so long a posthumous life?

NOTES

1. Originally published in *Balliol Studies* (ed. J.M. Prest, 1982).
2. R. Porter, 'The Crispe Family and the African Trade in the Seventeenth Century", *Journal of African History*, IX (1981), pp. 57-74; D. Brunton and D.H. Pennington, *Members of the Long Parliament* (1954), pp. 54-7; M.F. Keeler, *The Long Parliament* (Philadelphia, 1954), p. 147.
3. H.W.C. Davis, *A History of Balliol College* (revised by R.H.C. Davis and Richard Hunt, Oxford, 1963), pp. 104-5.
4. Brunton and Pennington, *op. cit.*, p. 59; D. Underdown, *Pride's Purge: Politics in the Puritan Revolution* (Oxford U.P., 1971), p. 234; B. Worden, *The Rump Parliament, 1648-1653* (Cambridge U.P., 1974), p. 224.
5. D. Lysons, *The Environs of London*, I (1792), p. 394; my *Economic Problems of the Church* (Panther edn.), p. 64 and Chapter XI, *passim*. It is possible indeed that Crisp may have been presented to Newington Butts by the Feoffees.
6. *D.N.B.* The reference to Crisp's refusal of advancement may be intended as retrospective rebuttal of the charge of simony.
7. See pp. 151-3 above.
8. Clarkson, *The Lost sheep Found* (1660), p. 9. See p. 146 above.
9. T. Crisp, *Christ Alone Exalted: in Seventeene Sermons* (1643), title-page. Subsequently referred to as *Seventeene Sermons*. The title-page says the sermons were preached in London, but presumably many of them had first been delivered at Brinkworth. Cf. [Anon], *A Memorial To Preserve Unspotted to Posterity the Name and Memory of Dr Crispe* (1643).
10. *Seventeene Sermons*, pp. 386-7.
11. *Crisp's Christ Alone Exalted, Being the Complete Works of Tobias Crisp, ... containing Fifty-Two Sermons* (ed. J. Gill, 1832), pp. 406-7. Hereafter referred to as *Fifty-Two Sermons*. The word in brackets occurs in the printed version, though presumably Crisp was not so specific in his manuscript. Cf. Milton's addition of an anti-episcopal headnote to *Lycidas* when he reprinted it in 1645.
12. T. Goodwin, *An Exposition of the Revelation*, in *Works* III, p. 174.
13. For one example among many of such anxieties shared by a layman of the sixteen-twenties, see R. Cust and P.G. Lake, "Sir Richard Grosvenor and the Rhetoric of Magistracy", *Bulletin of the Institute of Historical Research*, LIV (1981), pp. 42-53. See now the authoritative book by C. Hibbard, *Charles I and the Popish Plot, passim*.
14. *Seventeene Sermons*, p. 443. For the covenant theology see pp. 119, 127 above.
15. R.T. Kendall, *Calvin and the English Calvinism to 1649* (Oxford U.P., 1979), Chapter 13.
16. *Seventeene Sermons*, p. 60; cf. pp. 43, 58; and *Fifty-Two Sermons*, pp. 174-7.
17. *Fifty-Two Sermons*, pp. 86, 91.
18. *Seventeene Sermons*, pp. 89, 146-7.

19. Crisp, *Christ Alone Exalted*, III (1648), pp. 273-8. Hereafter cited as Vol. III.

20. *Seventeene Sermons*, pp. 87, 156. For Milton see pp. 153-4 above.

21. Vol III, pp. 129-30, 136; *Fifty-Two Sermons*, p. 22.

22. *Fifty-Two Sermons*, p. 411.

23. W. Walwyn, *The Power of Love* (1643), pp. 19-22, reprinted in Haller, *Tracts on Liberty*, II. See p. 127 above and pp. 166-9 below.

24. *Fifty-Two Sermons*, p. 14.

25. *Ibid.*, pp. 55, 106, 137, 190; II, p. 137.

26. *Seventeene Sermons*, pp. 409, 412.

27. *Ibid.*, p. 6.

28. *Fifty-Two Sermons*, p. 104.

29. *Seventeene Sermons*, pp. 16-17, 28, 452-3.

30. *Ibid.*, pp. 391, 446. This was a point later to be made very forcibly by the Ranter Abiezer Coppe, *A Fiery Flying Roll* (1649), pp. 5-9 and *passim*.

31. *Fifty-Two Sermons*, p. 143.

32. *Seventeene Sermons*, p. 182; cf. pp. 283-4.

33. Vol. III, p. 185.

34. Clarkson, *A Single Eye* (1650) and *The Lost sheep Found*, both printed in *A Collection of Ranter Writings from the 17th Century* (ed. N. Smith, 1983); Bauthumley, *The Light and Dark Sides of God* (1650), *ibid.*, pp. 243, 246, 259; cf. pp. 260-2 below. Sir Thomas Browne flirted with the doctrine in *Religio Medici*, as he did with mortalism; cf. Hotchkis, *op. cit.*, pp. 151-2.

35. *Seventeene Sermons*, pp. 319-26, 329.

36. *Paradise Lost*, Book III, line 210; Book XII, lines 401-4.

37. *Seventeene Sermons*, pp. 324, 332. Bunyan was equally barbaric: God "will burn sinners in the flames of hell ... with delight ... for the easing of his mind and the satisfaction of his justice" (*Works*, II, p. 111).

38. *Fifty-Two Sermons*, p. 191.

39. *Seventeene Sermons*, pp. 409, 412, 425-6; cf. Vol. III, pp. 174-9.

40. Vol. III, pp. 179-81.

41. *Fifty-Two Sermons*, pp. 114, 213; cf. pp. 202-3.

42. For Walwyn, see pp. 166-7 above.

43. Richard Sibbes, *Works*, II, p. 316. See pp. 173-5 below.

44. Thomas Washbourne, *Poems* (ed. A. B. Grosart, 1868), pp. 182-4. Washbourne — like Crisp, a Balliol man — survived to publish *The Repairer of the Breach. A Sermon Preached at the Cathedral Church of Gloucester* on 29 May 1661, which he dedicated to Charles II in a shameless bid for preferment: "to share in your triumphs as we had done in your sufferings". Washbourne's sufferings did not extend to loss of his living (A. G. Matthews, *Walker Revised*, Oxford U.P., 1948, p. 178).

45. Washbourne, *op. cit.*, p. 227; cf. *M.E.R.*, pp. 136-9.

46. *Fifty-Two Sermons*, p. 122.

47. *Seventeene Sermons*, pp. 156-9, 87.

48. *Fifty-Two Sermons*, pp. 224-6; cf. p. 131: even "a scandalous falling into sin" does not bring a believer under the curse. Cf. Adam Squire, sixteenth-century Master of Balliol: the Holy Spirit does not desert the elect when they sin (Anthony Kenny, "Reform and Reaction in Elizabethan Balliol, 1559-1588", in *Balliol Studies*, ed. J. Prest, 1982, p. 38).

49. *Seventeene Sermons*, p. 164; cf. Vol. III, pp. 105, 110.

50. Vol. III, pp. 113, 119-32, 167-8. Cf. note 22 above.

51. *Fifty-Two Sermons*, pp. 10, 43, 132; cf. pp. 15-18.

52. Vol. III, p. 326.

53. *Fifty-Two Sermons*, p. 328.

54. Vol. III, p. 362.

55. *Ibid.*, p. 359.

56. *Fifty-Two Sermons*, p. 133.

57. For initiatives by congregations, see p. 163 below.

58. Stephen Geree, *The Doctrine of the Antinomians ... Confuted* (1644), p. 41. Geree referred to Eaton as Crisp's "master" — *ibid.*, p. 5. But there is no evidence that they ever met, and Crisp's ideas must have been settled long before Eaton's writings were published. Eaton was twenty-five years Crisp's senior.

59. Kendall, *op. cit.*, pp. 185-8. See also R. S. Paul, *The Assembly of the Lord: Politics and Religion in the Westminster Assembly and the 'Grand Debate'* (Edinburgh, 1985), pp. 82-4.

60. S[amuel] C[risp], *Christ Alone Exalted in Dr Crisp's Sermons* (1693), p. 7.

61. Tobias Crisp, *Christ Made Sin* (ed. S. Crisp, 1691), p. 4.

62. Cowley, *The Civil War* (ed. A. Pritchard, Toronto U.P., 1973), pp. 110-11.

63. R. Baillie, *Letters and Journals* (Edinburgh, 1775), I, p. 408.

64. Samuel Rutherford, *A Sermon Preached to the Honourable House of Commons* (1644), pp. 32-7; cf. *The Tryal & Triumph of Faith* (1645), pp. 56-9, 111-12, 132, 169-71 — against Crisp.

65. Robert Baylie, *Satan the Leader in chief to all who resist the Reparation of Sion* (1644), pp. 25-6; H. Palmer, *The Glasse of Gods Providence towards his Faithfull Ones* (1644), pp. 54-5.

66. Edmund Calamy, *Englands Antidote against the Plague of Civil Warre* (1645), pp. 18-19; cf. William Jenkyn, *A Sleeping Sicknes the Distemper of the Times* (1647), Sig. A3.

67. Vol. III, pp. 28-9.

68. Bakewell, *A short View of the Antinomian Errors* (1643); *A faithfull Messenger sent after the Antinomians* (1644), esp. pp. 28, 35; *The Antinomians Confounded* (1644), esp. pp. 1-16, 28, 33 sqq.; T. Edwards, *Gangraena*, II, p. 6; cf. II, p. 146, III, p. 107.

69. *Op. cit.*, pp. 50-64. Bedford also attacked Henry Denne, pp. 25-33, 60-70.

70. Rutherford attacked Eaton, Towne, Saltmarsh and Dell as well as Crisp.

71. *Op. cit.*, Sig. B 3.

72. *Ibid.*, Sig A 2.
73. *Ibid.*, pp.1-2, 5, 26, 41, 46-8, 127, 133-4. For Brearley see p.163 below.
74. *Ibid.*, Sig. A 2.
75. Edwards, *op. cit.*, I p.97.
76. Clarkson, *op. cit.*, p.9.
77. Edwards, *op. cit.*, I. p.90. See p.146 above.
78. *The Testimony of William Erbery* (1658), p.68. For Erbery see *W.T.U.D.*, pp.192-7.
79. For Ranters see A.L. Morton *The World of the Ranters* (1970), and Frank McGregor "Ranterism and the Development of Early Quakerism", *Journal of Religious History* (Sydney, 1978), pp.349-63.
80. R.Towne, *The Assertion of Grace* (n.d.? 1644), p.23. See also Rutherford "A modest Survey of the Secrets of Antinomianism", printed with *A Survey of the Spirituall Antichrist*, pp.25, 71. See p.165 below.
81. Coppe, *op. cit.*, I, pp.1-5, 11.
82. For Bauthumley see *W.T.U.D.*, pp.219-20; for sin generally see *ibid.*, Chapter 8 *passim.*
83. Thomas Hotchkis, *An Exercitation Concerning the Nature and Forgivenesse of Sin* (1655), Sig. B 2, B 3v.
84. *Ibid.*, p.152.
85. Crisp, Vol. III, Sig. A 8v.
86. H.Pinnell, *A Word of Prophecy concerning The Parliament, Generall and the Army* (1648), p.49.
87. C.Webster, *The Great Instauration: Science, Medicine and Reform, 1626-1660* (1975), p.184.
88. Pinnell, *op. cit.*, pp.2-4, 7-10, 17, 74.
89. Webster, *op. cit.*, p.280. Crisp's successor as rector of Brinkworth was the Presbyterian John Harding, an even more active translator of Paracelsus, *ibid.*, p.281. Harding was expelled after the restoration.
90. D.Underdown. "The Chalk and the Cheese: Contrasts among the English Clubmen", *P. and P.*, 85 (1979), esp. pp.30, 39-40; *W.T.U.D.*, pp.46-7, 77, 109; cf. Buchanan Sharp *In Contempt of All Authority: Rural Artisans and Riot in the West of England, 1586-1660* (California U.P., 1980), *passim*, and *V.C.H. Wilts*, III p.102.
91. Hotchkis, *op. cit.*, pp.239, 291-2. For Coppin, see pp.194-6 below, and *W.T.U.D.*, esp. pp.220-3.
92. E. Stokes, *The Wiltshire Rant* (1652), pp.4, 14, 53, 61. Former Levellers in Wiltshire were alleged to have become Ranters (*W.T.U.D.*, p.239). For Salmon see *ibid.*, esp. pp.217-19.
93. Hotchkis, *op. cit.*, pp.172-6. Eyre's book (dedicated, rather late, to Barebone's Parliament) gave rise to an exceptionally tedious and long-winded controversy, in which Baxter mentioned Crisp as an antinomian of learning and judgment (*Richard Baxters Admonition to Mr William Eyre of Salisbury*, 1654, Sig. A3). John Graile (of Tidworth, Wilts.), another participant in the discussion, associated Eyre with Crisp's doctrines (*A Modest Vindication of the Doctrine of Conditions in the Covenant of Grace*, 1655, p.25; cf. pp.49, 57). I have not been able to

trace any relationship between the Rev. William Eyre and Colonel William Eyre the Leveller, also of Wiltshire. If there was any connection it was a distant one.

94. *W.T.U.D.*, p. 228.
95. M.E.R., pp. 303, 313-16.
96. Vol. III, pp. 346-7.
97. *Fifty-Two Sermons*, p. 27.
98. See chapter 11 below.
99. *M.E.R.*, pp. 303-5.
100. W. Empson, *Milton's God* (1961), pp. 130-46.
101. John Toland's first appearance in print arose from the Crisp controversy. Toland, still a very young man, rather unexpectedly "greatly liked" Daniel Williams's book, and made an abstract of it which Le Clerc published in his *Bibliothèque Universelle*, Tome XXIII, p. 505. Benjamin Furly, the Quaker patron of Toland and other radical thinkers, had three volumes of the first edition of Crisp's sermons in his famous library (*Bibliotheca Furliana*, Rotterdam, 1714, p. 143). The freethinker Anthony Collins had a copy of the 1690 edition of Crisp's works (T. Ballard, *Biblioteca Antonij Collins, Arm.*, 1731, pp. 36, 134).
102. Isaac Chauncy, *Neonomianism unmasked: or the ancient Gospel Pleaded* (1692), p. 2.
103. Quoted in W. M. Lamont, *Richard Baxter and the Millennium* (1979), p. 267; cf. *Reliquiae Baxterianae*, p. 43.
104. *Op. cit.*, pp. 3, 50, 54, 61. Crisp is (with Milton) one of the very few seventeenth-century Englishmen to have an '-ism' attached to his name (*M.E.R.*, p. 226n.)
105. Robert Nelson, *The Life of Dr George Bull, Late Lord Bishop of St David's* (1713), p. 260. John Mason, who proclaimed the millennium in Water Stratford in 1694, was "inclined to antinomianism" (H. Maurice, *An Impartial Account of Mr John Mason*, 1695, p. 27).
106. Tobias Crisp, *Christ Made Sin* (1691), Preface; S. C., *Christ Alone Exalted in Dr Crisp's Sermons* (1693), pp. 7-14.
107. *W.T.U.D.*, Chapter 8, *passim*; *M.E.R.*, Chapter 21, *passim*.
108. Volume III, p. 362.

10. *Antinomianism in 17th-century England*[1]

"That old leaven of innovations, masked under the name of reformation, ... was never wont so far to infect the whole mass of the nobility and gentry of this kingdom, however it dispersed among the vulgar."[*]

I

An unfriendly but moderately balanced anonymous pamphlet of 1644 summarized antinomian doctrines as: The elect are always beloved of God, who sees no sin in them even when by human standards they commit sin.[2] Antinomians stressed the complete freedom of the regenerate — restrained by no law, not even the Mosaic Law, by no rulings of churches, not even by the text of the Bible. The protestant concept of the priesthood of all believers abolished all mediators between man and God, whether the Virgin and the saints in heaven, or the hierarchy of the church on earth. The conscience of the individual believer was put in direct contact with God. This supremacy of the individual conscience facilitates ecclesiastical change in response to social pressures. In the first place it gives relatively little (if any) weight to the church and its ceremonies. Secondly, individual consciences are formed in a given society: what the conscience believes must bear some relation to the society in which it is formed. Believers living in the commercial strongholds of early protestantism found "the protestant ethic" written on their consciences — hard work in one's calling, frugality, accumulation, monogamy — the bourgeois virtues. It was to be different later when lower-class consciences also established a direct relationship with God.[3]

Antinomians carried this freedom for elect consciences to its

---

Eikon Basilike, The Portraicture of His Sacred Majestie in His Solitude and Sufferings (1649), p. 69. Attributed to Charles I, but almost certainly by John Gauden, later Bishop of Worcester. I cite from the edition of 1876.

extreme. For Luther the informed consciences of the godly were above the law — though of course because they were elect their consciences would be guided by God's will and so would *voluntarily* keep his commandments. But the important thing was their freedom of choice. "Whatsoever thou shalt observe of liberty and of love", Luther preached, "is godly; but if thou observe anything of necessity, it is ungodly". "If an adultery could be committed in the faith, it would no longer be a sin".[4] Luther no doubt intended this as a *reductio ad absurdum* for normal persons, though perhaps he had the difficult case of King David in mind too. Luther did after all authorize bigamy for Philip of Hesse. But seventeenth-century antinomian theologians pushed Luther's doctrine just a little bit further. Samuel Rutherford filled many score pages explaining away remarks by Luther which were susceptible of an antinomian interpretation.[5]

When antinomianism revived — or emerged from underground — in England, the urgent need seemed to be to liberate the consciences of the godly from external pressures, first of the Laudians, then of the Presbyterians. Antinomianism in England was a reaction against the alleged "works-mongering" of Laudians and covenant theologians, in the same way as Luther reacted against the formal ceremonial "works" of the Catholic church of his day. "The title of antinomian", said William Eyre sourly in 1654, "is by some of our new doctors appropriated to them who have most faithfully managed the protestant cause against the papists".[6]

It is difficult to estimate how much conscious antinomianism there had been in England before 1640. Roger Brearley's congregation at Grindleton was accused in 1617 of holding that "the Christian assured can never commit gross sin". It is indeed sinful to ask God's forgiveness, or to believe the Bible "without a motion of the spirit". The Christian assured "must never think of salvation".[7] Brearley's congregation seems to have carried his doctrines even further than he did. Thomas Shepard in 1622 was attracted by the Grindletonians, wondering "whether that glorious estate of perfection might not be the truth".[8] He decided it was not, and became a very orthodox New England divine; but Governor Winthrop attributed the heresies of Mistress Anne Hutchinson (which Shepard confuted) to Grindletonian doctrines.[9] Samuel Gorton, who carried another version of antinomianism to New England in 1636-7, came from Lancashire like Clarkson and Winstanley, but we do not know where he picked up his ideas.[10] John Cotton described them as "Familist".[11]

The almost immediate appearance of antinomianism in New England suggests that it may have been fairly widespread in England. Mrs Hutchinson was born in Lincolnshire, and returned there at the age of twenty-one after some years in London. In Lincolnshire she made contact with John Cotton, and followed him to New England in 1634. In England in 1607 Thomas Rogers was attacking antinomians.[12] Twenty-five years later a number of antinomians were brought before the High Commission. Samuel Pretty of London was charged with preaching that "a believer ought not to be sorrowful for his sins, nor to be grieved for anything". All the effects of sin are taken away for believers. He was imprisoned and degraded from the ministry.[13] Richard Lane, a conventicler, was alleged to have declared that "we are without sin", and that he himself was perfect God and perfect man. His group met at the house of one Westbrook, a tailor of Shoe Lane.[14] Another group of "plain men" were said to hold that justified persons cannot displease God, and that believers were justified before they had actual faith. "To the believer all things are pure": David when he committed adultery pleased God as well as when he danced before the Ark.[15]

In his *Antinomianisme Anatomized* of 1643 John Sedgwick begins his list of antinomians with the name of John Traske.[16] Traske obtained notoriety for his Judaizing opinions. For these Star Chamber in 1618 degraded him from the ministry, and ordered him to be whipped, nailed by the ear to the pillory, branded, fined £1000 and imprisoned for life. (By recanting he obtained his release in 1620, but his wife, made of sterner stuff, remained in jail till the sixteen-forties.)[17] Earlier and later Traske professed antinomian opinions: he was alleged to have said that the truly converted were "as free from sin as Jesus Christ". He ended life as a Baptist. While in prison he wrote a letter to the King in which he "thee'd" and "thou'd" him.[18]

The leading antinomian in this period seems to have been John Eaton, who was also the first antinomian whose works got into print after the liberation of the press in 1640. Eaton was born in Kent, and started his career as curate of St Catherine, Coleman St, a traditional radical area since Lollard times. Later he was vicar of Wickham Market, Suffolk. He was convicted in the High Commission "for preaching ... that God seeth no sin in his elect". In 1632, when John

Ettrall was up before the same court, Laud declared that Eaton was "your patriarch". Ettrall was certainly in touch with Eaton, who wrote urging him to resist — unlike Samuel Pretty, who was alleged to be wavering. In this letter Eaton sent greetings to "Mr. Towne" — possibly Robert Towne; and Laud stated that "one Townes" had held tenets similar to Pretty's.[19] John Cotton in 1635 or 1636 referred to "Mr. Townes of Nottinghamshire" as "a ringleader of that sect" of Familists. The county is wrong, but it is difficult to see who else could have been meant.[20] Robert Towne's whole career was in fact spent on the Yorkshire-Lancashire border in which the Grindletonians flourished and which was to be a centre of Quakerism in the sixteen-fifties. He was ultimately buried in Haworth, the Bronte's parish.[21] Towne declared: "I am a sinner and no sinner. Daily I fall in myself and stand in Christ for ever. My works fail, his never can, and they are also mine". "To faith there is no sin, nor any unclean heart".[22]

II

Because the elect are saved from all eternity, they are uninfluenced by what conservatives saw as the main social function of religion, the maintenance of standards of conduct by fear of penalties or hope of rewards in the after life. The antinomian godly knew their eternal reward was secure. Some few drew libertine conclusions from this — and of course the possibility was always heavily emphasized in the propaganda of their enemies. Other antinomians, conscious of the enormous love God had shown in choosing them, wished to reciprocate by living on earth as God would wish them to live. But this was not from fear of hell or hope of heaven: it was to satisfy their own consciences.

John Eaton was clear on this point. "Where there is any moral work commanded to be done upon pain of punishment, or upon promise of any reward either temporal or eternal, there is to be understood the voice of the Law". Only where promise of salvation is offered freely and unconditionally do we hear the doctrine of the Gospel, whether such promises occur in the Old or the New Testament. "There is no sin in the sight of God".[23] Like Crisp, Eaton was concerned to escape from the revival of justification by works which he saw in the covenant theology, and in particular from "the popish rotten pillar that God accepts the will for the deed".[24]

As the careers of Luther and John Cotton show, the border line between orthodoxy and antinomian heresy was often difficult to draw. Crisp appealed to Calvin against latter-day Calvinists, and so did Cotton.[25] Crisp alleged the authority of William Twisse, Pro-locutor of the Westminster Assembly of Divines, the custodian of authority, for the claim that justification might precede faith.[26] Cotton, defending himself against the attacks of Robert Baillie, also cited "Dr. Twisse (not suspected for an antinomian, much less for a Familist)".[27] So did William Eyre, Wiltshire antinomian.[28] Crisp faced the possible abuse of his doctrine by the licentious, but was himself convinced that the elect could never willingly sin. "The grass and the pasture is so sweet that he [God] put a believer into, that though there be no bounds to keep in such a soul, yet it will never go out of this fat pasture to feed on a barren common".[29]

III

One of the more interesting antinomians is William Walwyn. Unlike most, he accepted the label. "I . . . had long been established in that point of doctrine (called then antinomian) of free justification by Christ alone".[30] Like Crisp, Walwyn emphasized that Christ died for sinners, the ungodly, all the world.[31] "Your present comfort depends upon your believing; . . . yet the work of Christ depends not on your believing". It comes freely to all sinners.[32] Like Crisp too, Walwyn denounced hell-fire preachers with their harrowing effect on sensitive consciences. "Many of you may, through sense of sin and of wrath due for sin, walk in a very disconsolate condition: fears and terrors may abound in you". They are the product of "the grossest antichristian error, to think righteousness comes by the law". Wal-wyn was later to speak of "those yokes of bondage unto which sermons and doctrine mixed of law and gospel do subject distressed consciences".[33] Like Crisp, Walwyn attacked Perkins's doctrine that God accepts the will for the deed. No one "should so much as doubt of your salvation".[34] Neither infidelity nor impenitence nor un-thankfulness nor denying Christ "can separate you from his love".[35] As soon as men realise this they will lead good lives,[36] and — a characteristic Walwyn touch — "will be inflamed to fight against injustice". "True Christians are of all men the most valiant defenders of the just liberties of their country, and the most zealous preservers of true religion".[37] So Walwyn's support for the Levellers seemed to him to follow naturally from his religious principles. Samuel Ruther-ford may have been referring to Walwyn when he said that "sundry antinomians say Irish papists ought to have liberty of conscience".[38]

Like Crisp, Walwyn is ambiguous on the question of whether salvation is offered to all men. In *The Power of Love* he spoke of those liable to eternal death.[39] In *A Whisper in the Eare of Mr. Thomas Edwards, Minister*, Walwyn denied the salvation of all.[40] Yet *The Vanitie of the Present Churches* (1649), which may not be by Walwyn, but which he cited approvingly, speaks of "the love of God which bringeth salvation unto all men".[41] In *Tyranipocrit Discovered* (1649), which some have attributed to Walwyn, we are told that "God accepteth any man that desireth to be good".[42] "Neither doth God give more grace unto one man to be saved than he doth to all and every man".[43] But other theological statements in *Tyranipocrit* make me think it cannot be by Walwyn. The author appears to approve of the doctrine that God accepts the will for the deed, which Walwyn had attacked in *The Power of Love*.[44] The author of *Tyranipocrit* speaks of "working out of their salvation in fear and trembling".[45] "God hath given unto man a free power to will, and till man hath used his willing power in leaving such sins as are in his power to leave, God will not help him".[46] "God's predestination is no forcing power, but a prescience".[47] "He that teacheth an absolute predestination in God of man, without man, he cannot honour God nor comfort man".[48] If Walwyn wrote *Tyranipocrit*, he had abandoned his antinomianism of 1643-4, of which he had spoken without disapproval in May 1649.[49]

Henry Denne is another antinomian who was closely associated with the Levellers, until his recantation after playing a leading role in the Army mutiny which ended at Burford in May 1649 led them to denounce him as "Judas Denne". Although an ordained minister of the Church of England, Denne ultimately became a Baptist preacher. In *The Doctrine and Conversation of John Baptist* (1643) — a visitation sermon "contradicted by many of the auditors" — Denne argued that "the safest way is to say No" when asked "whether a desire to believe be faith itself".[50] "The poor man can tell you that to be rich and to desire to be rich are two things".[51] Two years later he put forward a familiar antinomian position. "God is freely reconciled to the elect, and loveth them in Jesus Christ, without any previous dispositions, without any qualifications, without any performances or conditions on their parts, unless to be polluted and sinful be a previous condition or qualification".[52] Grace was given before the world began, and God's love is just as great before as after our conversion.[53] He did not love us because he foresaw that we would repent and believe.[54] Free grace is a doctrine of liberty. Those who think "it were better to hide this from the people, and to terrify them with hell-fire, with wrath and judgment" aim "to keep them in bondage".[55] (Again the image of political liberty, which the Levellers were to take up.)

Denne was aware that he might "to many seem guilty of that crime which was laid against the Apostle, to turn the world upside down".[56] But he was unconcerned. All false religions, Denne argued, those of Jews, Turks, papists, pharisaical protestants and heathen, all these "propound in some degree or other an angry God", who has to be propitiated. For them, "the world would be saved by doing", not by reliance on Christ. All ask, as Bunyan's Pilgrim was soon to ask, "What shall I do to be saved?" In Denne's view, "there cannot be greater idolatry committed than to conceive a possibility of gaining the love and favour of God by works wrought in the creature".[57] So his was not a religion of doing: one begins to see the force of Winthrop's remark, "most of their tenets tended to sloth-fulness, and quench all endeavour in the creature".[58] This is something rather different from "the protestant ethic". But as early as 1643 Denne's was a socially conscious religion. In a dialogue he made a minister ask a man who claimed to be in a state of grace "Why have you not sold either the whole or half of your possessions and divided it among ... your brethren in great poverty?"[59] It was a theme which Abiezer Coppe and the author of *Tyranipocrit Discovered* were later to take up. Crisp similarly had argued that good works should be performed only because they are profitable to others, not with any idea that they confer merit on the doer.[60] Samuel Gorton asked indignantly "When and where have I lived upon other men's labours and not wrought with mine own hands for things honest in the sight of men?"[61] We recall Milton's slightly shame-faced admission that his "ease and leisure" came "out of the sweat of other men".[62]

In his own day John Saltmarsh, another Yorkshireman, had the greatest reputation of any antinomian. He conditionally accepted the label, though he himself preferred to speak of "free grace".[63] But his reputation was perhaps won by his literary qualities rather than by any novelty in his ideas: and I must say I prefer Walwyn as a writer. But Saltmarsh was also famous, or notorious, for his radical commitment, which culminated in his rising from his death bed and riding across southern England in December 1647 to denounce the generals for departing from God by dividing the Army and suppressing the Agitators.

It is indeed of Walwyn that Saltmarsh reminds us. "Love began all the work of salvation in God";[64] it is God's mercy, not his justice, that Saltmarsh stresses. Like Crisp, Saltmarsh was anxious to deny the allegation that "from free grace there will follow nothing but looseness and libertinism". "If any man sin more freely because of forgiveness of sins, that man may suspect himself to be forgiven".[65] Like Crisp, Walwyn and Denne, Saltmarsh had no use for the doctrine that God accepts the will for the deed: the preacher who "told me my desire to pray was a prayer" did not help him.[66] Saltmarsh had himself been in despair, with temptations to suicide, till he learnt that "no sin can make one less beloved of God or less in Christ".[67] "The promises of Christ are held forth to sinners as sinners, not as repenting sinners or humble sinners, as any condition in us upon which we should challenge Christ".[68] "A person justified, or in covenant, is as perfect in the sight of God as the righteousness of Christ can make him (though not so in his own eyes). ... No sin can make God love us less".[69] "There is no sin to be committed which Christ did not pay down the price of his blood for". A believer is "as free from hell, the law and bondage ... as if he were in heaven".[70]

William Dell's antinomianism is much less central to his thought, but he too proclaimed that we are free from the law and sin.[71] Dell was more interested in the independence of the congregational churches than anything else. "Our union with the church flows from our union with Christ", and not vice versa.[72] "The assemblies of the true church are all equal", and within them all believers are equal.[73] "If every free society hath power to choose its own officers, much more hath the true church, being ... the freest society under heaven".[74] Here we see how ideas about liberty and equality can be freely transferred from the spiritual to the secular sphere.

Thomas Collier, like Dell and Saltmarsh a former Army chaplain, was another man influenced by antinomianism. "As God writes his laws in the hearts of his people", he declared, "so shall they live above the Law in the letter, even of the gospel, yet not without it, for they have it within them, ... and so they are a law to themselves".[75] John Reeve, founder of what was later called Muggletonianism, held that "whosoever hath that true love of God in him, that man hath no need of man's law to be his rule, but he is a law to himself, and lives above all laws of mortal men". "And yet", he added, he "is obedient to all laws".[76] Milton held similar views.[77]

IV

Crisp had been aware that his doctrine could be interpreted as authorizing libertinism.[78] Thomas Shepard thought the ideas of New England antinomians were "mere fig-leaves to cover some distempers and lusts lurking in men's hearts".[79] In England in the mid-forties Samuel Rutherford and Robert Baillie,[80] the English Presbyterians Herbert Palmer, Edmund Calamy, John Sedgwick, Stephen Geree, Thomas Edwards and Thomas Bedford recognized that antinomian doctrines were "most plausible and pleasing to flesh and blood".[81] "Oh it pleaseth nature well, to have heaven and their lusts too", John Winthrop had said apropos New England anti-nomians in the sixteen-thirties.[82] The most frightening thing about antinomianism was indeed its appeal to natural man. It was, Richard Baxter argued, "so easy a way, which flesh and blood hath so little against, as being too consistent with men's carnal interest";[83] so "pleasing to the fleshly mind", said Thomas Symonds in 1657.[84]

Crisp announced that sin was finished.[85] Robert Towne declared in 1644 "if thou believe sin, death and the curse to be abolished, they are abolished".[86] Five years later the Ranter Abiezer Coppe repeated that sin was finished; God's service is "perfect freedom and pure libertinism". But he concluded from this that "I can ... love my neighbour's wife as myself, without sin". He claimed God as "that mighty Leveller".[87] When a very different character from Coppe, John Bunyan, declared that "no sin shall frustrate or make election void", he added: "the world, when they hear that God would have mercy offered in the first place to the biggest sinners, will be apt to think that this is a doctrine that leads to looseness and gives liberty to the flesh".[88] Bunyan had known Ranters in his younger days, and his ideas were perhaps sometimes closer to those of an antinomian like Crisp than is always recognized.

Laurence Clarkson was influenced by Crisp. He tried to become one of those in whom God saw no sin — or so he tells us.[89] In 1647 he wrote a Leveller tract. Two years later he was "Captain of the Rant", systematizing the ideas which critics of the antinomians had most feared. "There is no such act as drunkenness, adultery and theft in God", he wrote. "Sin hath its conception only in the imagination. . . . Which act soever is done by thee in light and love, is light and lovely, though it be that act called adultery. ... No matter what Scripture, saints or churches say, if that within thee do not condemn thee, thou shalt not be condemned".[90] He even claimed that "none can be free from sin till in purity it be acted as no sin".[91] The Ranter John Robins authorized his disciples to change their spouses, changing his own wife "for an example".[92] Samuel Gorton expressed a common Ranter view when he said that the clergy conspired "to press the poorer sort with the burdens of sins, and such abundance of servile obedience as to make them slaves to themselves and others".[93]

V

Now that we have seen the full development of antinomianism in the freedom of the sixteen-forties in England, it may be helpful to look back at its first appearance in New England in the thirties. "The late stirs in the New England churches, occasioned by Master Wheelwright, Master Hutchinson and their followers", an opponent of antinomianism declared, were greatly influenced by the "tenet 'No condition in the covenant', ... if it were not the main cause thereof".[94] Most English antinomian doctrines were present in embryo in the case of Anne Hutchinson — either taught by her or her adherents, or attributed to her by her enemies. She and her brother-in-law, the Rev John Wheelwright, "inveighed against all that walked in the covenant of works", among whom Mrs Hutchinson included many of the ministers.[95]

John Winthrop summarized "their opinions", clearly referring to wider circles than the supporters of Mrs Hutchinson and Wheelwright. Many of his points were to become familiar in England in the sixteen-forties. "No. 9: to question my assurance, though I fall into murder or adultery, proves that I never had true assurance".[96] "No. 18: God loves a man never the better for any holiness in him, and never the less, be he never so unholy. No. 19: Sin in a child of God must never trouble him".[97] Error 20 condemned by the New England churches was "to call in question whether God be my dear Father, after or upon the commission of some heinous sins (as murder, incest, etc.), doth prove a man to be in the covenant of works".[98] Among "unsavoury speeches" Winthrop cited: "I may know I am Christ's, not because I do crucify the lusts of the flesh, but because I do not crucify them, but believe in Christ that crucified my lusts for me". Unsavoury speech (2) suggested that "to evidence justification by sanctification or graces, savours of Rome".[99] One of Wheelwright's disciples was alleged to have said that the commandments ". . . were a dead letter . . .".[100] Mrs Hutchinson was accused of holding that "the law is no rule of life to a Christian". "Not being bound to the law, it is not transgression against the law to sin, or break it, because our sins they are inward and spiritual . . . and only are against Christ".[101] Error 49: "we are not bound to keep a constant course of prayer in our families or privately, unless the spirit stir us up thereunto".[102]

Winthrop did not fail to recall "the tragedy of Münster", which "gave just occasion to fear the danger we were in".[103] Peter Bulkeley provided this familiar slander with a theological basis by arguing that if our union with Christ were the only resurrection, "then all that are united are the children of the resurrection, and therefore are neither to marry nor to give in marriage, and so by consequence there ought to be community of women" — "that foul, gross, filthy and abominable opinion held by the Familists". It seems a far-fetched conclusion, but it shows the acute awareness of the ministers that a good man's theological theory may become a lewd man's immoral practice. Mrs Hutchinson, who did not deny that "we are united to Christ with the same union that his humanity on earth was with the deity",[104] indignantly repudiated the sexual consequences which Bulkeley asserted. But Cotton — once her friend — repeated it in his formal admonition to her on behalf of the church. That union with Christ amounted to a resurrection in this life was an "argument . . . which the Anabaptists and Familists use" to "set an open door to all epicureanism and libertinism".[105]

A further charge against Mrs Hutchinson was the heresy of mortalism, shared in England by Richard Overton the Leveller, Milton, Ranters and Muggletonians. Mrs Hutchinson admitted this accusation. She also admitted to having revelations: "if she had not a sure word that England should be destroyed her heart would shake" when she saw the "meanness" of New England.[106] "These disturbances that have come among the Germans", commented Deputy-Governor Dudley, "have been all grounded upon revelation".[107]

Samuel Gorton, who survived to sum up New England antinomianism, thought that "every believer, Godded, deified and anointed with the spirit, is Christ".[108] Heaven was to be found on earth in the hearts of men.[109] He questioned the existence of sin, suggesting that it had been invented by the privileged in order to control the lower classes.[110]

VI

Antinomianism drew on strong protestant traditions going back to Luther; it was anti-catholic and anti-Laudian. Its appeal to the individual conscience of those who felt themselves to be the elect was well calculated to attract members of congregations which had just come up from underground, or were newly formed around some charismatic mechanic preacher. It was, as an anonymous pamphlet of 1644 put it, a "doctrine of liberty".[111] "The antinomians were commonly Independents" Baxter wrote — much later, it is true.[112]

Antinomianism indeed cannot be divorced from the context of mid-seventeenth century England. Its adherents faced political problems; and their theology led many of them to radical conclusions. Until the breakdown of 1640 consensus politics had prevailed, at least among those who were able to express opinions. Since there was no police force, no absolute monarchy whose policies could be enforced by an Army and a bureaucracy, society was held together by the consent of "the political nation", of those gentry and merchants whose wealth and status gave them authority in normal times.

But stresses had been developing with the great economic divide of the two generations before 1640. Among the unprivileged classes the rich were getting richer, the poor poorer. It may well be that Sir Thomas More was right to see all commonwealths as conspiracies of the rich to oppress the poor,[113] but the legal aspects of this tyranny became more obvious with the development of the poor law, laws against vagrants, cottagers, etc. The bland Richard Hooker could claim that "laws they are not which public approbation hath not made so",[114] but this was consensus among the beneficiaries of society, J.Ps. and parish élites, and even as Hooker wrote it was wearing thin. Mr Tim Curtis has spoken of Elizabeth's government as "a beleaguered garrison"; Ralegh called J.Ps. "the garrisons of good order throughout the realm".[115] Well and good, so long as the garrison held together; but the sixteen-twenties saw a polarization, not only for or against the King's government, but also on attitudes towards poverty.[116] The traditional political consensus no longer seemed to work. The ultimate answer was that of Hobbes: law is the command of the sovereign, who is sovereign because he has power; and later still when consensus was restored again, law derives from

the social contract agreed by "the people", who are sharply differentiated from the poor.[117] But such ideas were far ahead in 1640.
What had men to hold on to?

Respect for the law — perhaps for a purged and purified law, not
for the actual law administered by Charles I's judges — is something
which historians cite as characteristic of Englishmen in the seventeenth century, just as they speak of "ages of faith", meaning the ages
from which nearly all surviving records were written by churchmen.
But as soon as men were free to speak, this respect for law seems to be
confined to the possessing classes. "Our very laws were made by our
conquerors", said Wildman in the Putney Debates. "The old kings'
laws", Winstanley agreed, "were the laws of a conqueror to hold the
people in subjection".[118] The young Milton had longed to be rid of
"this Norman gibberish".[119] Hence the continued opposition of the
propertied classes to suggestions that the law might be reformed.
Any questioning of its immemorial authority seemed to them risky.

The keystone of the arch holding propertied society together, as
both James I and Wentworth pointed out, was the King — an
anointed, semi-divine figure, aloof and intangible, above the law
which he enforced. From this point of view the greatest error of the
revolutionaries was to execute Charles I when he refused to accept
the position of constitutional monarch. Charles played magnifi-
cently on this stop at his trial — if power without law can do this to
the King, who is safe? — and so ensured Charles II's restoration in
1660 as the sanction of a deferential society — though by now the
King had accepted that he was above neither the law nor those who
enforced it.

Not only the law of Moses but all human laws were inapplicable to
the elect. Antinomianism thus helped to undermine the mystique of
law and of power. Its attractiveness to the unprivileged, to "natural
man", was very early revealed. The speculative theology of Brearley,
Eaton and Crisp was soon transformed by these popular overtones,
which Traske had foreshadowed. With the breakdown of traditional
controls after 1640, antinomian doctrines easily fused with the
radical tradition, which certainly goes back to sixteenth-century
Familists and perhaps to fifteenth-century Lollards.[120] Perfection is
attainable on earth, believers can be in heaven in this life. All men can
be saved, God is in all men, all men are Sons of God.[121] Consequently
all men can be above the law.

Antinomianism could appeal to very different social groups, who had in common only a feeling that the existing law thwarted their activities. For Anne Hutchinson and her female adherents in New England, it has been suggested, antinomianism was "an ideology through which the resentments they [women] felt could be focused and actively expressed".[122] Bernard Baylin suggested that support for Mrs Hutchinson came predominantly from merchants, and it seems clear that, although she had lower-class supporters, some of her partisans were well-to-do men who opposed the regulation of commerce in the interests of consumers and farmers and wanted greater freedom to use their elbows.[123] We may recall that Tobias Crisp came from a very rich merchant family and that in Barbados planters equated Independency with free trade.[124]

The accusation which contemporaries brought against antinomians was rather different. Their doctrine provided an excuse for the "slothful" to escape the demands of the law, said Thomas Shepard.[125] Winthrop agreed: "their way of life was made easy; if so, no marvel so many like of it". Hence its popularity in London among "carnal and vile persons". "Oh, it pleaseth nature well to have heaven and their lusts too". Mrs Hutchinson's was "a very easy and acceptable way to heaven, to see nothing, to have nothing, but to wait for Christ to do all". It appealed to "many profane persons" as well as to women.[126] "In the ordinary course of [God's] dispensation", the New England Synod told Mrs Hutchinson, "the more we endeavour, the more assistance and help we find from him".[127] Rejection of "the protestant ethic" suggests a plebeian version of antinomianism, such as was to flourish in England. John Trapp tells an anecdote of an antinomian servant girl who denied any personal responsibility for stealing: it was sin in her.[128] "The antinomian doctrine", wrote Baxter, "is the very same in almost every point which I find naturally fastened in the hearts of the common profane multitude".[129]

VII

When liberty of conscience was affected, the antinomian impulse led men to associate with other groupings to achieve political ends. But in general antinomianism was a dissolvent rather than a positive political creed. There was never a sect of antinomians. Their doctrine imposed no external constraints on the way in which they should act; they had no predetermined or planned political programme. Their liberty, like Milton's, was a negative liberty.[130]

Walwyn decided that discussion was a more important part of religious worship than preaching; like the antinomian Milton he advocated liberty of the press.[131] With Clarkson and Denne he supported the Levellers. Richard Overton, later a Leveller like Walwyn, attacked the dogma of universal human depravity and insisted that Christ died for all.[132] The anonymous pamphlet *Vox Plebis*, variously attributed to Overton and to Henry Marten, near-Leveller M.P., affirmed that "God created every man free in Adam: so by nature are all alike freemen born, and since made free in grace by Christ".[133] "The interest of the people in Christ's Kingdom", wrote John Saltmarsh, "is not only an interest of compliancy and obedience and submission, but of consultation, of debating, counselling, prophesying, voting, etc. And let us stand fast in the liberty wherewith Christ hath made us free".[134] William Dell drew less democratic but more revolutionary conclusions. If "the things of God" are determined "by the plurality of votes, . . . the greater part still overcomes the better". "According to our new or second birth . . . there is exact equality"; to faith nothing is impossible.[135] So antinomianism justified military dictatorship. An intense urge to secure freedom for the consciences of the elect was combined with considerable pragmatism about the means by which this freedom was to be attained.

So although contemporaries often linked antinomians with Levellers, antinomians who did not believe that God is in all men could justify minority dictatorship. Fifth Monarchist insurrection, Digger communism, the petty Hobbism of the Muggletonians, could all be so defended. After 1649, as the radicals lost their basis of popular support, their only hope seemed to lie in giving power to a godly minority. "How can the kingdom be the saints' when the ungodly are electors and elected to govern?" one of them pertinently asked in 1649.[136] Barebone's Parliament in 1653 failed to provide a solution. Milton was still trying to grapple with the problem in 1659-60.

Part of the difficulty was something which Crisp and Milton at least always shirked. Who are the elect whose freedom must be guaranteed? How are the unregenerate to be controlled? Crisp and Walwyn often speak as if grace was offered to all men.[137] Did they mean it? There were those who argued, in the words of John Goodwin, that "Christ . . . died intentionally to save all the posterity of Adam".[138] In controversies in Wiltshire in the sixteen-fifties antinomians and their opponents accused each other of opening the door to universal redemption.[139] Failure to ask such questions, still more to answer them, increased the liability of antinomianism to fragment when doctrines of universal grace and political democracy came to the fore. Intellectual antinomianism was essentially an élitist creed, calling for liberty for the elect. But the intensity of feeling about the necessity of such liberty tended to spill over into universal statements, just as many Parliamentarians called for liberty for "the people" when they were far from including the whole population in that undefined phrase.[140] So Milton in 1644 declared that "now the time seems come, wherein ... all the Lord's people are become prophets".[141] Nothing must be suppressed, lest God's truth should be lost. "The true church", wrote Dell in 1649, "is a kingdom of prophets", for Christ lives in his elect. In this church the learned have no advantage over the unlearned.[142]

Antinomianism was always potential within Puritan protestantism. It attended on Calvinism like a shadow. But the antinomian moment, like the universalist moment, was short-lived. The theoretical antinomianism of the theologians could fuse with traditional heretical doctrines only in conditions of upheaval, of revolution. Larzer Ziff suggested that New England antinomianism relied heavily on belief that the millennium was imminent.[143] Its supersession as millenarian hopes faded was perhaps natural, though the decline of popular antinomianism seems in fact to have occurred before Fifth Monarchism reached its peak. Richard Baxter modestly took some credit for this decline to "those ungrateful controversial writings of my own".[144]

Looking back, we can see why respectable contemporaries attached such importance to having only one religion in a society. More than one religion could lead to more than one centre of political power — as Hobbes noted. This was the case in France between the Edict of Nantes and Richelieu's suppression of the Huguenots' fortified towns: after that the Edict could be repealed whenever the government wished. This illuminates the importance which Bancroft, Elizabeth and James attached to getting the oath of allegiance accepted by as many papists as possible; it explains the danger seen in any foreign protection of recusants (or of Huguenots in France). It explains too the hostility of the radicals to the clergy who accepted a monopoly state church, and to the universities which trained them.[145]

The political and ideological exhaustion of the sixteen-fifties testifies to recognition of the magnitude of the task of totally reconstituting the ideas and institutions of society. It was too much for one generation. The changes ultimately came about by gradualist means after the revolutionaries had been defeated. They could come because the key institutions had been overthrown in 1641. There was insufficient agreement among those who criticized the old law, the old church. It was easier to unite the anti-revolutionaries than the revolutionaries.

The nonconformists' recognition that Christ's kingdom was not of this world was an acceptance of the fact that the elect could not be identified on earth, or at any rate that the visible elect would not challenge the laws of the state. The spiritual was segregated from the secular.[146] The restricted sphere of religion which this implied, the withdrawal of the clergy from aspirations to political power, brings us into the modern world.

Historians — myself included[147] — have perhaps been too apt to dwell on the sexual consequences of antinomianism — following too closely the emphases of contemporaries. Coppe and Clarkson are exceptionally quotable. But this is I think a mistake, comparable with the error which emphasizes the polygamy of the Münster Anabaptists to the exclusion of their other ideas and activities. Coppe and Clarkson, after all, were both highly political thinkers: sexual libertinism was only one part of their radical ideology. Such antinomians as Crisp, Walwyn, Denne and Saltmarsh (and many others) appear to have drawn no libertine conclusions from their similar starting point. The monogamous family was very important to the social stability of working householders. Immoralists were aristocratic rakes or the poor.

More important, perhaps, was the antinomian challenge to laws and institutions, though this lasted only as long as the political and social crisis lasted, whilst Cromwell was asking "What if a man should take it upon him to be King?" and others were looking to King Jesus to save them from King Oliver. When antinomians had an arbitrary sword in their hands, everybody else cried out for law. Harrington was right when he said that the call for restoration of monarchy in England was really a demand for restoration of known laws.[148] Popular antinomianism was permanent revolution reduced to the absurd: no accepted sanctions, no known authorities, no limits: and yet no agreement among the permanent revolutionaries. Antinomianism extended the principle of the priesthood of all believers to the kingship of all believers, the absolute sovereignty of the individual conscience. "Then every Christian in a commonwealth must be king and sheriff and captain and Parliament-man and ruler", snorted Edward Winslow.[149]

The question, as Albertus Warren put it, was not "whether we should be governed by arbitrary power, but in whose hands it should be".[150] "Better the Grand Turk than the rabble rout", an Independent observed in 1650.[151] The replacement of monarchy by military rule produced few lasting benefits for most of the population, and was much more expensive than any form of government previously known. The return to monarchy, to bishops, to the natural rulers, was also a return to belief in sin. Perfection, men discovered the hard way, was not to be found in this vale of tears.

NOTES

1. This piece is a by-product of Chapters 8 and 9 above.
2. [Anon], *A Declaration against the Antinomians and their Doctrine of Liberty* (1644), quoted by Gertrude M. Huehns, *Antinomianism in English History. With special reference to the period 1649-1660* (1951), p. 8. I have not always made specific references to this pioneering book, but I found it immensely useful in writing this essay, especially in directing me to sources.
3. See my *Change and Continuity in 17th-century England*, Chapter 3.
4. Martin Luther, *Thirty-four sermons* (trans. William Grace, 1747), p. 281; H. Haydn, *The Counter-Renaissance* (New York, 1950), p. 485. See pp. 170-1 above.
5. Rutherford, *A Survey of the Spirituall Antichrist* (1648), p. 87.
6. W. Eyre, *Vindiciae Justificationis Gratuitae: Justification without Conditions* (1654), Sig. a 3; cf. Sig. a 4v.
7. For the Grindletonians see p. 149 above, and *W.T.U.D.*, pp. 81-5. Baxter said there were links between William Hacket, executed in 1591, and the Grindletonians: see G.F. Nuttall, *The Holy Spirit in Puritan Faith and Experience* (Oxford, 1946), pp. 178-9. For Hacket see pp. 73, 84, 96 above.
8. "Autobiography of Thomas Shepard", *Publications of the Colonial Soc. of Massachusetts*, XXVII (1927-30), pp. 362-3.
9. Nuttall, *op. cit.*, p. 179.
10. Philip F. Gura, "The Radical Ideology of Samuel Gorton: New Light on the Relation of English to American Puritanism". *William and Mary Quarterly*, XXXVI (1979), pp. 80-1.
11. Hall, *The Antinomian Controversy*, p. 398.
12. T. Rogers, *The Faith, Doctrine and Religion, Professed and Protected in*

the Realm of England (Cambridge U.P. 1681), p. 39. First published 1607.

13. Ed. S. R. Gardiner, *Reports of Cases in the Courts of Star Chamber and High Commission* (Camden Soc., 1886), pp. 182-5, 275, 316-21.

14. *Ibid.*, pp. 191-4, 269, 275.

15. *Ibid.*, pp. 270-1, 313-14.

16. Sedgwick, *op. cit.*, p. 1; cf. p. 26.

17. *C.S.P.D.*, *1639*, pp. 466-7; cf. p. 40 above.

18. B. R. White, "John Traske (1585-1636) and London Puritanism", *Baptist Quarterly*, XX (1968), pp. 223-33; D.S. Katz, *Philo-Semitism and the Readmission of the Jews to England* (Oxford U.P., 1982), pp. 8-34.

19. *Ibid.*, pp. 316-21, 186. Wood says that Eaton died in 1641, but it was probably earlier. For Eaton see pp. 149-51 above, and Rutherford, *The Tryal &Triumph of Faith*, pp. 147-8; for Towne, *ibid.*, pp. 23-4, 114.

20. Hall, *op. cit.*, p. 32.

21. *W.T.U.D.*,p. 216; Nuttall, *op. cit.*, p. 179.

22. Towne, *The Assurance of Grace* (1644), pp. 40, 71; Rutherford, *A Modest Survey of the Secrets of Antinomianism*, p. 25, in *A Survey of the Spirituall Antichrist*. Cf. also p. 151 above.

23. Eaton, *The Honey-comb of free justification*, pp. 65-6, 62-3.

24. Eaton, *The Discovery of the most dangerous dead Faith* (1641), pp. 62-3.

25. Hall, *op. cit.*, p. 188; cf. E. Battis, *Saints and Sectaries: Anne Hutchinson and the Antinomian Controversy in the Massachusetts Bay Colony* (North Carolina U.P., 1962), pp. 18, 33. For departures from Calvinism by later "Calvinists", see Kendall, *Calvin and English Calvinists to 1649*, passim.

26. Cf. Crisp, *Fifty-Two Sermons*, pp. vi-vii.

27. Hall, *op. cit.*, p. 409; cf. Battis, *op. cit.*, p. 171.

28. Eyre, *op. cit.*, pp. 22, 174; T. Hotchkis, *An Exercitation Concerning the Nature and Forgiveness of Sin* (1655), p. 219. For Eyre see p. 153 above.

29. Crisp, *Christ Alone Exalted*, p. 39.

30. *Walwyns Just Defence* (1649), in Haller and Davies, *op. cit.*, p. 361; cf. *A Whisper in the Eare of Mr. Thomas Edwards, Minister* (1646), p. 6, in Haller, *Tracts on Liberty*, III, and *The Power of Love* (1643), Sig. A 5v., *ibid.*, II.

31. *The Power of Love*, pp. 24-5, 31.

32. *Ibid.*, pp. 32, 35; cf. *Walwyns Just Defence:* "God putteth away our sins out of his remembrance" (*op. cit.*, p. 378).

33. *The Power of Love*, pp. 19-22; *Walwyns Just Defence*, p. 361. He was replying to *Walwyns Wiles* (1649), in which he had been accused of rejecting prayer and Sabbath observance (Haller and Davies, *op. cit.*, p. 297).

34. *The Power of Love*, pp. 21, 27-8.

35. *Ibid.*, p. 30.

36. *Ibid.*, pp. 35-40.

37. *Ibid.*, pp. 39-41. Cf. *A Whisper in the Eare:* "I esteem it a high point of true religion to promote common justice" (p. 5).

38. S. Rutherford, *A Modest Survey of the Secrets of Antinomianism*, pp. 176-7.

39. *The Power of Love*, p. 18.

40. *Op. cit.*, in Haller, *Tracts on Liberty*, III, p. 327.

41. In Haller and Davies, *op. cit.*, p. 266.

42. *Op. cit.*, in *British Pamphleteers*, Vol. I, p. 94.

43. *Ibid.*, p. 110.

44. *Ibid.*, p. 92. Contrast *The Power of Love*, p. 21.

45. *British Pamphleteers*, p. 92.

46. *Ibid.*, p. 98.

47. *Ibid.*, p. 110.

48. *Ibid.*, p. 112. "He that saith that the mercy of God endureth for ever, and yet that it may fail a man in this life, *if he seeketh it*, maintaineth an absurd paradox" (*ibid.*, p. 111). The words I have italicized are hardly those of an antinomian.

49. *Walwyns Just Defence*, p. 361; cf. p. 378.

50. Denne, *op. cit.*, p. 51. Rutherford attacks Denne in *The Tryal & Triumph of Faith*, pp. 169, 287-91.

51. Denne, *A Conference Between a sick man and a minister*, p. 2.

52. Denne, *Grace, Mercy and Peace* (1645), printed in *Records of the Churches of Christ gathered at Fenstanton, Warboys and Hexham, 1644-1720* (ed. E. B. Underhill, Hanserd Knollys Soc., 1854), p. 378.

53. *Ibid.*, pp. 380, 384.

54. *Ibid.*, p. 388.

55. *Ibid.*, p. 398.

56. *Ibid.*, p. 422.

57. *Ibid.*, pp. 400-2.

58. Winthrop, *A Short Story of the Rise, raign and ruine of the Familists and Libertines* (1644), p. 32.

59. Denne, *A Conference Between a sick man and a minister*, p. 8.

60. See pp. 143-5 above.

61. Gura, *A Glimpse of Sion's Glory*, p. 93.

62. *M.C.P.W.*, I, p. 804.

63. Saltmarsh, *An End of One Controversie* (1646), p. 116; *Free Grace* (10th edn. 1700), Sig. A 3.

64. *Free Grace*, Epistle Dedicatory.

65. *Ibid.*, Sig. A 3.

66. *Ibid.*, pp. 22-3, 28-9.

67. *Ibid.*, pp. 47-8, 67.

68. *Ibid.*, p. 86.

69. *Ibid.*, p. 104.

70. *Ibid.*, p. 111. For Saltmarsh see A. L. Morton, *The World of the Ranters* (1970), pp. 45-69. Thomas Gataker's *Antinomianism Discovered and Captured* (1652) is directed against Saltmarsh: "Mr. Eaton's spirit seems to be revived in this man" (Sig. A2v, pp. 1, 35, and *passim*).

71. Dell, *The Crucified and Quickened Christian* (1652), in *Several Sermons*, pp. 316-18, 327-8.

72. Dell, *The Way of True Peace and Unity* (1649), in *Several Sermons*, p. 190.
73. *Ibid.*, pp. 192, 266-7.
74. *Ibid.*, pp. 246.
75. T. Collier, *The Marrow of Christianity* (1647), p. 68.
76. John Reeve, *A Divine Looking-Glass* (3rd edn., 1719), pp. 56-7. First published 1656.
77. See pp. 153-4 above. Cf John Smith: "It is not anything a man can do that makes him more or less beloved of God" (*Soul Reviving Influence of the Sun of Righteousness*, 1654, pp. 107-8, 160, 178-80).
78. See pp. 147-8, 155 above.
79. Gura, *A Glimpse of Sion's Glory*, p. 53.
80. Rutherford, *A Sermon Preached to the Honourable House of Commons* (1644), pp. 32-7; *A Survey of the Spirituall Antichrist, passim:* Baillie, *Satan the Leader in chief* (1643-4), pp. 25-6; *A Disswasive from the Errours of the Time, passim*.
81. Palmer, *The Glasse of Gods Providence* (1644), pp. 54-5; Calamy, *Englands Antidote*, pp. 1-19; John Sedgwick, *Antinomianism Anatomized, passim*; Edwards, *Gangraena, passim*; Bedford, *An Examination of the chief points of Antinomianism* (1647), *passim*; Geree, *The Doctrine of the Antinomians Confuted* (1644), Sig. A.2.
82. Winthrop, *A Short Story*, in Hall, *The Antinomian Controversy*, p. 204.
83. *Richard Baxters Confession of Faith* (1655), p. 3.
84. Symonds, *The Voice of the Just* (1657), pp. 3-4, quoted by Watts, *The Dissenters*, p. 202; cf. pp. 123-5, 147 above.
85. See pp. 144-5 above.
86. Towne, *The Assertion of Grace*, p. 73.
87. Coppe, *A Fiery Flying Roll*, I, pp. 1-5, 11. Cf Crisp, pp. 146-9 above, and pp. 329-30 below.
88. Bunyan, *Works*, I, p. 163.
89. Clarkson, *The Lost sheep Found*, p. 9.
90. Clarkson, *A Single Eye*, pp. 8-12, 16; Cf. *A Generall Charge* (1647), *passim*. This doctrine had been anticipated by a group of "plain men" in 1632 (see p. 164 above).
91. Clarkson, *The Lost sheep Found*, p. 24; cf. Bauthumley, quoted on p. 151 above.
92. J. Reeve, *A Transcendent Spiritual Treatise* (1711), p. 12. First published 1652.
93. Gorton, *An Antidote against the Common Plague of the World* (1655), quoted by Gura, *op. cit.*, pp. 298-9; cf. pp. 85-6. See p. 210 below.
94. John Graile, *A Modest Vindication of the Doctrine of Conditions in the Covenant* (1655), p. 93. Graile was minister at Tidworth, Wilts.
95. Hall, *op. cit.*, p. 7.
96. *Ibid.*, p. 202.
97. *Ibid.*, p. 203.
98. *Ibid.*, p. 224.
99. *Ibid.*, pp. 244. Cf. Crisp, p. 143 above.

100. *Ibid*, p. 278.
101. *Ibid.*, pp. 302-3, 352. Parallels could be found in almost any antinomian.
102. *Ibid.*, p. 232.
103. *Ibid.*, pp. 275, 304-5, 362-3.
104. *Ibid.*, p. 302.
105. *Ibid.*, pp. 363, 371-2.
106. *Ibid.*, pp. 216, 301, 304, 338. She also quoted Thomas Hooker's claim that "it was revealed to me that England should be destroyed", which derived from Hooker's *The Danger of Desertion: A Farewell Sermon* preached in 1641 before he left for New England. Revelations seem to have been no necessary part of English antinomianism; but Winstanley and Reeve also claimed to have had them, and Milton was visited nightly by his Muse.
107. Hall, *op. cit.*, p. 343. Dudley can hardly have thought this an explanation of the Thirty Years War. I suspect he was looking back to Münster again.
108. Gura, *op. cit.*, p. 294.
109. *Ibid.*, p. 89; cf. pp. 298-9.
110. *Ibid.*, pp. 85-6. Gorton's adherents were described as "not learned men" (L. Ziff, *Puritanism in America: New Culture in a New World*, New York, 1973, p. 95).
111. [Anon]. *A Declaration against the antinomians and their doctrine of liberty;* cf. Crisp, *Christ Alone Exalted*, Vol. III, p. 359.
112. *Reliquiae Baxterianae*, p. 111.
113. Sir T. More, *Utopia* (Everyman edn.), p. 112.
114. R. Hooker, *op. cit.*, I, p. 194.
115. I owe the phrase to discussions with Mr Curtis; Sir Walter Ralegh, *Works* (1751), II, p. 320.
116. Cf. B. Manning, *The English People and the English Revolution*, Chapter 6.
117. See my "The Poor and the People in 17th-century England", in *Political and Social Ideas in 17th-century England* (forthcoming).
118. Woodhouse, *op. cit.*, p. 65; Winstanley, *The Law of Freedom and Other Writings* (Cambridge U.P., 1983), p. 283.
119. See *M.E.R.*, pp. 100-1.
120. See Chapter 7 above.
121. Gura, *op. cit.*, p. 93. Gura notes that so well-informed a theologian as Roger Williams linked Gorton with the Familists (*ibid.*, p. 94), as Cotton did the Hutchinsonians (p. 164 above).
122. L. Koehler, "The Case of the American Jezebels: Anne Hutchinson and Female Agitation During the Years of the Antinomian Turmoils", *William and Mary Quarterly*, XXXI (1974), pp. 57-63.
123. B. Bailyn, *New England Merchants* (Harvard U.P. 1955), p. 40; L. Ziff, *Puritanism in America*, pp. 75-77; E. Battis, *Saints and Sectaries*, pp. 102-3. See G. F. Nuttall, *The Holy Spirit*, pp. 178-80, for links between the Hutchinsonians and the Quakers.
124. See my "Radical Pirates?", in *The Origins of Anglo-American Radicalism* (ed. M. and J. Jacob, 1984), Chapter 1.

125. Hall, *op. cit.*, p.18.
126. Hall, *op. cit.*, pp.204, 264.
127. Quoted by Perry Miller, *The New England Mind: from Colony to Province* (Harvard U.P., 1953), p.56.
128. J. Trapp, *Commentaries on the New Testament* (Evansville, 1958), p.501. First published 1647. For the appeal of "slothful" ideologies to those whom their betters believed to be the labouring classes, see *W.T.U.D.*, p.326.
129. *Richard Baxters Confutation of a Dissertation for the Justification of Infidels* (1654), p.288, quoted by Lamont, *op. cit.*, p.128; cf. p.143; Baxter, *The Holy Commonwealth*, pp.65, 92, 103, 203, 226-8.
130. *M.E.R.*, pp.262-7.
131. Walwyn, *The Vanitie of the Present Churches* (1649), in Haller and Davies, *op. cit.*, p.273.
132. R.O., *Mans Mortalitie* (Amsterdam, 1644). I quote from the reprint edited by H. Fisch (Liverpool U.P., 1968), pp.8-9.
133. *Vox Plebis* (1646), p.4.
134. Saltmarsh, *The Smoke in the Temple* (1646), p.184. Samuel Gorton published in 1655 *Saltmarsh Returned from the Dead*. Cf. A. L. Morton, *The World of the Ranters*, pp.60, 68.
135. Dell, *Sermons*, pp.253, 266, 342-3.
136. [Anon.], *Certaine Queries Presented by many Christian People* (1649), in Woodhouse, *Puritanism and Liberty*, p.246.
137. Crisp, *Fifty-Two Sermons*, pp.114, 213; cf. pp.202-3; for Walwyn see pp.166-9 above.
138. J. Goodwin, *Truths Conflict with Error* (1650), p.28.
139. Cf. W. Eyre, *op. cit.*, p.84.
140. See my "The Poor and the People", in *Political and Social Ideas in 17th-century England*.
141. *M.C.P.W.*, II, pp.355-6; cf. I, p.14.
142. Dell, *Sermons*, pp.275-6.
143. Ziff, *The Career of John Cotton* (Princeton U.P., 1962), p.156.
144. *Reliquiae Baxterianae*, p.111. In retrospect Baxter sounds almost sympathetic to antinomianism here. Perhaps he has been edited.
145. See chapters 2 and 4 above.
146. Woodhouse, *Puritanism and Liberty*, Introduction, *passim*.
147. Especially in *W.T.U.D.*
148. *The Political Works of James Harrington* (ed. J. G. A. Pocock, Cambridge U.P., 1977), p.49.
149. Winslow, *Hypocrisie Unmasked* (1646), p.44, quoted by Gura, *op. cit.*, p.81. Winslow was attacking Gorton.
150. Warren, *Eight Reasons Categorical* (1653), p.5.
151. John Price, *The Cloudie Clergy* (1650), p.14.

11. *The Religion of Gerrard Winstanley*[1]

"Some others of this age, by a new art of levelling, think nothing can be rightly mended or reformed unless the whole piece ravel out to the very end ... Say they, the law enslaves one sort of people to another. The clergy and gentry have got their freedom, but the common people are still servants to work for the other ... I wonder not so much at this sort of arguing as to find that they who have such sort of arguments should have spades in their hands ... *

I

INTRODUCTION

There have been two approaches to the religion of Gerrard Winstanley. One has stressed the modernity of his ideas, relating them forward to nineteenth- and twentieth-century socialism. In this perspective his theology seems relatively unimportant, the main problem being to explain how he broke sufficiently loose from the religious ideas with which he started to arrive at conclusions which are unprecedented in the seventeenth century. The other approach stresses the continuity of Winstanley's ideas, and sees him primarily as a religious thinker, whose communist ideas were the result of a mystical experience and of his study of the Bible. The digging at St George's Hill was "symbolic" rather than political.[2]

Each approach removes Winstanley from his historical context. The first exaggerates the break between the early ("mystical") and the later ("rationalist") Winstanley.[3] Adherents of the second view have rightly denied that Winstanley was a "seventeenth-century Marxist", though I do not know that anyone ever suggested he was.

---

* Anthony Ascham, *Of the Confusions and Revolutions of Governments* (1649), pp. 18-19. This clear reference to the Diggers was contained in a chapter added to the first version of Ascham's pamphlet, *A Discourse Wherein is examined, What is particularly lawfull during the Confusions and Revolutions of Government* (1648). This chapter, significantly, was entitled "The Originall of Property".

The second approach fails to emphasize the profoundly heretical nature of Winstanley's religion, and the extent to which he threatened the traditional orthodoxy of his time; and it underestimates the seriousness of the Diggers' political motivation. It leads to what Professor Hudson called "a mystifying paradox": "if the new order was dependent on God's decision, why should Winstanley embark upon a programme of practical action?" Professor Hudson's rather weak explanation is that the digging was intended as a "sign" demanding attention from the Lord.[4] Each of these approaches seems to me unsatisfactory, because Winstanley is treated in isolation. My object is first to relate him to the radical and heretical ideas of his predecessors and contemporaries, and then to show in what respects he broke away from them and was truly original.[5]

Historians pay perhaps too little attention to Winstanley's earlier pamphlets, and indeed they must yield in interest to those which deal with the digging and Winstanley's communism. Nevertheless many of his later ideas are already present in the early theological tracts, which seem to have been the more popular. There were two editions each of *The Breaking of the Day of God, The Mysterie of God, The Saints Paradise* and *Truth Lifting Up its Head above Scandals*. These four together with *The New Law of Righteousness* were reprinted, with a separate introduction, in *Several Pieces Gathered into One Volume* (December 1649). Eight years later the same pamphlets (except for *Truth Lifting up its Head*) were listed by William London in his *Catalogue of the Most Vendible Books in England*, whose object was to bring culture to the north.[6]

Part II of what follows briefly summarizes Winstanley's ideas as they had matured in his first four tracts. Part III relates these ideas to those of Winstanley's radical contemporaries and predecessors. Part IV discusses his conversion to communism, and Part V the evolution of his ideas after that turning-point. Part VI discusses some points on which I disagree with others who have written about Winstanley, and Part VII attempts to draw some conclusions.

II

BEFORE THE END OF 1648

Winstanley's early thinking, like that of most of his radical contemporaries, is concerned with explaining the existence of evil, with the relationship of man to God, with the Fall of man. "Mankind is a garden which God hath made for his own delight to dwell and walk in". But selfishness, the Serpent, rose up in Adam's heart, in the middle of the living garden.[7] Since the Fall, good and evil struggle together within man. God is not to be found "without you", "at a distance", "in some particular place of glory beyond the skies", nor is he to be known only after we are dead. He is to be known here and now within each one of us. Before Winstanley understood this, he tells us, he worshipped a devil and called him God. And so do most Englishmen still. "While ... I looked after a God without me, I did but build upon the sand, and as yet I knew not the rock". "He that looks for a God without himself, and worships God from a distance, he worships he knows not what, but is ... deceived by the imagination of his own heart". Worship of anything external must be idolatry, devil-worship.[8] But "he that looks for a God within himself ... is made subject to and hath community with the spirit that made all flesh, that dwells in all flesh and in every creature within the globe" The universe was created out of the substance of God.[9] When the spirit of the Father finally prevails over the evil in man, then that man becomes a saint and is one with Christ.

God is the sun of righteousness, burning up the dross and evil in man in order that pure gold may emerge. "This dross and gold in man is so mixed together that nothing can separate them but the fiery orb, which is the Father himself, that tries all things". "All must be burned herein, more or less, before they lie down quietly in the lap of providence".[10] Burning is an unpleasant process, which men often attribute to the devil. But the devil does not exist: the Serpent is "my own invention". Like God, he is within men and women. "The devil which thou thinkest is a third power, distinct between God and thee", is nothing "but the declaration of the rigour of the righteous law of God laying hold upon the corruption that is in the creature". The sinner cannot look upon the law and live; only when "the law of love hath swallowed that law of works that required perfection from the creature" and has changed "the man to the same nature and glory" can man behold God and live. Then "your eyes being opened, you shall see the King of Righteousness sit upon the throne within yourselves, judging and condemning the unrighteousness of the flesh". The Father dwells bodily in every man and woman: they become perfect when they are taken up into this spirit and live in the light of Reason.[11]

Few so far, Winstanley thought, have attained to this knowledge, but it is accessible. The beginning of wisdom is to reject traditions and hearsay, together with the hireling clergy who preach from books and other men's words. The spirit is a teacher within each one of us: "when your flesh is made subject to him, he will teach you all things ... so that you shall not need to run after men for instruction". Winstanley himself did not aspire to be a teacher, only to draw men's attention to this teaching within each one of them. "You may teach me, for you have the fountain of life in you as well as I". The poor and ignorant ("in men's learning") can "become abundantly learned in the experimental knowledge of Christ". "The spirit of righteousness within yourselves ... will bring you into community with the whole globe"; and then you will have peace, and will be freed from covetousness and the slavery of the flesh.[12]

This is the age in which God is beginning to gather his elect, to appear in the flesh of the saints.[13] The day of Christ is begun, Winstanley proclaimed in *Truth Lifting up its Head*.[14] Relying apparently upon the text, "Touch not mine anointed", which Winstanley like Milton interpreted as meaning "Touch not my saints",[15] Winstanley referred regularly to "the anointing which the saints receive from the Father" and which "doth teach them all things"; "the anointing, or that Son of God ruling as King of Righteousness and peace within you, that sets you free". This is not a wholly original concept,[16] but Winstanley gave it an unusual emphasis. There are two witnesses, he tells us: "the word of God, or the anointing in the person of Christ after the flesh, and the spirit of God, or the anointing in the flesh of the saints".[17] If the "anointing, or power and wisdom of God dwell and rule in you", as it did in the prophets and apostles, then you "can speak the mind of the Scriptures, though you should never see, hear nor read the Scriptures from men". "Anointing unites Christ in the saints": "faith, or the anointing in you". The anointing is Christ, "the wisdom and power of the Father". "When the anointing hath made a oneness ... God dwells and rules in man, and man lives in God". "The Father and you become one".[18] It is "the same anointing or spirit that was sent down" into the body of the historical Jesus Christ, and which will ultimately fill all men and women.[19] It is "God himself in man". "This anointing is said to be the earnest of an inheritance, that as the power of God did dwell in Jesus, ... even so the same power in the Father's times and seasons will bruise the same Serpent's head in every son and daughter of Adam".[20]

"If you cast your eyes abroad among the sons and daughters of men, you shall see very few that are saved, and very few in whom Christ dwells". This was conventional doctrine. But Winstanley added a millenarian note: the Son of Righteousness is coming, and ere long "the sweet song that is sung in private shall be sung publicly upon the house tops, Rejoice, for the Lord God omnipotent reigns".[21] Both in *The Mysterie of God* and in the final chapter of *The Saints Paradise* Winstanley argued a wholly unorthodox case for universal salvation: at the last, "Jesus Christ ... will dwell in the whole creation" and "every man shall be saved ... without exception". The Father "is not simply angry with his creatures, but with this sin or curse in the creature". To sin, and to sin only, "the Father will ever be a consuming fire"; "yet he will make his creature, man, one with him when the curse is swallowed up of life". The everlasting fire in which sin is consumed is not really everlasting: it will merely last for a long time.[22]

The anointing is "the power, life and peace of the Father; ... this is Christ in you, which is the hope of glory, or the earnest of the future inheritance". Jesus Christ or the anointing of flesh sets us free from the Serpent. Anointing unites Christ and the saints, "and makes them but one mystical body". "The anointing of the Son of God" is not one man only; Christ and all his saints "makes up but one Son of God". "The Father and the saints, ... being but one body, one man, ... one Son of God": this composite Christ, "this complete man or seed of the woman, shall break the Serpent's head".[23] "God now appears in the flesh of the saints". "Every particular saint is a true heaven or place of glory": the Father dwells in "this his Son", and he is in the Father. "And this is God's kingdom". When the sin against the Holy Ghost is mentioned in Matthew 12.31, the Holy Ghost means "the anointing, or the spirit ruling in flesh, either in the flesh of Christ or in the flesh of his saints". The sin against the Holy Ghost is a sin against a Son in whom the Father dwells bodily. " Every creature ... is a Son to the Father"; "perfect man is the Son of the Father in perfect glory".[24]

The concept of the anointing thus virtually equates the saints with Jesus Christ: Christ is regularly spoken of as a man. Even when Winstanley was trying to defend his orthodoxy in *Truth Lifting up its Head* it is fairly clear that he did not believe in the Trinity in any normal sense. "Jesus Christ ... was the first in whom the Father did appear bodily to dwell".[25] "Men that are wholly taken up into God

are called angels" — for example, Jesus Christ and Moses. Jesus
Christ "was the great prophet", and "the same anointing or power
and wisdom of God" that dwelt in the prophets and apostles can
dwell in the saints.[26] "Jesus Christ . . . is not a single man at a distance
from you, but . . . the wisdom and power of the Father . . . dwelling
and ruling King of Righteousness in your very flesh".[27] Christ
"cannot properly be called a perfect man if he should be separated
from the saints". To deny that the anointing is manifest in the flesh
of the saints is to deny that Christ is come in the flesh.[28]

Not only does Winstanley reject the orthodox doctrine of the
Trinity: he attaches more significance to his allegorical interpretation of the gospel story than to its historical truth. If you look for
Christ "under the notion of one single man after the flesh to be your
Saviour, ye shall never taste salvation by him". "His ascension, so
called", is an allegory of the spirit of the Father rising up "from under
the earthy imaginations and lusts of the sons of men, for mankind is
the earth that contains him buried". To expect Christ to "come in
one single person" is to "mistake the resurrection of Christ". "You
must see, feel and know from himself his own resurrection within
you, if you expect life and peace by him". "Everyone hath the light of
the Father within himself, which is the mighty man Christ Jesus. And
he is now rising and spreading himself in these his sons and daughters,
and so rising from one to many persons". This "spirit and power . . .
dwells in every man and woman". We are not "saved by believing
there was such a man that lived and died at Jerusalem". "A man filled
with the power of God . . . bears the name Christ".[29] "The Scripture", Winstanley declared, "is to me but the declaration of a
historical truth pointing out this higher mystery".[30]

Similarly the devil's temptation of Christ in the wilderness is a
dramatization of doubts and murmurings which appeared in the
human nature of Jesus. "But Jesus Christ gave no consent therunto,
as Adam the first man did".[31] The fall of the rebel angels occurs
"when Adam (or indeed any man or woman) doth give way to self "
and prefers it to the King of Righteousness in man. Milton too
compared heaven and earth apropos the fall of the rebel angels.
Winstanley refers to Adam's fall in the garden of Eden as "the
history"; but he is more interested in "the mystery", the allegory.
"We may see Adam every day before our eyes walking up and down
the street".[32]

If God and Christ are within us, not external, the day of judgment is to be taken as a metaphor. It may be a single day at the end of time, but it is also a series of events that take place within the saints during their life on earth, over a long period, "till the power of Christ do make it appear to the man's clear knowledge that self and flesh is the devil". "The ... salvation which is pointed at in the letter of the Scripture doth lie in the restoring of the creature, mankind, from the power" of evil.[33] "If you desire to know the Beast that treads you and the holy city underfoot, look first into your own hearts, for there She sits". "Wheresoever God dwells, ... that is called heaven". Heaven and hell signify the saints and the unregenerate.[34]

When in *Truth Lifting up its Head* Winstanley defended his belief in Jesus Christ, he treated the resurrection as an allegory; the "ascension, so called" was not a historical event but "was only a declaration in vision" to the apostles "of the spirit's rising up". Jesus was "*a man* [my italics] taken up to live wholly in the Father; or a meek spirit drawn up to live in the light of Reason". He appears to be everyman. When Christ rules in sons and daughters, then "the writings of the apostles and prophets ... are to cease", for they will be superseded by the internal spirit.[35]

What Winstanley has to say about God the Father is no less unorthodox. "This spirit or Father is pure Reason". Reason "gave being to all and ... knits all creatures together in peace". It "governs the whole globe in righteousness, ... and the light thereof discovers thy darkness".[36] Reason is the highest name that can be given to the Father. This Reason is to be found within every man and woman if only he or she will submit to it. "Let Reason rule the man, and he dares not trespass against his fellow-creature, but will do as he would be done unto. For Reason tells him, Is thy neighbour hungry and naked to-day, do thou feed and clothe him; it may be thy case tomorrow, and then he will be ready to help thee". The opposite of Reason is selfishness, the Serpent. In *Truth Lifting up its Head* Winstanley explained why he used the word "Reason" instead of the word "God". Partly it was because he had "been held under darkness" by the word "God". Reason is "that spiritual power that guides all men's reasoning in right order and to a right end ... It hath a regard to the whole creation, and knits every creature together into a oneness, making every creature to be an upholder of his fellow". Christ reconciles man to Reason.[37] In *Fire in the Bush* Winstanley equated God with universal love, righteous conscience and pure Reason.[38]

So, Winstanley concluded, we must always speak only from our own experience of God within us; the trade of preaching as practised by hireling parsons of the state church is useless and harmful. Indeed Winstanley rejected this church and its ordinances totally — prayer, preaching, holy communion, baptism, Sabbath observance.[39] Winstanley was to express anticlericalism more violently later; but from his earliest writings he seems to have held it as strongly as Milton did. It was wrong that "sharp punishing laws were made to prevent fishermen, shepherds, husbandmen and tradesmen from ever preaching of God any more", and that preaching was restricted to "scholars bred up in human letters".[40] Winstanley was already critical of the text of the Bible, and extended this to the antinomian position of rejecting the Ten Commandments as "the letter" to which the spirit is superior.[41] The Bible "shall cease" when the Lord rules in sons and daughters.[42]

It is hazardous to look for autobiography in Winstanley's theological writings, but let us see what we can find. His description of the inadequacy of Seekers, roaming in quest of religious fellowship, may well relate to his own experience.[43] So may his account of the satisfaction of being "taken off from either glorying in the presence or mourning in the absence of any creature-help or fruit. If you never see the faces of the saints, but live in prison, in a wilderness, or in some private place, yet you are at rest in God".[44] So may his description of the man who finds he cannot pray: "when people do not regard him for his preaching and praying, then he is troubled", though he will not yet accept that "he must cease praying and preaching and self-acting, and wait upon the Father for his pure teaching". (Winstanley may well have had a period of itinerant preaching.) He had been a cloth merchant, and this may be recalled in his account of the scruples of the man who asks "sometimes too little, as sometimes too much" for his wares.[45] He had been beaten out of this trade;[46] in 1660 he was still being sued for debts incurred before 1643, when he retired to Surrey to earn a difficult living as wage labourer. We may hear echoes of this when he writes of "sickness, frowns of friends, hatred of men, losses of his estate by fire, water, being cheated by false-spirited men, death of his cattle, or many such-like casualties whereby he becomes poor in the world" and has to endure "hard language, hungry belly, to be despised" and imprisoned. In April 1646 Winstanley with five others was in trouble at Cobham manor court for cutting peat from the waste.[47]

Winstanley was certainly no Fifth Monarchist. He had published all his pamphlets before the Fifth Monarchist movement started.[48] But with Milton and almost all the radicals he shared general millenarian expectations, foreseeing a time when God will reveal himself to "the despised, the unlearned, the poor, the nothings of this world". (Foxe's *Book of Martyrs*, the main source for such ideas, was the only book to which Winstanley referred.)[49] The very desperation of his own and England's plight suggested to Winstanley that the mystery of iniquity, the Beast, the Serpent who rules in flesh, was nearing the end of his reign; in his place God will dwell in flesh himself.[50] In May 1648, faced by "these uproar risings", when men sought to chain the Roundheads up under an ecclesiastical and state power, Winstanley believed that the last period of the Beast's reign had come — very hot but short.[51] The "wrath, bitterness and discontent that appears generally in men's spirits in England, one against another ... in the midst of these national hurly-burlies" suggested to him that "the Father hath cast England into the fire, and is purging the dross from the gold, that liberty is not far off, and that the plentiful pouring out of the anointing, even the spirit of love, truth and oneness is near at hand". England, Scotland and Ireland may be "the tenth part of the city Babylon that shall fall off first and bow down at the feet of the anointing, which is the wisdom and power of God that rules in flesh". Then national divisions will be swallowed up in brotherly oneness.[52]

Thus Winstanley's attitude towards millenarianism was complex. More specific than an expectation of the reign of Christ on earth in the near future, which was widespread in the exciting sixteen-forties, was the millenarian belief which often accompanied the heresies of the radical underground — that Christ would reign and judge the world in and through his saints.[53] "God the Father hath committed all judgment to the Son" is the same as saying he "hath engaged himself to subdue the Serpent's power under the feet of the saints".[54] Here too Winstanley's doctrine of Sonship was crucial. "The three days and a half or 42 months of the saints' captivity under the Beast" are "very near expired", declared the title-page of *The Breaking of the Day of God*. "Christ hath begun to reign in his saints". "Jesus Christ is upon his rising from the dead, and will rule King of Righteousness in flesh", treading "the powers of flesh under his feet". Since Christ is the saints and they are Christ, his "dominion over the nations of the world", we must suppose, would be exercised by them.[55] But Winstanley never envisaged the forcible rule of a godly minority, as the Fifth Monarchists (and perhaps William Erbery) were to do in the sixteen-fifties. For Winstanley believed that ultimately Jesus Christ "will dwell in ... every man and woman without exception".[56]

III

THE HERITAGE OF RADICAL THEOLOGY

It is difficult to decide which writers during the revolutionary epoch are producing original ideas, and which are expressing or recombining commonplaces. Before 1640 the censorship prevented unorthodox ideas getting into print: we hear of them only through the distorting medium of their enemies' attacks. But it is clear from the writings of Robert Baillie, Ephraim Pagitt, Samuel Rutherford, Thomas Edwards and other propagandists against the radicals that, before Winstanley wrote a line, many of the ideas which he was to make his own were circulating in the world of Familists, Hermeticists, Behmenists, General Baptists and Seekers. It would be difficult to find a single heresy of Winstanley's which was not adumbrated, however crudely, by someone reported by Edwards in *Gangraena* (1646). From this milieu were to come the ideas of Ranters, Quakers, Muggletonians and many others, as well as of Winstanley and the Diggers.[57]

  Winstanley rejected the doctrine of original sin. He has been classed with Richard Coppin as one of the first English universalists, who taught that all men would be saved.[58] They may have been the first to make the positive point in print; but the heresy was attributed to Elizabethan Familists, and John Penry said in 1587 that such beliefs were popular. They were held in Essex in 1592 and in 1646.[59] General Baptists preached universal redemption from at least the early seventeenth century. Belief that perfection could be attained in this life was attributed to London tradesmen in 1549, to Elizabethan Familists, and to Yorkshire Grindletonians in the 1620s. William Walwyn, Henry Denne, Mrs Attaway and William Jenny in the mid-sixteen-forties, were said to believe that it could not stand with the goodness of God to damn his creatures eternally. Tobias Crisp thought sin was finished; so did many Ranters.[60] The young Thomas Browne was a universalist as well as a mortalist. Giles Randall and

John Saltmarsh preached perfectibility on earth in the sixteen-forties, and Saltmarsh toyed with the idea of universal salvation.[61] Samuel Fisher tells us in 1653 that rejection of original sin was popular.[62] So when we find *Tyranipocrit Discovered* in 1649, Richard Coppin, Ranters and George Fox in the sixteen-fifties, and John Milton, holding similar beliefs, we need not attribute them to Winstanley's influence.[63] Even when Coppin and Milton speak of a Paradise within, happier far than the garden of Eden, to be attained in this life, we need not necessarily postulate Winstanley's influence, though we should note the similarity.[64]

The doctrine of perfectibility on earth is linked by Winstanley with the idea of the Sonship of all believers. This of course derives from the New Testament, and is to be found in orthodox Puritans. "If God be a Father and we are brethren", wrote Richard Sibbes, "it is a levelling doctrine".[65] In the sixteenth and seventeenth centuries Hermeticism contributed to the conception. *Pimander*, published in John Everard's translation in 1650, taught that men can again become like gods on earth;[66] Paracelsus held that man could become the Son of God and be united to God — a state higher than that of the angels.[67] So again the fact that — after Winstanley — Erbery, Morgan Llwyd, Ranters, Quakers and Milton held similar beliefs is no evidence of influence.[68] The idea that God was to be found within man was familiar to Familists, Boehme, John Everard, John Saltmarsh, Thomas Collier, Joseph Salmon, William Erbery, Jacob Bauthumley, Richard Coppin, John Pordage and Quakers.[69]

Fox proclaimed that he was the Son of God. As men became the Sons of God, "this would bring them into unity with the Son and with the Father".[70] James Nayler agreed that "the saints are all one in the Father and the Son". Nayler denied that Fox had claimed to be Christ, but did not query his assertion that, as a saint, he was "the judge of the world".[71] Fox spoke of "a teacher within thee, the anointing".[72] Samuel Rutherford attributed the phrase "the state of perfection or anointing" to the Familist leader Henry Niklaes.[73] A pamphlet of 1642 attacked those who "will turn a monarchy into a democracy" by claiming that the people are the Lord's Anointed.[74] George Wither and John Milton both referred to the elect as the Lord's Anointed.[75] In 1655 Richard Overton associated "the anointing" with anti-Trinitarianism.[76]

If the significant Christ is the Christ in us, then the Christ who died at Jerusalem diminishes in importance. Thomas Webbe made this point before Winstanley, and George Wither, John Pordage and many others after him.[77] Familists had long been accused of allegorizing the Scriptures, of making the Fall, the resurrection and the last judgment take place in this life only.[78] Mrs Anne Hutchinson was alleged to believe there was no resurrection but union to Christ Jesus.[79] John Everard, John Saltmarsh and Giles Randall before Winstanley, and William Erbery, Richard Coppin, Ranters and Quakers after him, taught similar doctrines. "Thou needest not go to Rome, Canterbury or Westminster", wrote Joseph Salmon in 1647, before Winstanley said something very similar, "but thou mayst find that Adam in thee, denying Jesus Christ to be come in thy flesh". "Thy heart is the temple where this great Whore sitteth". The day of judgment took place within each individual.[80] John Warr in 1648 thought that "the end of the world", "the resurrection from the dead" and "the world to come" all referred to changes in this life. "The highest pitch of a Christian life is Christ risen, or rather sitting at the right hand of God".[81] God "as really and substantially dwells in the flesh of other men and creatures as well as in the man Christ", declared Bauthumley in 1650. Where God dwells is "all the heaven I look ever to enjoy". At about the same time Richard Coppin taught that we come to a right knowledge of God through his resurrection in us, and then we have a fuller revelation than prophets and Apostles, returning to "a more excellent state" than the Paradise which Adam lost.[82]

Christ's coming in the flesh was but a figure, declared the Quaker Richard Hubberthorne. Bunyan in 1656-8 accused Ranters and Quakers of mocking the Second Coming.[83] For Collier and Erbery the Second Coming was "God appearing in the saints", who would rule on earth and judge the world.[84] John Cook argued that the court which sentenced Charles I "was a resemblance and representation of the great day of judgment, when the saints shall judge all worldly powers". John Canne and John Milton agreed with him.[85] For Ranters, Christ's Second Coming meant "his coming into man by his spirit", and that only.[86] Clarkson expected to "know nothing after this my being was dissolved".[87]

To men who thought along these lines, heaven and hell ceased to be geographical locations — an idea which the Copernican astronomy had already called in question. Elizabethan Familists had taught that heaven and hell were to be found in this world only, that the devil was not a real person.[88] Boehme also held that heaven and hell were in the conscience, doctrine later repeated by John Everard, Mrs Attaway, William Jenny, Richard Overton, William Walwyn and many others.[89] The young Thomas Browne disbelieved in a local hell.[90] In 1651 Henry Newcome in Cheshire was invoking the Rump's Blasphemy Act against an intruder who taught that God and hell existed only within the soul of man.[91] Clarkson rejected both God and the devil.[92] John Reeve thought that "the bottomless pit ... is in a man and not without a man".[93] Jacob Bauthumley and Richard Coppin were accused of holding similar views.[94] Sir Henry Vane rejected the idea of a material hell.[95] "There is no knowledge of heaven or hell", said Nayler, in words which may echo Winstanley or Clarkson.[96] What was new in Winstanley was the vigour with which, in *The Law of Freedom*, he denounced the evil effects on men and women of the fear of hell and the hope of heaven.[97]

If Christ was within men, then either men were gods or Christ was not God. The logical conclusion of elevating man to Sonship was to stress the humanity of Christ to the exclusion of his divinity. Anti-Trinitarianism has a long history in England, going back to the Lollards, the Marian martyrs, Familists and the last two heretics to be burned in England, in 1612. In the sixteen-forties the heresy was common among Baptists. It was shared by Milton. Again Winstanley was only one of many.[98]

Another consequence of the doctrine of Sonship was rejection of a separate clerical caste, insistence that laymen (and sometimes women) may preach, that a godly mechanic preacher is better than a university-trained hireling, that "experience is a copy written by the Spirit of God upon the hearts of believers".[99] Consequently the tithes which maintained parish ministers should be abolished. Evidence of such anti-clericalism in the sixteen-forties and early sixteen-fifties is overwhelming.[100] Winstanley and Milton are two of the fiercest exponents of an attitude which extended from Oliver Cromwell to William Walwyn.[101]

Hence rejection of the state church and its ordinances. These matters were much discussed in the late sixteen-forties and in the sixteen-fifties.[102] Coppe, Clarkson, Muggleton and "Jock of Broad Scotland" agreed with Winstanley in rejecting prayers; Salmon, Reeve, Erbery, Colonel Hutchinson, Milton and early Quakers agreed with him in withdrawing from church worship.[103] Another consequence was the passionate belief in liberty of conscience which Winstanley shared with Milton, Walwyn, Overton, Reeve and so many of the radicals.[104] Even when severely critical of the Ranters, Winstanley insisted that they were to be reasoned with, not forcibly repressed.[105] He had been attacking antinomian immoralism as early as 1648 — those who say "that which was sin formerly ... is now no sin while thou art under the law of love".[106] But rejection of the law of Moses was often taught — by Saltmarsh and Milton as well as by Winstanley, Coppe and Clarkson.[107]

Mortalism, the doctrine that the soul sleeps from death till the general resurrection (or dies with the body) frequently accompanied anti-Trinitarianism and rejection of a local hell. The heresy extended from Lollards through Familists to Richard Overton, Clement Wrighter, Mrs Attaway and William Jenny, Winstanley, Agricola Carpenter, Ranters, Muggletonians and Milton. Winstanley seems to me to imply mortalism in *The Mysterie of God*,[108] but his expression of it was not specific until 1652.

The mortalist doctrine that at death the body returns to the elements of which it was composed occurs in the Hermetic writings. Richard Overton, Winstanley, Bauthumley, Clarkson and the author of *Annotations upon All the Books of the Old and New Testaments* (1657) may all have got it from this source. An extreme version of mortalism was annihilationism — denial of any ultimate resurrection. This doctrine was being taught in London in the early sixteen-forties — long before Winstanley or Clarkson had written; in 1646 it was held by "some whole troops in the Army", Edwards thought.[109] Bunyan accused Quakers of denying the resurrection of the body.[110]

Another Hermeticist doctrine was that matter could not exist apart from God, from which it derived. The visible universe was the demiurge, the second God.[111] Winstanley, like Milton, believed that matter was created *ex deo*, not *ex nihilo*. George Fox's desire for unity with the creation, whether or not he got it via Winstanley, was almost certainly Hermeticist. Fox admitted to having been tempted to believe, as the Ranters did, that there is no God and that all comes by nature.[112] Bacon had taught that "to look for a first cause beyond the chain of natural causes is to abandon the principle of causation and to fly from solid knowledge into a realm of fantasy" — words which Winstanley appears to echo.[113] William Harvey recalls both writers when he told men not to look beyond the elements of which the body is compounded, nor "to fly up to heaven to fetch down I know not what spirits", to whom they ascribe "these divine operations" of the blood.[114] Winstanley, like the Ranters, believed that God was in all things, that the creation was the clothing of God. But this did not lead him to the pantheistic emphasis of Servetus in the sixteenth century and Jacob Bauthumley in the seventeenth (God is in "dog, cat, chair, stool", as well as in men). Winstanley's interest was mainly in God in humanity: on the title-page of *The Mysterie of God* he equated "the whole creation" with "mankind".[115]

Winstanley may have got his doctrine that God is a purging fire, burning up the evil in men, from John Everard. Everard believed that God was the sun, and no doubt took the idea from Hermes Trismegistus, whom he translated.[116] It was repeated by Saltmarsh and Coppin, and hinted at by George Fox.[117] The equation of God and Reason was another Hermeticist doctrine which Winstanley was using as early as 1648, together with the idea that Reason in men is itself drawn from the substance of God, so that those men and women in whom it is found are approaching the divine.[118] Winstanley might also have found the identification of God and Reason in Richard Overton's *Mans Mortalitie*. The Ranters were said to identify God and Reason too.[119] In 1648, a very sophisticated version of this doctrine appeared in John Warr's *Administrations, Civil and Spiritual*. For Warr, Equity or Reason is a divine principle in a man, telling him to "do as thou wouldst be done unto". When Reason rules within, "man becomes a law unto himself". "Reason hath been long out of the throne", replaced by Form. But "God himself is on Reason's side". Reason "is content to tarry the Lord's leisure"; but when the time comes, "Reason shall ride in triumph in the spirits of men". "When Reason ... rises from the dead" it will mean "the destruction of the world, or the present state of things". "When Equity itself comes, then the order, government and majesty thereof shall command the spirits of all ... . This will be a glorious time indeed", when every man shall be "a complete resemblance of divine wisdom, goodness and love". Till then "we shall never attain to perfect freedom".[120] Although it is impossible to be confident who influenced whom, Winstanley seems to have developed Warr's ideas.[121]

Winstanley held that the rising of Christ in sons and daughters was the victory of Jacob over Esau, of Abel over Cain, of the younger over the elder brother. This picked up a traditional popular metaphor, which Boehme used and which George Smith employed in 1645.[122] Mrs Attaway and William Jenny distinguished between

Esau's world and Jacob's world. When the latter replaced the former, then all creatures would be saved.[123] Coppe in 1649, Bauthumley in 1650, Wither in 1653, Vane in 1658, George Fox, Lodowick Muggleton and John Bunyan, all made use of the metaphor.[124]

Thus although Winstanley's theology had led him to very radical positions before the end of 1648, these views came out of a common pool of heretical ideas. What was uniquely novel in Winstanley was his association of the doctrine of Sonship with community of property, and the way in which he combined other ideas from the radical heritage into a single coherent theory. There was of course nothing new in advocacy of communal ownership, from John Ball through sixteenth-century Anabaptists to Walwyn, Coppe, Foster, Pordage and the author of *Tyranipocrit Discovered*.[125] Sir Thomas More had thought that communist ideas went naturally with anti-Trinitarianism.[126] The Hermeticist literature frequently attacked property, and argued that communion or fellowship drives out cupidity.[127] John Everard thought that not only "selfness" but also "property must be taken away".[128] It was a commonplace in orthodox Puritan writings that Sonship gave a special right to earthly possessions. In Jesus Christ, wrote John Ball, the author of *A Treatise of Faith*, "a son-like right and title to the creatures is restored, which by sin and disobedience was forfeited". Milton insisted that "the liberty we have in Christ" restores us "in some competent measure to a right to every good thing, both of this life and the other".[129] But in Winstanley this becomes something very different.

We now turn to the tracts in which Winstanley expressed his communist ideas.

IV

WINSTANLEY'S TRANCE

Before 1648 Winstanley had been through a period in which he was "a blind professor and strict goer to church, as they call it, and a hearer of sermons". He then "believed as the learned clergy ... believed". At some stage he had joined a Baptist church, but did not find satisfaction there.[130] It was after his financial ruin and flight to the country that he took to writing theological pamphlets. He may perhaps have been excommunicated either from his parish church or by a gathered congregation.[131] Aware possibly of a lack of verbal fluency to expound the tumultuous and complex ideas that were welling up inside him, he started to write in an obsessive way.[132] He had had trouble with the clergy in the Cobham area well before the digging began. This was, we must recall, before the 1650 Act had accepted the fact that it was no longer possible to force people to attend their parish churches if they did not want to. *Truth Lifting up its Head* is Winstanley's reply to accusations of blasphemy, of denying God and the Trinity, the Scriptures and all ordinances, brought against him and William Everard. Such charges might have carried a death sentence under the Blasphemy Ordinance of 1648, which became ineffective only after the Army's seizure of power in December of that year.

In *The Saints Paradise* Winstanley tells us that God sometimes speaks inwardly to believers, by voice, vision, dream or revelation.[133] In *The New Law of Righteousness* he claimed to have received in a trance the messages "Work together, Eat bread together"; "Let Israel go free; Israel shall neither give nor take hire".[134] I have been taken to task for suggesting that this may have been a seventeenth-century way of referring to a moment of clarification in a process of deep meditation.[135] But the *Oxford English Dictionary* appears to confirm this interpretaiton, quoting seventeenth-century examples of *trance* as meaning "a state of mental abstraction from external things". Richard Baxter described exactly this state; Sir Isaac Newton had similar trance-like revelations.[136] I referred to Lord Herbert of Cherbury, Descartes and Pascal (as well as Fox and Bunyan), in order to indicate that such claims were commonly made by men who are not normally regarded as religious mystics. I might have added John Sadler, friend of Milton and member of the Council of State, who was said to have had "a vision and a trance for three days together", holding communion with angels.[137] The phenomenon is of course familiar to anthropologists.[138] The Whig politician and financier, Goodwin Wharton, willed himself to hear divine voices in 1686 and later. This was at a time of tension, when he had attempted to solve his problems by communicating with God through his mistress, Mary Parish. Wharton undoubtedly believed that God spoke to him, both in dreams and in "waking visions"; he was taken aback by God's use of four-letter words and by his recommendation that Wharton commit incest.[139]

I am not quite sure what alternative explanation is proposed. That

Winstanley did receive a direct divine message? That would be difficult to prove. For a man to say "God hath spoken to him in a dream", as Hobbes put it in 1651, "is no more than to say he dreamed that God spake to him".[140] Winstanley himself contrasted "speaking inwardly ... by voice, vision, dream or revelation" with speaking "by the voice of a material man, standing before him". Milton's muse, we must suppose, did not speak "by the voice of a material woman". The authors of "Winstanley: A Case for the Man as He Said He Was" go so far as to speak of "a dialogue" between Winstanley and "a real visible God who could appear and speak to him with a real visible voice". The passage to which they refer, so far from describing the miracle of a dialogue with "a real visible voice", has Winstanley conducting a monologue "within my heart".[141]

If we do not accept a supernatural explanation, it is not enough merely to say that Winstanley had a mystical experience, as though that ended the matter. It is pertinent to ask why Winstanley, why in the winter of 1648-9, why this particular message. We know that he had the habit of working very intensively, forsaking "my ordinary food whole days together", ignoring cold when "the power of that overflowing anointing" took hold of him.[142] Most of us know from our own experience that when one has wrestled with an intractable problem for some time it may suddenly appear to solve itself, as though in a flash of intuition. For Winstanley the peat-cutting incident of 1646 may have initiated, or may have been part of, an intellectual wrestle with the compatibility of private property and communal welfare. And, we might add, we have Winstanley's own later statement of the ways in which traditional religion could make people believe they had seen visions.[143]

We know too that Winstanley thought it important that significant truths should be "a free revelation" from within, not taken from books or at second hand from the mouth of any flesh. "I have writ nothing but what was given me of my Father", he assured his fellow-Lancastrians in 1648.[144] (The Father, let us recall, is Reason within each one of us). In so far as Winstanley thought of himself at this stage as a prophet of God, some such form of communication as a vision or trance was appropriate to give special authority to the words spoken.[145] He was after all announcing a *new* law of righteousness, "that is to be writ in every man's heart, and acted by every man's hand", and would supersede the traditional Scriptures. It was necessary to support so major an undertaking "by vision, voice and revelation"; the later choice of St George's Hill for the digging was similarly supported.[146]

There are also factors which may have a bearing on the time of the trance. In *The New Law of Righteousness*, dated 26 January 1648/9, Winstanley said that it had occurred "not long since".[147] The winter of 1648-9 was a particularly cruel one. The disruption of the civil war had been followed by a succession of bad harvests; men were said to be starving in London. The economic crisis exacerbated and was exacerbated by the political crisis. The Army seized power in December; Charles I was executed four days after Winstanley had signed his preface to *The New Law*. Leveller agitation was at its height; it was soon to lead to Army mutinies. Radical ideas for relieving the poor were expressed by the regiment of horse for the county of Northumberland at the beginning of December, and by many others.[148]

Also at the beginning of December *Light Shining in Buckinghamshire* had drawn on Winstanley's (or Warr's) theology to define Reason in all men as the principle of co-operation, of doing as you would be done by. If Winstanley read the pamphlet — as is surely likely — he could have learned from it that men had certain birthright privileges, which included enjoyment of "the creatures, without property one more than another"; and he would have noticed the phrase "kingly power", which he was to use to good effect later. He might also have observed a reference to "freeholders which had their freedom of the Normans" and to the desirability of using church, crown and forest lands for the poor.[149] *Light Shining* is much more specifically anti-monarchical than Winstanley's early writings, more explicitly pro-Leveller; and it attacks the privileges of corporations in the name of property rights in a way Winstanley never did. A later pamphlet from the same group of Buckinghamshire Levellers promised help to the Digger colony, which had then been in existence for a month.[150] The three Buckinghamshire pamphlets were almost certainly not written by Winstanley; but it is difficult to suppose that he did not read them. They were produced, after all, less than forty miles from Cobham.

The point I wish to stress is that, whatever we make of Winstanley's trance, it is unlikely that his ideas were as completely original as he wished to suggest. His theological emphasis on Sonship was almost a commonplace in the radical milieu; communist ideas had been floating around for some time, and were appearing in print in the starvation winter of 1648-9. Winstanley put the two together.

But the juxtaposition led to novel conclusions. Sonship extends to all men and women, and the title to the creatures (that is, the right to enjoy what God has made as a common treasury for all) is a "creation-right" to be exercised collectively rather than individually.[151] The privilege and benefit of Sonship is to have free access to cultivate the earth. "The glorious liberty of the Sons of God", the Iver Digger pamphlet put it, "is equality, community and fellowship with our own kind".[152] If Winstanley's communism is immanent in his early theological tracts, we shall have to ask whether it was also immanent in the writings of all those others whom I have cited, with whom Winstanley had so much in common. Was their failure to press on to Winstanley's conclusion due to a failure of nerve? Or did Winstanley's experience as an unsuccessful merchant pushed down into the ranks of wage labourers force conclusions upon him? Or must we attribute it all to the caprice of that "visible voice"? These are difficult, perhaps unanswerable questions.[153]

From *The New Law of Righteousness*, his first tract after his trance, it appears that Winstanley expected a transformation of society to come swiftly and peaceably as a consequence of Christ rising in sons and daughters. Poor men and women (and not only the poor) would see what was the reasonable way out of their desperate situation. Universal love, as Winstanley put it in *A New-Yeers Gift*, will "make mankind to be all of one heart and one mind, and make the earth to be a common treasury".[154]

The pamphlets which Winstanley poured out during the next eighteen months were almost all propagandist appeals to specific audiences — *Letters* to Fairfax for the Army, *An Appeal* to the House of Commons, *A Watch-Word* for London and the Army, *A New-Yeers Gift* for Parliament and Army. Most important for our purposes is *Fire in the Bush*, whose date has now been established as the middle of March 1650: that is to say, towards the end of the Digger colony's existence. This date has proved embarrassing for those who wish to play down the theological element in Winstanley's thought.[155] But from our perspective there is no problem. *Fire in the Bush* appeared shortly after Winstanley had reprinted his first five tracts, with a preface stressing the continuity between his theological and his communist writings.[156] *Fire in the Bush* was written for the churches. It is possible that it may have been drafted earlier,[157] but Winstanley may well have felt in March 1650 that his recent propagandist writings had become excessively preoccupied with historical and legal arguments. He no doubt wished to sort out and complete his fusion of theology with economics, at a time when he was becoming aware that the Digger colony might fail.

Fire in the Bush is in no sense a retreat to "merely" religious themes; it is as fiery and fierce as any of his pamphlets, from its introductory denunciation of hypocrisy, in terms worthy of Milton, and of "murdering property". Jesus Christ is "the true and faithful Leveller". The God whom priests and professors worship is the devil. Law is "but the declarative will of conquerors, how they will have their subjects to be ruled". Winstanley admits that his doctrine "will destroy all property and all trading", all existing government, ministry and religion.[158] The tract ends by defining the two greatest sins in the world. "First for a man to lock up the treasuries of the earth in chests and houses ... while others starve for want to whom it belongs, and it belongs to all". Secondly, "for any man or men first to take the earth by the power of the murdering sword from others; and then by the laws of their own making do hang or put to death any who takes the fruits of the earth to supply his necessaries". *Fire in the Bush* is not different in spirit from *An Appeale to All Englishmen*, issued at the end of March 1650 as a last broadside appeal to the common people, "whether tenants or labouring men", provocatively inciting them to illegal action. "Will you be slaves and beggars still, when you may be free men? Stand up for your freedom in the land by acting with plough and spade upon the commons".[159] If we read *Fire in the Bush* carefully, we can I think detect in it some of Winstanley's answers to the weaker brethren in the Digger commune who were tempted to despair. Defeat need not mean surrender: it was the theme of Milton's *Paradise Regained*, of Bunyan's *The Holy War*.[160]

Professor Hudson argued that the Diggers "did not conceive of their venture as a means of affecting social change"; "the peace they experienced in their hearts was the *final* justification of the digging" (my italics).[161] One wonders how he knew that. It is not what Winstanley said. "The first reason is this, that we may ... lay the foundation of making the earth a common treasury for all". To fail to act was to "consent still to hold the creation down under bondage". "I command thee, to let Israel go free".[162] "As the Scriptures threaten misery to rich men ... surely all those threatenings shall be materially fulfilled, for they shall be turned out of all".[163] Clearly the Diggers' enemies did not regard them as merely making symbolic gestures. From *The True Levellers Standard Advanced* onwards

Winstanley called for rejection of landlordism and an economic revolution. "That Scripture which saith 'The poor shall inherit the earth' is really and materially to be fulfilled", he told Parliament, Army and preachers in *A New-Yeers Gift*. The transition would be peaceful, for "the people shall all fall off from you", and follow the Levellers; but in the colony's last weeks Winstanley was inciting to disobedience, and ominously repeating the denunciation of idle gentry to be found in the *Light Shining* pamphlets.[164] In March 1650 a new colony had been started at Wellingborough, with some co-operation from local farmers and in contact with the Diggers. It produced its own pamphlet. In May another pamphlet appeared from the colony at Iver, Buckinghamshire, the title of which was almost identical with that from Wellingborough. It revealed that in all some ten colonies had been set up, with others in prospect; Digger emissaries met with a successful reception in many places in the midlands.[165] The movement was spreading: it was time to respond to the demands of local landowners by suppressing the headquarters at Cobham.

The message that Winstanley received in his trance was that men should break bread together and work together, and that they should not take hire. They should live and work in community, rejecting wage labour.[166] It is important to grasp the significance of the second part of the divine message, for it was essential to the first. Winstanley always proclaimed that the Diggers had no intention of expropriating landlords: they should retain their enclosures, and the common people should cultivate the common lands, paying no rent for them.[167] But in so far as the ban on wage labour became effective — that is, as the spirit rose in sons and daughters — so the gentry would be unable to get their enclosures cultivated: they would effectively own no more than they could cultivate themselves, so living "freed from the straits of povety and oppression".[168] The point is spelt out most clearly by Robert Coster.[169] It was not expropriation, but it would have amounted to a piecemeal deprivation of the profits of ownership. So Winstanley's provision for the gentry to receive compensation if they wished to throw their lands into the common stock was a hard-headed realistic proposal: a life annuity in return for surrendering a capital asset on which no return could be expected.[170]

Moreover the Digger claim to common lands, for which no rent was to be paid, came to include the demand originally put forward in *Light Shining in Buckinghamshire* for confiscated church, crown and forest lands; and (in *The Law of Freedom*) for monastic lands too.[171] Realization of this claim would have amounted to a large-scale act of expropriation. To work "for another, either for wages or to pay him rent" lifts up the curse; "by denying to labour for hire ... men join hands with Christ, to lift up the creation from bondage" and restore "all things from the curse".[172] The common land is the due of the poor both "by right of creation and by the laws of a common-wealth".[173] Copyholds were "parcels hedged in and taken out of the common waste since the conquest"; the poor should be as free in them as lords of manors in their land after the abolition of feudal tenures.[174]

In *The New Law of Righteousness* the emphasis was still internal, but by April 1649 communal cultivation of the earth had for Winstanley become central to the overthrow of the curse. "All the prophecies, visions and revelations of Scriptures, of prophets and apostles, concerning the calling of the Jews, the restoration of Israel and making of that people the inheritors of the whole earth, doth all rest themselves in the work of making the earth a common treasury".[175] Private property in land is "rebellion and high treason against the King of Righteousness".[176] If they perished in the attempt, the Diggers told Fairfax, they would "die doing our duty to our Creator, by endeavouring from that power he hath put into our hearts to lift up his creation out of bondage". "True religion and undefiled is this, to make restitution of the earth".[177]

This conviction that they were about the Lord's work, and that Christ was already rising in sons and daughters, gave the Diggers a naïve confidence not only in the persuasiveness of their words and example, but also that, as they told Fairfax, the earth would be made fruitful when the curse was removed from the creation.[178] But manuring was part of cultivation: "true religion and undefiled", Winstanley came to think, "is to let everyone quietly have earth to manure, that they may live in freedom in their labours". To withhold it from them is sin.[179]

V

FROM RIGHTEOUSNESS TO FREEDOM

Winstanley devoted considerable attention to his titles: each contains something programmatic.[180] It is therefore not altogether without significance that his writings after his trance begin with *The New Law of Righteousness* and end with *The Law of Freedom*: a transition from theology to politics. In each case the law concerned is the law of Reason. Winstanley's intellectual evolution is towards a realization that lack of freedom impedes the rise of Reason within men and women. It is inadequate to say that "to Winstanley the only freedom that mattered was freedom from economic insecurity", or to deny to him any "respect for the individual"[181] and his freedom. This travesties the thought of the man who wrote "freedom is the man that will turn the world upside down"; "freedom is Christ in you and among you".[182] Like many thinkers after him Winstanley came to appreciate that it is not possible to be fully human so long as one is hungry, or indeed so long as anyone else is unnecessarily hungry. It is true Winstanley thought "there cannot be a universal liberty till this community be established". But freedom meant rather more than Mr Davis suggests. It is the rule of Reason, "the appearance of Christ in the earth". "When men are sure of food and raiment, their reason will be ripe, and ready to dive into the secrets of the creation".[183] In his final pamphlet Winstanley declared that "all the inward bondages of the mind" are "occasioned by the outward bondage that one sort of people lay upon one another".[184] It is a remarkable statement of apparent social determinism. This section attempts to explain how Winstanley's thinking about communism, which started from a vision, arrived at this anticipation of socialist materialism. The evolution, I believe, is less paradoxical than appears at first sight.[185]

In certain respects Winstanley's theology had advanced since his commitment to digging the commons. He made more precise his idea of the Second Coming as the rising of Christ in sons and daughters. The very extent of oppression and bondage was for him evidence that "it is the fullness of time for Jacob to arise. Extreme necessity calls for the great work of restoration". "We dig upon the commons to make the earth a common treasury", Winstanley told Fairfax, "because our necessity for food and raiment requires it".[186] Digging was no mere symbol: it was a political act, part of the rising of Christ in sons and daughters which would establish a just commonwealth on earth.[187] "Now the man of Righteousness shall take the kingdom". "The righteous judge will sit upon the throne in every man and woman", and this will be "the day of judgment". "The material earth shall be his possession".[188] "A few years now will let all the world see who is strongest, love or hatred, freedom or bondage".[189] "Before many years pass: ... I can set no time", wrote Winstanley less confidently ten months later, in April 1650.[190]

> And to the Son the Father hath
> All judgment given now

sang Robert Coster, having made it clear that the Son is Jacob, the younger brother. The Lord will make

> All tyrants servants to the Son
> And he the power will take.[191]

"The rising up of Christ in sons and daughters", Winstanley tells us as explicitly as possible, "is his Second Coming". "His ... Second Coming in the flesh ... is justice and judgment ruling in man". This spirit in "whole mankind ... becomes the alone King of Righteousness", who is "not one single person". It is difficult to understand how anyone who has read these passages can argue that Winstanley postulated "a literal Second Coming" of "a real personal Christ", "an external Christ" and "a God who existed beyond the realm of men and nature", "whose intervention was essential".[192] If we must use the technical terms of twentieth-century theology, Winstanley knew no transcendent God, only immanent Reason. Only if we forget that the Father is Reason and that Christ's Second Coming is in sons and daughters can we slip into thinking of an external God. We must continually pay close attention to what Winstanley says, and especially to his definition of terms. Professor C.H. George has demonstrated Winstanley's cavalier use of proof texts: they often make his point only if we assume the very special meaning which he gives to a term like the Second Coming, or to the liberation of the Jews signifying the establishment of a communist society in England. They make the point, that is to say, only if we assume it in advance. Winstanley uses Scripture to bolster up a position which he has already adopted.[193] The novelty came in *The True Levellers Standard Advanced*, where Winstanley specifically equated the rising Christ with Jacob the younger brother, "the poor people" who would be "the Saviours of the land". It is repeated in *Fire in the Bush*: Christ dwells among the poor, "Christ levelling".[194]

It is in this context that we must set Winstanley's conception of himself as a prophet, the mouthpiece of God. Jacob, Moses and David were Christ.[195] "Christ in that one body", the historical Jesus Christ, was "a great prophet". So is the man today who has "the light and power of Christ within".[196] Winstanley saw himself as one of the Sons in whom Christ had risen in these last days. It was his duty to proclaim the message of the Father, for the benefit of others in whom Christ was still to rise. His duty was not to preach, as hirelings did; but to testify, so that those who had the spirit of Reason within them could try Winstanley's spirit.[197] ("Oh that all the Lord's people were prophets!"). Hence the importance for Winstanley of stressing that "what I have spoken I have not received from books nor study, but freely I have received and freely I have declared what I have received".[198] for this was the *new* law of righteousness which would replace the old: the message from Christ rising in sons and daughters, before which Christ in one single person would fall back.

In *The New Law of Righteousness* and the pamphlets which followed, Winstanley envisaged the day of judgment more clearly as an internal event occurring to every man and woman during their lifetime, rather than as the end of the world.[199] He rejected Biblical history more firmly in favour of allegorical interpretations. "The public preachers have cheated the whole world by telling us of a single man called Adam, that killed us all by eating a single fruit called an apple".[200] There is no need "to go up into heaven above the skies to find Christ". In this world "few are saved, that is enter into rest and peace". To say that all will be saved means that all will "live in peace and rest". "The outward heaven ... is a fancy, which your false teachers put into your heads to please you with while they pick your purses". Heaven and hell are within us: we make our own hell. Heaven is "a comfortable livelihood in the earth". "The glory of Jerusalem" is not "to be seen hereafter, after the body is laid in the dust": the Diggers expected "Glory here!" "Whether there was any such outward things" as the Bible related "or no, it matters not much".[201] The Fall, the Virgin birth, the resurrection, the ascension, the Second Coming are likewise treated as allegories.[202] Professor Pocock, whose asides on Winstanley are very much to the point, said that for him "community of ownership of the earth and the resurrection of Christ are interchangeable concepts".[203] The War in Heaven "wherein Michael and the Dragon fights the great battle of God Almighty" takes place within "the living soul": we are reminded of Milton's

> What if earth
> Be but the shadow of heaven, and things therein
> Each to other like, more than on earth is thought?[204]

Winstanley advances to a more secure Bibilical criticism, possibly based on Clement Wrighter but more probably drawing on general sceptical discussions in radical circles.[205] Whether the earth should be free for all men and women to cultivate, Winstanley told Fairfax, is a question "not to be answered by any text of Scripture, or example since the Fall, but the answer is to be given in the light of itself, which is the law of righteousness, or that word of God that was in the beginning, which dwells in man's heart and by which he was made, even the pure law of creation". Arguments drawn from Biblical texts thus cut no ice with Winstanley himself, though he used them for specific audiences whom they might influence, as in *An Humble Request*. He virtually abandoned them in *The Law of Freedom*, where he adopted the position of Henry Parker and Milton, that we must interpret the Bible by reason, and not attribute to the Creator intentions contrary to the good of man, including his temporal good.[206] Winstanley's patronizing phrase, "there are good rules in Scripture if they were obeyed and practised", reminds one of Milton's "I am not one of those who consider the decalogue a faultless moral code".[207]

The New Law of Righteousness is perhaps a little more specific than its predecessors in asserting that the spirit shall "in these last days be sent into whole mankind", that "there is not a person or creature within the compass of the globe but he is a Son of the Father". The blessing which lies hid in Jacob "must be the alone Saviour and joy of all men", Winstanley assured "the twelve tribes of Israel".[208] Jacob, Moses and David will rise and reign in sons and daughters, who will live in the kingdom of heaven on earth.[209] Then "as Moses gave way to Christ", so the historical Christ will give way to the spreading of the spirit in sons and daughters. This will be the true Second Coming. "The spreading power of righteousness and wisdom" is to be "set ... in the chair"; "the ministration of Christ in one single person is to be silent and draw back". "Perfect man shall be no other but God manifest in the flesh".[210]

In the day of Christ, Winstanley had written in *Truth Lifting up its Head*, all created flesh shall be made subject to Reason, "so that the Spirit, which is the Father, may become all in all, the chief ruler in flesh". "Those sons and daughters in whom the Spirit rests cannot be deceived, but judge all things".[211] When "the Spirit . . . manifested in flesh ... draws all things back again into himself", then "the Son delivers up the kingdom to the Father; and he that is the spreading power, *not one single person*, becomes all in all in every person, that is the King of Righteousness in every one" (my italics). Then Moses and Christ will both yield place "as the earth grows up to be a common treasury for all", for the King of Righteousness will dwell in everyone, "the alone King in that living soul, on earth; or the five living senses".[212] The point could hardly be made more explicitly. As communist society develops, Christ and the Bible will be superseded, and there will be no authority greater than that of Reason in each human being, which alone can be called God.

What has been added to Winstanley's pre-1648 theology is the equation of the Second Coming with the establishment of a communist society on earth. In *Fire in the Bush*, when Winstanley writes "Christ the anointing spirit ... comes to set all free", he makes it quite clear that liberty includes free access to cultivate the earth.[213] But we must watch Winstanley's use of words rather carefully, since under the 1648 Blasphemy Ordinance he cannot express himself with complete freedom. In *Truth Lifting up its Head*, where he was defending himself against charges of blasphemy, for instance, he wrote: "I pray continually, calling upon the name of the Lord, in the manner I declared before". But the manner he declared before is in fact a rejection of prayer in the normal sense of the word. His statement, "I do walk in the daily practice of such ordinances of God as Reason and Scriptures do warrant", must be interpreted in the light of his rejection of prayer, preaching, holy communion, baptism, Sabbath observance.[214]

In *A New-Yeers Gift*, *Fire in the Bush* and *The Law of Freedom* Winstanley drew an analogy, which perhaps would not have occurred to him earlier, between the Calvinist doctrine that "some are elected to salvation, and others are reprobated" and the inheritance law of "the kingly power". But Christ, "the true and faithful Leveller", "will have all saved, that is, will have all live in peace and rest".[215] To speak of "Christ, the great prophet" only confirms the anti-Trinitarianism of the earlier tracts.[216]

"This particular property of mine and thine", Winstanley wrote in *The New Law of Righteousness*, "hath brought in all misery upon the people".[217] "When self-love began to arise in the earth, then man began to fall". "The Fall of man ... came in by the rising up of covetousness in the heart of mankind". "When mankind began to buy and sell, then did he fall from his innocency".[218] Winstanley's emphasis all through is on private property in land, on treating land as a commodity. "The first step of the Fall" came when "the stronger or elder brother" claimed a larger part of the earth than his younger brother; the second step was "to enclose parcels of the earth" as private property, which then were bought and sold. "When mankind began to quarrel about the earth, and some would have all and shut out others, forcing them to be servants: this was man's fall".[219] When Adam "consented to that serpent covetousness, then he fell from righteousness, was cursed, and was sent into the earth to eat his bread in sorrow; and from that time began particular property to grow in one man over another".[220] "The law of property is ... as far from the law of Christ as light from darkness".[221] This reverses the orthodox view that private property, inequality, and the state which protects them, were the consequences of eating an apple, however allegorically that action is interpreted. For Winstanley the establishment of private property in land, and freedom to buy and sell it, *was* the Fall; the abolition of private property was therefore necessary if pre-lapsarian freedom was to be restored. So long as landownership survives, "so long the creation lies under bondage". Any who will truly acknowledge Christ will set the earth free, "for the voice is gone out, freedom, freedom, freedom".[222] The government that maintains private property is "the government of imaginary, self-seeking Anti-christ", and "shall be rooted out". "The government of highway-men" is *The Law of Freedom*'s more succinct summary. "Buying and selling ... both killed Christ and hindered his resurrection" — that is, in sons and daughters. Freedom — "the man that will turn the world upside down" — "is Christ in you"; "this work of digging" is "freedom or the appearance of Christ in the earth".[223]

The New Law of Righteousness had proclaimed that "now the kingdom is delivered into the Father's hand, the one spirit that fills all and is in all"; and "this distinction of dominion in one single person over all shall cease". This is "the new heaven and earth", to be "seen by the material eyes of the flesh", not after death but "here in this earth while bodies are living upon earth".[224] "Kingly power is the old heaven and the old earth that must pass away", and be succeeded by community. The Diggers expected "glory here", on earth.[225]

After the Fall men who get riches and government into their hands aim to "suppress the universal liberty, which is Christ", to bring "the creation under the curse of bondage, sorrow and tears".[226] Landowners naturally become "justices, rulers and state governors, as experience shows". So one part of the creation is forced "to be a slave to another; and thereby the spirit is killed in both". The creation groans under this curse of "civil property", "waiting for deliverance". To maintain the curse, not to struggle against it, is to "sin against light that is given into us, and so through the fear of the flesh, man, lose our peace". Property derives from murder and theft, and is maintained by violence.[227] "By the law of righteousness . . . the poorest man hath as true a title and just right to the land as the richest man", and "the earth ought to be a common treasury of livelihood for all, without respecting persons". This is our creation-freedom.[228]

In *The New Law of Righteousness*, Christ spreading himself "in multiplicities of bodies" makes them "all of one heart and mind", acting in righteousness one to another. This unanimity of Reason in community will make government unnecessary.[229] Punishments should be inflicted only in order "to make the offender to know his maker [Reason], and to live in the community of the righteous law of love one with another".[230] By the time of *Truth Lifting up its Head* it is "when once the earth becomes a common treasury again" and mankind has "the law of righteousness once more writ in his heart" that all will be "made of one heart and one mind". Then "the love of Christ in us constrains all men to do his will".[231] "True freedom . . . lies in the community in spirit and community in the earthly treasury, and this is Christ, . . . spread abroad in the creation".[232] "To live in the enjoyment of Christ", Winstanley put it in *Fire in the Bush*, "will bring in true community and destroy murdering property". The battle is between property or the devil on the one hand, and community, called Christ or universal love, on the other. "There is but bondage and freedom", Winstanley maintained in *The Law of Freedom*, "particular interest or common interest".[233]

From the significantly entitled *The True Levellers Standard Advanced*, the millenarian aspect of Winstanley's thought fades into the background; economics and politics loom larger — the Norman Yoke, the Solemn League and Covenant, kingly power.[234] Or — more correctly perhaps — millenarian theology and politics fuse. The Second Coming, Christ rising in sons and daughters, would be equivalent to establishing "the state of community".[235] "The cause of those they call Diggers is the life and marrow of that cause the Parliament hath declared for, and the Army fought for; the perfecting of which work will prove England to be the first of nations, or the tenth part of the city Babylon that falls off from the Beast first". So ran the title-page of *A New-Yeers Gift*.[236]

Winstanley thus fitted the traditional Leveller theory of the Norman Yoke into his own theology. Overton and other Levellers had already advanced from a claim that Englishmen should be liberated from Norman bondage to a claim that all men had rights as men.[237] This theory appeared in *Light Shining in Buckinghamshire*, which referred to "the whole Norman power" and to "freeholders which had their freedom of the Normans". More specifically, *More Light* referred to "the Norman and Beastly power" — that is, Antichristian power.[238] Three weeks later Winstanley used the theory of the Norman Yoke for the first time; and it is already fused with his doctrine of the English as the chosen people. "The last enslaving conquest which the enemy got over Israel was the Norman over England, ... killing the poor enslaved English Israelites". Landlords are "the Norman power". In *A Declaration from the Poor Oppressed People*, six weeks later, the argument that the land belongs to the people because of the promises of the Solemn League and Covenant and Parliament's victory over the King is put before the arguments from Scripture and from "the righteous law of our creation", although Winstanley regarded the first two as "our weakest proofs", to be interpreted "in the light of Reason and Equity that dwells in all men's hearts".[239] At this stage he clearly regarded historical and constitutional arguments as secondary to theological, though useful for propaganda purposes.[240]

The stronger argument, for Winstanley, derived from "our privileges given us in our creation, which have hitherto been denied to us, and our fathers, since the power of the sword began to rule".[241] The reformation needed in England was "not to remove the Norman Yoke only" but to restore "the pure law of righteousness before the Fall, ... and he that endeavours not that is a covenant-breaker". The right to cultivate the earth had been regained "by the law of contract", for all those who had contributed by fighting or by paying taxes "to recover England out of bondage" in the civil war.[242] In *An Appeal to the House of Commons* of July 1649 the emphasis was mainly on historical and legal arguments: tithes are a part of the Norman Yoke.[243]

In *A New-Yeers Gift*, where Winstanley referred to "true public-spirited men called Levellers", the incorporation of the Norman Yoke theory into Winstanley's theology is complete.[244] England has lain "under the power of the Beast, kingly property"; but "if England is to be the tenth part of the city Babylon that falls off from the Beast first", then kingly covetous property must be cast out, and the crown set upon "Christ's head, who is universal love or free community". To restore the creation calls first for "community of mankind, which is comprised in the unity of the spirit of love, which is Christ in you, or the law within the heart, leading mankind into all truth and to be of one heart and one mind"; secondly, for community of the earth. "These two communities, or rather one in two branches, is that true levelling which Christ will work at his more glorious appearance". "Jesus Christ the Saviour of all men is the greatest, first and truest Leveller that ever was spoke of in the world". "Christ comes riding upon these clouds", upon the True Levellers.[245] To restore the earth from the bondage of property to true community "is the work of the true Saviour to do, who is the true and faithful Leveller, even the spirit and power of universal love, that is now rising to spread himself in the whole creation". "His appearance will be with power, ... this great Leveller, Christ our King of Righteousness in us". "Righteous conscience or pure Reason ... is now rising up to bruise the Serpent's head ... He is called the restorer, Saviour, Redeemer, yea and the true and faithful Leveller".[246] So Christ rising in sons and daughters (the True Levellers) becomes Jesus Christ the Head Leveller.

The phrase "kingly power" occurs in *The Saints Paradise*,[247] but the concept was not developed there as fully as in *Light Shining* and *More Light Shining in Buckinghamshire*. The last-named pamphlet associated lawyers with kingly power. Winstanley did not use the phrase again until *A Watch-Word* of August 1649, where it referred especially to the royalist cause in the civil war.[248] Only in *A New-Yeers Gift* did he develop the notion of kingly power as "covetousness ... or the power of self-love" and equate it with the Norman Yoke and with property. This recognition that buying and selling, lords of manors, lawyers, priests and the state all form one kingly power differentiates Winstanley from the many radicals who attacked lawyers and priests. The law is "the strength, life and marrow of the kingly power", Winstanley wrote; the power of lawyers is "the only power that hinders Christ from rising".[249] Buying and selling killed Christ, but now he is rising up in sons and daughters, and kingly power in all its branches must be "shaken to pieces at the resurrection of Christ ... when righteous community rises". A government that "gives liberty to the gentry to have all the earth and shuts out the poor commoners from enjoying any part, ... this is the government of imaginary, self-seeking Antichrist. And every plant which my heavenly Father hath not planted shall be rooted out". It is "unreasonable men, who have not faith in Christ" who "uphold the kingly power" which Parliament has voted down.[250]

It is worth trying to sort out Winstanley's attitude towards the government of the Commonwealth, and to government in general, since this has caused confusion. Some have seen Winstanley as an anarchist who came to believe in the necessity of political action and political power. Mr Davis has argued, on the contrary, that Winstanley always respected power and was never an anti-authoritarian; and that in his ideal community "slavery replaced imprisonment".[251] Such views seem to me to err in using the blanket concepts "authority" and "political power". Winstanley was always opposed to the laws which upheld covetousness. He distinguished between laws which maintain the power of the Serpent and those which uphold the power of Reason.[252] Even in the early *Truth Lifting up its Head* he accepted the necessity of punishing a man who walked "unrighteously towards his fellow-creatures *in civil matters*" (my italics).[253] The commonwealth envisaged in *The Law of Freedom* differs from any form of kingly power by the fact that there would be no buying and selling, no lawyers, no state church or clergy. Even under kingly power, Winstanley accepted, some good laws had been passed — Magna Carta, for instance. Yet "that enslaving covetous kingly power ... runs in every man's and woman's veins, more or less, till Reason the spirit of burning cast him out".[254]

Winstanley "was always against the Cavaliers' cause", and the Diggers "have been ever friends to the Parliament"; their song treats Cavaliers as the personification of kingly power.[255] But "truly tyranny is tyranny in one as well as in another; in a poor man lifted up by his valour as in a rich man lifted up by his lands" — that is, in the Rump of the Long Parliament supported by the Army as well as in the Cavaliers. "Where tyranny sits, he is an enemy to Christ, the spreading spirit of righteousness". "Justices and most state officers doth more oppress than deliver from oppression". *The True Levellers Standard Advanced* accused "the powers of England" of restoring bondage; "all thy power and wit hath been to make laws and execute

them against such as stand for universal liberty".[256] Winstanley saw
the second civil war as Dragon against Dragon, one Beast against
another: "and the King of Righteousness hath been a looker on".
But now (June 1649) the battle is of Lamb against Dragon.[257]
Winstanley frequently expressed his abhorrence of violence, but he
expected "the government of Esau" to be beaten down "by wars,
counsels or hands of men". He told "lords of manors and Norman
gentry" that they would lose their kingdom of darkness. "The power
that is in" the Diggers "will take the rule and government from you
and give it a people that will make better use of it".[258] That sounds
like a transfer of political power, though it was to be brought about
by passive resistance, not by fighting. "The people shall all fall off
from you, and you shall fall on a sudden like a great tree that is
undermined at the root". "This falling off is begun already, divisions
shall tear and torture you till you submit to community". And in *An
Appeale to All Englishmen* Winstanley went a long way in inciting to
disobedience. Copyholders, he wrote, "are freed from obedience to
their lords of manors" by the Rump Parliament's Act declaring
England a free commonwealth, which "breaks in pieces ... the laws
of the conqueror"[259]

Winstanley attached great importance to this Act of 19 May 1649,
and to the Act abolishing monarchy (17 March 1649), as well as to the
Engagement to maintain the present Commonwealth. "You have set
Christ upon his throne in England", he told the "rulers of England,
... by your promises, engagements, oaths", and by those two Acts of
Parliament which he interpreted as giving Englishmen the right to
exercise their creation-freedom by cultivating the common land.[260]
What are we to make of his attitude towards the Rump, which had
also passed an Act "to maintain the old laws"? Winstanley referred
disparagingly to this latter Act as "made by a piece of the Parliament"
and warned his countrymen to beware of the danger of allowing the
Norman and kingly power to reassert itself.[261] Yet he wrote *Englands
Spirit Unfoulded* to urge support for the Commonwealth, specifically
on the ground that the Parliament's two Acts "declare plainly what
this state government aims at, and that is that all Englishmen may
have their freedom in and to the land, and be freed from the slavery of
the Norman Conquest". Professor Aylmer rightly sees this as a
realistic acceptance of the lesser evil.[262]

If we try to penetrate Winstanley's mental processes, it is I think
clear that he initially expected a sudden conversion to Reason, a

universal acceptance of community, as Christ rose everywhere in sons and daughters, and this Second Coming ended disagreement. Monarchy was abolished, we may recall, a fortnight before the digging started; the declaration that England was a free Commonwealth came two months later. In the euphoria of the moment this might seem to fortify the conviction that the digging was to initiate the Second Coming in England. But as the experience of the colony soon taught him, Winstanley had underestimated the institutional power of the Beast, the hold of the Serpent over the minds of men. What he must have found most upsetting of all was the hostility of many local tenants to the Diggers, as well as the antics of Ranters in the Cobham community which he attacked in *Englands Spirit Unfoulded*. Clearly a period of education was needed before Christ arose in a sufficient number of sons and daughters to overthrow kingly power.

Yet his experience also taught Winstanley that there were divisions among the ruling powers; sometimes the Army was less hostile than the local gentry. Charles I had after all been executed, and the Parliament had proclaimed a republic. The generals had at one stage allied with the Levellers; circumstances might force them to do so again. As late as January 1650 Winstanley still seems genuinely to have hoped for Army support.[263] Meanwhile divisions among the rulers could perhaps be exploited. Winstanley seems to have hoped that the Rump would fill up its vacant seats;[264] he expected "successive Parliaments", and seems to have suggested that "treacherous Parliament-men" might be recalled and replaced.[265] Whether Winstanley really believed that Parliament's two Acts aimed at granting all Englishmen their freedom in his sense matters not much; it was a good propagandist tactic to say so. His habit of interpreting Biblical texts in the sense he chose to give them might naturally lead him to read Acts of Parliament in the same spirit.[266]

Here the theory of the Norman Yoke was useful. Winstanley perhaps originally adopted its phraseology for propagandist reasons; but to denounce the gentry as Norman invaders drew on ideas which were widespread, especially in London, Buckinghamshire and among the rank and file of the Army; so did denunciations of lords of manors as representatives of Antichrist. As long ago as 1646 Christopher Feake was reported as saying that there was an "enmity against Christ" in aristocracy and monarchy.[267] Winstanley's equation of the rights of Englishmen with the creation liberties of all men, including the descendants of the free Anglo-Saxons, drew on the same traditions.

Pending the Second Coming, perhaps the Norman kingly power could be sapped piecemeal, since those in office differed in the extent of their readiness to compromise with it. Such an approach made co-operation with Parliament possible, even though many members of the Rump adhered to the Dragon. Some Quaker leaders were to pursue a similar tactic in 1659-60.[268] Popular pressure for Winstanley's interpretation of the two Acts could be used as a lever against conservatives in the government. Winstanley may have envisaged a period of dual power, in which Christ rising in sons and daughters would slowly hem the lords of manors into their enclosures, deprive them of labour, and so peacefully establish true freedom. In such circumstances, to call for the restoration of the creation liberties of all Englishmen was at once good propaganda and an accurate description of Winstanley's goal.

Hence by the time he came to write *The Law of Freedom* his emphasis had changed in relation to law. In *The New Law of Righteousness* he had envisaged the law of kingly power collapsing and being succeeded by the unanimous agreement of sons and daughters in whom Christ had risen — the *new* law. But *The Law of Freedom* is a more gradualist document. *Pace* Mr Davis, Winstanley did not anticipate a society "engaged in endless combat with sin and wickedness", nor did he return to the concept of original sin.[269] Mr Davis attributes far too great stability to the gentry power in Winstanley's Utopia, because he has failed to grasp what Winstanley expected to be the consequences of the withdrawal of labour from the enclosures. I think he is mistaken in supposing that Winstanley postulated, even in this transitional period, two systems of law and government existing side by side. Copyhold was to be abolished. So were the laws which favoured lords of manors.[270] Once wage labour became illegal, the only private property which could have survived for any length of time was peasant proprietorship, the farm worked by the labour of members of the family. One of the two greatest sins in the world, Winstanley had insisted in *Fire in the Bush*, was to hoard up more of the fruits of the earth than could be used by one particular family.[271]

Winstanley was concerned in *The Law of Freedom* with a trans-itional period. "In time . . . this commonwealth's government . . . will be the restorer of long lost freedoms to the creation". But meanwhile "the rudeness of the people", whether browbeaten tenants or pseudo-liberated Ranters, was a major obstacle to the Second Coming of Christ in sons and daughters. Winstanley's experience at St George's Hill and Cobham Heath must have convinced him that it was not possible to pass directly to a libertarian society: it would take time for Christ fully to rise in all. Winstanley's appeal to Cromwell shows an awareness, hinted at in *Englands Spirit Unfoulded*, of the importance of political power. So "because offences may arise from the spirit of unreasonable ignorance, therefore was the law added", Winstanley told "the friendly and unbiased reader"; it was "added ... against the rudeness and ignorance that may arise in mankind", he insisted in "A Short Declaration to take off Prejudice".[272] In the same way the law of Moses had been necessary against the hardness of the hearts of earlier Israelites. "The law was added ... to preserve common peace and freedom", "to limit men's manners, because of transgression one against another".[273] (Note the convenient Pauline phrase "was added", which Winstanley repeats in all these early references to the law.)[274] Whenever reasonable arbitration could "put a stop to the rigour of the law", it should do so, since the law is added as a "bridle to unreasonableness", to "regulate the unrational practice" of "covetous, proud and Beastly-minded men". Sentence for any offence which does not incur the death penalty may be mitigated by the judge, "for it is amendment not destruction that commonwealth's law requires".[275] Meanwhile the education both of innocent children (to help them "to govern themselves like rational men") and of unregenerate younger brothers is of the first importance.[276] Idleness is unreasonable because it hampers co-operation; so are extravagance and waste. Laws will be needed against them until this is understood.[277]

In this light I think we may conclude that Mr Davis exaggerated a little when he wrote that "flogging, judicial violence and torture" as well as capital punishment "were accepted by Winstanley as essential *and continuing* parts of the machinery of social discipline" (my italics).[278] We may think Winstanley's punishments unduly severe, but "torture" is an unnecessarily emotive word. In his earlier pamphlets Winstanley had totally rejected the law and its punishments; to execute a murderer was to commit another murder. His acceptance now of the necessity of some coercion was a reversal of this position in the light of the Diggers' political experience.

Winstanley was endeavouring to be realistic, and intended his punishments to be corrective. Given his desire "to prevent the cruelty of prisons", [279] what alternative was there in the seventeenth century to corporal penalties as a means of ensuring that the law was enforced? Whipping and burning in the hand were still so frequent that John Bunyan regarded them as minor punishments.[280] Mr Davis disregards the passage in *A Watch-Word to the City of London* where Winstanley tells "the Norman gentry" that "all the harm I would have you to have" is "that you my enemies may live in peace".[281] Mr Davis's word "continuing" suggests that Winstanley supposed that "the spirit of unreasonable ignorance" would last for ever. But that contradicts what he actually said. Such a denial of the Second Coming would be the sin against the Holy Ghost.[282]

Winstanley lived in the same world as Hobbes. His Reason has the same sort of universal validity, whether men recognize it or not, as the scientific laws of nature which Hobbes described in *Leviathan*. But Winstanley regarded co-operation as the law of the universe, whereas Hobbes saw competition and fear of death as the universal principles.[283] Winstanley's Reason, I have suggested elsewhere, also has its analogies with Rousseau's General Will. Its light is in all men, but will not completely dominate the thinking of any single individual until Christ has risen. "Many times men act contrary to Reason, though they think they act according to Reason". Winstanley's laws fulfil something like the function of "forcing to be free".[284]

In *The Breaking of the Day of God* Winstanley had described how the clergy cunningly juggled a corrupt power "out of the hands of the civil magistrates of the earth, which is God's ordinance ... for the government of the world". Magistracy must stand, but "this ecclesiastical power was always a troubler of godly magistrates.[285] Winstanley came to see closer connections between kingly power and the clergy power, and went beyond the traditional radical solution of separating church and state. He came to accept that "most laws are but to enslave the poor to the rich";[286] but "most" implies that some were not. Winstanley never wholly despaired of using state power in the cause of Reason against the kingly and clergy power.

In *Fire in the Bush* Winstanley recalled how Daniel had seen the Beast, kingly power, "lifted up from the earth and made to stand upon the feet like a man, and a man's heart was given to it; that is, this power should be the image of true magistracy, and while the Beastly power of self-love rules in the hearts of mankind this kingly power should be the preserver of the meek in spirit" for a transitional period until Christ comes to reign.[287] True magistracy was to be sought "among the poor despised ones of the earth, for there Christ dwells", rising up to unite the creation against false magistracy.[288]

"The great lawgiver in commonwealth government is the spirit of universal righteousness dwelling in mankind, now rising up to teach everyone to do to another as he would have another do to him". This spirit has been buried "for many years past". But we may hope, "because the name of commonwealth is risen and established in England", that "we or our posterity shall see comfortable effects". "It is the work of a Parliament to break the tyrants' bonds, to abolish all their oppressing laws, and to give orders, encouragements and directions unto the poor oppressed people of the land".[289] "All laws that are not grounded upon Equity and Reason", Winstanley told Fairfax, "not giving a universal freedom to all but respecting persons, ought ... to be cut off with the King's head".[290] He presumably hoped that Parliament would do the cutting.

Winstanley's position in *The Law of Freedom* signified something of a retreat. In *An Humble Request* and *Fire in the Bush* he had referred to the law of Moses as "but the moderation or curbing in of the Fall of mankind".[291] Moses "gave way to Christ" as Christ would now give way to the spreading power of righteousness.[292] But since in the England of 1652 the Second Coming clearly was not imminent, guidance was needed: the law was the schoolmaster to bring us to Christ. *The Law of Freedom* was subtitled *True Magistracy Restored*: it was pointing a radical way forward by removing the usurpations of kingly power, against which the Parliament had adopted two good laws.[293] It might be persuaded to pass more — if not the full programme of *The Law of Freedom*, at least part of it. Former monastic lands might be put at the disposal of the people, as well as church, crown and royalists' estates. Winstanley hoped that Parliament would legislate against tithes and copyhold services — both of which would have amounted to a form of expropriation.[294] It was a slim hope, but it was all there was. In realistic terms, all depended on winning over Oliver Cromwell.

In the years from the battle of Worcester to the dissolution of Barebone's Parliament Cromwell seemed the last hope of the radicals. It looks absurd to us now, knowing as we do that he was to preside over the reunion of Cavalier and Roundhead gentry which was ultimately to lead to the Restoration. But in these two years, as anger and frustration grew in the Army, Cromwell may well have appeared an ally. He had succeeded Fairfax, to whom as head of the Army Winstanley had previously addressed appeals. In April 1653 Cromwell was associated with Harrison and the millenarians against a conservative Rump. It was only his disillusionment with Barebone's Parliament that finally allowed him to succumb to conservative pressures. Winstanley can hardly have been very optimistic in 1652, but there was no other hope left. "You have power, ... I have no power," he sadly wrote. Pending the Second Coming (in Winstanley's sense) power was the essential consideration. Kingly power had defeated the Diggers; only commonwealth power could curb the Norman and Antichristian gentry, as it had abolished the Norman and Antichristian monarchy and House of Lords. "O power where art thou, that must mend things amiss?" were almost Winstanley's last printed words.[295]

Officers in Winstanley's commonwealth play a role similar to that of the law: they bridge the gap between the present divided state of England and the unanimity which will prevail after the Second Coming. The law in the heart of every man will be a check on all officers. So will the provision that officers are to be elected annually, by all men aged twenty and over, and that they may not be immediately re-elected. Laws will be fully discussed by all before enactment, and will be "few and short and often read".[296] The provision that judges are to apply, not to interpret, the law was intended to have the same effect as the written constitutions put forward by Levellers and others: to guard against the tendency of power to corrupt, and to prevent judicial discretion being used to achieve political and social ends.[297] We may think Winstanley's solution to this problem unsatisfactory, but he provided a degree of flexibility by the possibility of appeals to his County Senate and to Parliament. The militia of citizens in arms — as unprofessional a body as possible — existed to protect laws derived from Reason against "the turbulency of any foolish or self-ended spirit that endeavours to break their common peace".[298]

"All armies", as Winstanley rather pointedly told Oliver Cromwell, "make some poor, some rich, put some into freedom and others into bondage". "In the days of a free commonwealth" there was to be no professional army. The army was all the citizens, and would "be used to resist and destroy all who endeavour to keep up or bring in kingly bondage again". If a land be "so enslaved as England was under the kings and conquering laws, then an army is to be raised with as much secrecy as may be, to restore the land again and set it free".[299] These circumstances would presumably arise if the republican government and the generals failed to carry out the Commonwealth programme. It is a significant modification of the passive resistance which Winstanley had advocated when writing about the period before a communist society had been established.

VI

SOME PROBLEMS

If the foregoing analysis is correct, the outspoken materialism of *The Law of Freedom* should not present the difficulties it does to some commentators. Those who see Winstanley using religious language as a cloak to conceal atheistic materialism suggest that he cast off the veil in *The Law of Freedom* — though this is rather surprising in a pamphlet which clearly aims at moderation of expression in order to win maximum support. Those who think Winstanley believed in a personal God outside the creation have a good deal to explain away in *The Law of Freedom*. Among the many relevant passages the most important are, first, the starting point — that freedom depends on use of the earth, since men cannot live without the fruits of the earth. Take these away "and the body languishes, the spirit is brought into bondage". "A man had better to have had no body than to have no food for it. ... Free enjoyment" of the earth "is true freedom".[300] This leads on, secondly, to the famous paean beginning "to know the secrets of nature is to know the works of God", for God cannot be known outside the creation, nor can we have any knowledge of life after death. The desire to seek for "spiritual things" elsewhere comes from the devil. Third is Winstanley's equally well-known denunciation of divinity, speculation about such unknowable matters; and his explanation of "this doctrine of a God, a devil, a heaven and a hell, salvation and damnation after a man is dead" in psychological terms.[301] Finally, Winstanley's flat statement "I am assured that if it be rightly searched into, the inward bondages of the mind, as covetousness, pride, hypocrisy, envy, sorrows, fears, desperation and madness, are all occasioned by the outward bondage that one sort of people lay upon another".[302]

This materialism in no way contradicts Winstanley's theology, rightly understood. As we saw, he shared the theological materialism of many radical heretics. The doctrine of creation *ex deo* (as opposed to the orthodox *ex nihilo*) was proclaimed as early as *Truth Lifting up its Head*, and was shared by Familists, Ranters and Milton.[303] The creation is the clothing of God. For Winstanley this doctrine *excludes* a personal God. There are no external Saviours, there is no God beyond the sky, no heaven or hell after death, no personal external devil.[304] This is the annihilationist mortalism shared by Clarkson and many others. Those who offer themselves as Saviours are personifications of the Serpent, varieties of kingly power.[305]

I have been upbraided for suggesting that Winstanley rejected a personal God: what he rejected was only "the clergy's version . . . of a capricious, arbitrary God".[306] We are in agreement at least on this rejection: Winstanley's God was Reason. But what remains of a personal God in his system of ideas? A man who "thinks God is in the heavens above the skies . . . worships his own imagination, which is the devil".[307] The spirit which will rule after the Second Coming is "not one single person".[308] Sincerity and love are God, "the King of Righteousness which is called conscience". "The same spirit that made the globe" is "the indweller in the five senses of hearing, seeing, tasting, smelling and feeling".[309] The "murdering God of the world", who defends property, who "appointed the people to pay tithes to the clergy" and is "the author of the creatures' misery" is "the God devil".[310] He sounds at times suspiciously like the God of the Old Testament.[311] "That God whom you serve, and which did entitle you lords, knights, gentlemen and landlords, is covetousness, the God of this world, . . . under whose dark governing power you and all the nations of the world for the present are under".[312]

This, the clergy's God, is no more a real person than Winstanley's Reason is. It is a "dark power", which bears sway within professors and whom they call God and Christ. "Indeed, Imagination is that God which generally everyone worships and owns; . . . they worship the devil and mere nothing".[313] "Your Saviour must be a power within you to deliver you from that bondage within; the outward Christ, or the outward God, are but men Saviours", comparable to Moses, Joshua and Judges; "and these Gods sometimes proves devils". Preachers who tell you "your God and Saviour is without" (not those who assert the capricious, arbitrary God of Calvinism) "are servants to the curse".[314] That is why the Diggers would "neither come to church nor serve their God".[315] Each man has "his God", his Reason, his conscience, which he must be free to follow to the best of his ability.[316] Winstanley associated himself with the man who is called an atheist "because he will neither preach nor pray"; he regarded punishment for denying God, Christ and Scriptures as totally wrong. Like "wise-hearted Thomas" men should "believe nothing but what they see reason for".[317]

Always in Winstanley's thought there is a dialectic between the inner spirit and the external world, as well as between Reason and the Serpent.[318] Property, kingly power and a state church are institutionalizations of the Serpent within man; but they also vigorously protect and defend the Serpent, propagate its values. The establishment of private property is the Fall, the institutionalization of evil which gives it lasting power. Hence the importance of setting men and women free from a state church[319] so long as it exists, and of abolishing a state church altogether in the society envisaged in *The Law of Freedom*. Here Winstanley called for righteous laws based on Reason, to guide and help the young, the weak and the wavering. Hence too the great significance which Winstanley attached to education, and to studying the secrets of nature experimentally; both fortify Reason, as surrender to external objects, improperly understood, or idle speculation, fortify the Serpent. For Winstanley, as for Milton, education was a means by which men could get back behind the Fall.[320]

From his own experience Winstanley knew that the rising of Christ in sons and daughters can be hindered and delayed by the power of institutions; outward bondage occasions the inward bondages. That is why it seems to me wrong to describe the digging on St George's Hill as a mere symbolic gesture.[321] The Serpent must be cast out "not in words only, as preachers do, but in action, whereby the creation shines in glory".[322] Every political concession extorted from kingly power makes it easier for Christ to rise in sons and daughters. The dialectic is similar to that of more orthodox Puritans who believed that God's omnipotent will could be furthered by keeping one's power dry. But Winstanley's Christ is no external Saviour: men's wills cannot be changed except by themselves. If Winstanley had succeeded in casting down the kingdom of darkness, he believed that this would also be to the advantage of the men of property who themselves suffered from the institutions of the Serpent, though they were not yet sufficiently ruled by Reason to appreciate the fact. It would "break the devil's bands asunder, wherewith you are tied, that you my enemies may live in peace".[323]

The authors of "Winstanley: A Case for the Man as He Said He Was" are quite right to argue that there is no reason for surprise if a day-to-day pamphleteer reacting to events is not absolutely consistent;[324] though in *The Law of Freedom*, when Winstanley is looking back in defeat, one might expect his position to be more rather than less self-consistent. But in fact, I am suggesting, a very great consistency of *attitude* can be traced as Winstanley's ideas developed, as he learned from events. He *experienced* the might of kingly power and its ideologists, priests and lawyers; he learned from *experience* that Christ rose slowly in sons and daughters, that many were seduced by false arguments. It is the devil who tells a man that he "must not trust his own experience".[325] Winstanley's incorporation into his theological system of the myths of the Norman Yoke and of Antichrist, with correspondingly greater emphasis on external institutions and powers, reflects the experience of the Diggers' struggle, the growing appreciation that Reason too must be institutionalized. Hence the laws in *The Law of Freedom*, the stress on education and on diffusion of scientific knowledge. But this is only a shift in emphasis, not a fundamental change. There is no inconsistency, no "paradox", once we grasp that the dialectic is there from the start, and that Winstanley's theology *precludes* external Saviours and a personal God.[326] He uses the Christian myth in the same manner as he uses the Norman Yoke — as a myth. God and Christ are no more persons for him than Antichrist. "God is an active power, not an imaginary fancy". In "the great battle of God Almighty, light fights against darkness, universal love fights against selfish power, life against death, true knowledge against imaginary thoughts".[327] Property, "called the devil or covetousness", fights against "community . . . called Christ or universal love".[328]

Winstanley's relationship to the Quakers has often been discussed. I was long unconvinced by the attempt to identify him with the Gerrard Winstanley who was a corn-chandler in 1666, and died a Quaker ten years later.[329] But new evidence presented by James Alsop leaves no doubt, I think, that the man who received Quaker burial in 1676 was our Gerrard Winstanley.[330] Exactly what this fact signifies remains to be assessed. The Gerrard Winstanley who was sued for debts in 1660 did not use Quaker language. If Winstanley was an active Quaker in the sixteen-sixties and seventies, no evidence of this has been found. In 1659 he was appointed waywarden for Cobham parish. He occupied this office and those of overseer and churchwarden at various dates until 1668. In 1671 and 1672 he was one of two chief constables of Elmbridge Hundred. This suggests that he conformed to the state church during those years. The christening of three children born in the sixties is recorded in the Cobham parish register.[331]

In 1653 Francis Higginson, in 1655 Ralph Farmer, accused the Quakers of being "downright Levellers", well versed in the "learning of Winstanley and Collier".[332] Also in 1655 Francis Harris suggested that many Quakers had been Diggers, and others Levellers.[333] Thomas Comber in 1678, Thomas Tenison in 1683 and Thomas Bennett in 1700 all asserted that "Winstanley published the principles of Quakerism".[334] There are indeed analogies between Digger ideas and those of early Quakerism, but these may just as well derive from a common radical milieu as from direct influence — except perhaps for the Quaker adoption of Winstanley's phrase "the children of light".[335]

Winstanley's Quaker burial is often used to argue if not that he was a pacifist (as clearly he was not) at least that his approach to politics was primarily religious. But this was certainly not Comber's point, and it is to misunderstand the early Quakers. Before 1660 they were not pacifists and did not abstain from political action. As late as 1659 Edward Burrough was negotiating with the Rump of the Long Parliament with a view to Quaker support for and possible participation in the republican government.[336] Burrough was one of the activists among the Quaker leaders. The only direct evidence of contact between Winstanley and Quakers has recently been discovered by Dr Reay. In a letter to Margaret Fell, probably of August 1654, Burrough wrote: "Wilstandley [*sic*] says he believes we are sent to perfect that work which fell in their hands. He hath been with us".[337] At that date Quakers were being denounced as Levellers: Winstanley's remark is no evidence that he then held the doctrines which the Quakers espoused after 1660. But where else could he go after it became clear that Christ was not going to rise in Charles II's England?

VII

CONCLUSION

In what I have written my object has been strictly limited. If I had intended a full-scale reassessment of Winstanley's intellectual position I should have had to place much more emphasis on the political and economic ideas which he developed in and after *The True Levellers Standard Advanced*. I have confined myself to an attempt to assess the role of Winstanley's theology in the evolution of his ideas, since this I believe has been misinterpreted by too static an approach. Winstanley was not a crypto-atheist. Neither was he a traditional Christian. His theology was that of a very radical heretic, and can best be understood in relation to the thinking of his contemporaries, though ultimately it transcended their world of ideas.

A chronological approach makes it clear that Winstanley's conversion to communism antedates his adoption of the Leveller theory of the Norman Yoke, and his adoption of the name "Leveller". Before December 1648 he was relatively conventional in suggesting that God's people must learn by suffering and then wait patiently upon the Lord, expecting their consolation later. But Winstanley's conversion to communism included a new conviction that "action is the life of all; and if thou dost not act thou dost nothing". Action took the form of digging at St George's Hill, and the rest followed from that. In *The New Law of Righteousness* "the greatest combat is within a man".[338] But Winstanley learned that the external enemies of Christ rising were at least equally serious. His colony was opposed by local landlords, parsons, lawyers, ultimately by the power of the state: by kingly power. The Diggers were supported by the Levellers of Buckinghamshire; the Leveller newspaper, *The Moderate*, reprinted one of their declarations and echoed Winstanley's ideas on property as the cause of sin.[339] Perhaps support came from other radicals in the City and southern England. It was natural to take over Leveller political arguments in this context. In February 1649 Winstanley and another future Digger, Henry Bickerstaff, acted as arbitrators chosen by John Fielder, miller of Kingston-on-Thames, who had been imprisoned for holding a conventicle. In 1650 Lilburne took over Fielder's defence, using the same arguments as Winstanley had used. They can hardly have failed to meet. Fielder, like Lilburne, became a Quaker later in the sixteen-fifties: his house was used for Quaker meetings.[340]

What is interesting is the ease with which Winstanley combined his theology with the historical myth of the Norman Yoke and with Leveller doctrines of natural rights. Here Winstanley is unique only in the comprehensiveness and intellectual power of his synthesis. Walwyn, one suspects, had similar ideas, but he did not express them in writing. The Clarkson of *A General Charge, or, Impeachment of High-Treason, in the Name of Justice Equity, against the Communality of England* (1647), the author of *Tyranipocrit Discovered* (1649), the Coppe of *A Fiery Flying Roll* (1649), combined some communist ideas with radical theology, but never synthesized them.[341] John Warr linked the radical theology with the Norman Yoke theory in an elegant synthesis, but does not seem to have thought that communism necessarily followed.[341] Winstanley's is the most complete and successful marriage of politics and economics to the radical theology, the key concept being that of kingly power — the institutionalized Serpent — and its representatives: landlords, lawyers, clergy.

The heretical theology, with its deep roots in English history, and the radical version of the Norman Yoke theory which evolved during the civil war, both circulated in the same circles of artisans and small producers. Communist ideas had flickered in the radical underground for a long time, but had never (so far as the record shows) been elevated to a theory. Winstanley linked the three. His extension of the symbolism contained in the word "hedge" shows how naturally they came together. The word was commonly used in the seventeenth century as a symbol for private property, which the Levellers were alleged by their enemies to wish to cast down. Marvell, probably at almost exactly the same time as Winstanley was writing *The Law of Freedom*, spoke of:

> ...this naked equal flat,
> Which *Levellers* take pattern at.

It was a slur which Oliver Cromwell was to repeat.[342]

"A hedge in the field is as necessary in its kind as government in the church or commonwealth", wrote the Reverend Joseph Lee in 1656.[343] Winstanley wanted to throw down hedges in the field. But he also saw that churches "in the Presbyterian, Independent, or any

other form of profession ... are like the inclosures of land which
hedges in some to be heirs of life, and hedges out others". So in a
single phrase he linked, and dismissed, landlordism and the traditional "particular churches". In *The Law of Freedom* he extended the
analogy to the doctrine of predestination which (he no doubt
thought) protected landlordism. "This is the mighty ruler, that hath
made the election and rejection of brethren from their birth to their
death, or from eternity to eternity. He calls himself the Lord God of
the whole creation".[344] The overt, explicit reference is to kingly
power; but it is difficult not to suppose that Winstanley also
intended a backhand blow at the orthodox "Lord God of the whole
creation", who of course could not be explicitly attacked. So the
hedge with which Norman freeholders shut us out of the earthly
community has its analogue in the barriers with which priests try to
prevent us realising the spiritual equality of all men and women. Both
are cast down by Christ the true Leveller, simultaneously.

In Winstanley's mythology, then, the Norman Yoke, radical
theology and his theory of communism came to be indissolubly
linked. Landlords, kingly power and priests will be overthrown
together as Christ rises in sons and daughters: there is no distinction between economic freedom, political freedom and spiritual
freedom.

If we stress the theological origins of Winstanley's ideas, therefore, we must also emphasize the unorthodoxy of the theology.
From the start it was barely compatible with traditional Christianity; it became little more than a metaphor when salvation meant that
all will live in peace and rest on earth, with no after life; and Christ
yields place to the spreading of Reason in men and women "as the
earth grows to be a common treasury for all".[345] Once Winstanley
had broken loose from orthodoxy his thinking developed rapidly.
He took over Leveller political ideas, and his communism became
steadily less theological and more materialist as he learned from the
power of the enemies he was up against. By 1652 his message could be
expressed in almost wholly secular terms. In his ideal commonwealth
men called ministers were retained, but there was no state church,
and the unpaid "ministers" were elected by all the parishioners for
one year only, to perform secular educational functions. We cannot
explain this development except by reference to the England in
which he had hoped to see Christ rising. "Never has the tendency
towards secularization been so clear as in the years 1649-52", wrote

Professor Lutaud, who knows Winstanley and his world better than most scholars.[346]

We have seen that Winstanley was not an isolated thinker, though he pushed on further and more consistently than most. Ideas such as his, if freely preached in the tense political climate of 1649-50, with no censorship or church courts, would threaten not only the existence of a state church but also the authority of traditional theology. Such a prospect might well terrify those contemporaries, whether former Roundheads or former Cavaliers, who had no wish to see a social revolution. Hence the successive forcible suppressions of the Levellers in 1649, of the Diggers in 1650, of the Ranters in 1651, and the savage sentence on James Nayler in 1656. The debates on Nayler in the second Protectorate Parliament reveal with great clarity the hysterical *social* anxieties of those who most feared the Quakers. Hence too the political philosophy of Hobbes, with its emphasis on the authority of the sovereign — any sovereign who protects established civil society — as the only safeguard against the fanatical enthusiasm of the proponents of the radical theology — against those who, like Winstanley, received subversive messages from what they held to be a divine authority. Hobbes was only one of many proclaiming such theories in the early sixteen-fifties.[347]

When Cromwell accepted the Petition and Advice, a state church with an orthodox theology (to be defined by Parliament) had apparently been established. But in the traumatic winter 1659-60 this control slipped again as the attack on tithes developed, as Levellers and Agitators reappeared, as Quakers were said to be taking to arms. Hence the panic rush to recall Charles II, a rush in which conservative Puritans joined traditional episcopalians.[348] At many points in the history of popular revolutions it has appeared that radical religion might lead to irreligion. In France in the fifteen-sixties the respectable in "communities that had finally driven out priests and smashed idols feared that the congregations were in danger of drifting into atheism or worse if pastors did not arrive promptly to reorganize religious life".[349] "Does one come to unbelief through the mediation of a religious sect?", Albert Soboul asked, apropos the French Revolution. Many were the pamphleteers after 1660 who claimed that, religion apart, the church was essential to the maintenance of social order.[350]

The failure of the millennium to arrive, and the futile Fifth Monarchist revolts of 1657 and 1661, made the former millenarians

John Owen and John Bunyan reconsider the time-table for the events prophesied in Daniel and Revelation.[351] The coming of Christ's kingdom was postponed to kingdom come, and any connection with "fanaticism" was disavowed. The sixteen-fifties brought a decisive change in the perspective of the radicals too; the Restoration totally and finally defeated their this-worldly hopes. The Quakers turned pacifist and abandoned any attempt to bring about by political means a better world on earth. The Muggletonians also gave up Reeve's millenarianism; whilst retaining much of the radical theology (and Reeve's pacifism) Muggleton recreated an arbitrary authoritarianism under the surviving prophet.[352] The Diggers had hoped for salvation and glory on earth, and their this-worldliness reinforced the secularizing trend of their theology. But after 1660 not only conservative but also radical dissenters — at all events, those who could be heard — abandoned earthly solutions. It is a very important turning-point, the exact mechanisms of which have not been fully explored. It was a symptom rather than a cause of the defeat of the radical revolution in England, but it ensured that that defeat lasted for a long time. For thirty-five years at least it was very risky to publish anything which would have continued the radical theological trend. When the press regained a measure of freedom after 1695, the new world had established itself. The old ideas had been firmly driven underground or into exile, perhaps out of existence altogether. Freer though England was after 1688, anti-Trinitarians still risked a death sentence. Eighteenth-century deism was so abstractly secular that it lacked the emotional appeal of Winstanley's ideas. Never again were serious revolutionary ideas to be expressed in religious form in England. With Winstanley the radical theology reached a peak at which it was trembling over into secularism; but the reaction was so strong that the advance to secularism was stopped short, abandoned and perhaps forgotten. Even Toland, who salvaged so much of the seventeenth-century radical heritage, nevertheless felt that he had to invent a new religion to express it. When radicalism revived in the later eighteenth century, theology had been left behind.[353]

The historical achievement of Christianity has been to provide western civilization with a moral code for living in society. Its main weaknesses have been its attempt to combine human equality with property rights, and its invocation of the after life to compensate for the consequent injustices of this world. So it has proved increasingly inadequate as society moved towards greater equality. Winstanley did not look for consolations after death. His philosophy was designed for living in this world. But if supernatural sanctions and the authority of priests are abolished, how are standards of conduct to be maintained? Winstanley's original answer was by Reason in the conscience of every man and woman. But he came to realise that Reason can prevail only in an equal society; and that this must mean the abolition of private property and the wage relationship. Then free discussion in communities of equals can lead to acceptance of Reason's rule. (There is no space to do more than draw attention to Winstanley's very remarkable stress on sexual equality. Traditional orthodox emphasis on the Sonship of man becomes Christ rising in sons *and daughters*.)

The trouble about our unequal society, which has lost its belief in supernatural sanctions, is that there is no general acceptance of standards of right and wrong, and therefore no satisfactory means of enforcing them. Winstanley's intuition gives at least a possible answer: that in a non-exploitative society Reason might have a chance of rising in men and women, on the basis of their own social experience, and of being universally accepted as a guide to conduct. The weakness of his position is that, as Hobbes saw, "commonly they that call for right reason to decide any controversy do mean their own".[354] But it is arguable that in an equal society these disagreements might be soluble by rational discussion, since no vested interests would prejudice the debate. One could deny this *a priori* only by asserting a doctrine of original sin. Whether it is now too late to construct a society which shall be both non-exploitative and organized in communities small enough to conduct rational discussion (as Rousseau wished) is another matter. In Winstanley's time the possibilities were greater, as they may be today in parts of the Third World.

Winstanley, it seems to me, was groping his way towards a humanist and materialist philosophy, in which there were no outward Saviours, no heaven or hell or after life, but only men and women living in society. We should not underestimate the difficulties of this quest. There may have been philosophical atheists in the seventeenth century, though Bunyan doubted it.[355] It is at least as likely that those whom their contemporaries called atheists were either deists or "couldn't-care-less" non-philosophical hedonists. Until the concept of evolution had been established, it was not easy to account for the existence of the universe without postulating a creator. Theological materialists like Milton, philosophical materialists like Hobbes, took for granted the existence of a creator-God. The Bible had been accepted for so long as the source of all truth and wisdom that it was difficult to escape from its myths: popular radicalism indeed in the century since the Reformation had drawn on the Bible to criticize existing authorities and institutions. The fact that Winstanley left the historical veracity of the Bible an open question is evidence of very daring intellectual independence. His Reason, which is both the creator of the universe and the spirit which dictates co-operation to men and women living in society, is an attempt to maintain the unity of mankind and the cosmos.

So it is perhaps irrelevant to ask whether Winstanley "believed" the Christian myths, or whether he used them only as a convenient mode of expression, a metaphor. The question imposes twentieth-century assumptions on him. This was the idiom in which men thought: so were the Norman Yoke and Antichrist. Whether the myths were historically true "matters not much". What did matter — for Winstanley as for Milton — was that through the myths truths about man, society and the universe could be poetically expressed, in a way that would inspire to action. The battles of God Almighty between Christ and the Serpent could be described more prosaically, but I do not suppose that Winstanley thought in prose and then wrote in poetic myth. He used the myths because they were for him the most accessible way of expressing profound truths about humanity.

But these truths were very different from traditional orthodox Christianity, and in so far as they denied a human Saviour, a personal God, they were in opposition to orthodoxy. Winstanley's system of ideas could be rewritten in the language of rational deism; had he lived fifty years later he might have so expressed them. But a great deal of their force and immediacy derives from the poetic, mytho-poeic style which came naturally to him. We should not classify him as a deist, still less as a seventeenth-century Marxist; but we should recognize the profound difference between the content of his ideas and that of traditional Christianity. His thinking was struggling towards concepts which were to be more precisely if less poetically formulated by later, non-theological materialisms.

NOTES

1. Originally published as *Past and Present Supplement*, No. 5 (1978). It was followed by a discussion in *P. and P.*, No. 89 (1980). This discussion raised no new issues, but I have incorporated in the present text a few passages from my "Rejoinder" (pp. 147-51) to the comment by L. Mulligan, J.K. Graham and J. Richards (pp. 144-6). Since this piece was written T. Wilson Hayes's *Winstanley the Digger: A Literary Analysis of Radical Ideas in the English Revolution* (Harvard U.P., 1979) has added greatly to our understanding of Winstanley in his radical heretical context.

2. W.S. Hudson, "Economic and Social Thought of Gerrard Winstanley", *Journal of Modern History*, XVIII (1946), pp. 1-21; L. Mulligan, J.K. Graham and J. Richards, "Winstanley: A Case for the Man as He Said He Was", *Journal of Ecclesiastical History*, XXVIII (1977), pp. 57-75.

3. George Juretic, "Digger no Millenarian: The Revolutionizing of Gerrard Winstanley", *Journal of the History of Ideas*, XXXVI (1975), pp. 268-70, 274-6, 280.

4. Hudson, *op. cit.*, pp. 7, 11, 21. Had the Quakers no practical intentions when they did things "for a sign"?

5. I have already written at some length on these matters in *W.T.U.D.*, in my Introduction to Winstanley's *The Law of Freedom and Other Writings* (Cambridge U.P., 1983; hereafter cited by title only), and in *M.E.R.*. Here I concentrate on Winstanley's religion in its historical context. Cf. also Chapter 7 above.

6. Gerrard Winstanley, *The Breaking of the Day of God* (1648; 2nd edn., 1649); Gerrard Winstanley, *The Mysterie of God, Concerning the Whole Creation, Mankind* (1648; 2nd edn., 1649); Gerrard Winstanley, *The Saints Paradise* (two editions, both undated, almost certainly 1648); Gerrard Winstanley, *Truth Lifting up its Head above Scandals* (1649; 2nd edn., 1650); Gerrard Winstanley, *The New Law of Righteousness* (1649); Gerrard Winstanley, *Several Pieces Gathered into One Volume* (December 1649); William London, *A Catalogue of the Most Vendible Books in England, Orderly and Alphabetically Digested* (1657). *Truth Lifting up its Head* and *The New Law of Righteousness* are both reprinted in *The Works of Gerrard Winstanley*, ed. G.H. Sabine (Cornell U.P., 1941; hereafter *Works*). Subsequent references to *The Breaking of the Day of God* and to *The Mysterie of God* are to the second editions of these works. I cite the edition of *The Saints Paradise* which has 134 pages. These last three works of Winstanley listed above are hereafter cited by title only.

7. *The Mysterie of God*, pp. 2, 4.

8. *The Saints Paradise*, Sigs. B, D, pp. 54-5, 89; cf. "Another Digger Broadside", ed. K.V. Thomas, *P. and P.*, No. 42 (1969), pp. 57-68 (hereafter *A Declaration ... [from] Iver*); *W.T.U.D.*, pp. 113-14; *M.E.R.*, p. 243.

9. *The Saints Paradise*, Sigs. B, C, pp. 85, 89-90, 98; *Works*, p. 107; cf. pp. 375, 441, and *M.E.R.*, Ch. 26. See p. 226 above.

10. *The Mysterie of God*, Sig. A 2v, pp. 14-15, 21; *The Breaking of the Day of God*, p. 130; *The Saints Paradise*, pp. 39, 88. For the Father as the sun, cf. *ibid.*, pp. 1, 17.

11. *The Mysterie of God*, pp. 10-11, 23, 26; *The Saints Paradise*, Sig. B, pp. 29-30, 32, 35-9, 44-54, 101, 105, 110-11.

12. *The Saints Paradise*, Sigs. A-B, D-E, p. 11; *The Mysterie of God*, pp. 33-5; *The Breaking of the Day of God*, pp. 22-3, 63-4, 79, 115, 123, 129-30.

13. *The Saints Paradise*, pp. 24, 27; *The Breaking of the Day of God*, pp. 10-12, 16; *The Mysterie of God*, pp. 31-2, 38, 41.

14. *Works*, p. 125.

15. Cf. *ibid.*, p. 332: "Doth the murderer's sword make any man to be God's Anointed?" See pp. 195-6 above.

16. *The Saints Paradise*, pp. 3, 6.

17. *The Breaking of the Day of God*, p. 16.

18. *The Mysterie of God*, pp. 33, 35, 38; cf. p. 40; *The Breaking of the Day of God*, Sig. A 3v, pp. 80, 120; *The Saints Paradise*, pp. 9, 14, 49-50, 111.

19. *Works*, pp. 112, 120-4.

20. *The Breaking of the Day of God*, p. 12; *The Saints Paradise*, p. 53; cf. *The Mysterie of God*, p. 28. For the anointing see *The Experience of Defeat*, pp. 304-6.

21. *The Saints Paradise*, pp. 120-1. For the meaning Winstanley was later to give to "salvation", see p. 210 above.

22. *The Mysterie of God*, Sigs. A 3-4, pp. 7-8, 15, 46-7, 50-1; *The Saints Paradise*, pp. 126-34.

23. *The Breaking of the Day of God*, pp. 10-11; cf. p. 6, and *The Mysterie of God*, p. 6; also *Works*, pp. 120, 166, 169. See *M.E.R.*, pp. 303-5, and pp. 153-4 above.

24. *The Saints Paradise*, pp. 118-19, 63-4, 132; *The Mysterie of God*, pp. 24-5, 31-2; *Works*, pp. 124, 131-2.

25. *Works*, pp. 112, 121, 131-2; cf. pp. 113, 118. For the radical doctrine of Sonship, see *M.E.R.*, Ch. 23; cf. pp. 203-4 above.

26. *The Saints Paradise*, pp. 66-7, 13-14. For Christ as the great prophet, see John Saltmarsh, *Sparkles of Glory, or Some Beams of the Morning-Star* (1648), p. 39; *M.E.R.*, pp. 392-3.

27. *Works*, p. 116; cf. p. 82.

28. *The Breaking of the Day of God*, pp. 34, 37; cf. p. 10.

29. *The Saints Paradise*, pp. 82-5; *The Mysterie of God*, pp. 67-9; *Works*, p. 114.

30. *The Saints Paradise*, p. 94; cf. *Works*, p. 116. On the familiar distinction between "the history" and "the mystery", see *The Mysterie of God*, pp. 3, 5, and *The Breaking of the Day of God*, p. 90; cf. *W.T.U.D.*, p. 261.

31. *The Saints Paradise*, pp. 51-3. It is not uninteresting to compare these pages with *Paradise Regained*, and Winstanley's doctrine of Sonship

with Milton's: *M.E.R.*, Ch. 23.

32. *The Saints Paradise*, pp. 68-9; *The Mysterie of God*, p. 4; *Works*, p. 120.

33. *The Saints Paradise*, pp. 72-3, 87; *The Mysterie of God*, pp. 8, 53, 82-3. Cf. pp. 209-10 above.

34. *The Breaking of the Day of God*, pp. 39, 62, 119; *The Saints Paradise*, pp. 76, 98. Cf. Joseph Salmon quoted on p. 196 above.

35. *Works*, pp. 112-15, 122, 127.

36. *The Saints Paradise*, pp. 93, 105-6.

37. *Ibid.*, pp. 122-5; *Works*, pp. 104-5, 109, 111, 124-5. Cf. *Light Shining in Buckinghamshire*: Reason in all men teaches them to do as they would be done by; and *More Light Shining in Buckinghamshire*: Reason equals co-operation: *Works*, pp. 611, 627. If Winstanley had any hand in these pamphlets, these passages might well have been written by him.

38. *Works*, pp. 451-3.

39. *The Saints Paradise*, p. 16; *Works*, pp. 136-44. One of the few respects in which Kevin Brownlow's admirable film *Winstanley* errs is in making Winstanley say grace before eating. In *The New Law of Righteousness* he rejects the practice: *Works*, p. 232.

40. *The Breaking of the Day of God*, pp. 79, 115, 123, 129-30.

41. *The Saints Paradise*, pp. 12, 30, 78; cf. *M.E.R.*, pp. 314-16, and pp. 210-12 above.

42. *Works*, p. 122.

43. *The Saints Paradise*, pp. 8, 15-16.

44. *Ibid.*, pp. 18-19. Did Winstanley feel that his move into Surrey had cut him off from some London congregation?

45. *Ibid.*, pp. 57-8; cf. p. 115, and *The Mysterie of God*, p. 59.

46. *Works*, p. 315.

47. *The Saints Paradise*, p. 60; cf. p. 33. I owe the peat-cutting to David Taylor, citing recently identified Cobham manorial court records for the period 1620-60.

48. Contrast Hudson, "Economic and Social Thought of Gerrard Winstanley", pp. 5, 7, 11, 17, 19. Professor Hudson believes that the dedicatory epistle to *The Law of Freedom* is "a clear indication that he had been converted to the Fifth Monarchy point of view", at least so far as methods were concerned. Having argued that "political action was irrelevant" for Winstanley, Professor Hudson had to find a way out of the "mystifying paradox" of his own invention. But there were no Fifth Monarchist methods in 1651, when Winstanley completed *The Law of Freedom*.

49. *The Breaking of the Day of God*, p. 133; cf. *Works*, p. 186. D.W. Petegorsky believed that Winstanley had read More and Bacon: Petegorsky, *Left-Wing Democracy in the English Civil War* (1940), p. 122. My guess would be the same; but he never mentions them. Cf. P. Zagorin, *A History of Political Thought in the English Revolution* (1954), pp. 53-4; and T.W. Hayes, "Gerrard Winstanley and Foxe's 'Book of Martyrs'", *Notes and Queries*, new series, XXIV (1977), pp. 209-12.

50. *The Saints Paradise*, pp. 21, 27; cf. *The Breaking of the Day of God*,

pp. 35, 50, 70, 91-2, 132-6, and *Works*, p. 188.

51. *The Saints Paradise*, Sig. A 2v-3, pp. 70, 86-9, 93, 106.
52. *Ibid.*, pp. 19, 62-3; *The Breaking of the Day of God*, Sig. A 3v-4v, pp. 79, 125-7.
53. Cf. *Antichrist in Seventeenth-Century England* (1971), *passim*. We might list William Aspinwall, John Brayne, Mary Cary, Collier, Erbery, Nathanael Homes, Robert Purnell, William Sedgwick, John Spittlehouse, Peter Sterry and many others.
54. *The Breaking of the Day of God*, pp. 1, 40; cf. p. 30. This tract takes the form of an exposition of Revelation XI, a favourite chapter with millenarians: cf. Lodowick Muggleton, *A True Interpretation of the Eleventh Chapter of the Revelation of St. John, and Other Texts* (1662); Hanserd Knollys, *An Exposition of the Eleventh Chapter of the Revelation* (1679).
55. *The Saints Paradise*, pp. 81-2; cf. *The Mysterie of God*, p. 6: "The mystery of iniquity will be subdued under the feet of his Son, the human nature".
56. *The Mysterie of God*, p. 7; *W.T.U.D.*, p. 193. See pp. 196, 211 above.
57. Thomas Edwards, *Gangraena*, I, pp. 87-8, II, p. 11, and III, pp. 26-7; *W.T.U.D.*, esp. pp. 35-8, 184-92; *M.E.R.*, Chs. 6, 8. Sabine is good on the religious flux from which Winstanley's ideas emerged: *Works*, pp. 22-39.
58. *Works*, pp. 493-4; Alexander Gordon's article on "Richard Coppin" in *D.N.B.*
59. John Penry, *Three Treatises concerning Wales* (ed. D. Williams, Cardiff, 1960), p. 33. See Chapter 7 above.
60. Burrage, *op. cit.*, I, Chapters 9-11; *W.T.U.D.*, pp. 165-6; cf. p. 102 above. Thomas Edwards and the 1648 Blasphemy Ordinance denounced universalism.
61. R.M. Jones, *Spiritual Reformers of the Sixteenth and Seventeenth Centuries* (1928), p. 254; *Works*, pp. 25-6, 29; Saltmarsh, *Sparkles of Glory*, pp. 145-6; cf. C.H. Firth, *Cromwell's Army* (1902), p. 400, and p. 128 above.
62. Samuel Fisher, *Baby-Baptism meer Babism* (1653), pp. 27-9, 105-6; cf. *W.T.U.D.*, p. 259.
63. [Anon.], *Tyranipocrit, Discovered with his Wiles, Wherewith He Vanquisheth* (Rotterdam, 1649); *W.T.U.D.*, pp. 166-7, 204-6, 220-1; George Fox, *Three General Epistles to be Read in all the Congregations of the Righteous* (1664), p. 5.
64. *W.T.U.D.*, pp. 220-1, 232; Milton, *Paradise Lost*, xii. 585-7; cf. *Works*, p. 481; Lutaud, *Winstanley*, pp. 270-1.
65. *W.T.U.D.*, p. 186; cf. Saltmarsh, quoted in *Works*, p. 31.
66. F. Yates, *Giordano Bruno and the Hermetic Tradition* (1964), pp. 8, 23; P.J. French, *John Dee: The World of an Elizabethan Magus* (1972), p. 74; W. Shumaker, *The Occult Sciences in the Renaissance* (California U.P., 1972), pp. 230-2.
67. *Philosophy Reformed and Improved in Four Profound Treatises* (by O. Croll and Paracelsus), trans. Henry Pinnell (1657), p. 65.

68. *W.T.U.D.*, pp. 233, 236; William Erbery, *The Testimony ... left upon Record for the Saints of Succeeding Ages* (1658), pp. 5-15, 23, 40; Fisher, *Baby-Baptism meer Babism*, pp. 511-13; for Morgan Llwyd see R. Tudor Jones, "The Healing Herb and the Rose of Love: the Piety of Two Welsh Puritans", in *Reformation, Conformity and Dissent* (ed. R.B. Knox, 1977), pp. 172, 175-6.

69. *W.T.U.D.*, pp. 188-97, 204-6, 217, 220-2, 224-5, 228, 236-7, 259, 264; cf. Winstanley, *Works*, pp. 28-30, 39; Jones, *Spiritual Reformers*, pp. 214-15; Saltmarsh, *Sparkles of Glory*, pp. 9-12, 18, and *passim*; *Short Journal and Itinerary Journals of George Fox* (ed. N. Penney, Cambridge U.P., 1925), pp. 13, 21, 41; John Everard, *The Gospel-Treasury Opened* (2nd edn., 1657-9), I, pp. 54-5, 60, 76-8; Collier, *A Discovery of the New Creation* (1647), in Woodhouse, *Puritanism and Liberty*, p. 390.

70. Fox, *Short Journal*, pp. 17, 31-2. The passages in which Fox made this claim on his own behalf were omitted from the *Journal* as printed in 1694.

71. Nayler, *Sauls Errand to Damascus* (1654), pp. 2, 5-6, 10-11; Nayler, *A Discovery of the Man of Sin* (1654), p. 14.

72. Fox, *Short Journal*, pp. 1, 16. (These passages were also omitted from the 1694 *Journal*).

73. Rutherford, *A Survey of the Spirituall Antichrist* (1648), pp. 59-68.

74. [Anon.], *The Sovereignty of Kings* (1642), Sig. A 1v, A 3.

75. Wither, *Fides Anglicana* (1660), p 22, in *Miscellaneous Works* (Spenser Soc.), V (1877); *M.C.P.W.*, IV, pp. 403, 499; *M.E.R.*, p. 302; Saltmarsh, *Sparkles of Glory*, pp. 155, 187-8.

76. R[ichard] O[verton], *Mans Mortalitie* (Amsterdam, 1644) (ed. H. Fisch, Liverpool U.P., 1968), p. 97, quoting Overton's *Man Wholly Mortal* (1655).

77. *W.T.U.D.*, pp. 224-7; cf. pp. 237-40, 261-2; Wither, *Fragmenta Prophetica* (1669), in *Miscellaneous Works*, VI (1878), p. 121.

78. William Perkins, *Works* (1609-13), III, p. 392; Rutherford, *A Survey of the Spirituall Antichrist*, pp. 9, 55-68; Ephraim Pagitt, *Heresiography* (2nd. edn., 1645), pp. 84-7; cf. pp. 104-5 above.

79. D.D. Hall, *op. cit.*, pp. 350-73, esp. pp. 361-2.

80. Jones, *Spiritual Reformers*, pp. 225, 245-6, 262; Erbery, *Testimony*, pp. 207, 217-20, 237; *M.E.R.*, pp. 312-13; Fisher, *Baby-Baptism meer Babism*, pp. 511-13; Saltmarsh, *Sparkles of Glory*, pp. 39, 187-8, 219 and *passim*.

81. Warr, *Administrations, Civil and Spiritual* (1648), pp. 28, 35-6, 40.

82. *W.T.U.D.*, pp. 178, 187, 219-22.

83. Nayler, *Sauls Errand to Damascus*, pp. 2, 8; Bunyan, *Works*, II, pp. 168, 177, 198, 210.

84. *W.T.U.D.*, pp. 193-4; *M.E.R.*, pp. 304, 309; Collier, in Woodhouse, *Puritanism and Liberty*, p. 390.

85. Cook, *King Charls His Case* (1649), p. 40; Canne, *A Voice from the Temple to the Higher Powers* (1653), p. 14; *M.E.R.*, p. 298. Cf. pp. 193-4 above.

86. *W.T.U.D.*, pp. 204-6; cf. Clarkson, *ibid.*, p. 338.
87. *M.E.R.*, p. 322.
88. *W.T.U.D.*., pp. 142-6; Winstanley, *Works*, p. 28; G. K. Hyland, *A Century of Persecution* (1920), pp. 103-12; cf. pp. 103-5 above.
89. *W.T.U.D.*, pp. 170-9, 191, 209, 225-6, 228; *M.E.R.*, p. 309; Jones, *Spiritual Reformers*, pp. 186-7, 251-2; Edwards, *Gangraena*, III, pp. 26-7; R.O., *Mans Mortalitie*, pp. 38-42; Haller and Davies, *op. cit.*, pp. 296-7.
90. J. N. Wise, *Sir Thomas Browne's 'Religio Medici' and Two Seventeenth Century Critics* (Missouri U.P., 1973), pp. 25-6, 149.
91. Henry Newcome, *Autobiography* (ed. R. Parkinson, Chetham Soc., 1852), II, p. 37.
92. Clarkson, *A Single Eye*, Sig. A lv.
93. *A Discourse between John Reeve and Richard Leader* (1682), p. 9.
94. *W.T.U.D.*, pp. 219-22.
95. F. J. C. Hearnshaw, *Life of Sir Henry Vane the Younger* (1910), p. 57.
96. Nayler, *Sauls Errand to Damascus*, p. 14.
97. *Works*, pp. 567-70; Lutaud, *op. cit.*, p. 367.
98. *M.E.R.*, pp. 72-3 and Chapter 23; Pagitt, *Heresiography*, pp. 84-7; cf. Emmison, *Elizabethan Life: Morals and the Church Courts*, p. 110, and p. 103 above.
99. V. Powell, quoted in Jones, "The Healing Herb and the Rose of Love", pp. 157-8; cf. George Starkey, quoted by R. L. Greaves, "The Nature of the Puritan Tradition", in Knox, *Reformation, Conformity and Dissent*, p. 272; Saltmarsh, *Sparkles of Glory*, pp. 79-101.
100. *M.E.R.*, pp. 71-2 and Chapter 8; Fisher, *Baby-Baptism meer Babism*, pp. 34-8, 553, 591-2; *W.T.U.D.*, Chapter 6, p. 214.
101. For more on Winstanley and the clergy see *Change and Continuity in Seventeenth-Century England*, pp. 142-8.
102. B. R. White, "Henry Jessey in the Great Rebellion", in Knox, *op. cit.*, pp. 142-3; Saltmarsh, *Sparkles of Glory*, pp. 280-2.
103. *W.T.U.D.*, pp. 187, 195-6, 209, 372; *M.E.R.*, pp. 112-13; Hill, *Irreligion in the "Puritan" Revolution* (Barnett Shine Foundation Lecture, 1974), p. 19; cf. pp. 212, 226-7 above. I cannot understand how Professor Hudson came to suppose that Winstanley made "provision for regular worship" in *The Law of Freedom*, nor for "sermons to deal with what we would call 'historical theology', 'natural theology' and 'philosophy of religion'": Hudson, "Economic and Social Thought of Gerrard Winstanley", pp. 19-20. This seems to me a very strained interpretation of the passages to which he refers: *Works*, pp. 562-4, 597.
104. John Reeve, *A Remonstrance from the Eternal God* (1653), p. 21; Reeve, *Sacred Remains* (1706), p. 46.
105. *Works*, p. 402.
106. *The Saints Paradise*, p. 7.
107. *M.E.R.*, pp. 211-16; Saltmarsh, *Sparkles of Glory*, p. 117; *Free Grace* (10th edn., 1700), p. 111: first published 1645. Cf. Chapter 10 above.
108. *The Mysterie of God*, pp. 18, 44-5; *Works*, pp. 565-6; N. T. Burns, *Christian Mortalism from Tyndale to Milton* (Harvard U.P., 1972),

pp. 232-3 and *passim*; *M.E.R.*, pp. 73-5 and chapter 25; Emmison, *op. cit.*, p. 110; D.E. Underdown, *Somerset in the Civil War and Interregnum* (Newton Abbot, 1973), p. 146; cf. pp. 103-4 above.

109. Edwards, *Gangraena*, III, p. 101; cf. I, p. 117; *W.T.U.D.*, pp. 207, 221; *M.C.P.W.*, VI, p. 409; R.O., *Mans Mortalitie*, *passim*.

110. Bunyan, *Works*, II, pp. 176-7, 200. Bunyan may have confused Quakers with Ranters or even Diggers: both were to be found in Bedfordshire in the early sixteen-fifties.

111. Shumaker, *The Occult Sciences in the Renaissance*, pp. 214, 223; Yates, *Giordano Bruno and the Hermetic Tradition*, p. 34; *M.E.R.*, pp. 330-1.

112. *W.T.U.D.*, pp. 179, 206, 209; Winstanley, *Works*, pp. 107-8; William Sewel, *The History of ... the ... Quakers* (1722), pp. 16-17; G.F. Nuttall, *The Puritan Spirit* (1967), pp. 194-203; cf. p. 104 above.

113. Francis Bacon, *Works* (ed. J. Spedding, R.L. Ellis and D.D. Heath, 1857-74), III, pp. 213, 377; cf. Winstanley, *Works*, p. 565.

114. Harvey, *Anatomical Exercitations Concerning the Generation of Living Creatures* (1653), pp. 456-7. This was the first English translation, so what Winstanley published in 1652 is unlikely to derive from Harvey: *Works*, p. 565.

115. See pp. 187, 226 above; *M.E.R.*, p. 330; *W.T.U.D.*, pp. 206, 219-20.

116. Everard, *The Gospel-Treasury Opened*, I, pp. 5-11, 71-7, 111-13; II, pp. 64, 361, 363, 373-5.

117. Saltmarsh, *Sparkles of Glory*, pp. 189-93; Richard Coppin, *Divine Teachings* (1653), II, *Antichrist in Man*, pp. 99-101; Fox, *Short Journal*, p. 4.

118. *W.T.U.D.*, pp. 148, 391-2.

119. John Holland, *The Smoke of the Bottomlesse Pit* (1651), p. 2; Edward Hyde, *A Wonder and Yet No Wonder* (1651), pp. 35 ff., both quoted by Theodor Sippell, *Werdendes Quäkertum* (Stuttgart, 1937).

120. Warr, *Administrations, Civil and Spiritual*, pp. 2, 5-6, 10-11, 13-15, 18.

121. See p. 223 above; and for Warr, see also *W.T.U.D.*, Chapter 12.

122. Jacob Boehme, *The Signature of All Things* (Everyman edn.; first published in 1621), pp. 218-19; George Smith, *Englands Pressures, or, The Peoples Complaint* (1645), pp. 4-5.

123. Edwards, *Gangraena*, III, pp. 26-7.

124. *W.T.U.D.*, pp. 146, 220; C.S. Hensley, *The Later Career of George Wither* (The Hague, 1969), p. 99; Sir Henry Vane, *The Retired Man's Meditations* (1655), p. 173; Lodowick Muggleton, *A True Interpretation ... of the Whole Book of the Revelation* (1665), pp. 66-7.

125. *W.T.U.D.*, pp. 114-21, 169, 223-7; see p. 100 above. An English translation of More's *Utopia* had been published in 1639.

126. See Sir Thomas More, *The Cofutacyon of Tyndales Answere* (1532), quoted in G.R. Elton, *Reform and Reformation* (1977), p. 44.

127. Shumaker, *The Occult Sciences in the Renaissance*, pp. 213, 231.

128. Everard, *The Gospel-Treasury Opened*, I, p. 293; cf. p. 236; II, pp. 159-211. Everard died in 1650.

129. John Ball, *A Treatise of Faith*, (2nd edn. 1632;), p. 363 (I owe this

reference to Dr David Zaret); *M.C.P.W.*, II, p.601. Cf.*W.T.U.D.*, 149-50 (Sibbes and Bolton).

130. *Works*, pp.101, 243, 141.
131. This is only an inference from *Works*, pp.209, 213, 232.
132. *Ibid.*, pp.139, 232; *The Law of Freedom and Other Writings*, pp.157-8.
133. *The Saints Paradise*, p.78.
134. *Works*, pp.190, 199.
135. By Mulligan, Graham and Richards, "Winstanley: A Case for the Man as He Said He Was", pp.65-7. At this and other points my critics might have been less severe if they had reflected that I was introducing Winstanley, as a Penguin *Classic*, to readers most of whom would be unfamiliar with seventeenth-century society.
136. Lamont, *Richard Baxter and the Millennium*, esp. pp.66-7, 298; F.E. Manuel, *A Portrait of Isaac Newton* (Harvard U.P., 1968), pp.29, 86-7. Cf. Thomas Patience, *The Doctrine of Baptism* (1654), Epistle to the Reader.
137. Ed. A. Macfarlane, *The Diary of Ralph Josselin* (1976), p.350
138. For a good example see Peter Webster, *Rua and the Maori Millennium* (Victoria U.P., New Zealand, 1979), p.63.
139. J. Kent Clark, *Goodwin Wharton* (Oxford U.P., 1984), pp.145, 164, 179, 182, 213 and *passim*.
140. Thomas Hobbes, *Leviathan* (Penguin, 1968), p.411.
141. *The Saints Paradise*, p.78; Mulligan, Graham and Richards, *op. cit.*, p.67; *Works*, pp.328-9.
142. *The Law of Freedom and Other Writings*, pp.155-7.
143. *Works*, pp.218, 567-8; cf. p.520. See p.192 above.
144. *The Mysterie of God*, Sig. A 2; cf. pp.9, 33. Are we to postulate "a visible voice" here too?
145. *Works*, pp.244, 315, 329; cf. *Fire in the Bush*, *Works*, p.445: "This following declaration of the word of life was a free gift to me from the Father himself; and I received it not from men". So he sent it to the churches.
146. *Works*, pp.195, 257, 260-2, 264; cf. p.164: visions and revelations have not ceased. John Reeve had a vision in February 1652 which differentiated him from other prophets (*A Divine Looking Glass*, 1719, p.111. This is a reprint of the original edition of 1656: Muggleton considerably altered it when he reissued it in 1661).
147. *Works*, p.190.
148. *W.T.U.D.*, pp.133-6, 146-8. See p.193 above.
149. *Works*, pp.611, 613, 622; cf. *More Light Shining in Buckinghamshire*, in *Works*, p.638 (30 March 1649). See pp.214-16, 223 above.
150. *Works*, pp.612-14, 619-20, 628, 636, 646-7.
151. *W.T.U.D.* pp.163, 393; cf. p.336 (Roger Crab in 1657).
152. *Works*, pp.185, 192, 198; *A Declaration ... [from] Iver*, p.62. See pp.211-15 above.
153. I elaborate these points in my "Rejoinder", pp.149-50.
154. *Works*, pp 380-1.
155. Keith Thomas, "The Date of Gerrard Winstanley's *Fire in the Bush*", *P*

and P., no. 42 (1969), pp. 160-2; Juretic, "Digger no Millenarian", p. 279.

156. *The Law of Freedom and Other Writings*, pp. 155-7.

157. *"England's Spirit Unfoulded, or An Incouragement to Take the 'Engagement':* A Newly Discovered Pamphlet by Gerrard Winstanley", ed. G. E. Aylmer, *P. and P.*, no. 40 (1968), pp. 3-15 (hereafter *England's Spirit Unfoulded*.

158. *Works*, pp. 448, 453-7, 464, 488, 471.

159. *Ibid.*, pp. 496, 408, 413-14.

160. *Ibid.*, pp. 460-3, 478-82, 494-7; cf. *M.E.R.*, Ch. 30.

161. Hudson, "Economic and Social Thought of Gerrard Winstanley", pp. 11, 21. Contrast pp. 227-8 above.

162. *Works*, pp. 257-8, 265; cf. pp. 260, 262-4, 271, 315-17, 395, and the passage cited at note 159 above.

163. *Ibid.*, p. 181.

164. *Ibid.*, pp. 260, 389, 432; cf. p. 378.

165. *Ibid.*, pp. 650, 439-41; *A Declaration* ... [from] *Iver*, p. 65.

166. *Works*, p. 194.

167. *Ibid.*, pp. 305, 513; cf. p. 597.

168. *Ibid.*, pp. 195, 262, 326.

169. *Ibid.*, pp. 656-7.

170. *Ibid.*, p. 266; cf. pp. 191, 205.

171. *Ibid.*, pp. 363-4, 513, 558; cf. pp. 616, 638, and *A Declaration* ... [from] *Iver*, p. 65 (refusal of rent). Fox took up the suggestion of using former monastic lands to relieve the poor, and added manorial fines, in his *To the Parliament of the Comon-Wealth of England* (1659), pp. 6-8.

172. *Works*, pp. 260, 262; cf. pp. 303, 505, 529, 568, and *A Declaration* ... [from] *Iver*, p. 65.

173. *Works*, p. 420; cf. *Change and Continuity in Seventeenth-Century England*, pp. 228-9.

174. *Works*, p. 387. "The conquest" is of course the Norman Conquest.

175. *Ibid.*, p. 260; cf. p. 253. Cf. also the dedication of *The New Law of Righteousness* "to the twelve tribes of Israel that are circumcised in heart", and Everard's and Winstanley's proclamation to Fairfax that they were "of the race of the Jews", that is of the chosen people: *ibid.*, p. 15.

176. *Ibid.*, p. 201; cf. p. 492. The words could hardly be stronger.

177. *Ibid.*, pp. 284, 373.

178. *Ibid.*, pp. 15, 186; cf. pp. 114-16, 221.

179. *Ibid.*, pp. 200, 373, 428; cf. *A Declaration* ... [from] *Iver*, p. 62.

180. The point is made in O. Lutaud, *Winstanley: socialisme et christianisme* (Paris, 1976), p. 448.

181. J. C. Davis, "Gerrard Winstanley and the Restoration of True Magistracy", *P. and P.*, no. 70 (1976), pp. 78, 92. "Respect for the individual" is Mr Davis's phrase, though he appears to attribute it to me, as he also appears to attribute to me the description of Winstanley as a "countercultural hero" — a phrase which I am so far from accepting that I am not sure that I know what it means: *ibid.*, pp. 76, 93.

182. *Works*, pp. 316-17.

183. *Ibid.*, *199*, 437, 580; cf. p. 225 above.
184. *Works*, p. 520; cf. pp. 225-6 above.
185. See p. 226 above.
186. *Works*, pp. 187-8, 344. Contrast Paul Elmen, "The Theological Basis of Digger Communism", *Church History*, XXIII (1954), p. 214.
187. See pp. 227-8 above.
188. *Works*, pp. 206-8, 217, 226; cf. p. 239.
189. *Ibid.*, pp. 254, 297; cf. pp. 263-4.
190. *Ibid.*, p. 432; cf. p. 532.
191. *Ibid.*, pp. 673-4. Professor Lutaud compared *Paradise Lost*, X 55-7: God transfers all judgment to the Son: Lutaud, *Winstanley*, p. 301. For Milton too the Second Coming meant an end to "all earthly tyrannies".
192. *Works*, pp. 162, 225, Mulligan, Graham and Richards, "Winstanley: A Case for the Man as He Said He Was", pp. 65, 68, 71, and *passim*. See my "Rejoinder", pp. 148-9, citing *Works*, pp. 385-6 and 487-8; cf. pp. 317, 496.
193. C.H. George, "Gerrard Winstanley: A Critical Retrospect", in C.R. Cole and M.E. Moody (eds.), *The Dissenting Tradition: Essays for Leland H. Carlson* (Athens, Ohio, 1975), pp. 215-16.
194. *Works*, pp. 264, 470-1, 473-4; cf. Coster, quoted on p. 209 above.
195. *Works*, p. 189.
196. *Ibid.*, p. 210; cf. p. 264.
197. *The Saints Paradise*, Sigs. A-B, D-E, p. 11; *The Mysterie of God*, pp. 33-5; cf. p. 188 above.
198. *Works*, pp. 204, 244.
199. *Ibid.*, pp. 206, 227. Only on p. 296 does he appear to speak of the day of judgment in the traditional sense.
200. *Ibid.*, pp. 176-7, 203, 210-12, 215-16. Cf. Satan's mockery in *Paradise Lost*, X 485-7.
201. *Works*, pp. 153, 211, 216-19, 223, 226-7, 377, 409, 454, 462-3, 484, 495. Cf. *The Saints Paradise*, pp. 21-3.
202. *Works*, pp. 480-8. The Bishop of Durham has recently announced a similar theological position.
203. Pocock, *The Political Works of James Harrington*, p. 96; cf. pp. 3, 80.
204. *Works*, p. 481; Milton, *Paradise Lost*, V., 574-6; cf. *M.E.R.*, p. 408.
205. *Works*, pp. 210, 255; cf. Elmen, "The Theological Basis of Digger Communism", pp. 209-10. But already in *Truth Lifting up its Head* Winstanley had commented on the uncertainty of the text of the Bible: *Works*, pp. 100, 128. See p. 192 above.
206. *Works*, pp. 289, 569; cf. *M.E.R.*, p. 247, and George, "Gerrard Winstanley: A Critical Retrospect", p. 216.
207. *Works*, p. 509; *M.C.P.W.*, VI, p. 711; cf. *M.E.R.*, p. 314.
208. *Works*, pp. 149, 168-9; cf. p. 175.
209. *Ibid.*, pp. 160-1, 189, 215-16, 234-5, 251, 460; cf. p. 484.
210. *Ibid.*, pp. 161-3, 166, 224-5; cf. pp. 204-5, 462-3.
211. *Ibid.*, p. 124.

212. *Ibid.*, pp. 162-4, 170, 486-7; cf. *M.E.R.*, pp. 304-5, for other examples of what Empson called the "abdication of God".

213. *Works*, pp. 447-8.

214. *Ibid.*, pp. 136-44; cf. pp. 223-4. See pp. 197-8 above.

215. *Works,* pp. 381, 445-6, 454, 530; cf. pp. 176-7, and pp. 231-2 above.

216. *Works.*, p. 160; cf. pp. 189-90 above.

217. *Works*, p. 201; cf. p. 204.

218. *Ibid.*, pp. 301, 323, 511; cf. pp. 253-4, 289-90, 376, 385, 531. I deal with Winstanley on the Fall at what may seem excessive length because the subject has been misunderstood: see *P. and P.*, 89, pp. 145-6, 150.

219. *Works*, p. 424; cf. my "Rejoinder", p. 150.

220. *Works*, pp. 289-90. Cf. Chapter 7 of *Fire in the Bush*, "How came man's fall at the first?" It starts from covetousness for outward objects (*Works*, pp. 489-97).

221. *Ibid.*, pp. 489-94; cf. pp. 197, 380, 423-4, 464-6, 655.

222. *W.T.U.D.*, p. 163; *Works*, p. 448; cf. p. 316. Anthony Ascham, almost certainly after reading Winstanley, wrote that Adam's "first sin was a sin against property and therefore theft, or at least a sin of ambition by theft" (*Of the Confusions and Revolutions of Governments*, pp. 21-2).

223. *Works*, pp. 316-17, 437, 472, 529, 580. Cf. T. Wilson Hayes: for Winstanley "the Fall constitutes the progressive destruction of innocence through the creation of private property" (*Winstanley the Digger*, pp. 201-3).

224. *Ibid.*, pp. 170, 153, 184, 410; cf. p. 406, and *The Saints Paradise*, p. 122.

225. *Works*, pp. 532; *The Law of Freedom and Other Writings*, p. 395.

226. *Works*, p. 158-9.

227. *Ibid.*, pp. 253-8, 309, 321, 329.

228. *Ibid.*, p. 508; cf. pp. 420, 529, and *Change and Continuity in Seventeenth-Century England*, pp. 228-9.

229. *Works*, pp. 183-4; cf. p. 455.

230. *Ibid.*, p. 193; cf. p. 197. Mr Davis thinks that Winstanley "always had a respect for power": Davis, "Gerrard Winstanley and the Restoration of True Magistracy", p. 78. I think Winstanley consistently rejected the government and laws of kingly power, but approved of laws which helped men "to live in the community of the righteous law of love". See pp. 223-4 above.

231. *Works*, pp. 253, 473; cf. pp. 380, 426.

232. *Ibid.*, pp. 316-17; cf. pp. 337 ("community and freedom which is Christ"), 427.

233. *Ibid.*, pp. 453, 493, 559; cf. p. 496.

234. See p. 203 above.

235. *Works*, pp. 76, 376-7. Cf. pp. 209-10 above.

236. *Works*, p. 74.

237. *Puritanism and Revolution*, pp. 58-125.

238. *Works*, pp. 613, 622, 637.

239. *Ibid.*, pp. 259-60, 276; cf. p. 285.

240. They are so used in the *Letter to Fairfax* delivered on 9 June 1649:

Works, p. 282; as well as in *A Declaration from the Poor Oppressed People*.

241. *Works*, pp. 271, 273; cf. p. 529: land is the younger brother's "creation birthright". The concept of "creation liberties" had been worked out by Lilburne in *The Free Mans Freedom Vindicated* (1646), pp. 11-12.

242. *Ibid.*, pp. 288, 292; cf. pp. 289-90, 370.

243. *Ibid.*, pp. 311-12. In *The New Law of Righteousness* Winstanley denounced tithes as "the greatest sin of oppression": *Works*, p. 238.

244. *Works*, pp. 332, 382.

245. *Ibid.*, pp. 385-6; cf. pp. 316-17. For England as the tenth part of the city Babylon, see p. 193 above.

246. *Works*, pp. 389-91, 453-4; cf. p. 471. Winstanley makes it clear that his reference is not to the fighting Levellers but to Christ levelling. In the French Revolution "Jésus était sans-culotte": R.C. Cobb, *Les armées révolutionnaires*, 2 vols. (Paris and The Hague, 1961-3), II, p. 679. See p. 339 below.

247. *The Saints Paradise*, p. 34: "The Power of my unrighteous flesh strives to maintain the kingly power in me".

248. *Works*, pp. 615, 630, 639, 645, 330; cf. p. 349.

249. *Ibid.*, pp. 353-7, 362, 364, 388; cf. pp. 238-41, 470, 527, 617, and *W.T.U.D.*, Chapter 12.

250. *Works*, pp. 369, 463-4, 466, 472, 488, 580.

251. Davis, "Gerrard Winstanley and the Restoration of True Magistracy", pp. 78-9, 90. See pp. 221-3 above.

252. Winstanley draws this distinction carefully in *Fire in the Bush: Works*, pp. 472-3.

253. *Works*, p. 130.

254. *Ibid.*, pp. 362, 303; *Englands Spirit Unfoulded*, p. 13. For Reason as the spirit of burning, see p. 187 above.

255. *Works*, pp. 301, 389; cf. pp. 360-1, 366-7; *The Law of Freedom and Other Writings*, pp. 393-5.

256. *Works*, pp. 198, 188, 255; cf. p. 258 for the corruption of these rulers.

257. *Ibid.*, p. 297; cf. p. 467: "Where you see army against army, it is but the kingly power divided, tearing and devouring itself". Cf. also *More Light Shining in Buckinghamshire*, in *Works*, p. 633.

258. *Works*, pp. 205, 333.

259. *Ibid.*, pp. 384, 390, 411-13, 429-30; cf. p. 456.

260. *Ibid.*, pp. 411-12, 386, 429-30; cf. pp. 353, 372, 507.

261. *Ibid.*, pp. 302, 330.

262. *Englands Spirit Unfoulded*, pp. 9-10, 5.

263. *Works*, pp. 395-6.

264. *Ibid.*, p. 289.

265. *Englands Spirit Unfoulded*, pp. 9-10, 12.

266. Cf. *Works*, p. 430.

267. Edwards, *Gangraena*, III, pp. 147-8.

268. See Reay, "The Quakers and 1659: Two Newly-Discovered Broadsides by Edward Burrough", *Journal of the Friends' Historical Soc.*, 54 (1977), pp. 101-11.

269. Davis, "Gerrard Winstanley and the Restoration of True Magistracy", pp. 92, 85. See pp. 221-2 above.

270. *Works*, pp. 83, 505-10, 533-5, 586-7, 592; cf. pp. 308, 387, and p. 220 above

271. *Ibid.*, pp. 496-7. Something rather similar took place in Russia in the nineteen-twenties.

272. *Works*, pp. 534-5, 515, 526-7; cf. the reference to Moses on p. 516.

273. *Ibid.*, pp. 536, 539.

274. Cf. *ibid.*, p. 539: "the unruly ones, for whom only the law was added"; p. 588: "this outward law ... is a whip for the fool's back, for whom only it was added".

275. *Ibid.*, pp. 545-8, 553, 583, 587-90, 594.

276. *Ibid.*, pp. 493-4, 576-80. See p. 227 above.

277. *Ibid.*, pp. 593-4, 599-600.

278. Davis, "Gerrard Winstanley and the Restoration of True Magistracy", pp. 78-9, 85, 90, 92. Cf. pp. 217, 220.

279. *Works*, pp. 553, 597-8. This was not new: cf. pp. 193, 197-8.

280. Bunyan, *Works*, II, p. 127; cf. *The Law of Freedom and Other Writings*, pp. 41-2.

281. *Works*, pp. 332-3.

282. See pp. 188-90 above.

283. See *W.T.U.D.*, Appendix I.

284. *Ibid.*, pp. 391-2; *Works*, p. 105.

285. *The Breaking of the Day of God*, pp. 88, 132-6.

286. *Works*, p. 388.

287. *Ibid.*, p. 465.

288. *Ibid.*, pp. 473-4. This makes very clearly the point that Mr Davis misses — that Winstanley was not for or against state power as such, but for and against particular kinds of state power. See pp. 214-18 above.

289. *Works*, pp. 534, 558.

290. *Ibid.*, p. 288. I suspect an echo of John Warr in the equation of Equity and Reason, as well as in the suggestion that the spirit of righteousness has been buried for many years. See p. 199 above.

291. *Works*, pp. 425, 490-1; cf. pp. 254-5.

292. *Ibid.*, pp. 161-2; cf. p. 516.

293. Cf. *A Declaration ... [from] Iver*, p. 63 (Parliament's three Acts).

294. *Works*, pp. 510, 587, 581.

295. *Ibid.*, pp. 510, 600: followed by "O death, where art thou?" Cf. p. 581.

296. *Ibid.*, pp. 537-41, 559, 590-1, 596; cf. Davis, "Gerrard Winstanley and the Restoration of True Magistracy", p. 86.

297. It appears to have been so used in Surrey (the Diggers' county) in the eighteenth century: those of whom the substantial members of the community did not approve fared worse in court than those for whom a gentleman or a parson put in a good word: J.M. Beattie, "Crime and the Courts in Surrey, 1736-1753", in *Crime in England, 1550-1800* (ed. J.S. Cockburn, 1977), pp. 170-86.

298. *Works*, pp. 554-6, 559, 562, 572-3.

299. *Ibid.*, pp. 513, 573. Perhaps the reading should be "king's and conquering laws".
300. *Ibid.*, pp. 519-20.
301. *Ibid.*, pp. 565-8.
302. *Ibid.*, p. 502. Cf. Sabine's comments on this: *ibid.*, p. 59. Contrast the embarrassed passages in Mulligan, Graham and Richards, "Winstanley: A Case for the Man as He Said He Was", pp. 71-3: "at most, this shows that Winstanley was capable of being inconsistent", and has shifted to a "new vision of the millennium".
303. See pp. 187, 198-9 above, and cf. *W.T.U.D.*, pp. 206-7 (Bauthumley, Coppin).
304. *Works*, pp. 451, 523, 565, 567-8. See pp. 187, 190-1 above.
305. *ME.R.*, Chapter 25; *Works*, pp. 362, 454-7, 496.
306. Mulligan, Graham and Richards, *op. cit.*, p. 71.
307. *Works*, p. 107; cf. pp. 168, 476.
308. *Ibid.*, pp. 162-4, 169-70; cf. pp. 208-10 above.
309. *Works*, p. 251.
310. *The Saints Paradise*, Sig. B, pp. 28, 75, 114, 118; *Works*, pp. 197, 219-20, 222, 532; cf. p. 327.
311. *Works*, p. 255: Aaron and the priests were the first that deceived the people: weakness of the Mosaic law.
312. *Ibid.*, p. 332; cf. p. 383.
313. *Ibid.*, pp. 447-8, 453-7; cf. p. 187 above.
314. *Works*, pp. 490-1, 496; cf. p. 530 (against predestination).
315. *Ibid.*, p. 434. Cf. the much earlier reference to "their God" in *Light Shining in Buckinghshire*, in *Works*, p. 614.
316. *Works*, pp. 129-30, 453, 591.
317. *Ibid.*, pp. 232, 509, 523.
318. Cf. T. Wilson Hayes: for Winstanley "no human act is caused by a mere inner compulsion or a simple outer force. He combines reference to internal and external forces whenever he gives causal explanations, and he holds to this dialectic throughout his writing career", starting from the theological pamphlets of 1648 (*op. cit.*, p. 15; cf. Lutaud, *Winstanley*, esp. Part 7). In my "Rejoinder", for the benefit of a member of the editorial board of *P. and P.* who pretended not to know what "dialectical" meant, I cited the *Oxford English Dictionary*: "pertaining to the process of thought by which contradictions are seen to merge themselves in a higher truth that comprehends them, and the world process which develops similarly" — though that is perhaps a too post-Hegelian definition ("Rejoinder", p. 151n.).
319. *Works*, pp. 238-41; cf. *Antichrist in Seventeenth-Century England*, p. 170.
320. *Works*, pp. 564, 576-80; cf. pp. 203, 238, 452-6, and *M.E.R.*, p. 158. See p. 221 above.
321. *Works*, p. 362. Cf. pp. 205, 208-9, 219-20 above.
322. *Works*, p. 290; cf. p. 475.
323. *Ibid.*, p. 333.
324. Mulligan, Graham and Richards, "Winstanley: A Case for the Man as

He Said He Was", p.73.

325. *Works*, p.566.
326. The authors of "Winstanley: A Case for the Man as He Said He Was" may have been misled by Professor Hudson's argument that for Winstanley "the power of Satan" (whose existence Winstanley specifically denied) could be extirpated "only by the direct action of a personal deity ... who intervened in the affairs of the world and who was tremendously concerned about the everyday actions of men". He would intervene "by sudden miracle" to establish the new order in society. Hudson, "Economic and Social Thought of Gerrard Winstanley", pp.5-6; cf. p.20. Careful attention to Winstanley's use of words shows all these statements to be incorrect.
327. *Works*, pp.579, 457; cf. pp.200, 315, 395, 409, 567.
328. *Ibid.*, p.493; cf. p.375.
329. R.T. Vann, "From Radicalism to Quakerism: Gerrard Winstanley and Friends" *Journal of the Friends' Historical Society*, 49 (1959-61), pp.42-4; R.T. Vann, "The Later Life of Gerrard Winstanley", *Journal of the History of Ideas*, 26 (1965), pp.133-6.
330. J. Alsop, "Gerrard Winstanley's Later Life", *P. and P.*, No.82 (1979).
331. D.C. Taylor, *Gerrard Winstanley in Elmsbridge* (1982), pp.4-5. I have benefited from discussing these matters with Mr Taylor.
332. F.H. Higginson, *A Brief Relation of the Irreligion of the Northern Quakers* (1653), p.16; R. Farmer, *The Great Mysteries of Godliness and Ungodliness* (1655), dedication. I owe Higginson and the following reference to Barry Reay.
333. F. Harris, *Some Queries* (1655), p.23.
334. Comber, *Christianity no Enthusiasm* (1678), pp.90-2, 181; Tenison, *An Argument for Union* (1683), p.8; Bennett, *An Answer to the Dissenters' Pleas for separation* (1700), p.4. I owe the reference to Tenison to Barry Reay.
335. *The Breaking of the Day of God*, Sig. A 2v; *Works*, p.127. But the phrase was used by Giles Randall (Jones, *Spiritual Reformers*, p.259) and no doubt by Familists.
336. Reay, "The Quakers and 1659".
337. Friends' Meeting House Library, William Caton MS., 3, p.147: I owe this reference to the kindness of Dr Barry Reay. For Quakers and politics, see *W.T.U.D.*, esp. Chapter 10.
338. *Works*, pp.315, 228.
339. *The Moderate*, 10-17 April, 31 July-7 August 1649; cf. Lutaud, *Winstanley*, pp.172, 178, 215-16.
340. L.F. Solt, "Winstanley, Lilburne and the Case of John Fielder", *Huntington Library Quarterly*, 47 (1984), pp.119-36.
341. Warr, *Administrations, Civil and Spiritual, passim.*
342. Marvell, *Poems* (ed. H.M. Margoliouth, Oxford U.P., 1971), p.76; *Writings and Speeches of Oliver Cromwell*, III, pp.435-6. The slur seems to modern historians very unfair; they distinguish sharply between Levellers and Diggers on the property issue. But the digging of the True Levellers was the last visible action of the radical groups,

and it would remain in the memory of conservative contemporaries because it confirmed their stereotype of "levelling". This would be reinforced perhaps by the opposition to fen drainage at the Isle of Axholme in 1651, in which Lilburne and Wildman played a part: J.D. Hughes, "The Drainage Disputes in the Isle of Axholme", *Lincolnshire Historian*, II (1954), pp. 13-14.

343. Joseph Lee, *A Vindication of a Regulated Inclosure* (1656), p. 28.

344. *Works*, pp. 445-6, 530. Cf. p. 212 above.

345. See pp. 210-11 above. "The religion expressed in *The Law of Freedom* was no longer Christian, despite its terminology", as Professor Zagorin rightly remarked: Zagorin, *A History of Political Thought in the English Revolution*, p. 57. Professor Zagorin seems to me to have understood Winstanley's religion much better than some of the later commentators whom I have cited. So did Petegorsky and Sabine.

346. Lutaud, *Winstanley*, p. 426.

347. Q. Skinner, "Conquest and Consent: Thomas Hobbes and the Engagement Controversy", in *The Interregnum: The Quest for Settlement, 1646-60* (ed. G.E. Aylmer, 1972), pp. 79-98, and references at pp. 208-9.

348. *W.T.U.D.*, pp. 344-8; *The Experience of Defeat*, pp. 282-8.

349. R.M. Kingdon, *Geneva and the Coming of the Wars of Religion in France, 1555-1563* (Geneva, 1956), p. 11.

350. Soboul, *Paysans, sans-culottes et jacobins* (Paris, 1966), p. 202; see chapters 2 and 4, pp. 131-4 above and p. 333 below.

351. *Antichrist in Seventeenth-Century England*, pp. 146-8.

352. See chapter 12 below.

353. *Change and Continuity in Seventeenth-Century England*, p. 268. Cf. chapter 15 below.

354. Hobbes, *The Elements of Law* (ed. F. Tönnies, Cambridge U.P., 1928), p. 150.

355. "If there be such a thing as an atheist in the world", he made his Mr Wiseman say: Bunyan, *Works*, III, p. 627.

IV *The Millennium and After*

Historians are coming more and more to appreciate the importance of millenarianism in the seventeenth century — for radical politics, for literature, for political ideas. The failure of Jesus Christ to arrive, and the re-establishment of censorship and a repressive political régime after 1660, marked the end of revolutionary millenarian activity. Henceforth discussion of the dating of the Second Coming appears to be restricted to innocent academics. But the absence of visible millenarian politics after 1660 may mean only that popular millenarianism was driven underground rather than destroyed. There is perhaps a book to be written on the subject from 1660 to the early nineteenth century.[1]

But organized political action to expedite the millennium certainly ceased. The small body of London Fifth Monarchists tried and failed in 1657 and 1661, and that was the end. Quakers, Muggletonians and other sects abandoned immediate millenarian expectations, and went in for a good deal of rewriting of their own history. Yet the millenarian rhetoric had given expression to forces in articulate English society which were too strong to be obliterated: in different forms a secularized millenarianism took their place.

1. Cf. J.F.C. Harrison, *The Second Coming: Popular Millenarianism, 1780-1850* (1979), *passim*.

12. *John Reeve, Laurence Clarkson and Lodowick Muggleton*[1]

> "Hail! prophets sublime,
>   Who hath brought truth divine
> From heaven's imperial throne;
>   Which the great prophet Reeve
>   In commission received
> And imparts to the faithful alone."*
>
> "When men of learning leave discerning,
>   Perfect truth then flourish shall,
> The laity then will be esteemed;
>   Now mark what then there will befall:
> No false speaking, no false seeking,
>   Will be heard any more at all;
> But upright dealing without stealing,
>   Evermore then flourish shall. ...
>
> Not many wise, not many noble,
>   E'er embraced Christianity;
> They gave the world the shadow of it,
>   But ever practised cruelty;
> The conscientious, not contentious,
>   Evermore were punished;
> No compassion, but proud passion,
>   Ever great men fancied."†

I

The reader finding the Muggletonians sandwiched between Winstanley and Marvell — one of the greatest political thinkers and one of the greatest poets of the seventeenth century — may well feel that my interest in the extreme radicals has destroyed all sense of

*James Miller, 86th Song (Tune: 'Young Nancy once more'), *Divine Songs of the Muggletonians* (1829), p. 240. Other references to Reeve alone will be found on pp. 142, 240, 281, 383, 432, 519.

†Thomas Turner, 46th Song, *Divine Songs*, pp. 136-7. For Turner see p. 257 below.

proportion. Yet in the sixteen-fifties the followers of Reeve and
Muggleton attracted more support than the Diggers did; the Muggletonian sect lasted for 327 years, whilst the Diggers were suppressed
after little more than 327 days. It is arguable that the *Divine Songs of
the Muggletonians* may have enjoyed a wider readership in the early
nineteenth century than Marvell's poems.

More seriously, the Muggletonians are of historical interest because they and the Quakers are the only sects which originated in the
radical milieu of the late sixteen-forties and early fifties, in the world
of Ranters and Seekers, to survive until the present century. (Baptists and Congregationalists had long pedigrees and were not all involved in the radical politics of the late forties and early fifties, as was
shown by their repudiation of the Levellers in 1649). After 1660 the
Quakers regarded the Muggletonians as their most dangerous rivals.
Both Quakers and Muggletonians revised their doctrines in the
period of the restoration, and substantially rewrote their history:
historians have only recently begun to recover the history of the pre-
pacifist Quakers.[2]

Unlike the Quakers, the Muggletonians retained sacred writings,
by Reeve and Muggleton, and (after some rewriting of Reeve by the
surviving Muggleton) these remained basic for the sect's theology.
Consequently they give us a unique glimpse of the radical theology of
the late forties and early fifties: the Quakers had no texts of
comparable authority. But the Muggletonians in their first decade
underwent crises, challenges and splits just as the early Quakers did.
What follows is an attempt to recover some aspects of the history of
these years.[3]

II

Muggleton is often spoken of as co-founder with John Reeve of the
sect which later bore his name: they were the Two Last Witnesses.
But every significant doctrine of the Muggletonians is to be found in
writings properly attributed to Reeve alone, even though after
Reeve's death in 1658 Muggleton tried to claim a share in these
writings, and equality for his commission with Reeve's.[4] The record
is against him.

It was to John Reeve alone that God spoke on 2-5 February 1652.
Long after the event Muggleton claimed that he too had had a series
of revelations "before John Reeve had any". So far as we know this

was never mentioned before Reeve's death. The claim was hinted at in 1662, in Muggleton's first published work,[5] but it was not formally made in print until 1699, in Muggleton's posthumous *Acts of the Witnesses of the Spirit*. This was a polemical work, written to establish Muggleton's position as the equal if not the superior of Reeve. It was greatly to his advantage to claim precedence in revelations, and to hint that Reeve had been jealous of his priority in the period immediately before Reeve received his divine commission. There is every reason to be sceptical about Muggleton's claim.

Many others in the seventeenth century saw visions and heard voices; but none claimed quite the same authority as Reeve, to whom God gave "understanding of my mind in the Scriptures above all men in the world". The Bible was cited by every squabbling sect to support its case, but from February 1652 John Reeve became its sole authorized interpreter. "All men in the world" must include Muggleton, whom God gave to Reeve "to be thy mouth". The Holy Spirit reminded Reeve of Aaron's relationship to Moses. A glance at Exodus 4 will make clear Aaron's inferiority: "He shall be to thee instead of a mouth, and thou shalt be to him instead of God".

God's next command to Reeve was to curse "Theaureaujohn" (Thomas Tany), taking Muggleton and Thomas Turner with him. "If Lodowick Muggleton deny to go with thee, do thou from me pronounce him cursed to eternity". God seemed to be more sure of Thomas Turner (otherwise known only as author of the hymn used as epigraph to this Chapter) than of Muggleton. God was right: the threat of damnation had to be used before the latter agreed to accompany Reeve. Reeve's account of these matters, published whilst all parties concerned were still alive, was never challenged: Muggleton himself regarded *A Transcendent Spirituall Treatise*, our source for these events, as an inspired work. He must at the time have accepted his inferior status as therein recorded.

Confusion has been caused for historians by the addition of Muggleton's name to the title-page of Reeve's tracts: this was always done when Muggleton reprinted them after Reeve's death, and occasionally earlier. Cataloguers add to the confusion by citing Muggleton as co-author with Reeve, though *The Short-Title Catalogue* corectly attributes all "Muggletonian" pamphlets published in or before 1658 to Reeve alone.

Reeve published eight pamphlets in his lifetime:

A Transcendent Spirituall Treatise (1652)
A Letter presented unto Alderman Fouke, Lord Mayor of London (1653).
A General Epistle from the Holy Spirit (1653).
A Remonstrance from the Eternal God (1653).
An Epistle from the Prophet Reeve (1656).
An Epistle to a Quaker (1656).
A Divine Looking-Glass (1656).
Joyfull Newes from Heaven (1658).

Muggleton later claimed all but the fifth and last of these as "written by us",[6] but that is clearly untrue. There are in addition many pieces by Reeve subsequently published in *Sacred Remains* (1706), and others collected in *Spiritual Epistles* (1755). These confirm Reeve's claim to special status.

A Transcendent Spirituall Treatise is described on the title-page as "by the hand of his [God's] own prophet, being his last messenger and witness". Later on the page Muggleton's name is added, confusingly, but Muggleton himself admitted that Reeve was the sole author.[7] The treatise is written entirely in the first person singular: "The Lord Jesus spake unto me", "I am the messenger of the holy invisible Spirit", "I declare by revelation from the Holy Spirit", "by virtue of my commission": "unto me, John Reeve", "the third and last witness by commission from the Lord".[8]

When Reeve and Muggleton were examined by the Lord Mayor, it is clear from Muggleton's later account that Reeve did all the talking, though this is obscured by Muggleton using the first person when Reeve is speaking.[9] Muggleton also tells us that Reeve wrote the *Letter to Alderman Fouke* whilst they were in prison,[10] though this is described on the title-page as "from the Two Witnesses and prisoners of Jesus Christ in Newgate", "the two last spiritual witnesses and true prophets by commission from the holy Spirit of the true God". The tract begins "by our commission received by voice of words from ... the only true God, ... we declare"; "God sent us". But Reeve soon takes over: "I gave you a full account of the Lord Jesus speaking unto me"; "what I have been made to write in this paper". Only at the end does he change to "the Holy Spirit that sent us. ... We pronounce you".[11]

A General Epistle and *A Remonstrance from the Eternal God* both refer on the title-page to "the two Last Spiritual Witnesses", but the text of *A General Epistle* starts off firmly "by virtue of my commission … I present this epistle", and continues "I declare by revelation from the Spirit …". "God spake to me, John Reeve, his third and last witness".[12] In *A Remonstrance* both "I" and "we" are used.[13] *An Epistle of the Prophet Reeve* and *An Epistle to a Quaker* are throughout clearly by John Reeve, and signed by him only: "the light in me bears witness".[14]

The more important work, *A Divine Looking-Glass* begins "I being a poor layman, … God spake unto me"; "by inspiration from the unerring Spirit I positively affirm …". "We came forth" as the result of a message "by voice of words spoken unto me". God gave me "understanding above all men in the world" of "his mind in the Scriptures".[15] (Reeve repeated this claim, with emphasis, in *A Letter to William Sedgwick*, 1657).[16] In "Another Epistle Annexed" to *A Divine Looking-Glass* Muggleton claimed to share this gift of understanding the Scriptures — a claim he made specific in 1668.[17] But the text of *A Divine Looking-Glass* states flatly "I John Reeve am the last commissioned prophet". "I have both tasted and seen with my spirit a greater measure of the eternal glory and shame to come than any creature now living". "In the name and power of the Lord Jesus, by whose … spirit I was inspiringly moved to write it". Muggleton's name is joined with Reeve's at the end — "the two last commissioned spirits or prophets".[18] To later editions Muggleton added his own Epistle, in which he claimed that God hath chosen "*us two* to be his last commissioned prophets".[19] But in an introductory epistle to the 1661 edition Muggleton himself attributed *A Divine Looking-Glass* to "the unerring spirit of God which was given unto John Reeve".[20]

The title-page of *Joyfull Newes* states that Reeve and Muggleton are "the last commissioned witnesses and prophets", but the tract was "printed for the author" in the singular and the text is in the first person singular throughout. "I shall write", "from an unerring spirit I confidently affirm".[21] "I say again from that God that sent me"; "when a man is chosen alone, having only but one companion given unto him".[22] At the very end the names of John Reeve and Lodowick Muggleton are appended. Only in editions published after Reeve's death did Muggleton put "by" before their names, but in *Acts of the Witnesses* he confirms that Reeve was the author.[23] Even *A Discourse between John Reeve and Richard Leader*, which purported to be "recited by Lodowick Muggleton" when it was printed (in 1682?), is also written in the first person singular by Reeve.[24]

III

Some time before Reeve's death in 1658 he converted Laurence Clarkson. Like Reeve and Muggleton, Clarkson was a former Ranter, and a much better-known — not to say notorious — figure in the world of radical religion.[25] In 1659-60 Clarkson published four tracts in which he assumed the role of spokesman for the sect, calling Reeve — as Reeve had called himself — "the last commissioned prophet of the Lord".[26] In *The Quakers Downfall* (1659) Clarkson claimed to have inherited Reeve's mantle. He styled himself "the alone true and faithful messenger of Christ Jesus", bearing "the last revelation and commission that ever shall be". The spirit was "more fully manifested" in Clarkson "than it was in the saints that gave forth the Scriptures".[27] His Quaker critic, John Harwood, reported that Clarkson, like Reeve before him and Muggleton after him, claimed to be "the judge of the Scriptures, and all must believe the meanings he gives unto them, yet would show no reason for it".[28]

In his autobiographical *The Lost sheep Found* (1660) Clarkson continued his bid for the succession to Reeve, claiming to have been "a fellow-labourer" with him "beyond all now living" — that is, beyond Muggleton, whom Clarkson did not even mention. Reeve, Clarkson said, had seen him as "a glorious instrument, ... the like should never come after me". Clarkson referred to "our last commission", meaning his and Reeve's, and declared that he was "the true and only bishop now living".[29] We should not take Clarkson's word about his relationship with Reeve, any more — I am suggesting — than we should take Muggleton's. But Clarkson did publish his version at the time: Muggleton's did not appear till forty years later.

A struggle followed, which lasted for four years. Muggleton excommunicated Clarkson, took away his power to pronounce sentence of damnation and cut off his allowance. Clarkson had joined the sect too recently to have acquired a significant following, and Muggleton finally won out. According to the latter, Clarkson repented and agreed not to write any more. He preserved silence until his death in 1667. Muggleton demonstrated his superiority by reversing a sentence of damnation which Clarkson had pronounced.[30] It is possible that Clarkson had been interested in the succession primarily for financial reasons, as well as from considerations of power. He made no bones about his readiness to lie and cheat on other occasions.[31] We do not know much about the Muggle-tonians' finances, but Muggleton may have stood to lose a good deal if Clarkson had ousted him.[32] That was the end of Clarkson, but it was not the end of Reeve.

With Reeve dead and Clarkson silenced, Muggleton ventured into print for the first time in 1662, with a 200-page *True Interpretation of the Eleventh Chapter of the Revelation of St. John*, in which he firmly placed himself at the centre of the picture as the survivor of the two Witnesses whom God had commissioned.[33] Three years later he followed it up with a still vaster tome, *A True Interpretation of all the chief texts ... of the Revelation of St. John*. "I can truly say with Moses, the prophets, apostles and saints blessed by the Lord God of truth, who hath revealed unto me the mystery of God" and many other mysteries "never revealed before unto prophet or apostle".[34]

In 1671 the self-elevated Muggleton had to face a more serious challenge from William Medgate and Walter Buchanan. Medgate, like Muggleton, called himself the prophet of the Lord. The rebels accused Muggleton of going about to overthrow John Reeve and substitute his own authority. Muggleton virtually admitted the charge, confidently claiming "John Reeve is dead, and those that wrote the Scriptures are dead, but ... God hath preserved [Muggle-ton] alive to be the judge of John Reeve's writings and of the writings of the prophets and apostles. ... I being chosen of God had power to contradict him [Reeve] in his judgment".[35]

The rebels challenged Muggleton's doctrine that God takes no notice even of believers, which they rightly saw as an innovation. The furthest Reeve had ever gone was to deny the value of outward (as against inward) prayer.[36] Later Muggleton claimed to have corrected Reeve on this point whilst he was still alive; but again we have no evidence to confirm this. The rebels associated the new doctrine with Clarkson.[37] The view that prayer was ineffective was familiar in the antinomian circles in which Clarkson had moved.[38] Clarkson first taught the doctrine, so far as we know, as long ago as 1650, in *A Single Eye*. He may well have got the idea from Tobias Crisp, whose sermons he had attended. But it was of long standing in radical circles, having been taught by Henry Niklaes.[39] Mrs Anne Hutchin-son and the New England antinomians of the sixteen-thirties were alleged to reject prayer.[40] Jacob Bauthumley, Joseph Salmon and John Smith all taught the doctrine.[41] Gerrard Winstanley thought prayer was useless.[42]

In 1659 Clarkson said that he could not "find that ever God did hear or give an answer to any private believer".[43] In *The Lost sheep Found* Clarkson asserted as "the highest pitch of revelation" that God does not hear even "us his last commissioners", let alone ordinary mortals.[44] That was printed in 1660, long before Muggleton publicly adopted the doctrine. It looks as though he took it over from Clarkson, a more experienced and sophisticated theologian, of whose abilities Muggleton remained in considerable awe long after Clarkson's death.[45]

The idea that God takes no notice of his creation may derive from Stoicism. Seneca was available in English translation from 1614.[46] Grotius had contemplated the possibility that God did not care about humanity.[47] We can find it in Fulke Greville and Robert South.[48] Rochester did not think "prayers were of much use", and he translated Lucretius to the effect that God was "not pleased by good deeds nor provoked by bad".[49] Stoical acceptance of the fact that God takes no notice may well have been reinforced by the experience of defeat, first by royalists, then by Parliamentarians, and by the waning of the millenarian hope in the years after Reeve's death. Muggleton assumed the role, attributed to Clarkson, of the prophet who would carry the burdens of the saints, provided they believed implicitly in him.[50]

If God takes no notice of our prayers, there is no check on the infallible interpreter of Scripture. Clarkson spotted this. "There is no going to God but by commissioners",[51] a point Muggleton was to use more crudely to his own advantage. He accused the rebels of 1671 of "minding God only and disobeying and rebelling against the prophet".[52] (In *The World of the Muggletonians* I compared, semi-seriously, Muggleton's rewriting of the history of the sect with Stalin's rewriting of the history of the Soviet Communist Party to put himself on an equality with Lenin.[53] I missed the further analogy that Muggleton had to overcome a challenge to his authority from a brilliant recent recruit to the sect, and then quietly took over some of Clarkson's ideas, as Stalin took over some of Trotsky's).

Another point which Muggleton held against the rebels of 1671 was that "they would make all the Lord's people holy if they were in the prophet's place".[54] Reeve indeed said that "God himself is the alone teacher of his elect only, by the immediate inspiration of his holy spirit", which was rather different from Muggleton's idea (and perhaps Clarkson's before him) that the prophet is the essential mediator between God and the elect.[55] Reeve's position is close to Ranterism and Quakerism. Perhaps Medgate thought all the Lord's people were prophets.

IV

Among Reeve's doctrines which Muggleton dropped was the former's belief in the imminence of the end of the world. Reeve did not expect a thousand-year rule of the saints.[56] But in 1656 he said that "the day of the Lord" is "near at hand", and in *A Remonstrance from the Eternal God* he had implied that "the dissolution of this vain world" would occur during the lifetime of himself and Muggleton. In private correspondence in 1656 he suggested that it was a matter of months.[57] By the time Muggleton reprinted *A Divine Looking-Glass* in 1661 it was fairly clear that the millennium was not coming: King Charles rather than King Jesus had taken the throne. Anxious no doubt — like Quakers and other sectaries — to dissociate the Muggletons from the few desperate Fifth Monarchists who revolted in 1657 and 1661, Muggleton deleted the millenarian passages: in 1665 he himself declared that the time of the end of the world was uncertain.[58] But as late as 1674 Thomas Tomkinson could still assert that "the time will not be long".[59] A century and a half later a poem on the title-page of *Divine Songs of the Muggletonians* spoke of "these last days". Millenarianism was not dead.

Reprinting *A Divine Looking-Glass*, Muggleton tells us, was "the first thing I did after Clarkson was put down".[60] The massive deletions were an exercise of power, though it was sensible to cut out Reeve's dedication to "most heroic Cromwell", hoping that "thou mayst in due season become ... a faithful defender and deliverer of all suffering peoples upon a spiritual account within thy dominions".[61] Muggleton also excised the passages in the text in which Reeve had defended Cromwell and attacked "all those powers which endeavour to exalt the Roman see of Charles's seed upon his throne again". "Who can tell for what end the Protector of heaven and earth hath so highly exalted [Cromwell]? It may be that God will "make use of Oliver Cromwell to be an instrument of general good beyond thy expectation". "I positively affirm, by an immediate commission from the Holy Spirit, that the God of glory hath exalted Oliver Cromwell ... into the throne of Charles Stuart, that the yoke of Jesuitical persecution for conscience sake may be utterly taken off the necks of his people in these three nations". God "hath delivered his innocent people by thy [Cromwell's] hand out of their spiritual and natural tyranny in many places". "There is a secret hope in me of better things concerning thee". "Blessed are all spiritual warriors, for their crowns are immortal and eternal".[62] The qualified hope recalls Marvell's "If these the times, then this must be the man" in *The First Anniversary*: though the qualifications are perhaps a little surprising in an infallible prophet. Clarkson also recalled Cromwell's tolerance gratefully: "had it not been for the late Lord Protector, whose soul was merciful to tender consciences, O ... what a bloody persecuting day had been in England!"[63] Muggleton's distrust of human reason (greater than Reeve's) may derive from Clarkson,[64] though it no doubt also relates to the discomfiture of all radicals by the inability of their theories to cope with the events of the late fifties and of 1660.

V

Muggleton overcame the rebels of 1671, and started to write *The Acts of the Witnesses* to establish definitively his position as Reeve's infallible successor and equal if not superior. Hence the strong emphasis on the priority of his revelations and on his corrections of Reeve; hence his rather unpleasant attempts to denigrate Reeve.[65] There are interesting analogies between George Fox's reorganization of the Society of Friends after 1661 and Muggleton's takeover after defeating Clarkson. Neither Fox nor Muggleton had been in a position of sole authority earlier, but after the deaths of James Nayler and John Reeve, and after Fox had defeated the Story-Wilkinson revolt as Muggleton defeated Medgate and Buchanan, each stamped his personality on his sect at a time when rethinking was the order of the day for all radicals. The millenarian hope had proved delusive: Fox and Muggleton set about organizing their followers to face life as it was in the post-restoration world.

Muggleton's strengths were his pragmatic common sense as moralist and counsellor, and his organizing ability, to which we paid tribute in *The World of the Muggletonians*. He had an easy-going attitude towards the peccadilloes, and worse, of members of his sect, so long as they retained faith in his commission.[66] This laissez-faire tolerance, indeed laxity, undoubtedly contributed much to the survival of the Muggletonians: we do not know whether Reeve possessed such gifts, or could have acquired them.[67]

Contemporaries had no doubt that until his death Reeve was the important figure. Edward Burrough's *Answer to John Reeve's Epistle from the Mighty Jehovah* of 1654 makes no mention of Muggleton.[68] George Fox was well aware of Muggleton's attempt to exalt himself and demote Reeve. The idea that "a commission was given to him and John Reeve", Fox observed, was contradicted by the fact that Reeve called Muggleton merely his mouth. Reve claimed to be the last messenger and witness: how then could Muggleton be the last witness?[69] William Penn in 1672, in what Muggleton called "a wicked Antichristian pamphlet", reiterated the charge that Muggleton contradicted the infallible Reeve.[70] Thomas Tompkinson, the most significant Muggletonian spokesman after Muggleton himself, had virtually nothing to say about the two last witnesses, and refers only once to "this commission", which "will last to the end of the world".[71]

Divine Songs of the Muggletonians present an agreeable picture of a cosy, friendly, self-contained community, mainly of London artisans. The hymns were set to popular tunes — an old radical protestant tradition — and at least a score of them were written by women. These hymns provide interesting evidence of the survival of attitudes deriving from the radical milieu of the Revolution. There is much about liberty, which in one sense is the freedom given by consciousness of salvation, of the "peace of mind" which Muggleton said mortalism had given him.[72] But it is also political libertarianism, a class-conscious alignment with the poor against the rich and powerful. The hymns are fiercely anti-clerical ("the fat-gutted priest") and against that other enemy of interregnum radicals, lawyers.[73] The whole effect is of comradeship and solidarity, informal and jolly, notwithstanding the Muggletonians' predestinarian theology. Or rather perhaps because of this theology: knowing they were of the right seed, they could place the bishops in hell with the same confidence and relish as the young Milton had done.[74]

The survival of this non-proselytizing sect for so long owes much to Lodowick Muggleton's down-to-earth qualities. I do not wish to underestimate these in trying to establish Reeve's priority as leader and thinker, and to show how Muggleton successfully imitated Clarkson in deliberately setting out to appropriate Reeve's legacy. Despite Muggleton's efforts, "Reevonianism" remained alive. In 1719 and 1760 Reeve's original version of *A Divine Looking-Glass* was reprinted, with Muggleton's cuts restored. Whenever there was a crisis within the sect, whether in the seventeenth, eighteenth or nineteenth centuries, it was accompanied by a "back-to-Reeve" movement.[75]

NOTES

1. Based on my contribution to a discussion in *P. and P.*, No. 104 (1984).
2. W.A. Cole, *The Quakers and Politics, 1652-1660* (unpublished Thirlwall Prize Essay, Cambridge University, 1954); Barry Reay, *The Quakers and the English Revolution* (1985), *passim*.
3. See the discussion in *P. and P.*, No. 104.
4. C. Hill, B. Reay and W. Lamont, *The World of the Muggletonians* (1983), pp. 64-110, esp. pp. 91-3.
5. Muggleton, *A True Interpretation of the Eleventh Chapter of the Revelation of St. John* (1751-3), p. 47. First published 1662.
6. Ed. A. Delamaine and T. Terry, *A Volume of Spiritual Epistles . . . by John Reeve and Lodowicke Muggleton* (1755), pp. 45-6.
7. *The Acts of the Witnesses of the Spirit* (1764), pp. 48-9. First published 1699.
8. *A Transcendent Spirituall Treatise*, pp. 1, 4, 7, 32, 35, 56, 58, 71 and *passim*.
9. *Acts of the Witnesses*, pp. 68-72.
10. *Ibid.*, p. 75.
11. *A Letter to Alderman Fouke*, pp. 1, 4-7.
12. *Op. cit.*, pp. 18-19, 22.
13. *Op. cit.*, pp. 3, 6, 10.
14. *An Epistle to a Quaker*, p. 8.
15. *Op. cit.* (1719), pp. 1, 5, 7, 9, 11, 17, 22, 26-7, and *passim*. The table of contents, presumably added by Muggleton when he reprinted the tract in 1661, says that p. 1 gives "the names of the two last witnesses and the time of their call", though it does nothing of the sort.
16. Reeve, *Sacred Remains*, p. 13.
17. *Spiritual Epistles*, p. 147.
18. *A Divine Looking-Glass*, pp. 183, 190, 194.
19. *Ibid.*, Sig. A 3. My italics.
20. *Ibid.*, (1661 edn.), Sig. A 4v. On p. 25 occurs what is described as "the Prophets prayer", on p. 99 "the Prophets interpretation" and on p. 199 "the Prophets heavenly conclusion". The absence of an apostrophe in the original leaves the faint possibility that "prophets'" rather than "prophet's" might be the correct spelling; but in later editions on p. 107 Muggleton changed "the Prophets great confidence" to "the last Witnesses'", which suggests that he understood the singular elsewhere.
21. *Op. cit.*, pp. 1, 11, 21, 32, 46.
22. *Ibid.*, pp. 33, 46.
23. *Acts of the Witnesses*, p. 79.
24. *Op. cit.*, p. 1.
25. B. Reay, "Laurence Clarkson", in *The World of the Muggletonians*.
26. Clarkson, *Look about you* (1659), Sig. B.
27. John Harwood, *The Lying Prophet Discovered and Reproved* (1659), title-page, Sig. A 2, p. 1, quoting *The Quakers Downfall*, p. 1.
28. Harwood, *op. cit.*, p. 15.

29. Clarkson, *The Lost sheep Found*, pp. 38, 42-6, 48, 50, 52-3, 59-60, 62-3.
30. Muggleton, *Acts*, pp. 81, 145; *The World of the Muggletonians*, pp. 97-8.
31. *The Lost sheep Found, passim.*
32. Reay, "The Muggletonians: an Introductory Survey", in *The World of the Muggletonians*, esp. pp. 36-7.
33. *Op. cit.*, esp. Chapters LXXIV-LXXXIV.
34. *Op. cit.*, p. 312.
35. *The Prophet Muggletons Epistle to the Believers of the Commission, Touching the Rebellion Occasioned by the Nine Assertions* (?1671), pp. 8-13, printed with Reeve, *Divine Looking-Glass* (1719 edn.); Muggleton, *Acts*, pp. vi, 144-52.
36. *Joyfull Newes*, p. 42.
37. *Muggletons Epistle to the Believers of the Commission*, pp. 2-5, 7-11.
38. *The World of the Muggletonians*, p. 95.
39. Cf. Jean Moss, "*Godded with God: Hendrik Niclaes and His Family of Love* (Transactions of the American Philosophical Soc., 1981), pp. 25-6, 58, 71. For Crisp see p. 146 above.
40. D.D. Hall, *The Antinomian Controversy*, p. 232. See p. 172 above.
41. Smith, *Ranter Writings*, pp. 243, 246, 257 (Bauthumley); 194 (Salmon); [John Smith], *Soule-Reviving Influences of the Sun of Righteousness* (1654), pp. 107-8, 160, 178-80.
42. See pp. 192, 239 above.
43. Harwood, *op. cit.*, p. 13, quoting *The Quakers Downfall*, p. 41.
44. *Op cit.*, p. 56: cf. pp. 59-62. See also *The World of the Muggletonians*, pp. 94-5, 141.
45. *Spiritual Epistles* (1755), pp. 467-8, 542, 555.
46. Seneca, *Naturales quaestiones, XXXV-XXXVI*, trans. T. Lodge, in *The Works of L.A. Seneca, Both Morall and Naturall* (1614).
47. R. Tuck, *Natural Rights Theories: Their origin and development* (Cambridge U.P., 1979), p. 76.
48. Greville, *Poems and Dramas* (ed. G. Bullough, Edinburgh, n.d., ?1939), I, p. 124; *The World of the Muggletonians*, p. 95.
49. G. Burnet, *Some Passages of the Life and Death Of the ... Earl of Rochester* (1774), p. 26: first published 1680; ed. D.M. Veith, *Complete Poems of ... Rochester* (Yale U.P., 1974), p. 35.
50. See p. 260 above.
51. *The Lost sheep Found*, p. 36; cf. *The World of the Muggletonians*, p. 94.
52. *Muggletons Epistle to the Believers of the Commission*, Sigs. A-Av.
53. *The World of the Muggletonians*, pp. 64, 101.
54. Lamont, "The Muggletonians, 1652-1979", *P. and P.*, No. 99 (1983), p. 30.
55. *Epistle to Believers*, pp. 11-13.
56. *A Divine Looking-Glass*, pp. 159-65; *The World of the Muggletonians*, p. 26.
57. *A Divine Looking-Glass*, p. 110; *A Remonstrance from the Eternal God*, p. 6; Lamont, "The Muggletonians, 1652-1979", p. 28.
58. *A True Interpretation of ... the Whole Book of the Revelation*, pp. 109-10.
59. Lamont, "The Muggletonians, 1652-1979", p. 28.

60. Muggleton, *Acts*, p. 82.
61. *A Divine Looking-Glass*, Sig. A 2v.
62. *Ibid.*, pp. 60, 62, 64-5.
63. Clarkson, *Look about you*, pp. 31-2.
64. *The World of the Muggletonians*, pp. 81, 176-8; Clarkson, *The Lost sheep Found*, pp. 54-8.
65. Muggleton, *Acts*, pp. 4-5, 7, 136-52; *Spiritual Epistles*, pp. 355-6; *The World of the Muggletonians*, pp. 98, 158.
66. *Op. cit.*, esp. pp. 34-46, 98-102, 142-53.
67. Lamont sees pragmatism on moral questions in *A Divine Looking-Glass*, though he is wrong in regarding it as "a joint work" ("The Muggletonians, 1652-1979", pp. 25, 38).
68. Burrough, *The Memorable Works of a Son of Thunder and Consolation* (1672), pp. 36-44; cf. Burrough and Francis Howgil, *Answers to Several Queries* (1654).
69. G.F., *Something in Answer to Lodowick Muggletons Book*, ... "*The Neck of the Quakers Broken*" (1667), p. 21.
70. W.P[enn], *The New Witnesses Proved Old Hereticks* (1672), pp. 43 sqq.; *Spiritual Epistles*, p. 367.
71. Tomkinson, *Truths Triumph: or, A Witness to the Two Witnesses* (1823), p. 421: written 1676; cf. *A System of Religion* (1729).
72. Muggleton, *Acts of the Witnesses*, p. 25. Reeve had proclaimed mortalism in *A Transcendent Spirituall Treatise* (pp. 71-6); it was the main theme of *Joyfull Newes*. Muggleton, as was to be expected, later claimed to have discovered the doctrine before Reeve (*Acts*, pp. 25-8).
73. See esp. 6th, 28th, 50th, 55th, 78th, 139th, 165th, 169th, 174th, and 193rd songs.
74. *M.C.P.W.*, I, pp. 616-17. Cf. pp. 51-2 above.
75. See Lamont in *The World of the Muggletonians*, pp. 128-9.

13. *"Till the conversion of the Jews"*[1]

"Had we but world enough, and time,
This coyness, lady, were no crime.
We would sit down and think which way
To walk and pass our long love's day.
Thou by the Indian Ganges side
Shouldst rubies find: I by the tide
Of Humber would complain. I would
Love you ten years before the Flood;
And you should, if you please, refuse
Till the conversion of the Jews."*

I

Nearly thirty years ago I published a 350-page book dealing with economic problems of the Church of England during its first century. I described it, a bit wrily, as a footnote to *Lycidas*. My present subject is a footnote to the opening lines of Marvell's 'To his Coy Mistress'.

If you try just to read the words on Marvell's page, much of his wit will escape you. That happened to John Crowe Ransom, no mean critic in his day, who accused Marvell in this poem of "indeterminacies that would be condemned in the prose of ... College freshmen". He criticized "the tide of Humber", as though Marvell were indulging in mere periphrastic poetic diction.[2] In fact the Humber is the greatest of all English tidal rivers. John Taylor the Water-Poet, when he crossed it in 1622, had never seen anything like the waves that "like pirates board our boat and enter".[3] Marvell's father was drowned when crossing the Humber in 1641, a few years before the presumed date of the poem. Marvell had reason to complain of Humber's tide. Ransom also objected to "Indian Ganges", since "Ganges has little need of a defining adjective"; and suggested that it ought to be balanced by "English Humber". No doubt twentieth-century American readers know more about the

* Marvell, 'To his Coy Mistress'.

Ganges than about the Humber, but the reverse was true of seventeenth-century Englishmen, for whom the Ganges must have been incredibly exotic, whilst the Humber was one of the three greatest rivers in England.

Of the lines "And you should, if you please, refuse/ Till the conversion of the Jews", Ransom said "refuse brings out of the rhyming dictionary the Jews, which it will tax the poet's invention to supply with a context. ... The historical period from the Flood to the conversion of the Jews ... is a useless way of saying ten thousand years, or some other length of time". It "seems disproportionate" to the mere "ten years before the Flood".

At first sight indeed Marvell's lines seem merely fanciful. He will love the lady for a long time in the past, she shall refuse him till a long time in the future. The two propositions appear to have no more in common than this. Ransom might indeed have noticed an apparent failure in the parallelism: the Ganges is far distant in space, as Noah's Flood is in time; but the Humber is just round the corner — especially if — as is highly likely — the poem was written either in Hull or in Fairfax's house in Yorkshire where Marvell was tutoring Mary Fairfax in the early sixteen-fifties. The parallel would be more exact if we could think of the conversion of the Jews as imminent — as near as Humber, so to speak.

That, I shall suggest, is exactly what many of Marvell's contemporaries did think. I want to look at seventeenth-century ideas about the conversion of the Jews.

II

The conversion of the Jews was seen in the sixteenth and seventeenth centuries as part of a package of events announcing the approach of the end of the world and the millennium. We need not bother with the detailed calculations, based on Daniel and Revelation, which occupied some of the best mathematicians from Napier in the late sixteenth century to Newton at the end of the seventeenth. The ultimately agreed consensus was that 1260 years ("a time, times, and half a time") should be added to the date at which Antichrist set up his power. Protestants took Antichrist to be the Pope, whose rise was estimated to have occurred in 390-6 A.D. Alternatively, 1290 years were to be added to the years 360-6 A.D., taken as the dates of Julian the Apostate and/or the destruction of the Temple at Jerusalem. Both these calculations pointed to the years 1650-56 for the destruction of Antichrist, the gathering of the Gentiles, the conversion of the Jews and their return to Palestine. If — as some did — you placed the usurpation of the Bishop of Rome in A.D. 400-6, then 1260 added to that gave the year 1666 as an alternative.[4]

The conversion of the Jews and the spreading of Christianity to all nations were necessary conditions without which the millennium could not take place. Another was the destruction of the Turkish Empire, which controlled Palestine and under whose rule most Jews lived. Some thought the Great Turk was Antichrist: Christianity could not spread over the whole globe so long as Turkish power survived. (China and India hardly occur in these discussions, so ignorant were most Europeans still of the significance of their vast civilizations).

This time-table is particularly associated with protestantism. Martin Bucer and Peter Martyr of Strasburg preached it in England in the reign of Edward VI. It was taken up by Béza, and the Geneva New Testament of 1557 expressed concern for the conversion of the Jews.[5] Catholics, naturally, did not accept the equation of the Pope with Antichrist. They held that Antichrist had not yet come; when he did appear he would be a Jew. This doctrine was proclaimed in England by the Laudian Robert Shelford.[6] The Laudian campaign to accept Rome as a true church and to reject the identification of the Pope with Antichrist helped to convince many protestants that Laud was preparing for a restoration of popery in England.

There are mediaeval heretical precedents for these protestant attitudes. Wyclif and Hus both interpreted literally the Biblical texts relating to the return of the Jews to Palestine. Fifteenth-century Hussites had been eager for the conversion of the Jews.[7] Lollards had no doubt that the Pope was Antichrist. But interest developed in England especially after the Reformation; it naturally heightened as the sixteen-fifties approached.

There was an additional pointer to the mid-seventeenth century as the time for the series of events leading up to the millennium. Protestant chronologers generally accepted that the date of Noah's Flood was *anno mundi* 1656. Matthew's Gospel said "as the days of Noah were, so shall also the coming of the Son of Man be".[8] Osiander argued from this analogy that the last judgment would come in or soon after 1656 A.D.: his book was translated by George Joye in 1548.[9] A century later this had become a commonplace. In 1639 Thomas Goodwin, writing in exile in the Netherlands, gave the parallel with Noah's Flood as a reason for expecting Antichrist's reign to end in 1655 or 1656.[10] In 1651 Samuel Hartlib published a translation of the anonymous *Clavis Apocalyptica* in which the parallel was drawn, though the years were given as 1655 a.m. and 1655 A.D.[11] On Guy Fawkes Day 1651 Peter Sterry, preaching to Parliament, dated the Flood 1656 a.m., and continued "How near is that year 1656. .... A flood of fire is coming upon all the world. The windows of heaven are already open". Luther, like Noah, had foretold the day of doom 120 years before it came.[12]

The millenarians John Tillinghast, John Rogers, Henry Jessey and Nathanael Homes, all expected "the flood of God's wrath upon the idolatrous Antichristian world" to be poured out in 1656: the redemption of Israel would follow.[13] "As in Noah's Flood, after the doors were shut up, there was no mercy. .... Haste — haste — haste" cried Rogers.[14] Robert Gell, in a sermon preached to the Lord Mayor of London and the Drapers' Company, published in 1655, said that the years from Adam to Noah were 1656, and "many believe that the next year [1656 A.D.] will bring with it a notable change in the world; yea, many place the end of the world in that year".[15] William Oughtred, a very serious mathematician, said — also in 1655 — that "he had strong apprehensions of some extraordinary event to happen the following year", because of the correspondence with the year of the Flood. Perhaps the Jews would be converted by "our Saviour's visible appearance".[16] Quakers shared the expectation that the conversion would begin in 1656.[17] Thomas Traherne experienced a spiritual crisis in 1656 which he associated with the Flood, the renewal of God's covenant and the forgiveness and restoration of the Jews.[18]

Andrew Willet in 1590 seems to have been the first English Biblical scholar to devote a whole treatise to the calling of the Jews.[19] But the subject was discussed by William Perkins, Richard Hooker, and many others from the turn of the century onwards.[20] Gradually an agreed time-table emerged. The great mathematician John Napier, inventor of logarithms, committed himself to the view that "the day of God's judgment appears to fall" between 1688 and 1700: 1786 was the latest date to which the world could continue.[21] But this date was soon brought forward.

The crucial figure for England was the learned Puritan Thomas Brightman, who made the most elaborate study of the last days to date. Brightman died in 1607. All his books appeared posthumously, and had to be published abroad. He wrote in Latin, but English translations were printed in the Netherlands from 1612, and no doubt circulated clandestinely in England. Brightman's *Revelation of the Revelation* was not published in England until 1644, after the episcopal censorship has broken down. Already by the early seventeenth century attempts to date the end of the world were regarded as seditious: so early had the Elizabethan consensus collapsed, and so important were eschatological studies in polarizing men's attitudes. Brightman's English translator claimed that Brightman "hath so cleared the point of the Jews' vocation as I have not seen any writer the like". Brightman put the calling of the Jews much nearer in the future than any of his predecessors, dating their full conversion to 1695, though their "first calling shall be about the year 1650". It would be a process occupying several decades. In 1650, Brightman believed, the Euphrates would dry up to facilitate the passage of the first party of Jews from the lost tribes returning to Jerusalem from the East. Their conversion would follow the destruction of Rome and coincide with the overthrow of the Turkish Empire, whose power would begin to reel in 1650 and would be utterly abolished by 1695. The reign of the saints would follow.[22]

Although Brightman's writings were illegal in England before 1640, they were clearly well-known and very influential there.[23] In 1610, for instance, the Hebrew scholar Hugh Broughton believed that the conversion of the Jews was imminent, and with it the culmination of human history.[24] After 1640 translations of Brightman's writings, abridgments and summaries began to appear in large numbers. But two other writers must be mentioned before we pass on to the revolutionary decades.

Sir Henry Finch was a graduate of Christ's College, Cambridge, Milton's College, and a lawyer of some standing. In 1621 he published *The Worlds Great Restauration or The Calling of the Jews*, the first whole book on the subject in English. It appeared under the auspices of the eminent Puritan divine William Gouge. Finch accepted Brightman's time-table: in 1650 the Euphrates would dry up and the gathering of the Jews would begin, together with the decline of Turkish power.[25] Gouge was imprisoned for nine weeks until he produced a recantation of his share in this publication.

The earlier date was reinforced by the cautious and scholarly work of Joseph Mede, Fellow of Christ's College, when Milton was up there.[26] He too had difficulties with the censorship, and refrained from publishing his major works during the sixteen-twenties and thirties. His *Key of the Revelation* (1627) appeared in English translation only posthumously in 1643, published by order of a committee of the House of Commons. A timid man, Mede was clearly, as his correspondence shows, terrified of reprisals from Laud if he spoke out on the subject of his research. In a tract written in 1625 but not published until 1650 Mede suggested a date between 1653 and 1715.[27]

In the sixteen-thirties the Puritans Richard Sibbes and Thomas Adams were convinced that the conversion of the Jews was imminent.[28] George Hakewill in 1627 had thought this conversion so assured that he used it as one of his many arguments that the world was getting better.[29] Even Hakewill's rival, the arch-conservative Bishop Godfrey Goodman, believed in 1653 that Christ would not long be absent.[30]

III

So when the censorship broke down after 1640, when Parliament itself provided for the printing of translations of Brightman and Mede, a great stimulus was given to thinking about the end of the world. It was shrewd policy to authorize publication of scholarly works discussing the coming millennium, since Parliament's case against a Divine Right monarchy could be legitimated only by appealing to the higher authority of God. If the last days were at hand, and with them the overthrow of the papal Antichrist, and if Charles's Laudian advisers — and later his military commanders — were no better than papists, then it was right to call on ordinary people to fight for their overthrow. The subversive possibilities of this approach had already been demonstrated in New England, where in 1637 John Wheelwright preached an inflammatory sermon which got him into trouble. In this he declared "We know not how soon the conversion of the Jews may come". It "must come by the downfall of Antichrist, and if we take him away, we must burn him; therefore never fear combustions and burnings".[31] The spread of popular millenarian doctrines in England was like fire along a well-laid trail of powder.

In 1639 Thomas Goodwin foreshortened the dating still further by placing the downfall of Turks and Pope, and the return of the Jews, in 1650 or 1656, at latest 1666.[32] The Jews themselves, he added, have an eye on 1650 for the appearance of the Messiah. Their conversion, Goodwin thought, may fall out even sooner.[33] Pamphlets such as *Napiers Narration* (1641) and *A Revelation of Mr. Brightmans Revelation* (1641), both in dialogue form, helped to popularize the idea. William Sedgwick in a Fast Sermon of 29 June 1642 referred to the forthcoming conversion of the Jews and their calling "to a happy estate in their own country", though since this latter point "is subject to controversy ... we will waive it".[34] In the same year the author of an anonymous pamphlet — an astrologer — said of the millennium "some do assign one year, some another, yet all agree ... that it is near and even at our doors".[35] Next year a pamphlet entitled *The Rev. Mr. Brightmans Judgement* thought that "Rome must be in the destroying in 1641 in some of his dominions"[36] — a reference presumably to events in England and Scotland, Robert Maton in 1642 advocated the return of the Jews to Israel.[37] So did Ephraim Huit's commentary, *The Whole Prophecie of Daniel Explained* (1644).[38]

So preachers and pamphleteers agreed on the years 1650-6 as the crucial period — John Archer in 1642, Raphael Harford in 1643, and many more, including John Cotton in New England.[39] In July 1644 Stanley Gower assured the House of Commons that the Jews would be converted in 1650. Next month William Reyner confirmed to them that the overthrow of Antichrist either had already begun or was imminent.[40] Thomas Shepard in 1647-8 expected the Jews to return to Zion within the next few years: so did James Toppe.[41] In 1650 Thomas Tany (Theaureaujohn) published a broadsheet *I Proclaime from the Lord of Hosts the Returne of the Jewes*, and did his best to speed the process.[42] Mary Cary, in *The little horns doome and downfall* (1651), looked for the conversion and return of the Jews in 1655-6, leading up to the millennium in 1701. Her book included introductory material by Henry Jessey, who was not absolutely convinced that 1656 was the year. But he knew the conversion would come before 1658.[43] In 1653 John Canne thought that in the year 1655 the Lord will "most eminently appear"; there will be "great revolutions ... everywhere in Europe". The Jews would return to their own country and there wage war against the Turks until 1700. Meanwhile the "Antichristian state shall be wholly destroyed before the year 1660".[44] In 1641 the great Czech reformer Comenius had plans for the conversion of the Jews, since the last days were imminent; but like all the schemes which he devised in England, this one was frustrated by the outbreak of civil war. His disciple Samuel

Hartlib accepted the year 1655, and Hartlib's friend John Dury in 1649 felt that "the conversion of the Jews is at hand".[45]

So the excitement originally built up by the scholarly chronologists and exploited by Parliamentarian publicists continued and expanded as millenarian radicals became more and more involved in politics. A pamphlet of 1648 referred indeed unsympathetically to "all these Cabbalistical Millenarians and Jew-restorers".[46] Among scores of divines and pamphleteers who accepted the mid-fifties (or 1666 at latest) as the time for the conversion of the Jews, many were indeed radicals.[47] But they also included such relatively respectable characters as Archbishop Ussher, John Cotton, the Presbyterians Samuel Rutherford, Edmund Hall and Christopher Love, and the Directory of the Westminster Assembly.[48] Even so hard-headed a figure as Benjamin Worsley, in or after 1647, noted that most divines conceive that the conversion of the Jews is shortly to be expected. He had no doubts himself.[49] In 1650 the diarist Ralph Josselin was much preoccupied with the subject: he thought 1654 might be the year in which the conversion would begin, to be completed by 1699.[50] In 1651 the Ranter Joshua Garment published *The Hebrews Deliverance at Hand*, and Nicholas Culpeper expected their conversion within the next five years.[51] Milton's friend, Moses Wall, also in 1651, looked for the conversion during "this present ... age in which we live", suggesting 1655 as the date.[52] Thomas Tomkinson, later a Muggletonian, had a dream early in 1652 telling him the "joyful news" that "the Jews are now called; ... the day of judgment is at hand".[53]

Among those who totally rejected a special conversion was the Scot Robert Baillie. Richard Baxter observed sceptically that it would take a long time to convert all the Jews.[54] A radical who believed "the day of the Lord" was "near at hand" but nevertheless rejected any "general visible calling of the Jews in all nations" was John Reeve, founder of the sect later to be called Muggletonians. "The Lord Jesus", he declared, "will never spiritually gather the seed of those Jews who rated a bloody Barabbas above the Lord of life". But Reeve also used the word "Jew" to cover those who justify religious persecution.[55]

IV

What we see then is a cumulative process. First the Biblical scholars and the mathematical chronologists evolve techniques for interpreting the prophecies which enable them to arrive at agreed conclusions about dating the events of the last days. These dates are progressively brought back to the first half of the sixteen-fifties. This date is seized upon by the popularizers, the pamphleteers, the Parliamentarian propagandists and preachers in an effort to whip up enthusiasm for the Parliamentary cause and an expectation of the millennium in the foreseeable future. For many radicals the conversion of the Jews was significant primarily as a harbinger of the reign of the saints on earth which was to proceed the Second Coming. Soon achieving this reign became an end in itself, by comparison with which the Jews fell into the background.

Gerrard Winstanley for instance equated the English with the Israelites, the chosen people, and declared that "all the prophecies, visions and revelations of Scriptures, of prophets and apostles, concerning the calling of the Jews, the restoration of Israel and making of that people the inheritors of the whole earth," referred to the coming communist society which the Diggers were starting to build in England.[56] Winstanley and Everard told Fairfax that they were "of the race of the Jews".[57]

Echoes of discussions on the conversion of the Jews can be heard in literature. Giles Fletcher the elder was an early believer in the restoration of the Jews, though his views on the subject were not published until 1677, and I can find no trace of them in the writings of his sons Phineas and Giles the younger.[58] Francis Bacon's Bensalem in *New Atlantis* (1627) was inhabited by converted Jews. Twenty years later, in Samuel Gott's *Nova Solyma* (1648), an ideal society was created after the restoration of the Jews. The Turks had been expelled and the Jews converted fifty years before they left for Palestine — by ship from Dover.[59]

In Sir William Alexander's *Dooms-day* (1637) the "signs foreshown" of that event included "some Jews convert".[60] Henry Vaughan in *Silex Scintillans* wrote of the conversion "sure it is not far".[61] The date of publication (1650) suggests that it must be nearly contemporary with Marvell's 'Coy Mistress'. Abraham Cowley, perhaps in Marvell's more sceptical vein, wrote in the Preface to his *Poems* (1656): "there wants, methinks, but the conversion of [poetry] and the Jews for the accomplishing of the kingdom of Christ".[62]

V

But other factors contributed to an interest in the conversion,
factors perhaps less immediately obvious. The conversion of the
Jews and "the gathering of the Gentiles" were necessary before the
millennium could arrive. This gathering could be furthered by
English acquisitions of territory in the New World. (Spanish
conquests in America of course only extended the kingdom of
Antichrist). Take, for instance, Thomas Cooper's *The Blessing of
Japheth, Proving The Gathering in of the Gentiles and Finall Conversion of the Jewes*, dedicated in 1615 to the Lord Mayor, Aldermen
and Sheriffs of London and the Commissioners for Plantations in
Ireland and Virginia. "As the Lord hath enlarged himself abundantly
unto this honourable City", Cooper said, so "your hearts and purses
are enlarged plentifully to the furtherance of this great and glorious
work of the gathering in of the Gentiles" by the colonization of
Ireland and Virginia. Not for the last time in English history, piety
and profit went hand in hand. "Can you do God better service than
in promoting his kingdom and demolishing daily the power of Satan?
Can you do better service unto yourselves than not only to ease the
land of that rank blood which threatens some great sickness, but
especially to provide some retiring place for yourselves if so be the
Lord for our unthankfulness should spew us out".[63] (Here Cooper
touches on two anxieties which beset his contemporaries and which
historians sometimes forget — fear of the hordes of unemployed
vagabonds, and of international Catholicism's threat to England's
protestant independence).

His immediate concern is to strengthen the political and economic
might of his country. "Hath the Lord begun to enlarge us far and
near to Virginia and Ireland, and are not their hopes vain that seek to
root God's church out of England? ... Hath not God wonderfully
preserved this little island, this angle of the world, that in former ages
was not known or accounted to be any part of the world? Have not
all the neighbour-nations taken hold of the skirts of an Englishman?
Have they not joined themselves to us because the Lord is with us?
Are they not happily sheltered under our gracious government?"
The reference is to the union of England and Scotland, and perhaps
looks forward to the sort of union with the Netherlands which the
Commonwealth government was to offer in 1651. Already, pres-
ciently, Cooper links Parliamentary government, protestantism,

liberty and trade. "So bless thou O Lord the holy meetings of the state that in continuance and increase of the liberty of the gospel we may secure our liberty and advance thy glory, we may provide for the liberty of our posterity, in conveying thy worship unto them, more glorious than we found it".[64]

Those are significant if cautious words: remember that the Parliament of 1614 had just been dissolved without doing anything to secure the liberty of posterity or to advance the glory of protestantism. But Cooper looks forward with confidence to unlimited economic expansion. "Should we not possess all things even when in a sort we have nothing? . . . Ought not then the church to strive even for the best with the best? Must she not so run that she may obtain?" (In Cooper's phraseology "the church" means "the commonwealth").[65] Despite Cooper's title, the Jews come in almost as an afterthought to this programme for British expansion: but they do come in. "The Jews shall then have a full and glorious conversion, before the Second Coming of the Lord Jesus. . . . Have we not daily experience of the Jews coming in again? . . . This great coming in of the Jew cannot be far off, seeing the fullness of the Gentiles is well-near come in". Meanwhile English merchants must soldier on.[66]

The economic basis of religious belief was not often so nakedly exposed. But John Rolfe in 1616 thought the English were "a peculiar people marked and chosen by the finger of God" to possess North America.[67] Conquest of America was linked more closely with the conversion of the Jews by the theory that at least some American Indians were descended from the lost tribes of Israel. This hare seems to have been started in the Netherlands. A Portuguese Jew swore that he had talked Hebrew to some Indians, and the idea spread that the lost tribes were living in America.[68] John Dury among others took the story up.[69] Thomas Thorowgood in *Jewes in America* (1650) (with introduction by Hartlib) linked religion and commercial expansion as crudely as Cooper had done. "Look westward then, ye men of war, thence you may behold a rising sun of glory with riches and much honour, and not only for yourselves but for Christ". The Spaniards are thin on the ground in North America: Indians, Creoles and negroes will turn against them.[70] It reads like a blueprint for Oliver Cromwell's Western Design of 1655. Major-General Harrison was said to have seen similar millenarian possibilities in the Anglo-Dutch war of 1652-4: "The Dutch must be destroyed and we shall have an heaven on earth," thanks to control of the seas.[71]

We are told that those seventeenth-century Puritans in North America who recorded their opinions believed "almost without exception" that the Indians were descended from the ten tribes.[72] This conviction inspired John Eliot, the "Apostle to the Indians", since their conversion would accelerate the Second Coming. Eliot contributed "Conjectures ... Touching the Americans" to the 1660 edition of Thorowgood's pamphlet, seizing the opportunity to distance himself from Thorowgood's commercial approach. "We chose a place where nothing in probability was to be expected but religion, poverty and hard labour, a composition that God doth usually take most pleasure in".[73] Thorowgood, in the less ebullient circumstances of 1660, echoed Cooper's vision of America as a refuge for the godly from "not the violence of enemies so much as our own national and personal sins". The threat now came not from the "encroaching innovations" of (presumably) the Laudians, but from "the falsehood and hypocrisy, the backsliding and apostacy, the avarice and selfishness, the pride and security" which had accompanied the last years of the Commonwealth and which "do portend no less than a deluge of destruction" unless we repent. Thorowgood seems to have been as unenthusiastic about the restoration as was Milton, whom some of these phrases recall.[74]

In 1649 Parliament established a Society for the Propagation of the Gospel in New England, which among other things subsidized John Eliot. Henry Whitfield in 1652 supported this society because he hoped that thereby "the calling of the Jews may be hastened".[75] It survived the restoration, and won the continuing support of Robert Boyle, among others.[76] As late as 1707 William Whiston argued on its behalf that spreading the gospel to all nations would quicken the conversion of the Jews.[77]

VI

"The chiefest place where the Jews live is the Turkish Empire", Menasseh ben Israel told Oliver Cromwell in 1655.[78] In the early seventeenth century English trade with the Levant was prospering, outstripping that of France and Venice, anticipating that of the Netherlands, thanks to expanding production of new draperies, light cloths suitable for a Mediterranean climate. As early as 1591 the condemned heretic John Udall was offered commutation of his death sentence if he would go to Syria as minister for the Turkey Company merchants there; but he died in jail whist negotiating.[79] By 1646 there were at least twenty-two English merchants in Smyrna alone. They normally conducted their trade through Jewish middlemen: there was little intercourse with Turks. The father of the future Messiah Sabbatai Sevi acted as agent for English merchants in Smyrna. The merchants were held responsible for the behaviour of all their countrymen, and made a point of entertaining English travellers. They would be relatively well-informed about Jewish affairs.[80] As English trade opened up, visits to the Levant became feasible. By 1640 there was an extensive literature dealing with the area, from Hakluyt and Purchas to Richard Knollys, William Biddulph, William Lithgow, George Sandys, Fynes Moryson and Sir Henry Blount. This helped to spread knowledge not only of the religion but also of the growing anticipations of the Jews for the coming of the Messiah, especially prevalent in the Near East.[81] The Zohar was said to have predicted a return of the Jews to Israel for 1648.[82]

Among English radical millenarians the idea of leading the Jews back to Jerusalem, or travelling there to assist in the restoration of the Jews, frequently recurs in the two generations before 1640. Ralph Durden in 1586, who thought that the Tudor monarchy was the Beast of Revelation, proposed to lead the Jews and all the saints to rebuild Jerusalem; after which they would defeat all the kings of the earth.[83] Francis Kett, burnt in 1589, grandson of the Norfolk rebel leader of 1549 and friend of Christopher Marlowe, claimed that Jesus was currently in Jerusalem gathering the faithful; all God's people should go and join him there. Whoever will be saved must go to Jerusalem before he died[84] — an interesting survival in a radical heretic of the mediaeval idea of pilgrimage.

Richard Farnham and John Bull, prophets who died in 1642, were believed by their supporters to have sailed away in a boat of bull-rushes to convert the lost tribes.[85] Mrs Attaway was said to have left London with William Jenny some time before 1646 to await the universal salvation in Jerusalem.[86] The Ranter John Robins was inspired by the Holy Ghost to lead 144,000 men to Palestine, and started training some of them for their arduous expedition on a diet of dry bread, raw vegetables and water.[87] His associate Thomas Tany (Theaureaujohn) learnt Hebrew with the object of leading the Jews back. In April 1650 he assumed the title of King of the Jews and issued a proclamation announcing the return of his people. Some time later — perhaps as late as 1668 — he was said to have disappeared in a small boat which he had built for himself in the hope of getting to

Palestine.[88] In the sixteen-fifties Quaker missionaries went to convert the Grand Turk — by whom they were received with more tolerance than in New England.

Intense interest in the return of the Jews led to many stories circulating, most of them without foundation in fact. On All Fools Day 1645 *The London Post* reported that the Jews had sent letters to collect themselves into one body to return to Palestine.[89] Four days later Ralph Josselin in Essex had heard rumours of the Jews' return, no doubt derived from *The London Post*. "Can it be?" he asked doubtfully.[90] In 1647 an anonymous pamphlet, *Doomes-Day: or the great Day of the Lords Judgement proved by Scripture*, announced that the Jews were assembling in Asia Minor, and that the final overthrow of Antichrist was "near, even at the door".[91] There were similar excited expectations in 1648.[92] In 1650 George Foster announced that the Jews were to meet in 1651 in Italy. The Pope would lose his life in 1654, the Head Turk in 1656; after that there would be no Pope, and a classless society would prevail.[93] Samuel Brett's *Narrative of the Proceedings of a great Council of Jews assembled in the Plain of Ageda in Hungary on 12 October 1650* (published in 1655) had a very circumstantial though largely apocryphal account of the meeting. The author regarded it as "a hopeful sign of the Jews' conversion". The Jews, he added, believe that England has a great love to their nation, because they pray for their conversion. The greatest obstacle to the conversion of the Jews is Rome's idolatry.[94] Johnston of Wariston had heard of this Council three years before the publication of *A Narrative*.[95]

VII

Millenarian excitement and commercial interests both contributed to demands for a militant foreign policy which would expedite Antichrist's overthrow, the gathering of the Gentiles and the conversion of the Jews. In 1643 Robert Leslie, commanding the Scottish army in England, was reported as advocating ultimate use of his army to "go to Rome, drive out Antichrist and burn the town".[96] John Eachard in 1645 wrote that "the civil war [now] begun shall last till Rome be burnt and the Jews called". With this magnificent prospect it was absurd for Presbyterians and Independents to squabble among themselves.[97] Peter Bulkeley in *The Gospel Covenant* (1646) similarly anticipated the imminent conversion of the Jews and fall of the Great Turk.[98] The radical Puritan Robert Parker, who died in exile in 1614, left a pamphlet called *The Mystery of the Vialls opened*. Unpublishable before 1640, it appeared opportunely in 1651. Parker argued that England would soon take the lead in sacking Rome and converting the Jews — the former a theme of some of Milton's university writings.[99]

Peter Sterry in 1649 told Parliament that "the outward calling though not the inward conversion of the Jews" was expected near this time, adding that "perhaps the affairs of Constantinople, as they now stand, may make way to this desired conclusion".[100] In 1651 the astrologer William Lilly foretold that "we Christians shall recover the Holy Land ... out of the hands of the Turks; then also shall almighty God by miracle withdraw the people of the Jews from their hard-heartedness, and from the several parts of the world where they now live concealed, and they shall believe in the true Messias".[101] A year later John Owen, preaching before Parliament, rebuked M.P.s for their inactivity: "the Jews not called, Antichrist not destroyed. ... Will the Lord Christ leave the world in this state and set up his kingdom here on a molehill?"[102] A Fifth Monarchist preacher proclaimed whilst Barebone's Parliament was in session that Blake's fleet would carry the gospel "up and down to the Gentiles".[103] Morgan Llwyd and the Fifth Monarchists Christopher Feake, John Rogers and John Tillinghast, all promised that the Army of the saints would overthrow the Turks and the Pope and his helpers.[104] In 1657 George Fox — not yet a pacifist — rebuked Cromwell's Army for its failure to attack Rome.[108]

The Jews' potential usefulness to the development of a forward colonial and commercial foreign policy was an additional reason for English interest in them. As early as 1643 Jews in the Netherlands were said to be financing Parliament. Their command of bullion was enormous; they controlled the Spanish and Portuguese trades; the Levant trade was largely in their hands; they were interested in developing commerce with the East and West Indies. To governments they could be useful as contractors and as spies.[106] If the ambitious scheme for Anglo-Dutch union put forward by the Commonwealth in 1651 had come off, then the Jews in the Netherlands would have been taken over together with the Dutch colonial empire and its trade. When the Dutch refused to be incorporated into the British Empire, Dutch merchants were totally excluded from all British possessions by the Navigation Act of 1651. This development made many Jews in the Netherlands — especially those trading with the West Indies — anxious to transfer to London; and it redoubled the interest of the English government in attracting them there.[107] The policy paid off: Jewish intelligence helped the preparations for Cromwell's Western Design of 1655.[108]

VIII

So we come to Menasseh ben Israel's attempt to get the Jews formally readmitted to England, from which Edward I had expelled them. In 1648 a pogrom had driven Jews from the Ukraine. It was for them as well as for Jewish refugees from the Iberian peninsula that Menasseh hoped to find a home in England.[109] There was a contradiction in English attitudes which the Leveller Richard Overton noted in 1645: "our kings and our rulers, our bishops and our priests", would not "suffer a Jew by authority to live amongst them". "What hopes then", he asked, "is there the Jews should be converted?"[110] "We have prayed these 80 years for the conversion of the Jews", William Erbery was reported as saying in 1647; "yet we will not suffer a Jew to live amongst us". Selden's friend Christian Ravis made a similar observation in 1648.[111]

Robert Maton in 1642 had combined philo-Semitism with millenarianism, attacking those — too numerous among Christians, he thought — who condemn or revile the Jews.[112] In 1644 Bishop Griffith Williams had called for full toleration for the Jews in England, as a step towards their conversion.[113] In January 1649 a petition on behalf of the Jews was presented to the Army leadership.[114] The English delegation to the Netherlands in 1651, and especially its secretary John Thurloe, saw a great deal of Menasseh ben Israel. Menasseh's *Declaration to Parliament* of 1655 stressed that both Jews and Christians "believe that the restoration time for our nation into their native country is very near at hand". To admit Jews to England might expedite their conversion, he hinted, and so hurry on the last days.[115]

The cause of the Jews had many advocates. Moses Wall translated Menasseh ben Israel's *The Hope of Israel* in 1650, and added his *Considerations Upon the Point of the Conversion of the Jews* to the second edition (1651). The influential John Dury was a staunch supporter. In 1652 Robert Norwood and Thomas Collier called for permission for the Jews "to live peaceably amongst us, ... whose conversion is promised and we pretend to expect it".[116] So did Roger Williams and William Strong.[117] Samuel Hering told Barebone's

Parliament to call the Jews to England "for their time is near at hand".[118] J. W. in 1653 wanted "the Jews to be admitted".[119] In 1655 Ralph Josselin heard "great rumours of the Jews being admitted into England, in hopes thereby to convert them".[120] Henry Jessey argued for admission, speaking of "hopes of their conversion, which time (it's hoped) is now at hand, even at the door".[121] Margaret Fell, who later married George Fox, was the most active Quaker propagandist for the conversion of the Jews. Between 1656 and 1677 she wrote no less than five pamphlets addressed to the Jews, whilst Fox wrote two.[122]

George Wither advocated complete toleration for the Jews in England

> More than most nations we are thought
> Their restoration to have sought;

but when it came to the push "we/ Grow fearful what th'events may be".[123] In 1657 Henry Oldenburg, future Secretary of the Royal Society, was discussing the coming of the Messiah with Menasseh ben Israel.[124] By 1656 the Jews' admission was being officially considered. There was alleged to have been a proposal to this effect in Barebone's Parliament. Pressure for their admission was said to have given a fillip to Fifth Monarchists and other sectaries;[125] but the reasons for considering it were not merely religious or political. It was a development from the economic policy initiated by the Navigation Act of 1651.[126] "Doubtless, to say no more", commented Major-General Whalley, "they will bring very much wealth into this Commonwealth".[127]

Edward Nicholas, in *An Apologie for the Honourable Nation of the Jews* (1648), had deplored "the strict and cruel laws now in force" against the Jews.[128] But in fact the judges advised, no doubt under pressure from Cromwell, that there were no legal obstacles to their admission.[129] Jews had long been in England unofficially. In 1652 Elias Ashmole arranged to take lessons in Hebrew from Rabbi Solomon Frank.[130] No official decision to admit the Jews was taken, but Cromwell extended his personal favour to cover *de facto* admission, despite strong and unpleasantly anti-Semitic opposition from William Prynne and others. Permission was given for building a synagogue in London.[131] The wider implications for religious toleration of admitting the Jews were raised in the Nayler debates of 1656-7. "Will you suffer the Jews to walk upon the Exchange that

deny Christ", expostulated Bodurda, "and put this man to death
that acknowledgeth Christ?"[132] Harrington in 1656 saw Ireland as a
possible refuge for Jews;[133] many in fact settled in British colonies in
Surinam and the West Indies.[134]

IX

So I see converging trends. First the chronological experts fixed on
the early sixteen-fifties, and the religious and political propagandists
used this in support of Parliament's cause, especially radicals hoping
for the rule of the saints. Secondly, from the time of Richard
Hakluyt men had advocated an expansionist policy in North
America which would extend God's kingdom and bring profits to
Englishmen. Thomas Cooper in 1615 associated this with the
conversion of the Jews, an association later reinforced by the idea
that the American Indians were the lost tribes. Others, at least from
Robert Parker, who died in 1614, called for an aggressive policy in the
Mediterranean against Pope and Great Turk. This would protect
exporters of new draperies as well as being a necessary preliminary
to the conversion of the Jews. Finally there was the campaign for the
admission of the Jews to England, in which commercial motives
were once more mixed with those of religious radicalism.

By 1656 the Jews had been admitted *de facto*, Cromwell's Western
Design had given England a foothold in the Caribbean, and Blake's
fleet dominated the Mediterranean. Millenarian expectations of the
conversion of the Jews had stirred up popular excitement and hopes.
But as the crucial dates passed in the sixteen-fifties with no sign
of the millennium, and as the rulers of the Commonwealth grew
increasingly conservative, so active millenarianism rapidly declined.
In 1658 the Independents' Savoy Declaration of Faith spoke of "the
latter days, Antichrist being destroyed and the Jews called", but it
gave no dates. Charles II did not become "the great deliverer of the
Jews", as Arise Evans and Walter Gostelow had predicted; the
thought was repeated by a royalist pamphleteer in 1660.[135] Charles's
restoration put "enthusiasm" of any kind out of favour. The time-
table had to be recalculated. Owen, Bunyan and no doubt many
others came to think such calculations had perhaps been mistaken in
themselves.[136] A certain interest attaches to Edward Lane's *Look
unto Jesus*, published in 1663, since he had been a school-fellow of
Milton's. His book contained an appendix showing the certainty of
the calling of the Jews.

The brief career of Sabbatai Sevi in 1665-6, and the exploits of Valentine Greatrakes in England, caused a flutter of millenarian excitement around the year 1666, but it was short-lived.[137] In 1665 Increase Mather heard "rumours of motions [towards conversion] among the Jews in several parts of the world", which gave him hopes that the millennium might be coming.[138] In December 1665 the Secretary of the Royal Society was asking Spinoza for information about rumours that the Jews were about to return to their country.[139] The Rev. Samuel Lee in 1677 still believed in the restoration of the Jews to Palestine, but by now the date had been moved forward until 1766-1811.[140] It was not until the next great revolutionary age, the seventeen-nineties, that millenarians who favoured the French Revolution hoped that it would give occasion for the conversion and calling of the Jews.[141] Napoleon in Egypt at least got nearer to Palestine than Cromwell did. When in the present century a Jewish national state was established in Israel it did not coincide with "the conversion of the Jews".

X

The conversion of the Jews had been eagerly expected until about 1656 — a date after which it is unlikely that 'To his coy mistress' was written. So we come back to Marvell. He might, I hope you will agree, have heard of the conversion of the Jews. His contemporaries, accustomed to thinking in analogies, would naturally expect Noah's Flood to lead on to the conversion of the Jews. It is not, *pace* Ransom, "the logic of a child", but of a sophisticated seventeenth-century wit; not "disproportionate" but carefully calculated. "Ten years before the Flood" would be *anno mundi* 1646. 'To his Coy Mistress' was hardly written before 1646 A.D. If the end of the world is coming in 1656, Marvell's lady may not have so long as we thought for her refusal, or indeed as she may have thought. "And *the last age* should show your heart" (my italics). I am not suggesting that Marvell himself expected the conversion in 1656. We do not know, but my guess would be that he did not. An interesting paper by Hugh Ornsby-Lennon recently suggested that in 'Upon Appleton House' Marvell plays with modish alchemical ideas in a way that seems serious but is almost certainly ironical.[142] That is exactly what I am suggesting he does with fashionable millenarian ideas in 'To his Coy Mistress'.

The conversion of the Jews would have a clear connotation for

Marvell's contemporaries, and its association with the Flood would
in no way surprise them. Stanzas LIX-LXI of 'Upon Appleton
House' perhaps repeat the connection.[143] So the light elegance of the
opening of 'To his Coy Mistress', with its contemporary relevance,
leads up to the ironically courtly couplet:

> For lady you deserve this state;
> Nor would I love at lower rate.

It hardly prepares us for the clutch at the throat in the terrifying lines
which follow, the axis upon which the poem turns.

> But at my back I always hear
> Time's winged chariot hurrying near.

In the Bible chariots of fire could be images of God's power to rescue
his people (II Kings 6. 17; Psalm 68. 17); but they were also a symbol
of hostile might, Egyptians trying to prevent the Israelites from
leaving for the promised land (Exodus 14.7; I, Samuel 13.5; II, Samuel
10. 18; Psalm 20.7). Marvell's chariot carries not the Messiah but
Death, and a death which appears to offer no immortality:

> Yonder all before us lie
> Deserts of vast eternity.

C. S. Lewis called Milton our first poet of space.[144] Marvell has some
claim to be our first poet of an eternity which is associated neither
with the bliss of heaven nor with the torments of hell. Its blankness
and emptiness correspond to the blank infinity of the Copernican
universe. Marvell's lines recall Pascal's cry as he contemplated the
consequences of the new astronomy: "le silence éternel de ces espaces
infinis m'effraie", "ces effroyables espaces de l'univers qui m'enfer-
ment", "abîmé dans l'infinie immensité des espaces que j'ignore et
qui m'ignorent".[145] Pascal was writing at almost exactly the same
time as Marvell.

We had been prepared for the vastness of space by Marvell's
reference to the Ganges[146] — a river so remote that Marvell has to tell
his readers where it is — and by the lines about the poet's vegetable
love growing "vaster than empires, and more slow". The conversion
of the Jews, contemporaries would need no reminder, will come at
the same time as the overthrow of the papacy, the fourth vast

(Roman) empire, and will usher in the Fifth Monarchy, the kingdom of Christ on earth.

Marvell returns to this theme in 'The First Anniversary of the Government under O.C.' The ponderous movements of "heavy monarchs, ... more slow and brittle than the China clay" impede Oliver's millenarian potentialities, just as the vegetable growth of empires was contrasted with the love that could make the sun run. 'The First Anniversary' begins, unexpectedly, by picturing human life as a weight dropped into a smooth stream. "Like the vain curlings of the watery maze", man

> disappears
> In the weak circles of increasing years;
> And his short tumults of themselves compose,
> While flowing Time above his head does close.

This leads on to a contrast between ordinary men and the heroic Oliver, who

> The force of scattered Time contracts,
> And in one year the work of ages acts.

"Princes and cities" had made the protestant reformation. If princes all over Europe would only co-operate with Oliver's efforts

> Fore-shortened Time its useless course would stay,
> And soon precipitate the latest day.

We can perhaps trace analogies between the "private" love poems and the public poems. The slow movements of Time culminating in death frustrate the eager lover; the possibility of influencing the great world of affairs seems to offer an alternative to a perhaps illusory private happiness. Marvell makes the contrast in 'The Garden', the Mower poems, 'An Horatian Ode' and 'Upon Appleton House'. In 'An Horatian Ode' the poet applauds Cromwell's necessary emergence from

> his private gardens where
> He lived reserved and austere,
> As if his highest plot
> To plant the bergamot.

Cromwell urged his "active star"; his "industrious valour" made him "the force of angry heaven's flame" which ruined "the great work of Time".[147] In 'Upon Appleton House', less confidently, Marvell accepted Fairfax's withdrawal from activity. "The world will not go the faster for our driving", as he put it philosophically and (as usual) ambiguously in the much later *The Rehearsal Transpros'd*.[148]

In the contrast between public activity and private happiness Marvell mostly comes down on the side of public activity, despite his sympathy for Fairfax. The 'Horatian Ode' seems to give expression to a turning point in Marvell's own life: the forward youth henceforth sought public employment. Maria Fairfax is a much less convincing heavenly force than Oliver Cromwell in the 'Horatian Ode'. She recalls rather the somewhat perfunctory "Pan met me" in 'Clorinda and Damon'; the couple decide to commit suicide in order to get to heaven quickly.

But in the conflict between *carpe diem* and eternity the outcome is even less clear-cut. Marvell's attitude in 'To his Coy Mistress' has been called Puritan rather than libertine. The strategy of the poem is for lovers to take the counter-offensive against Time and so avoid languishing in his slow-chapped power.

> Pretty surely 'twere to see
> By young Love old Time beguiled,

as the poet put it in 'Young Love'. But, as Marvell tells us in 'The Unfortunate Lover', lovers cannot

> to that region climb
> To make impression upon Time.

'To his Coy Mistress' offers no really consoling conclusion. The lovers in their private world may temporarily triumph over circumstance by making their sun run, but the gates of life remain iron. The ultimate privacy is the grave; and "none I think do there embrace".[149]

XI

By 1656 the millennium had not come, nor had there been conversions in any significant number of either Jews or American Indians. But the new English foreign policy had been triumphantly achieved by the Navigation Act, by Blake's fleet in the Mediterranean, by the conquest of Jamaica in 1655. The Jews had been unofficially admitted to England. Their conversion seemed less urgently relevant.

What survived was a secularized millenarianism in which the conversion of the Jews plays little part, and English commercial enterprise is central.

The 'Horatian Ode''s lines,

> As Caesar he ere long to Gaul,
> To Italy an Hannibal,

perhaps catch something of the earlier revolutionary internationalism. But in 'The First Anniversary of the Government under O.C.' Marvell recognized that millenarian hopes were now doubtful.

> If in some happy hour
> High grace should meet in one with highest power ...
> Fore-shortened Time its useless course would stay
> And soon precipitate the latest day.

Cromwell was the obvious focus for such hopes:

> If these the times, then this must be the man.

But too many

> Unhappy princes, ignorantly bred,
> By malice some, by error more misled,
> Indians whom they should convert, subdue;
> Nor teach, but traffic with, or burn, the Jew.
> Hence that blest day still counter-poised wastes,
> The ill delaying what th'elected hastes.

It is the only mention of Jews in the poem: note their association with Indians.

What matters now is England's national power and national trade. In this respect Charles II could easily succeed to Oliver Cromwell. Dryden, like Marvell a former Cromwellian civil servant, resumed the theme of national commercial greatness in 'Annus Mirabilis', whilst ignoring any idea of an anti-Catholic crusade or the conversion of the Jews. After Dryden pseudo-millenarian predictions of a glorious imperial and trading future for London and England became common form.[150] We are back where we started, with Thomas Cooper. Just as the defeat of "the Puritan Revolution" allowed the Church of England to take over Sabbatarianism and "the protestant ethic", so the secular content of the millenarian foreign policy could be taken over once millenarianism was no longer dangerous.[151]

Milton was much less committal on the conversion of the Jews than he was on most theological subjects. In his *De Doctrina Christiana* he merely cited the relevant texts and said "some authors think" that the calling of the Jews will be a further portent of the Second Coming.[152] In *Paradise Regained* the Son of God leaves the question open:

> Yet he himself, time to himself best known
> May bring them back repentant and sincere.[153]

Milton's eager millenarian expectations had been disappointed so many times that his caution is understandable. Yet I should like to end by recalling Northrop Frye's argument that "the prophecy of Michael in *Paradise Lost* presents the whole Bible as a miniature contrast-epic, with one pole at the apocalypse and the other at the Flood".[154] The pattern does not depend on the dating 1656 a.m./1656 A.D.; but it is a suggestive thought for our theme. If the whole Bible proceeds from Flood to conversion of the Jews, Marvell hardly needed his rhyming dictionary: nor was it very difficult to supply a context for the Jews.

NOTES

1. Based on a Clark Lecture, delivered at the Clark Library, Los Angeles, in 1981.
2. J.C. Ransom, *The New Criticism* (1941), pp. 311-13.
3. Taylor, *A Very Merry Wherry-Ferry-Voyage* (1622), pp.18-19, in *Works of John Taylor* (ed. C.Hindley, 1872).
4. E.Rogers, *Some Account of the Life and Opinions of a Fifth Monarchy Man* (1867), pp.12-13, 148-51; Capp, *The Fifth Monarchy Men*, p.192. Since I wrote this piece, David S. Katz's *Philo-Semitism and the Readmission of the Jews to England, 1603-1655*, has added greatly to our knowledge of the subject.
5. B.W.Ball, *A Great Expectation: Eschatological Thought in English Protestantism to 1660* (Leiden, 1975), p.107n.; A.R.Dallison, "Contemporary Criticism of Millenarianism", in *Puritans, the Millennium and the Future of Israel* (Ed. P. Toon, 1970), pp.104-14.
6. R.Shelford, *Five Pious Learned Discourses* (1635), p.314. For Shelford see my *Antichrist in Seventeenth-century England*, pp.38, 180.

7. Ruth Gladstein, "Eschatological Trends in Bohemian Jewry during the Hussite Period", in *Prophecy and Millenarianism: Essays in Honour of Marjorie Reeves* (ed. A. Williams, 1980), p. 248; cf. M. Vereté, "The Restoration of the Jews in English Protestant Thought, 1790-1840", *Middle Eastern Studies*, January 1972, p. 14.

8. Matthew 24. 37. John Tillinghast made the point that the precise date of Christ's death was uncertain, and so calculations might be a couple of years out at the start; 1654 rather than 1656 might be the operative date (*Knowledge of the Times, Or, The Resolution of the question, how long it shall be unto the end of the wonders*, 1654, pp. 303-8).

9. Joye, *The coniectures of the ende of the worlde* (Antwerp, 1548), Sig. B i-iii.

10. T. Goodwin, *Works* (Edinburgh, 1861-3), III, p. 196.

11. *Op. cit.*, p. 34. John Dury contributed a preface, accepting the date 1656. *Clavis Apocalyptica* was probably written by Abraham von Franckenburg, a great admirer of Jakob Boehme. Cf. Elizabeth Labrousse, *L'Entrée de Saturne en Lion: L'Eclipse de Soleil du 12 Août 1654* (La Haye, 1974), p. 7.

12. P. Sterry, *Englands Deliverance from the Northern Presbytery* (1652), pp. 43-4.

13. Tillinghast, *Knowledge of the Times*, pp. 41-97, 306; *Generation-work: Or, An Exposition of the Prophecies of the Two Witnesses*, Part III (1655), pp. 22, 122; Homes, *The Resurrection Revealed* (1654); R. H. Popkin, "Rabbi Nathan Shapira's Visit to Amsterdam in 1657", in *Dutch Jewish History* (ed. J. Michman, Jerusalem, 1984), p. 187. For further examples of parallels between 1656 a.m. and 1656 A.D., see Labrousse, *op. cit.*, pp. 7-8.

14. Rogers, *Sagrir or Doomes-day drawing nigh*, quoted in E. Rogers, *op. cit.*, p. 83. Lady Eleanor Davies also expected a new Flood in 1656 (Theodore Spencer, "The History of an Unfortunate Lady", *Harvard Studies and Notes in Philology and Literature*, XX, 1938, p. 58).

15. Gell, *Noahs Flood* (1655), p. 17.

16. Ed. E. S. de Beer, *Diary of John Evelyn* (Oxford U.P., 1955), III, p. 138. See now Katz, "English Redemption and Jewish Readiness in 1656", *Journal of Jewish Studies*, XXXIV (1983), pp. 73-6.

17. R. H. Popkin, "Spinoza and the Conversion of the Jews", in *Spinoza's Political and Theological Thought* (ed. C. De Deugd, Amsterdam, 1984), p. 171.

18. Traherne, *Poems, Centuries and Three Thanksgivings* (ed. A. Ridler, Oxford U.P., 1966), pp. 409-13; cf. D. Brady, "1666: the year of the Beast", *Bulletin of the John Rylands University Library*, No. 61 (1978-9), p. 334, quoting Sprat in 1692. Cf. my *Writing and Revolution in Seventeenth-Century England* (1985), p. 231.

19. Willet, *De Judaeorum vocatione* (Cambridge U.P., 1590). Cf. Mayir Vereté's important article, "The Restoration of the Jews in English Protestant Thought", p. 15. See also T. K. Rabb, "The Stirrings of the 1590s and the return of the Jews to England", *Transactions of the Jewish Historical Soc. of England*, XXVI (1974-8).

20. Perkins believed that "it is not possible for any to find out the time of the end of the world" (*Works*, 1609-13, III, p. 467). Cf. T. Draxe, *The Worlds Resurrection or the generall calling of the Jewes* (1608), Elnathan Parr, *A Plaine Exposition upon the 8, 9, 10, 11 chapters of the Epistle of St. Paul to the Romans* (1618), Thomas Sutton, *Lectures upon the eleventh chapter to the Romans* (1632).

21. J. Napeir, *A Plaine Discovery of the whole Revelation of St. John* (1593), esp. pp. 12, 16, 179-80.

22. Brightman, *The Revelation of St. John Illustrated* (4th. edn., 1644), pp. 518-19, 543-5, 555, 781, 808, 836, 894, 967. For Brightman see Vereté, *op. cit.*, pp. 16, 30.

23. In 1612 Nicholas Fuller, Puritan lawyer, also expected the return of the lost tribes from the East. He had no doubt been reading Brightman.

24. Broughton, *A Revelation of the Holy Apocalypse* (1610), pp. 50, 264, 269; M. Reeves, "History and Eschatology: Medieval and Early Protestant Thought in Some English and Scottish Writings", *Medievalia et Humanistica*, N.S., No. 4 (1973), p. 112 and *passim*.

25. Finch, *op. cit.*, esp. pp. 3, 59-60. For Finch see Vereté, *op. cit.*, pp. 16, 30 and W. R. Prest, "The Art of Law and the Law of God", in *Puritans and Revolutionaries* (ed. D. Pennington and K. Thomas, Oxford U.P., 1978), pp. 94-117. The Puritan judge, Sir Henry Yelverton, heard a sermon during James I's reign on the signs of the coming millennium: "remaineth but a full conversion of the Jews" (Cliffe, *The Puritan Gentry*, p. 206).

26. Milton asked in his Seventh Prolusion — why seek fame on earth when "there will be few succeeding generations to remember us?" (*M.C.P.W.*, I, p. 302). Already Christ appears to be "shortly expected King". It is hardly likely that Milton was unaware of Mede's views.

27. J. Mede, *Remains, or Some Passages in the Apocalypse*, in *Works (1672)*, pp. 600, 766-7, and *passim*, Cf. Vereté, *op cit.*, pp. 17-18, 48.

28. Sibbes, *Works*, I, p. 99; Adams, *A Commentary or Exposition upon the Divine Second Epistle General, written by ... St. Peter* (1633), pp. 1136-8.

29. Hakewill, *An Apologie or Declaration of the Power and Providence of God* (3rd. edn., 1635), p. 549.

30. Goodman, *Trinity and Incarnation* (1653), p. 192.

31. Wheelwright, *A Fast-Day Sermon*, in Hall, *The Antinomian Controversy*, p. 165; cf. P. Greven, *The Protestant Temperament* (New York, 1977), p. 118. See also p. 130 above.

32. T. Goodwin, *Works*, III, pp. 28-9, 72, 157, 201-2. Goodwin quoted Mede for 1656 (*ibid.*, III, p. 196).

33. *Ibid.*, pp. 196, 202-3; *A Glimpse of Syon's Glory* (1641), in Woodhouse *Puritanism and Liberty*, pp. 233-41. Goodwin may have been reading Sir Henry Blount's *A Voyage into the Levant* (1636) — see p. 281 above. Or he may have talked to Dutch traders.

34. W. Sedgwick, *Zions Deliverance and her Friends Duty* (1642), pp. 5, 21-2.

35. [Anon.], *The Worlds Proceeding Woes and Succeeding Joyes* (1642), Sig. B.3.

36. *Op. cit.*, Sig. A 3v-A 4v.

37. Maton, *Israels Redemption* (1642).

38. *Op. cit.*, esp. pp. 58-63.

39. Cotton, quoted in Zakai, *Exile and Kingdom*, p. 383.

40. Gower, *Things Now-a-days, or The Churches Travail Of the Child of Reformation now-a-bearing* (1644), pp. 11-12, 18, 41-2; Reyner, *Babylons Running-Earthquake and the Restauration of Zion* (1644), pp. 28-33.

41. J. F. Maclear, "New England and the Fifth Monarchy: The Quest for the Millennium", in *Early American Puritanism: Essays on Religion, Society and Culture* (ed. A. T. Vaughan and F. J. Bremer, New York, 1977), p. 76. Toppe, *Christs Monarchicall and Personall Reigne uppon Earth* (?1648), quoted in *Biographical Dictionary of British Radicals*, III, p. 249.

42. For Tany see *Puritanism and Revolution*, p. 143; *W.T.U.D.*, pp. 225-6.

43. *Op. cit.*, pp. 207-9; B. R. White, "Henry Jessey: A Pastor in Politics", *Baptist Quarterly*, XXV (1973), p. 101.

44. Canne, *A Voice from the Temple to the Higher Powers* (1653), pp. 28-30, 20-1.

45. Ball, *op. cit.*, p. 108; G. H. Turnbull, *Hartlib, Dury and Comenius: Gleanings from Hartlib's Papers* (Liverpool U.P., 1947), pp. 257-8, 261-2, 267.

46. [Anon.], *The Great Day at the Dore* (1648), title-page.

47. For example, William Aspinwall, John Carew, Henry Danvers, John and Thomas Goodwin, Nathanael Homes, Henry Jessey, Morgan Llwyd, Robert Norwood, Robert Purnell, John Rogers, John Sadler, Thomas Shepard, John Spittlehouse, William Strong, John Tillinghast.

48. Ball, *op. cit.*, pp. 147, 150; Dallison, *op. cit.*, pp. 107, 112-14; E. H[all], *A Scriptural Discourse of the Apostasie and the Antichrist* (1653), pp. 72-3; Love, *Heavens Glory* (1653).

49. C. Webster, *The Great Instauration*, pp. 381, 565.

50. Josselin, *Diary*, pp. 227-8; cf. pp. 257, 266, 268; Lamont, *Richard Baxter and the Millennium*, p. 41.

51. Capp, *Astrology and the Popular Press*, p. 172.

52. M. Wall, *Considerations upon the Point of the Conversion of the Jewes*, in Lucien Wolf, *Menasseh ben Israel's Mission to Oliver Cromwell* (Jewish Historical Soc. of England, 1901), p. 53.

53. Quoted by Lamont, "The Muggletonians: A 'Vertical' Approach", *P. and P.*, No. 99 (1983), p. 26.

54. Baillie, *A Disswasive from the Errours of the Time* (1645), *passim*; Lamont, *Richard Baxter and the Millennium*, p. 56; cf. T. Hayne, *Christs Kingdom on Earth* (1645), *passim*.

55. Reeve, *A Divine Looking-Glass* (3rd. edn., 1719), pp. 184-5.

56. Sabine, *op. cit.*, pp. 260-1. Cf. p. 207 above.

57. *Ibid.*, p. 15. Winstanley's *The New Law of Righteousness* (1649) was dedicated to "the twelve tribes of Israel that are circumcised in heart".

58. Vereté, *op. cit.*, pp. 31-2, 49. Fletcher's *The Tartars or Ten Tribes* was

published in Samuel Lee's *Israel Redux; Or the Restoration of Israel* (1677).

59. I owe this point to J. C. Davis, *Utopia and the Ideal Society: A Study of English Utopian Writing, 1516-1700* (Cambridge U.P., 1981), pp. 113-15, 146.

60. Quoted by Ball, *op. cit.*, p. 90. Cf. George Herbert, 'The Jews'.

61. Henry Vaughan, *Works* (ed. L. C. Martin, Oxford U.P., 1914), II, p. 499.

62. A. Cowley, Preface to *Poems* (1656), reprinted in *Poetry and Prose* (ed. L. C. Martin, Oxford U.P., 1949), p. 71.

63. *Op. cit.*, Sig. A 2-3.

64. *Ibid.*, pp. 33-5

65. *Ibid.*, pp. 33-4, 42-3.

66. *Ibid.*, pp. 53-5. Cooper, agreeably enough, defended moderate usury (*The Worldlings Adventure*, 1619, pp. 63-4).

67. Quoted by A. Calder, *Revolutionary Empire: The Rise of the English-Speaking Empires from the Fifteenth Century to the 1790s* (1981), p. 141.

68. Wolf, *Menasseh ben Israel's Mission to Oliver Cromwell*, pp. xxiv, 1-8, and *passim*; Vereté, *op. cit.*, p. 49.

69. See p. 276 above. Dury published *An Information Concerning the Present State of the Jewish Nation* in 1658.

70. *Op. cit.*, Sig. c 3v. Much later the radical Quaker Benjamin Furly and the freethinking deist Anthony Collins each had Thorowgood's book in his library (See p. 198 above).

71. B. Capp, "The Fifth Monarchists and Popular Millenarianism", in McGregor and Reay, *op. cit.*, p. 188.

72. Alden T. Vaughan, *New England Frontier: Puritans and Indians, 1620-1675* (New York, 1979), pp. 19-20. Cf. Thomas Shepard, *The Clear Sun-shine of the Gospel breaking forth upon the Indians in New England* (1648); Gura, *op. cit.*, pp. 133-4.

73. Thorowgood, *Jewes in America* (2nd. edn., 1660), p. 23.

74. *Ibid.*, p. 51. Cf. *The Experience of Defeat*, pp. 281-2.

75. Whitfield, *Strength Out of Weaknesse* (1652), Sig. a, quoted by Ball, *op. cit.*, p. 109.

76. J. R. Jacob, *Robert Boyle and the English Revolution*, *passim*.

77. M. C. Jacob, *The Newtonians and the English Revolution* (1976), p. 167. Sir Hamon L'Estrange wrote a pamphlet entitled *Americans no Jews*, published in 1652.

78. Wolf, *op. cit.*, p. 85.

79. *D. N. B.*, s.v. Udall.

80. A. C. Wood, *A History of the Levant Company* (Oxford U.P., 1935), pp. 43-4, 73, 214, 219-20, 235-6; Gerschom Scholem, *Sabbatai Sevi: the Mystical Messiah, 1626-1676* (1973), p. 107. I am grateful to Richard Popkin for advice about Sabbatai Sevi.

81. Blount, *A Voyage into the Levant* (1636), pp. 102-3. See S. P. Chew, *The Crescent and the Rose: Islam and England during the Renaissance* (New York, 1937), esp. Part I, Chapter 3.

82. [J. Sadler], *Rights of the Kingdom: Or, Customs of our Ancestours*

Touching The Duty, Power, Election or Succession of our Kings and Parliaments (1649), pp. 38-48; cf. *Nova Solyma* (1648) (ed. W. Begley, 1902), I, Excursus F. This was by Samuel Gott, though Begley attributed it to Milton.

83. Capp, *The Fifth Monarchy Men*, p. 29.
84. W. Burton, *Davids evidence, or the Assurance of Gods love* (1592), p. 125, quoted by D. D. Wallace, "From Eschatology to Arian heresy: the Case of Francis Kett (d. 1589)", *Harvard Theological Review*, 67 (1974), pp. 461-2.
85. Ed. J. Lindsay, *Loving Mad Tom: Bedlamite Verses of the XVI and XVII centuries* (1969), p. 104; K. V. Thomas, *op. cit.*, p. 135. Cf. J. Reeve, *A Divine Looking-Glass* (1661), p. 10.
86. T. Edwards, *Gangraena*, III, pp. 26-7. For Mrs Attaway see pp. 102, 199-200 above.
87. G. H., *The Declaration of John Robins the false Prophet* (1651), pp. 4, 6.
88. See my *Puritanism and Revolution*, p. 143, and references there cited.
89. In J. Frank, *The Beginnings of the English Newspaper* (Harvard U.P., 1961), p. 83.
90. Josselin, *Diary*, p. 38.
91. Ball, *op. cit.*, p. 153.
92. See G. Nuttall, *Visible Saints: The Congregational Way, 1640-60* (Oxford, 1957), p. 144. At least one Jew was converted to Christianity, and there was one false conversion.
93. G. Foster, *The Pouring Forth of the Seventh and Last Viall* (1650), pp. 64-6.
94. In *Harleian Miscellany* (1744-6), I, pp. 369-75. There had in fact been a Jewish Council late in 1650 to deal with the consequences of the Ukranian massacres of 1648 (R. H. Popkin, "Jewish Messianism and Christian Millenarianism", in *Culture and Politics: From Puritanism to the Enlightenment*, ed. P. Zagorin, California U.P., 1980, p. 78).
95. Ed. D. H. Fleming, *Diary of Sir Archibald Johnston of Wariston*, II *(1650-1654)* (Scottish History Soc., 1919), p. 178.
96. Ed. J. G. Fotheringham, *The Diplomatic Correspondence of Jean de Montereul* (Scottish History Soc., 1888-9), II, p. 550.
97. Eachard, *Good Newes for all Christian Souldiers* (1646), Sig. A 4v, pp. 1, 3.
98. The passage was dropped from the 1651 edition of this tract.
99. Parker, *op. cit.*, p. 11.
100. Sterry, *The Comings Forth of Christ* (1650), p. 11.
101. W. Lilly, *Monarchy or no Monarchy in England* (1651), p. 55.
102. J. Owen *A Sermon Preached to The Parliament, October 13, 1652* p. 126.
103. My *Puritanism and Revolution*, p. 134; cf. p. 136.
104. Tillinghast, *Knowledge of the Times* (1654); Capp, *The Fifth Monarchy Men*, p. 151.
105. *Puritanism and Revolution*, p. 146.
106. Wolf, *op. cit.*, pp. xviii-xix, xxx.

107. *Ibid.*, pp. xxx-xxxi, xl-xli.
108. *Ibid.*, pp. xxxvi-vii.
109. *Ibid.*, pp. xxxvi-ix.
110. R. Overton, *The Araignement of Mr. Persecution* (1645), in Haller, *Tracts on Liberty*, III, p. 233; cf. p. 225.
111. F. Cheynell, *An Account Given to the Parliament by the Ministers sent by them to Oxford* (1647), p. 35; Christian Ravis, *A Discourse of the Orientall Tongues* (1648), pp. 61, 70; cf. H. Peter, *A Word for the Armie* (1647), pp. 11-12.
112. Maton, *Israels Redemption.*
113. G. Williams, *Jura Majestatis, the rights of kings both in church and state*, quoted by W. K. Jordan, *The Development of Religious Toleration in England (1640-1660)*, II, pp. 433-4.
114. C. V. Wedgwood, *The Trial of Charles I* (1964), p. 89.
115. Wolf, *op. cit.*, p. 79; cf. p. 53.
116. Norwood, *Proposals for the propagation of the Gospel, Offered to the Parliament* (1651[-2]), p. 17; Collier, *The Pulpit Guard Routed* (1652), p. 41.
117. R. W[illiams], *The Fourth Paper, Presented by Maior Butler* (1652), p. 9; Strong, "The Doctrine of the Jews Vocation", in *XXXI Select Sermons* (1656), esp. pp. 287-91. Strong died in 1654.
118. Ed. J. Nicholls, *Original Letters and Papers of State Addressed to Oliver Cromwell* (1743), pp. 99-100.
119. J. W., *A Mite to the Treasury* (1653), p. 17.
120. Josselin, *Diary*, p. 358. In 1656 Josselin dreamt that Thurloe was a Jew (*ibid.*, p. 337).
121. Jessey, *A Narrative of the late proceedings at Whitehall concerning the Jews* (1656), quoted by B. R. White, *The Separatist Tradition*, p. 107. Even a conservative like Thomas Barlow, Bodley's Librarian, urged "the toleration of the Jews" (Nuttall, *Visible Saints: The Congregational Way*, 1640-1660, Oxford, 1957, p. 146).
122. Isabel Ross, *Margaret Fell, Mother of Quakerism* (1949), pp. 89-97.
123. G. Wither, *Vaticinia Poetica, or, rather A Fragment of some Presages long since written* (1666), pp. 13-21, in *Miscellaneous Works* (Spenser Soc.), IV (1875). Joseph Frank records an anonymous work of this title as published in 1656 (*Hobbled Pegasus*, New Mexico U.P., 1968, p. 357). From internal evidence that would seem to be the correct date of first publication of Wither's poem.
124. Ed. A. R. Hall and M. B. Hall, *The Correspondence of Henry Oldenburg*, I, *1641-1662* (Wisconsin U.P., 1965), pp. 123-5.
125. Ed. T. Birch, *Thurloe State Papers* (1742), I, p. 387; Wolf, *op. cit.*, pp. xxxvi-vii.
126. Wolf, *op. cit.*, p. xli.
127. *Thurloe State Papers*, IV, p. 108.
128. Nicholas, *op. cit.*, p. 4. Nicholas expected his book to be attacked by "the Pope and his clergy", especially Jesuits. For Jews, like Puritans, hate idolatry (*ibid.*, p. 14).
129. See *A Collection of Original Letters and Papers* (ed. T. Carte, 1739),

I, p. 233, for a curious suggestion in 1648 that Parliament "had revoked the laws that were made against the Jews".

130. Ed. C. H. Josten, *Elias Ashmole (1617-1692)* (Oxford U.P., 1966), I, p. 92; II, pp. 560, 606, 609; cf. C. Roth, *The Resettlement of the Jews in England in 1656* (Jewish Historical Soc., 1960), pp. 10, 19, 23.

131. W. Prynne, *A short demurrer to the Jews long discontinued remitter into England* (1655), pp. 65-6, 89-90; Wolf, *op. cit.*, pp. lvii-ix, lxvii. John Sadler was said to have helped to win permission for the synagogue (A. Woolrych, *Commonwealth to Protectorate*, Oxford U.P., 1982, p. 207).

132. Burton, *Parliamentary Diary*, I, p. 121.

133. J. Harrington, *Political Works* (ed. J. G. A. Pocock, Cambridge U.P., 1977), p. 159.

134. J. A. Williamson, *English Colonies in Guiana and on the Amazon (1604-1688)* (Oxford U.P., 1923), pp. 164-5; Wolf, *op. cit.*, pp. xxxvi-vii; C. and R. Bridenbaugh, *No Peace Beyond the Line* (New York, 1972), pp. 147, 199, 326-7.

135. Gostelow, *Charles Stuart and Oliver Cromwell United* (1655); my *Change and Continuity in 17th-Century England* (1974), pp. 55, 58, 70-1, 77, 158, 310. See Popkin, "Rabbi Nathan Shapira's Visit", p. 188; cf. p. 204 for continuing hopes in 1662. Menasseh ben Israel quoted a Frenchman who thought that the King of France would be leader of the Jews "when they returned to their country" (Wolf, *op. cit.*, p. 124). Traditional nationalism is taking over from the religious internationalism of the interregnum radicals.

136. See pp. 233-4, 253 above.

137. Capp, *Fifth Monarchy Men*, pp. 213-14; cf. Ida Macalpine, "Valentine Greatrakes", *St. Bartholomew's Hospital Journal*, LX (1956), pp. 361-8. Marvell was a co-signatory with Boyle and others of Greatrakes's *Brief Account* (J. R. Jacob, *Henry Stubbe*, Chapter 3). Cf. R. H. Popkin, "Jewish Messianism and Christian Millenarianism", pp. 67-90, and p. 334 below.

138. D. Levin, *Cotton Mather: The Young Life of the Lord's Remembrancer, 1663-1703* (Harvard U.P., 1978), p. 5. Cf. Vavasor Powell, *The Bird in the Cage, Chirping* (2nd. edn., 1662), Sig. A 6; [Anon.], *The Life and Death of Mr. Vavasor Powell* (1671), pp. 44-5.

139. Oldenburg, *Correspondence*, II, pp. 635-7.

140. Lee, *Israel Redux*, pp. 120-2. Lee's book was reprinted several times. Cf. Vereté, *op. cit.*, pp. 31-2, 49.

141. Vereté, *op. cit.*, pp. 10-13, 26-7, 39-41.

142. Ornsby-Lennon, *Futurist Poets of the English Civil War* (xerox, 1981), I am grateful to Mr Ornsby-Lennon for allowing me to read this article.

143. Cf. A. E. Berthoff, *The Resolved Soul: A Study of Marvell's Major Poems* (Princeton U.P., 1970), p. 187.

144. C. S. Lewis, *Words* (Cambridge U.P., 1960), p. 251.

145. Pascal, *Pensées*, Nos. 194, 205-6 in Brunschwigg's edition.

146. Why does the lady find rubies by the side of the Ganges? No doubt Marvell had read some travel book associating rubies with India. In

seventeenth-century lore rubies divert the mind from evil thoughts (Brewer, *Dictionary of Phrase and Fable*, s.v.); the philosopher's stone sought by alchemists, Sir Epicure Mammon declared in *The Alchemist*, "the perfect ruby which we call elixir,/ ... Can confer honour, love respect, long life" (II, i). And, as the Bible tells us, wisdom and a virtuous woman's price are both above rubies (Job 28. 18; Proverbs 3. 15, 8. 11, 31. 10).

147.. Cf. T. W. Hayes, "The Dialectic of History in Marvell's *Horatian Ode*", *Clio*, I (1971), p. 34.

148. *The Rehearsal Transpros'd* (ed. D. I. B. Smith, Oxford U.P., 1971), p. 135. Marvell is cautiously defending the Good Old Cause. Cf. W. Chernaik, *The Poet's Time: Politics and Religion in the work of Andrew Marvell* (Cambridge U.P., 1983), esp. pp. 39-41.

149. Many poets made time run. Marlowe's Edward II told "bright Phoebus" to gallop apace ... through the sky" to "shorten the time"; his Faustus called on the "ever-moving spheres of heaven" to stand still when his time ran out. Cartwright thought Sir Henry Spelman's researches made the sun "backward run" (*To the Memory of the Most Worthy Sir Henry Spelman*), and Crashawe tells us that love "lends haste to heavenly things"; Christ "spurns the tame laws of time and place" (*Against Irresolution and Delay in Matters of Religion*). Cf. Joseph Hall, *Meditations: the First Century* (1605), in *Works* (Oxford, 1837), VIII, p. 6. In 'Last Instructions to a Painter' Marvell called for the obliteration of the day of England's defeat:

Thee, the year's monster, let thy dam devour.
And constant Time, to keep his course yet right,
Fill up thy space with a redoubled night (lines 737-42).

It all goes back to Joshua 10 and II Kings 20. Cf. Ruth Nevo, *The Dial of Virtue: A Study of Poems on Affairs of State in the Seventeenth Century* (Princeton U.P., 1962), Chapter 4.

150. McKeon, *op. cit.*, pp. 63, 153, 174-5, 249, 268-81.
151. *Society and Puritanism in Pre-Revolutionary England*, pp. 490-4.
152. *M.C.P.W.*, VI, pp. 617-18.
153. Milton, *Paradise Regained*, Book III, lines 433-4.
154. Northrop Frye, *Anatomy of Criticism: Four Essays* (Princeton U.P., 1957), p. 324, quoted by J. A. Wittreich, *Visionary Poetics* (San Marino, 1979), p. 266.

14. *Occasional Conformity and the Grindalian Tradition*[1]

"We ourselves, every Justice of Peace in his station, must make it his business strictly to find them [nonconformists] out; for the country people are generally so rotten, that they will not complain of them, though they see and know of these seditious meetings before their eyes daily."*

Occasional conformity, the dissenting habit of going to a service of the Church of England once or so a year, has been much maligned. In the later seventeenth and eighteenth centuries nonconformists qualified themselves for state or local government office this way. Without occasional conformity Tories might well have established permanent control of most boroughs, and so guaranteed themselves a permanent majority in the House of Commons. Hence their repeated attempts to make the practice illegal.[2] Consequently it suited them to denounce occasional conformity as a hypocritical practice, as no doubt it often was. Contemporary dissenters may have thought it essential to the survival of such toleration as the act of 1689 vouchsafed them. But the practice was not new. It had been advocated by the Independent Henry Jacob in 1616, long before there was anything to be gained by it: it has a very respectable intellectual ancestry. I want to try to put it into some sort of historical perspective.

We may find one clue in the fact that the fiercest opponents of occasional conformity came from the extremes of the political spectrum. Quakers denounced it as a cowardly compromise; a high Tory like William Bromley spoke of "that abominable hypocrisy, that inexcusable immorality".[3] Occasional conformists saw themselves as following a *via media*.

---

*Ed. E. M. Halcrow, *Charges to the Grand Jury at Quarter Sessions, 1660-77, by Sir Peter Leicester* (Chetham Soc., third series, V, 1953), p.91: charge at Nether Knotsford, Cheshire, 2 October 1677.

On Guy Fawkes Day, 1709, Henry Sacheverell preached a sermon before the Lord Mayor and the London City Fathers which was to become famous, or notorious. His main target was occasional conformity. He took for granted the wickedness of dissent, of separation from the national church. But he delivered a rather surprising backhand blow at one of Queen Elizabeth's Archbishops of Canterbury, whom Sacheverell even down-graded — "that false son of the church, Bishop Grindal". Against Sacheverell's rejection of Archbishop Grindal we may set John Owen's claim that he and his fellow dissenters "do sacredly adhere unto ... the doctrine of the Church of England ... as it is contained in the Articles of Religion, the Books of Homilies, and declared in the authenticated writings of all the learned prelates and others for sixty years after the Reformation."[4] He was claiming that dissenters were the true Church of England, the successors of Archbishops Grindal and Abbott.

Sacheverell's hero would presumably have been Laud, an Archbishop of Canterbury whose concept of the church was very different from that of Grindal or John Owen. Two years after Laud's death the Presbyterian Francis Cheynell declared that it was the Archbishop who had been "schismatical, imposing such burdens, [rather] than the people in separating from external communion".[5] And — to round off my argument that the idea of continuity from the pre-Laudian church to dissent had a long history — Henry Jessey as early as 1633 was recalling nostalgically Grindal's stand for preaching, Michael Sparke in 1652 looked back to the days of "that learned, pious, painful preaching Bishop Abbott".[6] The perspective in which I want to put the practice of occasional conformity goes back for 150 years before Sacheverell's sermon.

There were problems about a protestant state church. Calvinists had a dual concept of the church — in one sense it was the whole community, in another it was the true believers only. In Geneva, Scotland or Massachusetts the dualism could be resolved to the extent that church and state worked closely together: by excommunication and exclusion from the sacraments, and by stressing the authority of elders, the sovereignty of the godly within the church could be upheld. But in England, where discipline was imposed from above by bishops and their deputies, the situation was less satisfactory: there were Calvinists (as well as Anabaptists) who advocated separation from the national church *in order that* the congregation might be able to excommunicate the ungodly. Bishops were able to score many valid debating points against the Puritan demand for the right of congregations to elect their own ministers — a practice recommended by Luther, Tyndale and Calvin. How absurd to entrust the election of ministers to the ungodly dregs of the population, said Whitgift.[7] The negative point was more effective than the positive argument that in England the patron "represented" the congregation when he presented a minister to a living; no bishop, said one of them in 1570, would think of accepting a minister not presented by a nobleman or a rich gentleman.[8] Presbyterian Puritans were reduced to protesting that by election they did not mean selection by the people proper, but by the well-to-do and godly members of the congregation, with all the difficulties which even they recognized in equating these two categories. They at once laid themselves open to attack from Brownists, though of course the latter no more believed in the democracy of all parishioners than prelatists or Presbyterians: theirs would have been a democracy of the *separated godly*, not of the whole people. This seems the logical conclusion to draw from the two propositions that (i) ministers should be elected and (ii) the mass of the people are unregenerate. But most Calvinists managed to avoid this logic, so strong was the surviving ideal of a national church.

If the visible church must consist of believers only, then the godly should logically contract out of the state church, to reunite as a voluntary congregation. But constructing models like this is a way in which historians deceive themselves. Looking through the wrong end of the telescope the distinction between national church (all inhabitants) and sect (the separated godly) seems clear, simple and absolute. But history was not like that. A missing term is millenarianism, the belief that in the very near future *all* will be believers — either forcibly under the rule of the saints, or convinced by Christ's Second Coming. So separation from the national church is a short-term operation, not an end in itself: withdrawal in order to return, just as many of those who went into exile in the Netherlands or New England hoped to come back to a better England in the very near future. Hankerings after a national church lurked in most of those to whom posterity looks back as the founders of separatist sects, to be shed gradually only as their millenarian hopes faded into the light of common day. Historians have a natural tendency to read back what later became self-evident truths (the millennium is not just round the corner) into the men of the sixteenth and seventeenth centuries, by whom these truths were discovered, if at all, only after long and painful search.

It seems obvious to us that an appeal to Scripture is an appeal to the anarchy of individual consciences: that men have an infinite capacity to read into Scripture what they want to find there. But our recognition of this fact is the result of much disillusioning experience. In the sixteenth century, with the long-secret text of the Bible at last made available, it seemed crystal clear to its readers. Similarly in mid-seventeenth-century England many men believed that once episcopal hindrances had been abolished, it was only a matter of time before all good men agreed on what the Bible said. The spirit of Christ *must* be the same for all men; otherwise why should God allow the Scriptures to be translated, bishops to be overthrown? University-educated divines might try to confuse simple Bible-readers: but in the apocalyptic atmosphere of the sixteen-forties there was widespread confidence in the clarity of the text for honest mechanics, such as the Apostles themselves had been. The early Christian belief that the time was short reappeared: separation or exile would be only of brief duration. Our knowledge of the end of the story is an obstacle to understanding.

Let us remind ourselves of the historical sequence of events. Many of the sincerest English reformers were disappointed with the half-way and erastian nature of the English Reformation, which allowed the survival of bishops and patronage and failed to use church property for education or poor relief. The experience of the years 1547 to 1559 led them to hope for continuing reformation. After surviving the testing period of Mary's reign, convinced protestants, whether they had been exiles or had remained at home, soon felt that Elizabeth's settlement did not go far enough. Once it was clear that she would survive, inevitably schemes for further reformation were put forward.

Grindal's elevation to the see of Canterbury in 1576 and his "opening to the left" seemed to offer prospects of a Scottish type of episcopacy modified by Presbyterian institutions — the social pretensions of the higher clergy reduced, the shire rather than the diocese the unit of church administration, weaker church courts working with the natural rulers of the countryside, the J.Ps., the Geneva Bible replacing the Bishops' Bible. Elizabeth's suspension of Grindal in 1577 was a parting of the ways. His successor, Whitgift, was soon accused of setting "himself against the gentry".[9]

Presbyterianism was predominantly a clerical movement. But its sponsors needed the magistrate's support, since otherwise there would be no coercive power behind the church's discipline once bishops lost their political power. Hence the hope for reform by Parliament. When, as in the classis movement, local groups tried to introduce a form of Presbyterian discipline in advance of Parliamentary legislation, they soon found that their censures could be effective only if backed by the authority of a friendly J.P. or even a bishop.[10] But Elizabethan Presbyterians were never a sect: they hoped for the transformation of the English church into a Presbyterian church. They were perfectly straightforward in their appeals to Queen and Parliament against bishops. They had no more wish to abolish the Church of England than had Henry VIII and Cranmer; like them, the Presbyterians wished to change its government, in a further (and final) instalment of national reformation.

In the nineties the bishops broke up the classis movement, and drove some of its supporters into separatism, or into appealing for popular support. This in its turn lessened Parliamentary enthusiasm for the movement. By the end of the century the hierarchy's counter-attack, backed up by Hooker's theoretical statement, had been very successful; and this produced a new situation. The Marprelate Tracts' mocking exposure of the defects of the bishops and their government was intended to bring the whole hierarchy into disrepute. They contributed to drive many to believe that the Church of England was so fundamentally corrupt that reform from within was hopeless: that the only correct solution was withdrawal. Browne was followed into sectarianism by John Penry, probably at least part author of the Marprelate Tracts. On the other hand the scurrility and popular appeal of the tracts shocked and frightened some clerical and gentlemen supporters of the Presbyterian movement (including Thomas Cartwright himself); together with the rise of separatism this helped to complete the rout of its defenders in Parliament. The appeal to the people failed to produce rapid reformation; the Presbyterian policy of reform by political coup had failed. Only two alternatives remained — separatism, which might mean exile and would certainly involve persecution; or conformity and a longer-term, slower policy of permeation from within by preaching, moral reform, self-discipline.

For those who clung on to reformation from within there were many possibilities, varying from inaction to what was later to be called non-separating congregationalism. A congregation could often *in fact* (though not in theory) control its own affairs in many ways. There were some urban livings (fourteen or so in London) where patronage lay in the parishioners or the town corporation. The patronage of a friendly gentleman could on occasion be used: advowsons could indeed be bought.[11] In a poor living (and there were many such) judicious granting and withholding of an augmentation to the minister's stipend made it easier to obtain a man with the right theological outlook. Where it was impossible to influence the incumbent of the living, members of the congregation could subscribe to bring in a lecturer who would meet their doctrinal wishes. As Professor Haller put it, "every Puritan group which at any time joined together to engage a lecturer tended to become a gathered church".[12] This *de facto* Independency was expressed by Henry Jacob and William Bradshaw, insisting on the right of each congregation to control its own affairs under the King, who would be the head of the churches in England rather than of the Church of England.

So far we have been looking at the disintegration of what we may call "official" Puritanism — the nonconformity of clergymen, gentlemen and merchants. But we must not forget — as contemporaries never forgot — the much older stream of lower-class heresy, into contact with which the separating congregations inevitably came after the watershed of the nineties. In England we can trace, from Lollards through Marian martyrs to Elizabethan Familists and the radical sectaries of the sixteen-forties and fifties, a tradition of hostility to the state and its church, to clerical pretensions, to tithes, church courts and oaths, to military service. The state existed to maintain privileges. The radical sects were the organizations of the unprivileged. They were far more difficult to suppress than a national Presbyterian movement. The fact that they lacked the backing of a Walsingham or a Leicester was a help rather than a hindrance: they had to exist underground. As units the congregations might be broken up or driven into exile, but only as units. The movement could not be utterly stamped out, since it met deep spiritual and social needs of the people.[13]

Conformist Puritans differentiated themselves sharply from lower-class sectaries, and indeed claimed that their preaching, their discipline, would help to protect the English church and state from this threat no less than from that of papistry. Even a Commonwealth man like John Hales thought that Anabaptists and libertines, who "would have all things in common", had helped to cause the English risings of 1549.[14] Anabaptism became a shorthand expression for traditional lower-class rejection of the state church, though rejection of tithes was no Anabaptist innovation, going back at least to the Lollards. But anyone who believed in adult baptism would naturally have scruples about paying tithes. This challenged the economic stability of the state church at its most sensitive point. The claim to collect tithes held by many thousand impropriators made their rejection seem a threat to lay as well as to clerical property. All commentators agree that separatists were drawn from and attempted to appeal to the poorer classes. Henry VIII spoke sharply of those who "whilst their hands were busied about their manufactures had their heads also beating about points of divinity".[15] A rare point of agreement between Archbishop Laud and Roger Williams was that "most of the separation" were "of the lower sort of people". John Lilburne described Brownists as "the base and obscure fellows of the world".[16] An early Baptist like Leonard Busher, writing in 1614, was concerned with social reform for the benefit of the poor — the abolition of hanging for theft and of whipping, and putting an end to begging and to the exploitation of the poor by usury and low wages.[17] Walwyn and Winstanley, the most radical reformers, and the men of greatest social compassion who wrote during the interregnum, came from Baptist circles.

For many years the bishops and their supporters had been arguing that "if you had once made an equality ... among the clergy, it would not be long or you attempted the same among the laity".[18] It was perhaps an unfair argument for Elizabethan bishops to use against those who wanted to establish a Presbyterian discipline; but the events of the sixteen-forties were to show that opponents of religious toleration had a case. Even Lord Brooke in 1641 distinguished between those Anabaptists who "hold free will; community of all things; deny magistracy; and refuse to baptize their children" on the one hand, and the other sort "who only deny baptism to their children till they come to years of discretion, and then they baptize them; but in other things they agree with the Church of England". The former type were "heretics (or atheists)"; the latter were to be pitied. Brooke was quite clear about the "twofold" nature of the sect.[19] Unlike Oliver Cromwell later he felt that no toleration should be vouchsafed to its seditious lower-class wing.

It is worth emphasizing the deep historical roots of the Puritan *via media*, of the call for further reformation *in order* (among other things) to avoid the threat from socially subversive sectaries. Calvin himself began his chapter "Of Civil Government" by observing that he wrote at a time when "on the one hand, frantic and barbarous men are furiously endeavouring to overturn the order established by God", whilst on the other hand "the flatterers of princes, extolling their power without measure, hesitate not to oppose it to the government of God". He thought it his duty to "meet both extremes". But he first demonstrated the necessity for a coercive state machine, against "those who would have men live pell-mell like rats among straw".[20] Calvin's object was to show that true religion is completely consistent with the maintenance of private property, and yet does not necessitate an entirely uncritical acceptance of the existing state.

So when the bishops' campaign of the fifteen-eighties and nineties forced Puritans to choose between submission and separation, most educated, middle-class responsible Puritan laymen chose the former and so avoided being forced into the company of seditious sectaries. It was a preview of the dilemma of 1662, and on both occasions there was much disagreement among those who were faced with it. We must understand the position of "non-separating congregationalists" in this light. They wanted to preserve links with the state church, for social as well as for theological reasons. Even though tarrying for the magistrate had failed, and some with Robert Browne argued for reformation without tarrying for any, the ultimate hope of most of those whom we call Congregationalists was still to take over and modify the state church. Browne himself — Lord Burghley's cousin — returned to the fold. Others went to New England, where they made it clear that they wished to maintain a state church and that they had no use for religious toleration. The settlement of New England was at first envisaged as a sort of revolution by evasion: many New Englanders did in fact return to England in the sixteen-forties and fifties.

Attitudes towards conformity among the respectable separatists varied. Henry Jacob and his church allowed occasional conformity. John Robinson and his followers could hear preaching in the Church of England, but would communicate only privately with godly members of that church. Thomas Hooker also thought it lawful to hear preaching in the state church, but not to communicate either with that church or with Brownists. Henry Ainsworth and Francis Johnson were against any form of occasional conformity.[21] Helwys criticized refusal to break away from the national church.[22]

In 1610 James I appointed an Archbishop of Canterbury in the Grindal tradition, George Abbott; and for nearly two decades life was relatively easy for those who still hoped for further reformation of the national church. But the advent of Laud changed all that. He suppressed the Feoffees for Impropriations who were buying in patronage and augmenting livings; he forced subscriptions of conformity on ministers who were anxious only to have a blind eye turned on them; he suppressed lecturers, driving many of them into exile; his effective control of King and government made it clear that a loose federation of fairly self-governing congregations under the royal supremacy was no longer practical politics. Laud seemed to Puritans the true schismatic, not only because of his attempt to enforce new doctrines and ceremonies, but also because he ended intercommunion with the Dutch and Huguenot churches. This isolated England from the Calvinist international at a time when the threatened advance of Catholicism in the Thirty Years War seemed to make unity among protestants politically as well as theologically essential. Oliver Cromwell thought of emigrating; in fact he stayed on and led the policy of co-operating with lower-class sectaries to rescue England from what was seen as the threatened return of popery.[23]

It is in this perspective that we must see the conflict between those whom we too loosely call Presbyterians and Independents in the sixteen-forties. Both groups wanted to shift the centre of government of the Church of England so as to incorporate Calvinist Puritans. But the experience of the Dedham Classis[24] and New England — and of Scotland — had shown that the full discipline could be established and maintained only with the aid of the civil magistrate. "Presbyterians" were those who feared the social consequences of religious toleration most of all: "Independents" would ideally have favoured a system of congregational Presbyterianism such as existed in New England, but when they were forced into accepting more radical allies they had sufficient social confidence to believe that they could ride the storm. They had no wish to replace the tyranny of old priest by that of new presbyter: there was never much support for Presbyterian discipline from lay members of congregations. Before 1640, by temporarily withdrawing from the state church, and either going into exile or risking persecution at home, the congregations ensured — however unintentionally — that they were composed exclusively of picked and devoted men and women; they acquired confidence, determination, experience in self-government and an ability to manoeuvre and compromise without fear of being swamped. When the Revolution came "Independents" led its radical wing with assurance: "Presbyterians" on the contrary always had one eye looking backwards to the church and state machine within which they had flourished, and which they had only wished to modify to their own advantage. They could, in fact, regain the position they had held from 1644 to 1648 only by restoring monarchy and bishops to check the lower orders.

So both "Presbyterians" and "Independents" proved right, the former in believing that religious toleration would threaten the existence of a state church subordinated to the natural rulers, "Independents" in believing that in the long run they could contain the radicals and win through to a state church which would neither be clerically dominated nor wield a strict coercive discipline. That is why so many "Independent" M.P.s became elders when a Presbyterian state church was set up after 1646. They had wanted a greater share for laymen in running the episcopal Church of England, and certainly did not want to abolish a national church. If a Presbyterian establishment was the best that could be had, it was their duty to help to run it in the hope of continuing reformation.[25]

But these experiments were not carried out in a vaccum, and here "Presbyterian" fears proved more justified than "Independent" confidence. The *de facto* religious toleration of the sixteen-forties allowed the really radical sects to emerge from underground, to meet and discuss in public, to organize themselves under mechanic preachers, free from all control, either of the state church or of their social superiors. Liberty of the press, and the cheapness of publishing, allowed their views to be printed: the New Model Army spread these views across the country as it advanced to victory. Separatism ceased to be what it had been for the respectable godly, a regrettable necessity forced on them by the bishops; it became a principle, as it long had been for the radical sectaries. In the liberty of the forties and fifties the latter were able to work out a much more sophisticated theology and theory of church organization.

So the real dividing question was nakedly revealed: a state church or none? The leading "Presbyterians" and "Independents" came from social groups which could hope to control a state church, either from on top through Parliament, or by infiltration from below, through patronage and local influence. Most of those who whole-heartedly believed in religious toleration came initially from social groups which had no such aspirations — at least not until there had been a radical reform in the state as well as in the church, such as Levellers and others came to advocate.

I express this in what some may consider excessively sociological terms, in deliberate reaction against those denominational historians who are apt to push the origins of their own sect *in an organized form* too far back. The Dissenting Brethren in the Westminster Assembly in 1643, for instance, still envisaged a state church.[26] The New Model Army's Heads of Proposals of 1647 shared the Dissenting Brethren's attitude to the church which they nevertheless wished to retain: there should be no coercive jurisdiction, no penalties for failure to attend parish churches, the Solemn League and Covenant should not be enforced. Liberty not to attend parish churches, legally esta-blished from 1650, was denounced by Presbyterians as schism, just as Whitgift had denounced their practice of electing ministers as schism.

Barebone's Parliament of 1653 contemplated abolishing tithes and patronage. But the moderates, in reaction against what they regarded as the "excesses" of Ranters and Quakers, forced a change of attitude. Masson was quite right to say that "the protectorate came into being in the interests of a conservative interest generally, and especially for the preservation of an established church and the universities".[27] Cromwell's state church reunited moderate Epis-copalians, Presbyterians and many Congregationalists, together with some Baptists, in a loose federation of fairly independent congregations; it preserved tithes (until some better form of main-tenance could be devised) and patronage. It would have perpetuated a more liberal form of the *de facto* Independency which many congre-gations had enjoyed in the pre-Laudian church. There was a great extension of election by parishes. Triers were not empowered to impose any doctrinal test. John Gauden, a Presbyterian who later became a bishop, tells us that in 1656 Episcopalians, Presbyterians and Independents were in a fair way to be reconciled and "upon a very calm temper".[28] It has been estimated that nearly a quarter of the 1760 ministers ejected after 1660 were Congregationalists. Cromwell's church also contained Baptist ministers: six out of thirty-eight of the Triers of 1654 were Baptists.[29] But we should

remember that Baptists and Congregationalists were still not precisely differentiated; inter-communion was frequent. In 1672 John
Bunyan described himself as a Congregationalist.[30] Many ministers
who objected on principle to tithes were prepared to accept state
stipends financed from confiscated church lands, as ministers in New
England received stipends from towns, not tithes from parishioners.

Cromwell's was a last attempt at a broad-based national church,
under lay control. Parliament repeatedly tried under the Protectorate to narrow the standards of orthodoxy to be imposed on
ministers before they were eligible for public maintenance; and
Quakers and the radicals among the Baptists fiercely attacked the
whole conception of a state-endowed church and a professional
ministry. So the lines of division hardened. Any Parliament elected
on a property franchise insisted on some ecclesiastical jurisdiction,
on the maintenance of tithes, patronage and professional clergy
against the mechanic preachers of the radical sects. In 1656 the
Nayler case was a turning point, convincing conservatives that a
definition of orthodoxy enforced by persecution was the only alternative to anarchy and social unrest. It split the radicals, many of
whom felt Nayler had gone too far. It finally destroyed the illusion
that agreement could be reached among God's people. Presbyterians
and Independents clung on to the idea of a state church; receipt of
public maintenance was accepted in the Independent Savoy Declaration of 1658.[31]

Even the Levellers (in the 1649 Agreement of the People), Winstanley and Harrington had favoured some sort of national church
whose ministers should be elected by parishioners (all of them, not
only the godly). Those who rejected a national church were those
who rejected a professional clergy, carrying the priesthood of all
believers to the logical conclusion that a church can exist without a
minister. If there were ministers, they should (in the words of the
London Baptists in 1660), "freely minister to others", and the
congregation ought in return "freely to communicate necessary
things to the ministers (upon the account of their charge)".[32]

In time the sects abandoned hope of recapturing the state church
from which they had seceded. The unique freedom of the forties and
fifties hastened acceptance of a more permanent sectarian status by
enabling far more national organization than had ever before been
possible. The Particular Baptists for instance had a confession by
1644. But in the fifties Baptists were still quarrelling among them-

selves about the lawfulness of taking tithes — which means about the lawfulness of a state church.[33] By the end of the fifties Quakers, General and Particular Baptists were organized as sects. The Westminster Assembly of Divines produced a Presbyterian confession which it had hoped would be accepted as that of the Church of England. The Congregationalists significantly adopted no separate confession till 1658, when they were rightly becoming nervous about the future of the state church to which they had hitherto accommodated themselves.

Who gained from the Restoration? Sociologically it represented a reunion of the natural rulers against the radical lower orders. The royalist/Anglican position had always been clear and consistent. Edward Hyde in the early forties was unable to conceive how religion could be preserved without bishops, who were necessary to control the lower clergy who control the people; nor could the law and government of the state subsist if the government of the church was altered.[34] This social argument for episcopacy was often used. Henry Oxinden in 1643 called on all gentlemen "rather to maintain episcopal government ... than to introduce I know not what Presbyterial government, which will ... equalize men of mean conditions with the gentry".[35]

In 1660 the lay descendants of the conformist Puritans got a national church purged of its dependence on a would-be absolutist monarchy and of divine-right bishops: a church subordinated to Parliament. The political "Presbyterians" were the real beneficiaries of the Restoration, but they owed their victory to their own earlier defeat by "Independents" and sectaries; and they accelerated their triumph by sacrificing those who had made that victory possible, together with the Presbyterian clergy. The latter, however, were relieved at the restoration of their fear of the radicals. Richard Baxter told the House of Commons in April 1660 that now "the question is not whether bishops or no but whether discipline or none".[36] The point was vividly put by Henry Newcome, looking back after his dispossession: "Though soon after the settlement of the nation [note the phrase] we saw ourselves the despised and cheated party, ... yet ... I would not change conditions ... to have it as it was then, as bad as it is". For then "we lay at the mercy and impulse of a giddy, hot-headed, bloody multitude" and faced "a Münsterian anarchy ... far sadder than particular persecution".[37]

The restoration purges, and especially the Corporation Acts, checked the spread of radical sectarianism in towns; reassertion of the rule of parson and squire, plus the Act of Settlement, stopped the sects from spreading to the countryside. As a contemporary put it, "conventicles can be suppressed in the country where the gentry live and the people have a dependence on them, ... but in corporations it will never be carried through by the magistrates or inhabitants, their livelihood consisting altogether in trade, and this depending one upon another, so that when any of these shall appear to act in the least measure, their trade shall decline, and ... their credit with it".[38] Tithes were preserved.

The saints had tried and failed to build God's kingdom on earth. After 1660 Puritanism subsided into nonconformity: the sects were more concerned to disclaim responsibility for the execution of Charles I than with positive political ideals. Pacifism and withdrawal from politics became the order of the day, reinforced by the Clarendon Code's exclusion of dissenters from national and local politics, and from the universities. The Calvinist international no longer existed, and indeed religion had ceased to be a prime mover in international affairs. The French Huguenots were as anxious as English dissenters to proclaim that theirs were peace-loving, non-political bodies. A further factor in the retreat of aggressive Puritanism was the fact that the state church quietly stole many of its clothes. Bishops no longer discouraged preaching and sabbatarianism, and the bourgeois virtues secured the patronage of men like Archbishop Tillotson, who thought that "virtue promotes our outward temporal interests".[39] The thinking of those whom we call Latitudinarians (many of them former Presbyterians) retained much of the social content of Puritanism. Refusing to be excluded from the state church, they continued the Elizabethan struggle on two fronts, against popery and against enthusiasm.[40]

Clearly neither Presbyterians nor Independents could any longer aspire to control the Church of England. Yet neither took kindly to the status of sectary. Twelve days after St Bartholomew's Day, 1662, Henry Newcome and his Presbyterian friends in Cheshire resolved "to stick close to the public ordinances, and not to separate" from the national church.[41] In the same year the Presbyterian Philip Henry was "loath ... to encourage the people to separation", even though he himself felt constrained to resign his living. When Charles II issued his Declaration of Indulgence ten years later, Henry feared that "the danger is lest the allowance of separate places help to overthrow our parish-order … and beget divisions and animosities amongst us which no honest heart but would rather should be healed". He faced a "trilemma" — "either to turn flat Independents, or to strike in with the conformists, or to sit down in former silence and sufferings till the Lord shall open a more effectual door". The Independents, in Henry's view, "unchurch the nation; … they pluck up the hedge of parish order". Henry's choice of words is significant. He remained an occasional conformist.[42] Baxter continued in the sixteen-sixties and seventies to discuss with John Owen and other leading Independents the conditions for re-inclusion.[43] Andrew Marvell, friend of both Baxter and Owen, defended against Samuel Parker the doctrines held by "most of our ancient and many of the later bishops nearer our times".[44]

Attitudes towards the restored church among those "who separate, or are rather driven from, the present worship",[45] varied even more dramatically than they had varied after the fifteen-nineties. Some ministers managed to retain their livings without conforming at all — for example Henry Swift at Peniston, Yorkshire, who had the support of the chief families in the parish. Richard Heyricke continued Warden of Manchester collegiate church. The Latitudinarian Bishop Wilkins of Chester, who conformed in 1660, was very helpful to his old Puritan friends in such matters. Ralph Josselin in Essex for two decades avoided wearing the hated surplice.[46] Other clergymen, like John Ray, resigned their benefices and became lay conforming members of the Church of England. Presbyterians favoured occasional conformity more than others: there were no Presbyterian ordinations before 1672. Baxter, William Bates, Thomas Manton, Francis Chandler, Thomas Jolly and the members of his church, were all occasional conformists. Oliver Heywood attended his parish church from time to time.[47] John Humfrey, although pastor to a nonconformist congregation, was "a conformist parishioner", who never received the sacrament elsewhere than at his parish church.[48]

In 1702 Calamy and other dissenters told Bishop Burnet that occasional conformity had been "used by some of the most eminent of our ministers since 1662, with a design to show their charity towards the church".[49] Norman Sykes observes that it is likely that acceptance of occasional conformity as a test for office took this practice into account. "No man," said John Howe sensibly, "can allow himself to think that what he before accounted lawful is by this supervening condition become unlawful." Occasional conformity no doubt increased when the laws were more strictly enforced between the mid-seventies and mid-eighties.[50] Pressure to accept a separatist position perhaps came from the Presbyterian laity rather than from the clergy. Congregations, wrote Joseph Williamson in 1671, "are now come to ride their teachers and make them do what they will . . . . All the Presbyterians are grown to Independents, and so must the teachers".[51]

Among the Independents, Thomas Goodwin thought that in most parishes, "where ignorance and profaneness overwhelm the generality, scandalousness and simony the ministers themselves", occasional conformity was inadmissible. But in others there were godly members of congregations, under a godly minister whom they had chosen to cleave to. With such it was lawful to communicate, as with the reformed churches on the continent. It was indeed a duty to "break down this partition wall"; "nothing provokes more than . . . to deny such churches to be true churches of Christ." John Owen, however, after arguing the case at length, came down against occasional conformity.[52] William Bridge threatened to excommunicate members of his flock who even went to hear an Anglican service. Philip Nye thought it was not only lawful but a duty to *hear* ministers of the state church, though not to join in common prayer or communion. His son Henry favoured occasional conformity. Some Baptists even were occasional conformists — John Tombes and Thomas Grantham, for instance.[53]

Patriotism came into it too. The breach with Rome had been a national act, or at least was so represented. Under Elizabeth and again in the sixteen-twenties and fifties Puritans had been the spearhead of English patriotism against Spain and the Pope. Under Laud, patriotism and prelacy seemed to be diametrically opposed. But in the sixteen-seventies and eighties the Church of England revealed itself as firmly anti-Catholic, anti-French and therefore patriotic. The trial of the Seven Bishops probably did more to make occasional conformists than the mere desire for office. Presbyterians were eager to be comprehended in the Church of England after 1688.[54]

After 1660 England again enjoyed a "balanced constitution". The existence of nonconformity checked effective reform of the Church of England; but the strength of urban dissent made the state church necessary to prevent any spread of radicalism to the countryside. The

Tory/Anglican gentry bitterly resented the existence of dissent, which prevented the balance being tipped their way. In 1664 Elias Ashmole had told his Presbyterian brother-in-law Henry Newcome that "nonconformity could be nothing but in expectation of a change". A change may have seemed likely to alarmed Tories in 1679-81, when the number of dissenting M.Ps. increased significantly.[55] They therefore had the less objection to governmental interference with borough charters, until James II actually began to flirt with Quakers and to re-open local government to real radicals.[56] The one constant factor from 1640 to 1689 is that any House of Commons elected on the traditional franchise favoured persecution, at least of radical sectaries.

Surveying the period from 1559 to 1689 we might again conclude that the first century of the Church of England was also its last. After 1660 the state church was no longer inclusive of the whole nation. Some of the most truly religious English men and women had chosen to withdraw from it, or had been driven out of it. The failure of the millennium to arrive and of the revolutionaries to implement their ideals led to the exclusion of their successors from the main stream of national, political and intellectual life. Nonconformity was forced into a position in which it became provincial, "sectarian" and "Puritan" in the pejorative sense of those words.

One of the problems which Puritans failed to solve was the relation of the godly minority to the ungodly masses of the population. Puritans and sectaries had seemed to threaten the traditional rural way of life, its (pagan) festivals, its cakes and ale and cock-fighting. Presbyterians wanted the lower orders to be more severely disciplined; the sects would have offered them preaching, but would not have compelled them to come in. In the late forties and fifties we often find conservative Puritans like Baxter complaining that the ungodly rabble hankered after the old episcopal church.[57] They had their revenge in 1660. The Church of England survived primarily because of its deep roots among the landed ruling class, whose interests it shared in so many ways; but also because "the rabble" preferred its conservative laxity to an enforced Presbyterian discipline, or the voluntary self-discipline of the sects. In the last resort the main numerical support for the episcopal church may have come from those who least believed in his doctrines. The church and king mobs which bawled for Sacheverell in 1709 came from parts of London where there were fewest parish churches. Outside

London, his strongest backing came from the Welsh border region.[58]

The sects, despite many attempts, never succeeded in reuniting: they managed to survive in so far as they got respectable middle- or lower-middle-class support; and nearly died of it in the eighteenth century. Those which lacked such support — Muggletonians and the like — continued to exist only in a vestigial form. Wesley had to start from scratch in appealing to the lowest classes; and there was no room for Methodism in the state church either.

After 1660 the radical sectaries were driven out of politics, into which they had intruded during the revolutionary decades. They abandoned political aspirations, partly because of their own recognition that Christ's kingdom was not going to be realised on earth now, partly because three decades of fierce persecution weeded out all but the most convinced believers, at a time when belief was becoming more other-wordly. The final result was a disastrous split in English social and educational life, the consequences of which are still with us. The Church of England defined the privileged sector. Chamberlayne's *Angliae Notitia* of 1669 complained that "it hath been observed even by strangers, that the iniquity of the present times in England is such that of all the Christian clergy of Europe . . . none are so little respected, beloved, obeyed or rewarded as the present . . . clergy of England".[59] The practice of occasional conformity was not only a way of qualifying insincere merchants for membership of town corporations; it was also a last symbolic attempt to bridge the gulf between the two cultures and proclaim the unity of the protestant nation.

NOTES

1. First printed in *Reformation, Conformity and Dissent: Essays in honour of Geoffrey Nuttall* (ed. R.B. Knox, 1977).
2. G.F. Nuttall. "Nonconformists in Parliament, 1661-1689", *Baptist Quarterly*, XX (1970); D.R. Lacey, *Dissent and Parliamentary Politics, 1661-1689* (Rutgers U.P., 1969), appendix III.
3. G. Holmes (ed.), *Britain after the Glorious Revolution* (1969), pp. 167-8.
4. H. Sacheverell, *The Perils of False Brethren* (1709), p. 135; J. Owen, *Works*, VII, pp. 74-6, 133, 249; cf. III, pp. 243-5; V, pp. 164, 174; XV, pp. 184-5.
5. F. Cheynell, *The Rise, Growth and Danger of Socinianism* (1648), pp. 62-6.
6. *Collections of the Massachusetts Historical Soc.*, Fourth Series (1863), p. 458; M. Sparke, *Crumms of Comfort*, Part II, 1652, Sig. para., pp. 7-8,

quoted in J.S. McGee, *The Godly Man in Stuart England* (Yale, U.P., 1976), p.76.

7. Whitgift, *Works* (Parker Soc., 1851-3), pp.308, 405-6.

8. Cf. *The Writings of John Greenwood, 1587-90*, ed. L. H. Carlson (1962), pp.247-50.

9. I have drawn heavily in this paragraph on Collinson, *The Elizabethan Puritan Movement*, esp. pp.164-7, 185-9 and 334. Cf. Chapter 6 above.

10. R. G. Usher (ed.), *The Presbyterian Movement in the Reign of Queen Elizabeth* (Camden Soc., third Series, VIII, 1905), pp.53-7, 102, and *passim*.

11. Cf. G. F. Nuttall, *Visible Saints*, pp.23-4; my *Economic Problems of the Church*, Chapter 4.

12. W. Haller, *Liberty and Reformation in the Puritan Revolution* (New York, 1955), p.119.

13. For this and the following paragraph see Chapter 7 above.

14. H.C. White., *Social Criticism in Popular Religious Literature of the Sixteenth Century*, p.121.

15. Quoted in R.M. Jones, *Studies in Mystical Religion* (1909), p.402.

16. Roger Williams, *The Bloody Tenent of Persecution*, 1644 (Hanserd Knollys Soc., 1848), p.425; J. Lilburne, *Come out of her my people*, (1639), p.19.

17. L. Busher, *Religious Peace* (1614), pp.70-1.

18. Whitgift, *op. cit.*, II, p.398. See pp.55, 58 above.

19. Brooke, *A Discourse ... of ... Episcopacie*, p.96, in Haller, *Tracts on Liberty*, II.

20. J. Calvin, *The Institutes of the Christian Religion* (trans. H. Beveridge, 1949), II, pp.651-4.

21. C.E. Burrage, *Early English Dissenters*, I, pp.171, 293, 305; II, pp.163, 301-2.

22. T. Helwys, *The Mistery of Iniquity* (1612), pp.86-94, 101-23. I quote from the Baptist Historical Society's reprint, 1935.

23. Cf. Cliffe, *The Puritan Gentry*, Chapter 10.

24. Usher, *op. cit., passim.*

25. Cf. J. Hexter, "The Problem of the Presbyterian Independents", in *Reappraisals in History* (1961), pp.163-84.

26. J. Waddington, *Congregational History, 1567-1700* (1874), p.426; cf. p.430 and p.6 above.

27. D. Masson, *Life of Milton* (1859-80), IV, pp.566-8.

28. *Thurloe State Papers* (1742), pp.598-601. Gauden was the author of *Eikon Basilike*.

29. Nuttall, op. cit., pp.22-6, 37-8, 135-41; A.C. Underwood, *A History of the English Baptists* (1947), pp.80, 96, 103-5; A.G. Matthews (ed.), *Calamy Revised* (Oxford U.P., 1934), pp.xiii and xli.

30. Cf. B.R. White, "Henry Jessey in the Great Rebellion", in *Reformation, Conformity and Dissent: Essays in Honour of Geoffrey Nuttall* (ed. R.B. Knox, 1977), pp.140, 150.

31. R.W. Dale, *History of English Congregationalism* (1907), pp.387-8; cf. Nuttall, *op. cit.*, pp.64-8, 99-100.

32. Nuttall, *op. cit.*, pp. 85-8; R. Barclay, *The Inner Life of the Religious Societies of the Commonwealth* (1876), p. 338; E.B. Underhill (ed.), *Confessions of Faith ... of ... the Baptist Churches of England in the Seventeenth Century* (Hanserd Knollys Soc., 1854), p. 115.

33. Nuttall, *op. cit.*, pp. 135-41.

34. Clarendon, *History of the Rebellion* (1888), I, pp. 406-7. See pp. 57-8 above.

35. D. Gardiner (ed.), *The Oxinden and Peyton Letters, 1642-1670* (1937), pp. 36-7.

36. R. Baxter, *A Sermon of Repentance* (1660), p. 43.

37. H. Newcome, *Autobiography* (Chetham Soc., XXVII, 1852), p. 118-19.

38. *C.S.P.D.*, *1675-6*, p. 1. Cf. the epigraph to this Chapter.

39. J. Tillotson, *Sermons on Several Subjects and Occasions* (1748), IX, pp. 134-6.

40. M.C. Jacob, *The Newtonians and the English Revolution*, Chapter I *passim*, pp. 189-96, 266.

41. H. Newcome, *Diary* (ed. T. Heywood, Chetham Soc., XVIII, 1849), pp. 119-20.

42. Ed. M.H. Lee, *Diaries and Letters of Philip Henry* (1882), pp. 99, 250, 277, 328-9.

43. Lamont, *Richard Baxter and the Millennium*, pp. 210-19.

44. Marvell, *The Rehearsal Transpros'd*, p. 33. He was echoing views held by a great many nonconformists (see my *The Experience of Defeat*, pp. 307-9).

45. Owen, *Works*, XV, p. 102.

46. Josselin, *Diary*, pp. 627-8.

47. C.E. Whiting, *Studies in English Puritanism from the Restoration to the Revolution, 1660-1688* (1931), pp. 32-3, 60-1; Joan Thirsk (ed.), *The Restoration* (1976), p. 63.

48. Matthews, *op. cit.*, pp. 284-5; Lacey, *Dissent and Parliamentary Politics in England*, *p. 23*.

49. E. Calamy, *An Historical Account of My Own Life* (ed. J.T. Rutt, 1829), I, p. 473.

50. N. Sykes, *From Sheldon to Secker* (Cambridge U.P., 1959), pp. 96-7; Lacey, *op. cit.*, p. 26.

51. *C.S.P.D.*, *1671*, p. 496. For the influence of lay members of congregations before 1640 see pp. 69, 78 above.

52. T. Goodwin, *Works*, I, pp. 557-8; Owen, *Works*, XV, pp. 65-8, 345-58, 378-9; XVI, pp. 241-53.

53. Lacey, *op. cit.*, p. 17; See p. 9 above.

54. See p. 9 above.

55. Newcome, *Autobiography*, I, p. 145; Lacey, *op. cit.*, p. 119.

56. For examples see J. Miller, *Popery and Politics in England, 1660-1688* (Cambridge U.P., 1973), pp. 209, 219-22.

57. Cf. J. Morrill, "The Church in England, 1642-1649," *passim*.

58. G. Holmes, *The Trial of Dr Sacheverell* (1973), Chapters 7 and 10.

59. Edward Chamberlayne, *Angliae Notitia* (1669), p. 401; see pp. 58-9 above.

15. *God and the English Revolution*[1]

"When they [the Jews in the Old Testament] *had a mind to change the government, to enter into civil war, to change a royal family, to reform religion, and to dismember their kingdom, ... they presently had a voice from heaven to assure their actions and secure their courses."**

"When the Fifth Monarchy Men ... raised a rebellion against King Charles for the restoring King Jesus, ... everyone was crying out, it was a senseless, mad action, unaccountable and preposterous. 'Ay', says the old woman, 'that's true; but what should we have called it if it had succeeded?'"†

"Take heed of hooking things up to heaven."‡

From way back in the nineteenth century, and still when I was at school, the seventeenth-century English Revolution used to be known as the Puritan Revolution. This name lost favour after Marx, Weber, Tawney and many others taught us that religion was not a self-sufficient motivating factor. Yet even Marxists have been known to speak of Puritanism as the ideology of the English Revolution. God still has a role in seventeenth-century politics. I want to conclude by looking at the effects of God on this Revolution, and its effects on God.

God was not only on the side of the Parliamentarians. Far from it. There seem indeed to have been three gods — a trinity — at work during the Revolution. First there was the God who blessed the established order, any established order, but especially that of England. Kings and bishops ruled by Divine Right, the clergy had a Divine Right to collect ten per cent of their parishioners' income as tithes — so conservatives said. The Elizabethan Homilies extolled

---

*Anthony Ascham, *Of the Confusions and Revolutions of Governments*, p. 109.

†Daniel Defoe, *Review*, I, p. 127, quoted by F. Bastian, *Defoe's Early Life* (1981), p. 19.

‡Marvell to Samuel Parker, *The Rehearsal Transpros'd*, p. 255.

the existing hierarchical social structure, the great chain of being which ran through nature and society, and which Shakespeare stated — probably ironically — in *Troilus and Cressida.* "Take but degree away, untune that string/And hark what discord follows". All change was bad and dangerous, because the mass of mankind had been irredeemably wicked since the Fall of Adam. The state exists to prevent the horrors which sinful humanity — and especially the lower orders — would perpetrate if not held in by law and power.

The second God, the God of the Parliamentarians, was also in favour of order; but he stressed justice rather than mere defence of the *status quo.* The Hebrew prophets in the Bible denounced the injustices of rulers and called for reformation. But only certain kinds of change were permissible: reformation should go back to Biblical models, to the primitive church of the New Testament. The Bible was used as litmus paper to test existing institutions. Were bishops to be found in the New Testament? If not, they should be abolished. This was a dangerously wide-ranging principle.[2] Milton and many others could not find the Trinity in the Bible. Colonel Rainborough in 1647 searched the Scriptures in vain to find a justification for the 40/- freeholder Parliamentary franchise. This did not lead him to reject Parliaments, but to call for manhood suffrage. Others, more conscious of the risks of uncritical application of the Bible to seventeenth-century society, thought that change, however desirable, could be justified only if supported by the authority of the magistrate. Lesser magistrates might take the initiative if the sovereign did not, Dutch and French Calvinists thought. So they authorized revolt if supported by the respectable classes. Calvinists also found the protestant ethic in the Bible — thrift, sobriety, frugality, discipline, hard work, monogamy: a discipline which it was the duty of the magistrate to enforce on the labouring classes lest social chaos should result.[3]

But in the course of the Revolution some people discovered a third God, a God who — like the Holy Ghost — was to be found in every believer. And since it was difficult to ascertain who were true believers, this came to mean that God could be found in every man (some daring spirits said in every woman too). The full horrors of this doctrine were plumbed only in the sixteen-forties, but worshippers of the second, Calvinist, God were early aware of the existence of this third deity, and from the first tried to safeguard against his emergence. The Bible after all said many things, and untutored readers of it might draw very remarkable conclusions. Arise Evans, a Welsh-man, tells us of the impact that coming to London made on his thinking. "Afore I looked upon the Scripture as a history of things that passed in other countries, pertaining to other persons; but now I looked upon it as a mystery to be opened at this time, belonging also to us". In Amos and Revelation he found descriptions of what was happening in revolutionary England. In Amos 9.1 the Lord said "smite the lintel of the door, that the posts may shake"; Evans thought this could only refer to Speaker Lenthall.[4] Others used Biblical texts for more consciously subversive purposes.

The God within sometimes looked like a God of pure anarchy: there might be as many gods as there were men, as Fulke Greville and Gerrard Winstanley both came to the recognize, the former with disapproval, the latter with approval.[5] But this is something which developed fully only after the breakdown of all authority in the sixteen-forties, when lower-class sects of every heretical kind could meet and discuss freely. The three gods favoured different forms of worship. The first liked ritual and ceremonies; the second preaching; the third discussion and participation by the congregation in church government. So the first god attached most importance to the institutional church and its clergy; the second to an educated mini-stry; the third had no real use for ministers at all.

There is of course nothing surprising in this many-facedness of God. Any state religion which survives for any length of time has to perform a multiplicity of tasks: it has to console the down-trodden as well as to maintain the mighty in their seats. It has to persuade the rich to be charitable as well as the poor to be patient. Usually orthodox Christianity had interpreted the consolatory passages in the Scriptures as referring to an after life. But this is sometimes difficult to square with the Biblical text. As the Bible became available in English after the Reformation, and as literacy moved down the social scale, so men and women began to take literally the more subversive texts of the Bible which their betters preferred to read allegorically.

In the century before 1640 many had seen England as a chosen nation, which God continually intervened to protect. In 1588 he blew with his winds and the Spanish Armada was scattered; a century later the protestant wind wafted William of Orange safely over to England to replace the papist James II. Even the revolutionary Great Seal of the English Commonwealth claimed that freedom had been "by God's blessing restored." But great favours entailed great responsibilities.

God punished both individuals and societies for their misdeeds. Sylvester translated Du Bartas's explanation of a plague epidemic:

> For our sins, so many and so great,
> So little moved with promise or with threat,
> Thou now at last (as a just jealous God)
> Strik'st us thyself with thine immediate rod,
> Thy rod of pestilence.[6]

Lancelot Andrewes confirmed that "sin provokes the wrath of God, the wrath of God sends the plague among us".[7] One reason for emigration to New England in the sixteen-twenties and thirties, to which historians perhaps do not attach sufficient importance, was a desire to escape from the wrath to come. Thomas Cooper in 1615 reminded the Lord Mayor, Aldermen and Sheriffs of London of the need "to provide some retiring place for yourselves if so be the Lord for our unthankfulness should spew us out".[8] Fourteen years later John Winthrop, soon to be first Governor of Massachusetts, was "verily persuaded God will bring some heavy afflictions upon this land, and that speedily". "God is packing up his Gospel", said Thomas Hooker in 1631, "because nobody will buy his wares". "God is going from England".[9]

So God regularly showed his approval and disapproval of human actions, particularly those of rulers. One way of propitiating the God who was angry with our sins was to hold a private fast, as Alexander Leighton did in 1624, Hugh Peter in 1626. Such a fast might be semi-public. But "a land or nation ... must be longer in the fire than one particular person".[10] Parliaments of the sixteen-twenties implied criticism of the government by calling for a public fast. Laudians thought fasting "as hateful as conventicles," and sought to suppress fasts in Essex and East Anglia. Their discouragement of fasting deprived the godly of what seemed to them the most hopeful way of averting the calamities which threatened the nation.[11] The Long Parliament made the point neatly when it met in November 1640. It proclaimed a day of national humiliation, to be held on Queen Elizabeth's accession day, 17 November. The sermons preached on that day did not fail to make the contrast between the victorious protestantism of Good Queen Bess and her successors' ineffective

Laodiceanism.[12] Fast sermons preached during the civil war continued to be used to whip up support for the cause. On the eve of Charles I's trial Thomas Brooks reminded the House of Commons that "execution of justice and judgment will free you from the guilt of other men's sins".[13]

One problem was to interpret the signs so as to understand God's wishes. For many, success seemed evidence of God's support, and failure witnessed to divine disapproval; but sometimes, confusingly, it was left to a tiny remnant of the faithful to preserve the truth in secret. Arguments of this type were naturally used when convenient as the fortunes of civil war swayed backwards and forwards between 1642 and 1645. After Brilliana Harley's Brampton Brian had surrendered, triumphant royalists asked the defenders where their God was now?[14] In 1645 preachers before Parliament attributed the defeat of the Earl of Essex in Cornwall to God's objection to toleration of heretics. John Goodwin on the contrary suggested that it was God's judgment against Parliament's intolerance.[15]

In September 1641 Stephen Marshall doubted "whether God ever did such a thing for matter and manner in these two unworthy nations, ... giving us in one year a return of the prayers of forty four years".[16] "A miracle of Providence", Jeremiah Burrough called it; "a mercy that is a foundation of mercy to the generations to come, ... to the Christian world".[17] "It is the Lord's great work that is now a-framing", Brilliana Harley had told her son in May 1642.[18]

In retrospect Parliamentarians came to claim that it was God, not man, who called the Long Parliament in 1640; that God, not man, created the New Model Army and brought about the trial and execution of Charles I in 1649. The Fifth Monarchists Thomas Harrison and John Carew, no less than the Quakers Francis Howgil and Isaac Penington, all saw "the finger of God" in England's deliverances: "the Lord hath appeared in our day to do great things", declared the republican Edmund Ludlow. Even a relative conservative like the Scottish Presbyterian Robert Baillie told the Westminster Assembly that "the Lord ... has led us by the hand and marched before us" against the prelates.[19] "The God of the Parliament ... hath gone with you", the Independent divine John Owen assured Parliament in a sermon preached in June 1649 to celebrate the defeat of the Levellers at Burford. Oliver Cromwell believed that the Army had been "called by God", and fiercely defended "the revolutions of Christ himself", God's "working of things from one period to another". "God hath done great and honourable things" by the agency of the Long Parliament, the Quakers Edward Burrough and Miles Halhead admitted: the Bristol Baptist Robert Purnell, the Fifth Monarchist John Tillinghast, the Independents Thomas Goodwin and John Cook, the antinomian William Dell, the Quaker George Bishop, all agreed.[20]

William Sedgwick, famous Army preacher, in December 1648 denounced the Army's intervention in politics, since it prevented a peaceful settlement with the King which he had hoped would reunite the country. But a few months later he completely reversed his position. The trial and execution of the King, the establishment of the Commonwealth, the abolition of the House of Lords — these events overwhelmed him by their sheer magnitude. *Because* the Army's actions had been so unprecedented they must have been inspired by God. The only problem, as Sedgwick saw it, was to bring this fact home to the generals so as to make them live up to their responsibilities now that God "is upon motion, marching us out of Egyptian darkness and bondage into a Canaan of rest and happiness".[21] "You are the rod of God", Joseph Salmon told "the commanding powers in the Army". "In this day of the Lord's wrath you strike through King, gentry and nobility, they all fall before you".[22] God's people, George Joyce agreed, were going to do "such things as were never yet done by man".[23] We may compare Marvell's sense of Cromwell as "the force of angry heaven's flame", which "'Tis madness to resist or blame".[24] Even royalists, Baxter assures us, were "astonished at the marvellous providences of God, which had been against that family [the Stuarts] all along".[25]

The ultimate in divine intervention would be the Second Coming. Prophecies in Daniel and Revelation established that a great conflagration will mark the end of the world. Any Christian who takes these prophecies seriously must be anxious to ascertain when the holocaust will take place. I believe many middle-western American Christians are today looking forward with relish to helping to expedite it with nuclear warfare.[26] In the late sixteenth and early seventeenth centuries there seemed to be good reasons for supposing that the end of the world was imminent. When John Milton in 1641 spoke of Christ as "shortly-expected King", he was probably thinking of the sixteen-fifties, though he may have extended the possibilities a decade or two.[27]

For Milton the Second Coming would put "an end to all earthly tyrannies", including that of Charles I. It involved political revolution. Here we come to a great divide. The orthodox view was that after the destruction of the world a new heaven and a new earth would be created, in which the elect would henceforth lead blissful and quite different lives: it was a totally other-worldly concept. Many millenarians however interpreted the Biblical prophecies to mean that after Christ's Second Coming he would rule on earth for a thousand years (the millennium). Whether Christ would rule in person or through the saints was a question: radicals tended to foresee a rule of the saints (i.e. themselves). One can see how such widely held ideas could turn into theories justifying a dictatorship of the godly minority. Millenarian ideas could lead to rejection of régimes which seemed to be excluding Jesus Christ from his proper authority. For many — like William Sedgwick — the execution of Charles I only made sense if it cleared the way for King Jesus. When the Army went to conquer Scotland in 1650 its watchword was "No King but Jesus". But only three years later the Fifth Monarchist Vavasor Powell had to tell his congregation to ask God "Wilt thou have Oliver Cromwell or Jesus Christ to rule over us?"[28]

Millenarian ideas could also beget a sort of revolutionary internationalism. Hugh Peter told Parliament in December 1648 that "this Army must root up monarchy, not only here but in France and other kingdoms round about". Marvell foresaw Cromwell in this liberating role:

> As Caesar he ere long to Gaul,
> To Italy an Hannibal,
> And to all states not free
> Shall climacteric be.

In 1651 Admiral Blake, commanding the world's strongest fleet, said on Spanish territory that monarchy was on the way out all over Europe — in France as well as in England. He gave it ten years in Spain, a slower-moving country. John Rogers the Fifth Monarchist declared in 1653 "We are bound by the law of God to help our neighbours as well as ourselves, and so to aid the subjects of other princes that are either persecuted for true religion or oppressed under tyranny". Part of the English Army should be sent to France or Holland, to conduct a revolutionary war. The Quaker leader George Fox many times in the late sixteen-fifties rebuked the Army for not going to Spain, to overthrow the Inquisition. "Never set up your standard until you come to Rome", he urged, in words which show that he was not yet a pacifist.[29]

But God could also speak directly to private individuals. Lady Eleanor Davies, a slightly eccentric person, in 1633 prophesied that Charles I would come to a violent end. She was sent to Bedlam, but was taken more seriously after the King's execution.[30] In the political freedom of the forties and early fifties quite humble men and women could be entrusted by God with political messages. Gerrard Winstanley heard a voice telling him to set up the communist colony whose necessity to solve England's economic problems he had long been working out.[31] In 1652 John Reeve received a special commission from God, and he went on to found the sect later known as the Muggletonians, which lasted until 1979.[32] God dictated reams of rather mediocre verse to Anna Trapnell. George Fox and John Bunyan received messages, as did innumerable less well-known characters.

It was thus *natural* for perfectly normal people to hear God speaking to them: it was not, as it would be today, *prima facie* evidence of insanity. This followed indeed from what I described as the third manifestation of God, the theological assumption that God dwells in all his saints, perhaps in all men and women. The early Quakers became the best-known exponents of this theology, but it was widespread during the revolutionary decades. Gerrard Winstanley believed that God was the same thing as Reason; the Second Coming was not Jesus Christ descending from the clouds but Reason rising in sons and daughters[33]. So the logic of protestant heresy led to something very like secularism.

Political discussion was invariably carried on in religious language and imagery. Winstanley used the stories of Cain and Abel, Esau and Jacob, to express his class analysis of society: the younger brother would overcome his oppressing elder brother. David and Goliath, Samson and the Philistines, were symbols of revolt against tyranny. Existing corrupt society was designated as Sodom, Egypt, Babylon. The Pope had been Antichrist for Foxe and many protestants, as he had been for Lollard heretics earlier. Winthrop hoped that New England would become a "bulwark against the kingdom of Antichrist".[34] The Parliamentarian revolutionaries saw their royalist adversaries as "the Antichristian faction". Stephen Marshall, in a famous sermon preached to the House of Commons in February 1642, declared that "many of the nobles, magistrates, knights and gentlemen, and persons of great quality, are arrant traitors and rebels against God". What more desperate incitement to class war than that? "The question in England", he said in 1644, "is whether Christ or Antichrist shall be lord or king". In the same year some Parliamentarian soldiers believed that "the people, the multitude" would pull down the Whore of Babylon; "we are the men that must help to pull her down".[35]

But soon Parliament itself was being called Antichristian, and the adjective was applied to Presbyterianism in the sixteen-forties, to Cromwell in the fifties. Any national church was Antichristian, many sectaries asserted. Cromwell himself said that the distinction between clergy and laity was Antichristian. Richard Overton and Henry Denne thought intolerance Antichristian: Baptists said the same of infant baptism. Bunyan put the social point more subtly by describing Antichrist as a gentleman.[36] For Winstanley covetousness, buying and selling, were Antichristian: property was the devil, Christ community.[37] There was a whole code of Biblical shorthand on which (among many others) Winstanley and Milton drew with great effect. Winstanley argued that all the Scripture prophecies "concerning the calling of the Jews," foretold the work which the Diggers were carrying on.[38] Milton could not attack monarchy directly in *Paradise Lost*, since he was a marked man who had been lucky to escape execution in 1660; instead he merely recalled that monarchy had been founded by a rebel "of proud ambitious heart", who

> not content
> With fair equality, fraternal state,
> Will arrogate dominion, undeserved,
> Over his brethren.[39]

Milton did not even need to name Nimrod, of whom Charles I had spoken with approval: he could rely on his readers' Biblical knowledge.

During the Revolution the idea that God might be in every believer, or indeed in every man and woman, worked powerfully against traditional social deference, and for human equality: the eighteenth-century Great Awakening may have had similar effects in preparing for the American Revolution.[40] In England in the sixteen-forties and fifties God said unexpected things to and through his saints. The Ranter Abiezer Coppe, for instance, announced that God, "that mighty Leveller", would "overturn, overturn, overturn".

"The neck of horrid pride" must be chopped off, so that "parity, equality, community" might establish "universal love, universal peace and perfect freedom". "Thou hast many bags of money, and behold I (the Lord) come as a thief in the night, with my sword drawn in my hand, and like a thief as I am — I say deliver your purse, deliver sirrah! Deliver or I'll cut thy throat. ... Have all things common, or else the plague of God will rot and consume all that you have".[41]

George Foster had a vision of a man on a white horse who cut down those higher than the middle sort and raised up those that were lower, crying "Equality, equality, equality. ... I, the Lord of Hosts have done this. ... I will ... make the low and poor equal with the rich. ... O rich men, I will utterly destroy you". For Foster too God was "that mighty Leveller".[42] Laurence Clarkson preached a permissive morality. "Till you can lie with all women as one woman, and not judge it sin, you can do nothing but sin". Coppe had a similar libertine theology. "External kisses have been made the fiery chariot to mount me swiftly into the bosom of ... the King of Glory. ... I can kiss and hug ladies, and love my neighbour's wife as myself, without sin".[43]

Clement Wrighter and the Quaker Samuel Fisher argued that the Bible was not the infallible Word of God but a historical document to be interpreted. Some radicals rejected the immortality of the soul, heaven and hell. "When men are gazing up to heaven", Winstanley argued, "imagining a happiness or fearing a hell after they are dead, their eyes are put out, that they see not ... what is to be done by them here on earth while they are living".[44] To Winstanley the personal God above the skies, the God of priests and landlords, looked like the devil.

Conservatives began to feel freedom could go too far, that it was time to stop God communicating through the common people, or at least prevent his words being freely discussed, verbally and in print. Hence the suppression of Levellers, Diggers, Ranters and Fifth Monarchists and the restoration of censorship in the sixteen-fifties. Hence the move to restore authority to the state church. Alderman Violet made the point succinctly in May 1650, reporting upon the economic crisis to the Committee of the Mint: "I propose as remedies, first, to settle able and godly ministers in all churches throughout the nation, that will teach the people to fear God, to obey their superiors and to live peaceably with each other — with a competent maintenance for all such ministers".[45] He had got his priorities right. Ten years later Richard Baxter justified the restoration of episcopacy in the interests of discipline.[46]

One can see too why men desperately searched for certainty. There were so many rival accounts of God's wishes, so many differing interpretations of the Bible, that men sought either an infallible interpreter of God's will, or some other way of replacing the old certainties with a new consensus. The episcopal church had collapsed, and no single church took its place. An infallible prophet like John Robins or John Reeve, or the infallible inner light, were possible saviours. But prophets died, and the inner light said different things to different people. Winstanley rejected human Saviours, but his Reason was as difficult to define as the inner light.[47]

A more promising alternative was to look for secular solutions, for a science of politics which would guide human action. Thomas Hobbes in *Leviathan* (1651) argued that a ruler could claim the allegiance of his subjects only in so far as he could protect them. When Charles I was defeated in the civil war, he could no longer do this, and so subjects had a *duty* to switch their allegiance to the *de facto* power of the commonwealth. Political obligation had nothing to do with claims by Divine Right; it was a question of fact: could the sovereign do his job by protecting his subjects? Hobbes destroyed claims by any group to rule because God favoured them: the restoration of monarchy in 1660 in any case made nonsense of such arguments by Parliamentarians. So Hobbes undermined all traditional theories of obligation based on the will of God. It is the beginning of modern secular political theory. Every individual has a right to his own ideas; no subject and no church can claim a right in God's name to subvert the *de facto* sovereign. But Leviathan the mortal God also supplanted the third God who had rejected deference and promoted revolt.

In 1656 the republican James Harrington advanced his own science of politics — the idea that political structures depend on economic structures, that when the economic base changes the political superstructure (Harrington's word) must change too. During the English Revolution, he argued, there had been a transfer of power to those who had amassed landed property in the century before 1640: no government could be stable which did not recognize their right to rule. The events of 1660-88 appeared to confirm Harrington's analysis, and hammered another nail into the coffin of religious theories of political obligation and resistance. "A commonwealth is not made by man but by God", declared Harrington piously; but God acted through secondary causes, through the balance of property.[48]

The return of Charles II in 1660 ended the Revolution by restoring monarchy to preside over the rule of the propertied. When men took stock, these secular theories seemed to make sense. Charles was proclaimed King by the grace of God, but everyone knew that God had needed earthly agents to get Charles restored. Clarendon said of the restoration "God Almighty would not have been at the expense and charge of such a deliverance but in the behalf of a church very acceptable to him".[49] But that was in November 1660. During the interregnum each party had claimed God on its side in the hour of victory; each side had to rethink its position in the years of defeat, including no doubt Clarendon himself after he had been driven into exile in 1667. Either God was very unstable and erratic, or his ways were incomprehensible to mere human intelligence: better to leave him out of account altogether. This sceptical trend was strengthened by the alarm which the third God had caused, the God within the consciousness of lower-class sectaries. So the keynote of upper-class thinking after 1660 is opposition to "fanaticism", "enthusiasm", to claims to inspiration, whether in literature or in religion or politics. The royalist Sir William Davenant described inspiration as "a dangerous word".[50] Claims to literary inspiration fell out of fashion until they revived with romanticism after the French Revolution. It was Hobbes's undermining of deference that seemed to Clarendon his greatest betrayal of "the nobility, by whose bread he hath bin always sustained".[51] The restoration of the episcopal church confirmed the presence in every parish of an authorized, approved interpreter of the Scriptures, and confirmed the survival of the universities which trained these interpreters. God is one thing, the church is another.

For those Parliamentarians who believed they had been taking part in the revolutions of Christ, the total defeat which the restoration implied was a shattering blow. "The Lord had spit in their faces", Major-General Fleetwood wailed.[52] In December 1659, when Sir Arthur Haslerig seized Portsmouth on behalf of the Rump against the Army, he acknowledged that "the Lord hath wonderfully appeared with us in this business". Just one year later Sir Arthur died in prison; the Rump and the Army were no more.[53] A condemned regicide found it difficult to answer the question "Have you not hard thoughts of God for this his strange providence towards you?"[54] Men had to stress the justice of an avenging God rather than his mercy. "God did seem to be more cruel than men", Muggleton admitted. Milton was thus only one of a large·number who found it necessary to justify the ways of God to men, to account for the apparent triumph of evil over good. God was on trial, for Traherne, Bunyan, Rochester and Dryden as well as in *Paradise Lost* and *Samson Agonistes*.[55]

It is a turning-point in human thought. After 30 January 1649 kings never forgot that they had a joint in their necks. And God was never quite the same again after he had been put on trial in popular discussion. He slowly withdrew into the Newtonian stratosphere.[56] The idea that God watches over each individual's actions is perhaps more plausible within a small community. Once we get trade on a world scale God's immediate interest is more difficult to imagine. Would he organize a storm in the Indian Ocean in order to punish a London merchant with the loss of his ship? God may favour a particular nation, but belief in his direct intervention in the everyday affairs of individuals varies, as Adam Smith nearly said, with the extent of the market.

The belief that God might be in all men, rather than a distinct person above the skies, diminished the likelihood of a personal devil, and so of witchcraft. The former radical John Webster published a definitive *Displaying of Supposed Witchcraft* in 1677. *The Decline of Hell*, which Mr Walker has traced in the seventeenth-century, accompanied the decline of the torture chamber after the abolition of Star Chamber and High Commission. Fasts and fast sermons had faded out in the sixteen-fifties; in 1657 an M.P. was jeered at when he "cited a Scripture to confirm what he said".[57] Judicial oaths and oaths of allegiance could be taken seriously only if the religious sanction behind them was generally accepted. John Locke would refuse toleration to Roman Catholics and atheists because the former owed allegiance to a foreign power; the latters' oaths could not be trusted because they did not believe in the rewards and punishments of an after life. So long as church and state were one, oaths harnessed God to their use. But the existence of permanently organized dissent created new problems: Quakers refused oaths on principle, and ultimately had to be accommodated by a statutory declaration. It was another advance to secularism through religious radicalism.[58]

The God of early eighteenth-century England bore as little resemblance to his predecessor of a century earlier as Archbishop Tillotson did to Archbishop Laud; though Tillotson was rather more approachable than the Supreme Being. After Charles II's reign bishops no longer participated in government, and the state ecclesiastical itself had lost its coercive power. Divine Right, whether of bishops or kings, was forgotten; sovereignty belonged to secular Parliaments, and ecclesiastical law was finally subordinated to the common law.

After 1660 the restored episcopal church was slowly taken over by "Latitudinarians", mostly former Puritans, who abandoned Divine Right claims for bishops and tithes, and based their claims on the law of the land. The Latitudinarians played a prominent part in the newly-founded Royal Society, whose scientists also did much to talk down "fanaticism" and "enthusiasm". Their rejection of "extremes", their stress on moderation, common sense, etc., etc., helped to hold scientific thought within acceptable bounds.[59] Charles II was wise to become patron of the Royal Society as well as head of the Church of England. Here too the intellectual climate favoured a secular science of politics, an empirical probabilism. Common sense of course led to intellectual muddles. Some Fellows of the Royal Society proclaimed a belief in witchcraft, based on the evidence of the senses and the authority of the Bible. "No spirit, no God", declared Henry More, later F.R.S.[60] "No devil, no witches", was in effect Webster's retort. The lives of lonely old women as well as the existence of God were at stake.

The point is made by Eamon Duffy in a discussion of Valentine Greatrakes, whose cures by stroking were admitted by the Royal Society to be "stupendous performances". But his successes made people wonder about the exclusive royal touch for curing the King's evil (which Greatrakes claimed to cure), and even ask how Greatrakes's cures differed from those of Christ in the New Testament. Moreover, Greatrakes had a radical past; and in 1666-7 there was a great deal of renewed millenarian excitement, which Greatrakes shared. It was all very embarrassing for the Latitudinarians. "The development of a particular religious point of view", Duffy concludes, "is never a matter of intellect or spirit alone; the reactions to his cures were dictated as much by fear of democracy or anarchy, of popery or religious enthusiasm, of the upsetting of the Restoration social, political and religious order, as by the intellectual demands of science or reason. Rational theology was the lubricant for a piece of social engineering."[61]

In the early fifties the Ranters had abolished sin. But history abolished the Ranters, and sin came back in strength after 1660. The Quakers, who had denounced the state clergy for preaching up sin, found a place for it in their post-restoration theology. James Nayler had been feeling his way towards such a conclusion after his "fall" in 1656.[62] The sinfulness of the mass of humanity had always been used to oppose change. Even Milton, in *Paradise Lost*, explained the defeat of the Revolution by the sinfulness of the English people, who had failed to live up to the high ideals and aspirations put before them.

Dissenters, excluded from the state church, now formed a separate nation, huddled into their self-supported congregations, desperately concerned with survival in a hostile world. They were cut off from national political life and the national universities. Most of the sects followed Muggletonians and Quakers into pacifism and abstention from politics. Their God now presided over a provincial, stunted culture; he was no longer capable of transforming nations. Accepting that religion should not concern itself with high politics, the sects' emphasis henceforth fell more on questions of conduct and personal morality, such as arose in the confusing growth of capitalist society with its new standards. As they adapted themselves to this new world, the sects became — to adapt Lenin's phrase — schools of capitalism. The nonconformist conscience was to revive as a political force only after internalization of the work ethic had helped many dissenters to prosper: but that was far ahead in 1660.

For those whose lack of property put them below the line which marked off "the political nation", restoration of the familiar, consoling rituals of the traditional church may have been acceptable. Others no doubt just opted out. Church courts no longer enforced church attendance; but perhaps Sir Roger de Coverley's watchful eye over his tenants was more effectual in ensuring their presence. Parson and squire collaborated to keep the rural poor in order. Dissenters could not be suppressed in towns, but church and king mobs could always be used against them.[63] After 1672 the practice of licensing dissenting ministers ensured that nonconformist congregations too were presided over by some sort of recognized interpreter of the Scriptures; they could not now be mere discussion groups chaired by an elected mechanic preacher. The strenuous virtues which Milton had expected of the English people were no longer demanded. They lapsed into the old assumption that politics was for their betters. Church and state, King and country, the royal touch healing scrofula, monarchy as spectacle, after 1688 safely controlled by the King's ministers.

1640 was the last national revolution whose driving ideology was religious. Milton's *De Doctrina Christiana* was so heretical that it could not be published, even in Latin. When his literary executor tried after his death to publish it in the Netherlands, all the power of English diplomacy was exerted to prevent it. The confiscated manuscript lay among the State Papers until 1823. When it was published — on the orders of a King, translated by a bishop — the dynamite of the sixteen-sixties had become a damp squib. Since the American and French Revolutions revolutionary doctrines were no longer expressed in religious idiom. The Revolution had no need of God.

What remained after 1660 was a secularized version of the myth of the chosen people, which Charles II still proclaimed.[64] The millenarian Thomas Goodwin had wanted England to be "top of the nations".[65] The republican James Harrington had advocated "a commonwealth for increase". "The late appearances of God unto you" were not "altogether for yourselves". If "called in by an oppressed people" (Scotland? Ireland? France?) England had a duty to respond. "If you add unto the propagation of civil liberty ... the propagation of liberty of conscience, this empire, this patronage of the world, is the kingdom of Christ".[66] As we saw, Marvell, and Dryden in *Annus Mirabilis*, took up the idea, the latter with minimal religious underpinning.[67]

Ireland — the first English colony — was a case in which the Cause of God got hopelessly mixed up with economic and strategic considerations. Most of the English revolutionaries believed that Charles I and Laud had been part of, or at least had connived at, an international Roman Catholic plot for the conquest of England and the subversion of protestantism. In this plot Ireland's role was crucial. It was an open back-door to foreign Catholic invasion. Spanish troops had landed there in the fifteen-nineties, French troops would land there in the sixteen-nineties in an attempt to restore James II to the English throne. The collapse of English power in Ireland in 1640 unleashed the rebellion of 1641, which was soon headed by a Papal Nuncio. So the Cromwellian re-conquest of

Ireland seemed a necessary defensive blow against Antichrist, to prevent the restoration of monarchy by invasion through Ireland. The radicals, fiercely attacking Cromwell on internal matters, offered no real opposition to the conquest and enslavement of Ireland — with a few notable exceptions, such as the Leveller William Walwyn.[68] The English republic, in Karl Marx's pregnant phrase, "met shipwreck in Ireland". "The English reaction in England had its roots ... in the subjugation of Ireland".[69] If ever God showed himself a conservative it was in thus allowing religion to mislead the radical revolutionaries.

So God played many parts in the English Revolution. First came the landslide of 1640-1, when suddenly the apparently all-powerful government of Charles and Laud found itself unable any longer to persecute the saints: and when by overwhelming majorities in Parliament the repressive machinery of the prerogative courts was swept away. When the King tried to resist, God raised up an army against him; when stalemate seemed likely to occur, God and Oliver Cromwell created the New Model Army. After bringing about the second great revolution of 1648-9 God continued his favour by permitting the conquest of Ireland and Scotland, the Navigation Act of 1651 and the consequent successfully aggressive colonial foreign policy — Dutch War, Spanish War, Dunkirk seized, piracy brought under control. In turn the events of 1660 came to seem as providential as those of 1640-1 and 1648-9. But with a difference. In 1649 the Army had acted positively as God's instrument, had brutally but effectively shattered the image hitherto worshipped as divine: in 1660 it was the return of the traditional rulers that seemed providential.

> Neither man's power nor policy had place; ...
> The astonished world saw 'twas the mighty work of heaven,

sang Sir Francis Fane.[70] God had changed sides, and was now overwhelmingly on the side of the traditional establishment, as he had previously been on the side of shocking innovation: the restoration came in spite of rather than because of the royalists. Those who had been the instruments of the omnipotent God in 1648-9 were now revealed as impotent mortals, for whom the God of history had no more use.[71]

The Glorious Revolution of 1688 was an additional providence, another landslide like those of 1640 and 1660, another reassertion of the predetermined social order. It also confirmed England's new right to rule the world. Further confirmation came from the Industrial Revolution, another unplanned gift from heaven. The secular millenarian interpretation of England's manifest destiny was validated by these providential social transformations.

In the sixteen-forties the belief that men were fighting for God's Cause had been a tremendous stimulus to morale. A popular slogan in the north said that "God is a better lord than the Earl of Derby".[72] The theoretical duty of a feudal lord was to protect his underlings; what impressed them was his ever-present power. If you lived in Lancashire or on the Isle of Man it was difficult to think that there could be a greater power than the Earl of Derby. Yet in the sixteen-forties confidence in God's overlordship gave the Puritan citizens of Lancashire towns courage to resist even the Earl of Derby, who ultimately in 1651 was executed "for treason and rebellion ... in a town of his own", Bolton.[73] It seemed a great blow against traditional deference. Yet in 1660 his son reappeared in Lancashire to wield much of his father's old authority: in the long run God proved the weaker lord.

After 1660 a new ruling-class consensus formed, when a more remote God again presided over the established order, and sanctified it. To suggest "that religion is a cheat", Chief Justice Hale declared in 1676, "tends to the dissolution of all government and therefore is punishable here" — i.e. in the common-law courts.[74] Religion must not be allowed to decline with church courts. God = history = what happens. So the Revolution, which at one time looked like a historic triumph for the third God, ended with his utter defeat. Mammon, Winstanley's God of this world, who played a very covert role in the initial stages of the Revolution, fared much better in the end.

One conclusion we may perhaps draw is that any religion can serve any social purpose, because of the ambiguity of its basic texts. Enemies of the revolutionary radicals noted the similarity of many of their theories to those of the Jesuits. We should not think of protestantism as causing the rise of capitalism, but rather of protestantism and Puritanism being moulded by capitalist society to suit its needs. After 1660 God continued to offer consolation in the after life to those who were unhappy on earth. But between 1640 and 1660 God had also stimulated protest, rejection of an unjust society and its laws; he had legitimized movements for change. "True religion and undefiled", Winstanley said, "is to let everyone quietly have earth to manure, that they may live in peace and freedom in their labour".[75] Land for all might have been the basis for a different consensus. Collective farms making two blades of grass grow where one grew before might have led England out of scarcity into abundance without the expropriation of smallholders in the interests of large-scale capitalist agriculture, without the disappearance of the peasantry. But the victorious God willed otherwise.

How much of the radical tradition survived underground we do not know, for censorship closed down again after 1660, and victors write history. At the end of *Samson Agonistes* Milton envisaged God's Cause as an undying Phoenix; "and though her body die, her fame survives,/ A secular bird, ages of lives".[76] I do not myself think that ideas like those of the radicals get totally forgotten: men were discussing Winstanley's writings in a Welsh valley in the seventeen-nineties — an interesting place and an interesting time.[77] In 1850 God was called the first Chartist,[78] just as Italian socialists in 1893 thought "Jesus was a true socialist".[79] In Blok's *The Twelve* the revolutionary soldiers were led by Jesus Christ. A popular song of the Spanish civil war celebrated Christ as a revolutionary, contrasted with the fascist clergy. God the great Leveller who wants everything overturned is active today in Latin America and parts of Africa. But in England he seems no longer to exercise his power of stirring masses of men and women up to political action.

NOTES

1. This chapter is based on a lecture given at a History Workshop and printed in *History Workshop Journal*, 17 (1984).
2. Cf. pp. 37-8 above.
3. See pp. 123-5 above.
4. Evans, *A Voice from Heaven to the Commonwealth of England* (1652), pp. 26-7, 33, 45, 74-5; *An Eccho to the Voice from Heaven* (1653), p. 17, quoted in my *Change and Continuity in 17th-century England*, pp. 59-60.
5. "No man shall be troubled for his judgment or practice in the things of his God" (Winstanley, *The Law of Freedom and Other Writings*, p. 379; Fulke Greville, "A Treatise of Religion", in *Remains*, ed. G. A. Wilkes, Oxford U.P., 1965, p. 207).
6. *Du Bartas his Divine Weekes and Workes* (translated by Joshua Sylvester), in Sylvester, *Complete Works* (ed. A. B. Grosart, 1880), I, p. 224.

7. Andrewes, *Works* (Oxford U.P., 1854), V, pp. 224, 234. Cf. R. Sibbes, *Works*, VI, pp. 153-4, and E. K. Chambers, *The Elizabethan Stage* (Oxford U.P., 1923), IV, p. 197.

8. See p. 278 above.

9. Collinson, *The Religion of Protestants*, p. 283; E. S. Morgan, *The Puritan Dilemma: the Story of John Winthrop* (Boston, Mass., 1958), p. 40. It was suggested to Sir Simonds D'Ewes in 1638 that he should "make provision of refuge for harsh times, if they should happen in England" by a plantation in Massachusetts (ed. E. Emerson, *Letters from New England: The Massachusetts Bay Colony, 1629-1638*, Massachusetts U.P., 1976, p. 225).

10. S. Foster, *Notes from the Caroline Underground*, pp. 17, 50; S. Rutherford, *The Tryal & Triumph of Faith* (1645), p. 30.

11. Hunt, *The Puritan Moment*, p. 274.

12. They were preached by Cornelius Burges (*The First Sermon*) and Stephen Marshall (*A Sermon*). For fasting see pp. 129-30 above.

13. Brooks, *Gods Delight in the Progresse of the Upright* (1649), pp. 17-18; cf. pp. 46-7.

14. *H.M.C., Bath MSS.*, I, pp. 29-32.

15. J. C. Spalding, "John Goodwin", *Biographical Dictionary of British Radicals*, II, p. 16.

16. Marshall, *A Peace-Offering to God* (a sermon preached before the House of Commons, 7 September 1641) (1641), pp. 3, 40; cf. pp. 45-6.

17. J. Burrough, *Sions Joy* (1641), pp. 43-4, 49-50; cf. p. 38. Preached on the same day as Marshall's sermon.

18. Ed. T. T. Lewis, *Letters of the Lady Brilliana Harley* (Camden Soc., 1854), pp. 157-8.

19. W. Sewel, *The History of the ... Quakers* (1722), p. 87; Baillie, *Letters and Journals* (Edinburgh, 1775), II, p. 86. Cf. Johnston of Wariston, quoted in *The Experience of Defeat*, pp. 79-80.

20. I give evidence in *The Experience of Defeat*, pp. 86, 173, 319-20; ed. Abbott, *Writings and Speeches of Oliver Cromwell*, I, pp. 696-8, III, pp. 590-3; Dell, *Sermons*, esp. pp. 71-6; Sewel, *op. cit.*, pp. 215, 513. Cf. R. Fitz-Brian, *The Good Old Cause, Dressed in its Primitive Lustre* (1659), *passim*.

21. Sedgwick, *Justice upon the Armie Remonstrance* (1649), *passim*; and *A Second View of the Army Remonstrance* (1649), p. 15 and *passim*.

22. Salmon, *A Rout, A Rout* (1649), p. 4.

23. C. H. Carlton, "Joyce", *Biographical Dictionary of British Radicals*, II, p. 148.

24. Marvell, *An Horatian Ode upon Cromwels Return from Ireland*.

25. *Reliquiae Baxterianae*, I, p. 100.

26. See a forthcoming article by Richard H. Popkin, "The Triumphant Apocalypse and the Catastrophic Apocalypse".

27. See pp. 270-4 above.

28. E. Rogers, *Life and Opinions of a Fifth-Monarchy Man*, p. 127; S. R. Gardiner, *The Commonwealth and Protectorate* (1903), III, p. 5.

29. *Puritanism and Revolution*, pp. 133-4, 140; G. Fox and E. Burrough,

Good Counsel and Advice Rejected by Disobedient Men (1659), pp. 26-7, 36-7; G. Fox, *To the Counsell of Officers* (1659), pp. 2, 8; Fox, *Gospel-Truth* (1706), pp. 196-7; M. R. Brailsford, *A Quaker from Cromwell's Army: James Nayler* (1927), pp. 23-5.

30. T. Spencer, "The History of an Unfortunate Lady", pp. 43-59.
31. See pp. 202-7 above.
32. *The World of the Muggletonians*, pp. 23, 64. See Chapter 12 above.
33. Pp. 191, 208-12, 226-7 above, and references there cited.
34. Morgan, *op. cit.*, p. 40.
35. *Antichrist in Seventeenth-Century England*, pp. 79-82, 86. Cf. Feake, quoted on p. 219 above.
36. *Antichrist in Seventeenth-Century England*, pp. 93-6. 108, 110, 121-3; Bunyan, *Works*, II, p. 54.
37. Pp. 214, 216 above.
38. Winstanley, *The Law of Freedom and Other Writings*, p. 88.
39. Milton, *Paradise Lost*, XII. 24-37.
40. Patricia V. Bonomi, "'A Just Opposition': The Great Awakening as a Radical Model", in *The Origins of Anglo-American Radicalism*, pp. 243-56.
41. Coppe, *A Fiery Flying Roll* (1649), in Smith, *A Collection of Ranter Writings*, pp. 86-8, 90, 100-1.
42. G. Foster, *The Sounding of the Last Trumpet* (1650); *The Pouring Forth of the Seventh and Last Viall* (1650), both quoted in *W.T.U.D.*, pp. 210-11.
43. Clarkson, *A Single Eye* (1650), in Smith, *op. cit.*, pp. 169-73, 180-1; Coppe, *op. cit.*, ibid., pp. 107-8. See pp. 170-1 above.
44. *W.T.U.D.*, Chapter II; Winstanley, *The Law of Freedom and Other Writings*, p. 353.
45. *C.S.P.D., 1650*, p. 180.
46. See p. 313 above.
47. See pp. 39, 47 above for this and the following paragraphs.
48. Harrington, *Political Works*, p. 704.
49. R. W. Harris, *Clarendon and the English Revolution* (1983), p. 301.
50. Davenant, *Gondibert*, 1651 (ed. D. F. Gladish, Oxford U.P., 1971), p. 22; cf. P. W. Thomas, "Court and Country under Charles I", pp. 192-3.
51. Clarendon, *A Brief View and Survey of the dangerous and pernicious errors ... in Mr. Hobbes's ... Leviathan* (Oxford U.P., 1676), pp. 181-2.
52. *Clarke Papers* (ed. C. H. Firth, Camden Soc.), IV (1901), p. 220; *Clarendon State Papers*, III, p. 633.
53. D. Dymond, *Portsmouth and the Fall of the Puritan Republic* (Portsmouth, 1971), pp. 9-11.
54. H. G. Tibbutt, *Colonel John Okey, 1606-1662* (Bedfordshire Historical Record Soc., XXXV, 1955), p. 154.
55. *The Experience of Defeat*, pp. 307-8; *M.C.P.W.*, VI, pp. 397-8; *M.E.R.*, pp. 351-2, 358-60.
56. Very slowly, we must emphasize. As late as the sixteen-eighties a Whig politician heard God's voice advising him on his speculations, his bets,

his sex-life. He planned to marry the Queen of the fairies. The fact that both God and the fairies repeatedly let him down did nothing to diminish Goodwin Wharton's belief in either (J. Kent Clark, *Goodwin Wharton*, Oxford U.P., 1984, *passim*). Cf. Wildman, quoted on pp. 135-6 above.

57. *The Diary of Archibald Johnston of Wariston*, III, *1655-1660* (Scottish History Soc., 1940), p. 71; cf. p. 120.

58. Cf. pp. 131-4, 233 above.

59. J.R. Jacob, *Robert Boyle and the English Revolution, passim*; M.C. Jacob, *The Newtonians and the English Revolution, passim*.

60. H. More, *An Antidote to Atheism* (1653), p. 164; cf. Joseph Glanvill, F.R.S., *Sadducismus Triumphatus* (1666), *passim*.

61. Duffy, "Valentine Greatrakes, the Irish Stroker: Miracle, Science and Orthodoxy in Restoration England", in *Religion and Humanism* (ed. K. Robbins, Ecclesiastical History Soc., 1981), p. 273 and *passim*. For Greatrakes see J.R. Jacob, *Henry Stubbe*, Chapter 3 and Epilogue.

62. I. Breward, "James Nayler", in *Biographical Dictionary of British Radicals*, II, p. 258.

63. See pp. 132, 313-14 above.

64. *The Experience of Defeat*, pp. 248-9. See p. 30 above.

65. T. Goodwin, *A Sermon of the Fifth Monarchy* (1654), p. 18.

66. Harrington, *Political Works*, pp. 329-33.

67. See chapter 4, p. 314 above.

68. [Anon.], *Walwyns Wiles* (1649), in Haller and Davies, *op. cit.*, pp. 288-9, 310; cf. H.N. Brailsford, *The Levellers and the English Revolution* (1961), pp. 501-5.

69. K. Marx and F. Engels, *Correspondence, 1846-1895: A Selection* (ed. D. Torr, 1934), pp. 279, 281; cf. p. 264. See now my "Seventeenth-century English radicals and Ireland", in *Radicals, Rebels and Establishment* (ed. P.J. Corish, Belfast, 1985).

70. Quoted by James Sutherland, *English Literature of the Late Seventeenth Century* (Oxford U.P., 1969), p. 3.

71. *The Experience of Defeat*, pp. 321, 323-5.

72. See my *Economic Problems of the Church*, p. 23, where I acknowledge discussions with Mervyn James on this point. See also pp. 27-8 above.

73. The shocked words are those of Edward Hyde, Earl of Clarendon, in his *History of the Rebellion*, V, p. 184.

74. Quoted by Susan Staves, *Players Scepters*, p. 290; cf. p. 263.

75. See pp. 207-8 above.

76. Milton, *Samson Agonistes*, lines 1706-7.

77. P. Jenkins, *A Social and Political History of the Glamorganshire Gentry, c. 1650-1720* (Cambridge University Ph.D. Thesis, 1978), p. 298. Cf. pp. 108-9 above.

78. *The Northern Star*, 26 October 1850, quoted by John Saville, *Ernest Jones, Chartist* (1952), p. 112.

79. Eric Hobsbawm, *Primitive Rebels* (Manchester U.P., 1959), p. 183.

Index

Abbott, George, Archbishop of Canterbury, 75, 79-81, 302, 309

Adam, 46-7, 100, 118, 176, 187-8, 190, 196, 210, 213, 247, 272, 322

Adams, Thomas, 23, 274

Adams, — of Cambridge, 76

Admonition to Parliament, The (1572), 23

Africa, 141, 339

Agitators, 152, 169, 233

Agreement of the People, the, 312

Ainsworth, Henry, 309

Aldgate, London, 153

Ale-houses, 107

Alexander, Sir William, 277

Alsop, James, 228

America, 29, 94, 108-9, 278-80, 286, 326, 339

Ames, William, 93

Anabaptists, 38, 72, 80, 90, 93, 97-9, 101-2, 107, 122, 126, 149, 172, 178, 200, 302, 306-7

Andrewes, Lancelot, Bishop of Winchester, 54, 120, 324

Anglo-Saxons, see Norman Yoke, the

Anne, Queen of England, 59, 108

Anointing, the, 188-90, 195, 238

Antichrist, the Beast, 29-30, 45, 78, 105, chapter 11 *passim*, 270-2, 274-5, 278, 281-3, 286, 328-9, 337

Anti-clericalism, 94, 119, 177, 192, 197, 216-17, 222, 232, 265

Antinomianism, antinomians, 97, 105-6, 119, chapters 8-10 *passim*, 198, 261

Anti-Trinitarianism, anti-Trinitarians, chapter 7 *passim*, 190, 195, 197-8, 234, 322

Apostles, the, 133, 168, 196, 304

Apostolic Succession, the, 38, 47

Archer, John, 275

Arianism, Arians, 102, 104, 149

Armada, the Spanish, 73, 323

Arminianism, Arminians, 32, 66, 76, 78-80, 101-2, 104, 106, 119, 127, 129, 132-6, 143

Arnold, Matthew, 47

Arthington, Henry, 96

Articles, the Thirty-nine of the Church of England, 13, 17, 66, 100, 102, 302

Articles, the Forty-two of the Church of England, 100, 102

Ascham, Anthony, 185, 247

Ashford, Kent, 92-3

Ashmole, Elias, 23-4, 285, 317

Aspinwall, William, 240, 295

Astell, Mary, 46-7

Aston, Sir Thomas, 100

Atheism, atheists, 105, 124, 133, 227, 235, 252, 307

Atherton, John, Bishop of Waterford and Lismore, 55

Attaway, Mrs., 102, 194, 197-9, 281

Augustine, St., 97-8

Axholme, Isle of, 97, 252

Aylmer, Gerald, 218

Aylmer, John, Bishop of London, 29, 53, 56, 83

Ayrshire, 97-8

Backster, Margery, 104

Bacon, Sir Francis, Lord Verulam, 14, 17, 119, 198, 239, 272

Baillie, Robert, 149-50, 166, 170, 194, 276, 325

Bakewell, Thomas, 150

Bale, John, Bishop of Ossory, 29

Ball, John, peasant leader (1381), 65, 93, 100-1, 200

Ball, John, 17th-century theologian, 200

Balliol College, Oxford, 141, 158-9

Bancroft, Richard, Bishop of London and Archbishop of Canterbury, 14, 17, 31, 44, 53-4, 64-5, 72-80, 84, 177

Baptists, 5-9, 28, 44, 92, 95-7, 102, 107, 109, 129, 134, 142, 164, 194, 197,

343

200, 256, 307, 311-13, 316, 326, 329
Barbados, 175
Barberini, Antonio, Cardinal, 33
Barclay, Robert, 132
Barnabees Journal (1636-6), 106
Barrow, Henry, Barrowists, 39-40, 45, 97, 99-100
Barrow, Isaac, 58-9
Bartas, Guillaume Salluste du, 324
Barwick, John, 57, 79
Basle, 30
Bates, William, 315
Bath, 108
Bauman, Richard, 47
Bauthumley, Jacob, 146, 151, 195-200, 261
Baxter, Richard, 7-8, 26, 56, 69, 75, 104, 120, 125, 130, 151-4, 160, 170, 173, 175, 177, 179, 184, 201, 276, 313, 315, 317, 326, 331
Baylin, Bernard, 175
Beast, the, see Antichrist
Becon, Thomas, 27
Bedell, William, Bishop of Kilmore, 54
Bedford, 5
Bedfordshire, 243
Bedford, Thomas, 150, 170
Bedlam, 328
Behmenists, see Boehme, Jakob
Bendich, Mr., 28
Bennett, Thomas, 229
Berkshire, 97-8
Bernard, Richard, 29
Béza, Theodore, 76, 144, 271
Bible, the, 16, 22, 25-7, chapter 4 *passim*, 92, 95-6, 100-1, 104-5, 109, 122, 126, 131, 134, 162-3, 165, 192, 196, 201-2, 206-7, 210-12, 219, 226, 236, 257, 260-1, 271, 276-7, 288, 300, 304, chapter 15 *passim*
Bible, the Geneva, 25, 41, 271, 304
Bickerstaff, Henry, 230
Biddulph, William, 281
Bidle, John, 96, 103, 128
Bishop, George, 326
Bishops, 6-9, 15, 19, 21, 43, 45, 47, chapters 5 and 6 *passim*, 90, 99, chapter 14 *passim*, 321
Bishops, the Seven, 9, 316
Black Country, the, 108
Blackburne, Robert, 58-9
Blake, Robert, Admiral, 283, 286, 290 327
Blake, William, 108, 136

Blasphemy Act (1650), 197
Blasphemy Ordinance (1648), 102, 130, 201, 246
Blok, Alexandr, 339
Blount, Sir Henry, 281, 294
Bodurda, Griffith, 284-5
Boehme, Jakob, Behmenists, 195-7, 199, 293
Bohemia, 31-2, 81
Bolingbroke, Henry St. John, Viscount, 132-3
Bolton, Lancashire, 338
Bowling, William, 104
Boyle, the Hon. Robert, 134, 140, 280, 299
Bradford, Yorkshire, 96, 106
Bradshaw, William, 41, 306
Brampton Brian, Herefordshire, 325
Brayne, John, 240
Bread St., London, 141
Brearley, Roger, 78, 149-50, 163, 174
Brett, Samuel, 282
Bridge, William, 316
Bridgewater, 68
Brightman, Thomas, 54, 86, 272-5
Brinkworth, Wiltshire, 142, 151-2, 157, 160
Bristol, 5, 97, 326
Broadmead Baptist Church, Bristol, 5
Bromley, William, 301
Brooke, Fulke Greville, Lord, 6, 15, 19, 59, 307
Brooks, Thomas, 325
Broughton, Hugh, 273
Browne, Robert, Brownists, 5, 8, 40, 71, 74, 92, 97, 303, 305, 307-9
Browne, Sir Thomas, 104, 158, 194, 197
Brownlow, Kevin, 239
Bucer, Martin, 30, 271
Buchanan, Walter, 261, 264
Buckinghamshire, 56, 95-6, 105, 203, 206, 215-16, 219, 230
Buckingham, George Villiers, Duke of, 32, 80, 97, 107
Bulkeley, Peter, 172, 282
Bull, George, Bishop of St. David's, 155
Bull, John, 281
Bullinger, Henry, 30
Bunting, Jabez, 136
Bunyan, John, 5, 7, 16, 56, 120, 135, 158, 168, 170, 196, 198, 200-1, 205, 222, 234-5, 243, 286, 312, 328-9, 333

Burford, 167, 325
Burges, Cornelius, 130, 340
Burghley, Sir William Cecil, Lord, 40, 53, 71, 73, 308
Burnet, Gilbert, Bishop of Salisbury, 13, 26, 59, 125, 315
Burns, N.T., 103
Burns, Robert, 108
Burrough, Edward, 229, 264-5, 326
Burrough, Jeremiah, 325
Burton, Henry, 6, 79
Burton, Robert, 11
Busher, Leonard, 307
Butler, Samuel, 58-9
Byllynge, Edward, 45

Cade, Jack, 45, 91, 100
Calais, 30
Calamy, Edmund, 130, 150, 170, 315
Calne, Wiltshire, 141
Calvin, John, Calvinism, Calvinists, 27, 30-2, 45, 73, 76, 79, chapter 8 *passim*, 143-4, 166, 177, 180, 212, 302-3, 308-9, 314, 322
Cambridge University, 44-5, 76, 84, 93, 106, 132, 141, 153, 273
Cambridgeshire, 97-8
Canne, John, 196, 275
Canons of 1604, the, 77, 79
Canons of 1640, the, 55
Canterbury, 196
Carew, John, 295, 325
Caribbean, the, 286
Carlyle, Thomas, 108
Carpenter, Agricola, 198
Carter, Anne, 94
Cartwright, Thomas, 29, 41-2, 73, 75, 305
Cartwright, William, 300
Cary, Mary, 240, 275
Catholics, Roman, Catholicism, 4, 13, 19-20, 24, 26, 30-1, 33, 37, 59, 63-6, 69, 76-7, 80, 98, 109, 120, 124, 126, 134, 143, 163, 168, 263, 271, 274, 278, 291, 306, 309-10, 316, 333, 336
Cavaliers, see Royalists
Cecil, Sir Robert, later Earl of Salisbury, 14, 55
Cecil, Sir William, see Burghley, Lord
Censorship, 90, 127, 131-2, 135-6, 142, 233-4, 253, 273-4
Chamberlain, John, 75
Chamberlayne, Edward, 318
Chandler, Francis, 315

Chapman, George, 125, 139
Charles I, King of England, 20, 28, 30, 32-3, 40, 52, 55-6, 58, 65, 76-7, 79, 81, 91, 94-5, 143, 162, 174, 196, 203, 215, 219, 223, 263, 274, 314, chapter 15 *passim*
Charles II, King of England, 12, 16, 30, 40, 59, 130, 134, 158, 174, 229, 233, 286, 291, 314, 332, 334, 336
Charles IV, King of Spain, 17
Chartists, the, 108, 339
Chelmsford, 45, 95, 100
Cheshire, 197, 314
Chestlin, Robert, 56
Cheynell, Francis, 6, 80, 302
Chichester, 98
Chillingworth, William, 26, 33
Chiltern Hills, Hundreds, 95-6
China, 22, 271
Christ's College, Cambridge, 93, 141, 153, 273
Church courts, 23, 78, 89-90, 101, 132, 135, 233, 306, 338
Church of England, the, Parts I and II, *passim*, 106, 132, 134, 136, 167, 233, 269, 291, chapter 14 *passim*, 334
Civil War, the second, 193, 218, 248
Clarendon, Edward Hyde, Earl of, 57-8, 313, 332, 342
Clarendon Code, the, 314
Clark, Peter, 92
Clarkson, Laurence, 106-7, 128-9, 136, 142, 146-8, 151, 163, 170-1, 176, 178, 196-8, 226, 231, chapter 12 *passim*, 330
Cleveland, John, 91, 100
Clubmen, the, 152
Cobham, Cobham Heath, Surrey, 192, 201, 203, 206, 219, 221, 229, 239
Coke, Sir Edward, 99
Colchester, 93-4, 98, 102
Coleman St., London, 97, 164
Colesbourn, Gloucestershire, 96
Collective Christ, the, 153-4, 189-90
Collier, Jeremy, 16
Collier, Thomas, 101, 169, 195-6, 229, 240, 284
Collins, Anthony, 108, 161, 296
Collinson, Patrick, 4, 10, 20, 30, 43, 52, 54, 67-9, 74-5, 78, 80, 82-3, 92, 122-3
Collop, John, 91
Colpeper, Sir John, 58
Comber, Thomas, 229

Comenius, Jan Amos, 275
Commons, the House of, 14, 22, 24, 31, 51, 54, 64, 66, 68, 73, 76-7, 204, 215, 274-5, 301, 313, 317, 325, 328
Commonwealth of England, the, 141, 217-20, 222-3, 225, 278, 280, 283, 286, 323, 326
Communism, communists, 13, 106, 122, chapter 11 *passim*
Congregationalism, congregationalists, *see* Independency, independents
Constantinople, 283
Convocations of Canterbury and York, 51, 77
Cook, John, 79, 101, 196, 326
Cooper, Thomas, later Bishop of Winchester, 52-3, 55, 72-3
Cooper, Thomas, preacher, 278-80, 286, 291, 296, 324
Copernicus, Nicholas, Copernicanism, 196, 288
Coppe, Abiezer, 100, 106, 147, 151-2, 158, 168, 170, 178, 197-8, 200, 231, 329-30
Coppin, Richard, 128, 152-3, 156, 194-7, 199
Coppinger, Edmund, 73, 96
Copyhold, copyholders, 135, 207, 218, 220, 223
Cornwall, 325
Corporation Acts, the, 313
Corpus Christi College, Cambridge, 132
Cosin, John, 31
Coster, Robert, 206, 209
Cottagers, 91, 93
Cottington, Francis, Lord, 14
Cotton, John, 164-6, 172, 183, 275-6
Counter-Reformation, the, 32-3, 65
Covenant, the Solemn League and, 214-15, 311
Covenant theology, the, 23, 30, 119, 127, 143-4, chapters 9 and 10 *passim*
Coventry, 97
Coverley, Sir Roger de, 335
Cowley, Abraham, 91, 149, 277
Cranmer, Thomas, Archbishop of Canterbury, 305
Crashawe, Richard, 300
Crashawe, William, father of the above, 26
Crisp, Ellis, 141
Crisp, Sir Nicholas, son of the above, 141

Crisp, Samuel, son of Tobias, 155
Crisp, Tobias, son of Ellis, 127, chapter 9 *passim*, 165-70, 174-7, 194, 261
Croll, Oswald, 152
Cromwell, Oliver, General and Lord Protector, 7-9, 16, 28, 33-4, 54, 69, 97, 107, 136, 152, 178, 197, 221, 289-91, 307, 309, 311-12, 325-7, 329, 336-7
Crowley, Robert, 12, 96
Culpeper, Nicholas, 276
Cumberland, 108
Curtis, Tim, 173

Daniel, Colonel William, 28
Danvers, Henry, 295
Davenant, Charles, 48
Davenant, Sir William, 332
Davies, Lady Eleanor, 328
Davies, Sir John, husband of the above, 120
Davies, John, of Hereford, 157
Davis, J.C., 208, 217, 220-2, 245, 247, 249
Dean, Forest of, 96-7
Dedham classis, the, 309
Defoe, Daniel, 108
Deism, deists, 109, 117, 132, 135, 234
Dell, William, Master of Gonville and Caius College, 44, 91, 136, 151, 169, 176-7, 326
Denne, Henry, 28, 149, 167, 169, 176-7, 194, 329
Derby, James and Charles Stanley, seventh and eighth Earls of, 338
Dering, Edward, 67
Descartes, René, 201
Devonshire, Charles Blount, Earl of, 60
D'Ewes, Sir Simonds, 340
Dickens, A.G., 89, 96, 104
Digby, George, later Earl of Bristol, 58
Diggers, the, 28, 90, 92, 95-7, 100, 107, 131, 136, 147, 176, chapter 11 *passim*, 256, 277, 329-30
Dissenting Brethren, the Five, 6, 311
Divine Right, 16, 31, 64-5, 74, 79, 274, 313, 321, 331, 334
Divorce, 54, 106, 153
Donne, John, 104, 120
Dort, Synod of, 32, 79, 123
Dover, 103, 277
Downame, John, 129
Downing, Calibute, 56

Drake, Sir Francis, 22
Draper, Augustine, 101, 104
Drapers' Company, London, 272
Dryden, John, 22, 30, 121, 130, 291, 333, 336
Dublin, Archbishop of, 54
Dudley, Thomas, Deputy Governor of Massachusetts, 172, 183
Dudley's Conspiracy (1556), 98
Duffy, Eamon, 334
Dunkirk, 337
Durden, Ralph, 281
Dury, John, 276, 279, 284, 293

Eachard, John, 282
Earle, Sir Walter, 56
East Anglia, 97, 324
East Indies, the, 283
Eaton, John, 149-51, 159, 164-5, 174, 180-1
Edinburgh, 34
Edward I, King of England, 284
Edward VI, King of England, 11, 29-30, 40, 92-3, 98, 100-2, 271
Edwards, John, 132
Edwards, Thomas, 44, 92, 95, 102, 106, 128, 150-1, 167, 170, 194, 198, 240
Egypt, Egyptians, 287-8
Eliot, Sir John, 14
Eliot, John, 280
Elizabeth I, Queen of England, 4-6, 11, 14, 19, 27-8, 30, 40, 42-3, 56, chapter 6 *passim*, 91, 93, 97-8, 103, 120, 122, 173, 177, 194, 196, 273, 302, 304-7, 314, 316, 321-2, 324
Elmsbridge Hundred, Surrey, 229
Elton, G.R., 89, 107
Ely, Isle of, 97
Empson, Sir William, 154, 247
Enclosures, 94, 97
Erasmus, Desiderius, 25
Erbery, William, 151, 194-7, 240, 284
Essex, 27, 30, 93-5, 97-106, 122-3, 194, 282, 315, 324
Essex, Robert Devereux, second Earl of, 80
Essex, Robert Devereux, third Earl of, 54, 325
Ettrall, John, 164-5
Euphrates, river, 273
Evans, Arise, 286, 323
Evans, J.T., 97
Eve, 46, 100, 118

Everard, John, 93, 102, 107, 195-7, 199-200
Everard, William, 201, 245, 272
Everitt, Alan, 91
Eyre, the Rev. William, 153, 160-1, 163, 166
Eyre, Colonel William, 160-1

Fairfax, Maria, 270, 290
Fairfax, Sir Thomas, Lord, General, father of the above, 28, 204, 207-8, 211, 223-4, 245, 270, 277, 290
Fairstead, Essex, 93
Falkland, Lucius Cary, Viscount, 57
Fall of Man, the, 118, 125, 136, 186-90, 196, 210-11, 213, 223, 227, 247, 322
Familists, Family of Love, 80, 93, chapter 7 *passim*, 122, 126, 164-6, 172, 174, 194-8, 226, 251, 306
Fane, Sir Francis, 337
Farmer, Ralph, 229
Farnham, Richard, 281
Fasting, fasts, fast sermons, 129-30, 149-50, 275, 325, 333
Fathers, the Christian, 25, 133
Feake, Christopher, 219, 283
Fell, John, Dean of Christchurch, 134
Fell, Margaret, 29, 229, 285
Feoffees for Impropriations, the, 142, 157, 309
Field, John, 73, 83, 100
Fielden, John, 230-1
Fielding, Henry, 108
Fiennes, Celia, 97
Fifth Monarchism, Fifth Monarchists, 97, 101, 120, 176-7, 193-4, 233-4, 239, 253, 263, 283, 285, 289, 321, 325-7, 330
Filmer, Sir Robert, 121
Finch, Sir Henry, 273
Firth, Katharine R., 29
Fisher, Samuel, 46, 92, 105, 129, 195, 330
Fitz, Richard, 29
Five Members, the, 95
Flanders, 126
Fleetwood, Major-General Charles, 7, 332
Fletcher, Giles, 277, 295-6
Fletcher, Giles, son of the above, 277
Fletcher, Phineas, son of Giles the elder, 277
Flood, Noah's, chapter 13 *passim*
Foster, George, 100, 200, 282, 330

Fouke, Fowke, Alderman John, Lord Mayor of London, 258
Fox, George, 5, 8, 96, 101, 129, 132, 195, 198-201, 241, 245, 264-5, 283, 285, 327-8
Foxe, John, 16, 29-30, 90-1, 97, 193, 328
France, the French, 30-1, 63, 80, 177, 233, 280, 299, 314, 316, 322, 327, 336
Frank, Rabbi Solomon, 285
Frankfurt, 30
Frederick, Duke of Saxony, 38
Frederick, Elector Palatine, 32
Freke, Edmund, Bishop of Norwich, 71
French prophets, the, 108
Fry, Northrop, 292
Fuller, Nicholas, 294
Fuller, Thomas, 30, 65, 84, 100, 103
Furly, Benjamin, 108, 161, 296

Galileo Galilei, 46
Ganges, river, 269-70, 288, 299
Garment, Joshua, 276
Gauden, John, later Bishop of Worcester, 162, 311
Gaunt, John of, 73
Gell, Robert, 272
Geneva, 30, 76, 122, 125, 302
George, C.H., 209
Geree, John, 150
Geree, Stephen, brother of the above, 150, 159, 170
Germany, the Germans, 31-2, 126, 143, 172
Giffard, George, 120
Giggleswick, Yorkshire, 96
Gloucestershire, 96-7, 103
Godwin, Francis, 53
Goldsmith, Oliver, 108
Goodman, Godfrey, Bishop of Gloucester, 77, 126, 274
Goodwin, John, 129, 176, 295, 325
Goodwin, Thomas, 121, 143, 271-2, 274-5, 294-5, 316, 326, 336
Gorton, Samuel, 104, 163, 168, 171-2, 183-4
Gospel, Society for the Propagation of, 280
Gostelow, Walter, 286
Gott, Samuel, 277, 297
Gouge, William, 273
Gower, John, 105
Gower, Stanley, 275
Graile, John, 160, 182
Grand Remonstrance, the (1641), 79

Grantham, Thomas, 9, 316
Great Bumstead, Essex, 106
Great Marlow, 95
Greatrakes, Valentine, 287, 299, 334
Greek, 42, 49
Green Ribbon Club, 108, 115
Greenham, Richard, 53
Greville, Sir Fulke, Lord Brooke, 262, 323
Grindal, Edmund, Archbishop of Canterbury, 27, 31, 59, chapter 6 *passim*, 96, 301-2, 304, 309
Grindleton, Yorkshire, Grindletonians, 78, 96, 98, 102, 105, 149, 151, 163, 165, 179, 194
Grotius, Hugo, 262

Hacket, William, 73, 84, 96, 99, 179
Hakewill, George, 274
Hakluyt, Richard, 281, 286
Hale, Sir Matthew, Chief Justice, 47, 338
Hales, John, Commonwealthsman, 307
Hales, John, the ever-memorable, 123
Halhead, Miles, 326
Halifax, 69
Halifax, George Savile, Marquis of, 125
Hall, Edmund, 276
Hall, Joseph, Bishop of Worcester, 23, 28
Hall, Thomas, 38
Haller, William, 5, 15, 29, 306
Hampden, John, 93, 95
Hampton Court Conference (1604), 21, 73
Harding, John, 160
Harford, Raphael, 275
Harley, Brilliana, Lady, 325
Harrington, James, 178, 286, 312, 331, 336
Harris, Francis, 229
Harrison, Major-General Thomas, 224, 279, 325
Harsnett, Samuel, Bishop of Norwich, later Archbishop of York, 79
Hart, Henry, 102, 122
Hartlib, Samuel, 272, 275-6, 279
Harvey, William, 198, 243
Harwood, John, 260
Haslerig, Sir Arthur, 332
Hatton, Sir Christopher, 70, 73, 76-7
Haworth, Yorkshire, 165
Heads of Proposals, the (1647), 311
Heaven, 12, 90, 117, 165, 170, 190-1, 196-7, 210, 225, 321

Hebrew, 42, 273, 279, 281, 285
Heidelberg, 31
Hell, 12, 90, 92, 105, 117, 120, 131-2, 134-5, 156, 165-6, 168-9, 191, 196-7, 210, 225
Helwys, Thomas, 309
Henrietta Maria, Queen of England, 33
Henri IV, King of France, 31
Henry VIII, King of England, 13, 19-20, 37-9, 41, 63, 66, 71, 100, 105, 107, 305, 307
Henry, Philip, 9, 314-15
Herbert of Cherbury, Edward, Lord, 201
Hering, Samuel, 284-5
Hermes Trismegistus, Hermeticism, Hermeticists, 194-5, 198-200
Hertford, Edward Seymour, Earl of, 72
Heyricke, Richard, 315
Heywood, Oliver, 315
Hibbard, Caroline, 80
Hickes, George, 29-30
Hieron, Samuel, 120, 124
Higginson, Francis, 229
High Commission, the, 71, 74, 99, 132, 164-5, 333
High Wycombe, 95-6
Highworth, Wiltshire, 152
Hobbes, Thomas, Hobbism, 12, 15, 22, 34, 38-9, 44, 47, 121, 132-4, 173, 176-7, 202, 222, 233, 235-6, 331-2
Hobson, Paul, 151
Holland, see Netherlands, the
Hollis, Thomas, 108
Homes, Nathanael, 240, 272, 295
Homilies, of the Church of England, the, 11-13, 26, 39, 123, 302, 321-2
Hooker, Richard, 14, 26, 54-5, 73, 76, 80, 125-6, 173, 272, 305
Hooker, Thomas, 183, 308, 324
Horne, George, Bishop of Norwich, 108
Hotchkis, Thomas, 151-3
Hotham, Durant, 99
How, Samuel ("Cobbler"), 56
Howe, John, 315-16
Howgil, Francis, 325
Hudson, Anne, 105
Hudson, river, 108
Hudson, W.S., 186, 205, 239, 242, 251
Huehns, Gertrude M., 179
Huguenots, French, 31-2, 177, 309, 314, 322
Huit, Ephraim, 275
Humber, river, 269-70
Humfrey, John, 315

Hungary, 31
Huntingdon, Henry Hastings, fifth Earl of, 28
Hus, Jan, Hussites, 99, 271
Hutchinson, Mrs. Anne, Hutchinsonians, 104, 163-4, 171-2, 175, 183, 196, 261
Hutchinson, Mrs. Lucy, 7
Hutchinson, Colonel John, husband of the above, 7, 197
Hutchinson, William, husband of Anne, 171
Hyde, Edward, see Clarendon, Earl of

Iconoclasm, 26, 94, 101
Impropriations, 20, 307
Independents, Independency, 6-9, 69, 74, 78, 134, 142, 149, 154-5, 231, 256, 286, chapter 14 *passim*, 326
India, 271, 299
Indians, American, 279-80, 286, 290-1
Indulgence, Declaration of (1672), 314
Inquisition, the Spanish, 327
Inverness, 108
Ireland, the Irish, 20, 63, 76, 108, 167, 193, 278, 286, 336-7
Ireton, Henry, 7
Israel, 30, 201, 205, 207, 215, 275, 277, 287
Israel, Menasseh ben, 280, 284-5, 299
Italy, 282, 327, 339
Iver, Buckinghamshire, 96, 204, 206

Jacob, Henry, 8, 301, 306, 308
Jamaica, 290
James VI, King of Scotland, and I, King of England, 21, 30-2, 39, 41, 46, 52, 54-5, 58, 64-5, 73-5, 77, 79-80, 105, 120, 122, 164, 174, 177, 294, 309
James II, King of England, 9, 20, 68, 107, 317, 323, 336
Jefferson, Thomas, 108
Jegon, John, 27
Jenny, William, 102, 194, 197-9, 281
Jerusalem, 195, 210, 270, 273, 281
Jessey, Henry, 272, 275, 285, 295, 302
Jesuits, 263, 298, 338
Jewell, John, Bishop of Salisbury, 26
Jews, the, Judaizing, 30, 109, 164, 168, 207, 245, chapter 13 *passim*, 321-2, 329
"Jock of Broad Scotland", 197
Jolly, Thomas, 315
Johnson, Francis, 309

Jonson, Ben, 300
Jordan, W.K., 97
Josselin, Ralph, 276, 282, 285, 298, 315
Joyce, Colonel George, 326
Joye, George, 271
Julian the Apostate, 270
J.Ps., 90, 107, 132, 173, 301, 304-5

Kent, 70, 75, 91-3, 95-6, 102, 104, 106,
    109, 128, 164
Kett, Francis, 101, 103-5, 281
Kett, Robert, grandfather of the above,
    Kett's rebellion (1549), 93, 103, 281,
    307
Kidderminster, 120
Killick, Yorkshire, 149
King's evil, the, 334, 336
King's Lynn, 125
Kingston-on-Thames, 230
Knevet, Ralph, 55
Knightley, Sir Richard, 98
Knollys, Sir Francis, 64-5, 70-1
Knollys, Richard, 281
Knowles, John, 96
Knox, John, 27, 30, 39
Kyle, Scotland, 97

Lacock, Wiltshire, 153
Lake, Arthur, Bishop of Bath and Wells,
    75
Lamb, Thomas, 128
Lambeth Decrees (1595), 76
Lambeth Palace, 86
Lancashire, 46, 105, 163, 165, 202, 338
Lancaster, Robert, 149-50
Lane, Edward, 286
Lane, Richard, 164
Langley Burhill, Wiltshire, 152-3
La Rochelle, 126
Lasco, John à, 30
Latimer, Hugh, Bishop of Worcester,
    23
Latin, 40-2, 45, 49, 273, 336
Latitudinarians, 16, 46, 132, 314-15, 334
Laud, William, Archbishop of
    Canterbury, Laudians, 5-6, 8, 15, 20,
    32-3, chapters 5 and 6 *passim*, 94, 102,
    127, 136, 142-3, 156, 163, 165, 173, 271,
    280, 302, 307, 309, 316, 324, 334, 336-7
Law, common, lawyers, 24, 47, 119, 174,
    178, 205, 216-17, 220-4, 338
Leach, Sir Edmund, 106
Leader, Richard, 259
Lecturers, lectureships, 80, 309

Ledbury, Herefordshire, 108
Lee, Joseph, 231
Lee, Samuel, 287, 299
Legate, the brothers, 93, 103
Leicester, Robert Dudley, Earl of, 68, 71,
    73, 80, 306
Leicestershire, 83, 97
Leighton, Alexander, 29, 324
Lenin, V.I., 335
Lenthall, William, Speaker of the Long
    Parliament, 323
Leslie, General Robert, 282
L'Estrange, Sir Hamon, 296
Levant, the, 280-1, 283
Levellers, the, levelling, 9, 24, 42, 56,
    chapter 7 *passim*, 128, 131, 135-6, 145,
    147, 151-2, 160-1, 163, 165-8, 170,
    172, 176, 203, 206, 209, 215-16, 219,
    224, 229-33, 248, 251-2, 256, 284,
    311-12, 325, 329-30, 337, 339
Lewis, C.S., 288
Lewis, John, 99
Libertines, libertinism, 104, chapters
    8-10 *passim*, 296, 307
Licensing Act, lapse of (1695), 136
Lilburne, John, 91, 99-100, 152, 230-1,
    248, 252, 307
Lilly, William, 283
Lincolnshire, 97, 164
Lithgow, William, 281
Little Horsted, Sussex, 92
Llwyd, Morgan, 195, 283, 295
Locke, John, 22, 76, 121, 333
Lollards, Lollardy, 4, 25, 37, 41, 73, 80,
    chapter 7 *passim*, 122, 164, 174, 197,
    271, 274, 306-7, 328
London, Londoners, 21, 30-1, 57, 69, 74,
    81, 93, 95, 97-8, 102, 107-8, 122, 126,
    128, 130, 134, 141-2, 149, 153, 155, 164,
    198, 203-4, 230, 239, 253, 265, 272, 278,
    281, 284-5, 291, 306, 312
London, Lord Mayor of, the, 38, 95, 258,
    302, 324
London Post, The, 282
London, William, 186
Long Island, 107
Lords, House of, 45, 51, 54, 58, 77, 90,
    224, 326
Louis XIV, King of France, 59
Love, Christopher, 276
Lucretius, Carus, 262
Ludlow, Edmund, 101, 325
Lutaud, Olivier, 233
Luther, Martin, Lutherans, 16, 25, 32,

38-9, 41, 63, 91, 97, 99, 133, 154, 163, 272, 303

McCarthy, Joseph, 74
McFarlane, Bruce, 107
McKenna, J.W., 29
Magna Carta, 217
Manwaring, Roger, Bishop of St. David's, 79
Major-Generals, the, 107
Malcolm, Joyce, 57
Man, Isle of, 38
Manchester collegiate church, 315
Manning, Brian, 99
Manton, Thomas, 315
Marlowe, Christopher, 11, 15, 103-4, 139, 281, 300
Marprelate, Martin, Marprelate Tracts, the, 28, 54, 72-5, 82, 84, 96, 98, 305
Marriage, 105-6, 117-18, 162, 171-2, 178, 322
Marshall, Stephen, 29, 40, 325, 328, 340
Marten, Henry, 104, 176
Martin, —, M.P., 54
Martindale, Adam, 85
Martyr, Peter, 30, 271
Martyrs, the Marian, 4, 90-3, 99, 103, 197, 306
Marvell, Andrew, 18, 231, 255-6, 264, chapter 13 *passim*, 315, 326-7, 336
Marx, Karl, Marxism, 22, 321, 337
Mary I, Queen of England, 19, 32, 63, 68, 102, 122, 304
Mary, Queen of Scots, 39, 70
Mason, John, 161
Massachusetts, 92, 103, 125, 302, 324, 340
Masson, David, 311
Master, Robert, 92
Materialism, 104, 106, 225-6
Mather, Increase, 287
Maton, Robert, 275, 284
May, Sir Humphrey, 53
Mede, Joseph, 273-4, 294
Medgate, William, 261, 263-4
Mediterranean, the, 284, 286, 290
Melville, Andrew, 31
Methodism, see Wesleyanism
Mildmay, Sir Walter, 44, 69
Milford, Essex, 94
Millenarianism, Millenarians, 101, 106,

109, 136, 177, 193-4, 233-4, 250, Part IV *passim*, 326-7
Milton, John, 6, 24, 26, 29, 38, 44-6, 51-2, 68, 90, 99, 101-6, 128-9, 131, 136, 141, 144, 147-8, 153-4, 156-7, 161, 168-9, 172, 174-7, 183, 190, 192-3, 195-8, 201-2, 205, 210-11, 226-7, 236, 238-9, 246, 265, 269, 273, 276, 280, 283, 286, 288, 292, 294, 297, 322, 326-7, 329, 333, 335-6
Mitchell, Sir Francis, 107
Mompesson, Sir Giles, 107
Monck, General George, later Duke of Albemarle, 28
Montague, Richard, Bishop of Chichester, 32, 79
Montagu, James, Bishop of Winchester, 75
More, Henry, 334
More, Sir Thomas, 106, 173, 200, 239, 243
Morrill, J.S., 119
Mortalism, chapter 7 *passim*, 198, 226
Morton, A.L., 108
Morton, Thomas, Bishop of Durham, 75
Moryson, Fynes, 281
Muggleton, Lodowick, 197, 200, 234, 244, chapter 12 *passim*
Muggletonians, the, 92, 95, 103-4, 146, 169, 172, 176, 194, 198, 234, 253, chapter 12 *passim*, 276, 318, 328, 333
Mun, Thomas, 133
Münster, 90, 105, 172, 183, 313
Müntzer, Thomas, 25, 105

Namier, Sir Lewis, 20
Nantes, Edict of, 31, 177
Napier, John, of Merchiston, 270, 272, 275
Napoleon I, Emperor of the French, 287
Nash, Beau, 108
Nashe, Thomas, 45, 72, 83, 106
Navigation Act, the (1651), 283, 285, 290, 337
Nayler, James, 96, 105-6, 130, 195, 197, 233, 264, 285, 312, 335
Neile, Richard, Bishop of Durham, later Archbishop of York, 54, 79, 103
Netherlands, the, 5, 30-2, 55, 70, 123, 126, 271, 273, 278-80, 283-4, 303, 309, 327, 336-7
Newbury, Berkshire, 97

Newcastle, 24
Newcastle, William Cavendish,
    Marquis of, 12, 40
Newcome, Henry, 192, 313-14, 317
New England, 5, 8, 78, 85, 97, 104,
    107, 109, 120, 125, 130, 163-4,
    169-72, 177, 183, 261, 274, 280, 282,
    303, 308-9, 312, 324, 328
Newgate, London, 258
Newington Butts, 142, 157
Newman, Humphrey, 98
New Model Army, the, 40, 130-1, 152,
    169, 198, 201, 203-4, 206, 217-19,
    224-5, 283-4, 310-11, 325-7, 333, 337
Newton, Sir Isaac, Newtonianism,
    Newtonians, 133-4, 201, 270, 333
Nicholas, Edward, 285, 298
Niklaes, Henry, 195, 261
Nineteen Propositions, the (1642), 91
Non-Jurors, the, 59
Norfolk, 67, 103, 105, 281
Norman Yoke, the, 100, 174, 203,
    214-16, 218-20, 222, 224, 228, 230-2,
    236
North, Dr. John, 135
Northamptonshire, 128
Northumberland, 203
Northumberland, John Dudley, Duke
    of, 80
Norwich, 9, 32, 97, 99-101, 105, 108,
    115
Norwood, Robert, 284, 295
Notestein, Wallace, 36
Nottinghamshire, 108, 165
Nye, Henry, 316
Nye, Philip, father of the above, 316

Oates, Samuel, 101, 128
Oates, Titus, son of the above, 101,
    128
Occasional conformity, 8, chapter 14
    passim
Ochino, Bernardino, 30
Oldenburg, Henry, 285
Ornsby-Lennon, Hugh, 287
Osborne, Francis, 40
Osiander, Andreas, 271
Oughtred, William, 272
Overbury, Sir Thomas, 22
Overton, Richard, 9, 50, 90-1, 104,
    172, 176, 194, 197-9, 215, 284, 329
Owen, John, 8, 51, 126, 234, 283, 286,
    302, 315-16, 326
Owen, Sir Roger, 54

Oxford University, 44-5, 106, 151
Oxinden, Henry, 313

Pagitt, Ephraim, 194
Palestine, 271, 277, 281-3, 287
Palmer, Herbert, 150, 170
Paracelsus, Theophrastus, 152, 160,
    195
Paradise within, a, 118, 126, 195-6
Paris, 32
Parish, Mary, 201
Parish élites, 67-8, 78, 93, 119
Parker, Henry, 123, 211
Parker, Matthew, Archbishop of
    Canterbury, 29, 53, 68
Parker, Robert, 282-3, 286
Parker, Samuel, later Bishop of
    Oxford, 16, 315
Parliament, the Reformation (1529-36),
    37-8
Parliament of 1584-5, the, 67
Parliament of 1604, the, 77
Parliament of 1614, the, 279
Parliament of 1628, the, 53
Parliament of 1640, the Short, 141
Parliament of 1640, the Long, 24, 43,
    54, 80, 95, 129-30, 141, 143, 149,
    152, 274, 299, 324-6, 329
Parliament, the Rump, 197, 204, 206,
    217-20, 223-4, 229, 272, 280, 283,
    325, 327, 332
Parliament, Barebone's (1653), 105,
    176, 223-4, 283-5, 311
Parliament of 1656, the, 130, 233, 333
Parliamentarians, the, 13, 15, 79, 193,
    262, 277, 286, 321-2
Pascal, Blaise, 201, 288
Paul, St., 221
Pelagianism, 68, 92, 122-3, 133
Penington, Isaac, senior, 95
Penington, Isaac, son of the above,
    96, 325
Peniston, Yorkshire, 315
Penn, William, 96, 265
Pennines, the, 96, 98
Penry, John, 27, 71, 74-5, 79, 194, 305
Pepys, Samuel, 56
Perfectibility of man, 90, 102, 164, 174,
    195, chapter 11 *passim*
Perkins, William, 31, 123-5, 127, 143-4,
    166, 272, 294
Peter, Hugh, 324, 327
Petition and Advice, the Humble
    (1657), 233

Petty, Sir William, 12, 140
Philip of Hesse, 163
Philpot, John, 102
Pickering, Colonel John, 152
Pilkington, James, Bishop of Durham, 27, 30
Pinnell, Henry, 151-2
Pocock, J.G.A., 210
Polygamy, 106, 148, 153, 178
Ponet, John, Bishop of Winchester, 122
Poor, the permanent, 118-19
Poor law, poor relief, 22, 68, 93, 119, 304
Pope, the, 32, 37-9, 47, 65-6, 73, 270-1, 274, 282, 286, 298, 316, 328
Popish Plot of the sixteen-thirties, the, 33, 59, 80
Pordage, John, 195-6, 200
Portsmouth, 332
Portugal, the Portuguese, 279, 283
Powell, Vavasor, 327
Prayer, the Book of Common, 20, 30
Preaching, 22, 30, 77, 80, 106-7, 117, 192, 197, 212, 306, 314, 323
Predestination, 76, 80, 102, 117, chapters 8-10 *passim*
Prendergast, William, 108
Presbyterianism, Presbyterians, 6-9, 32, 43, 59, 73-4, 80, 83, 100, 109, 134-5, chapter 10 *passim*, 163, 170, 231, 276, 282, chapter 14 *passim*, 325, 329
Preston, John, 143
Pretty, Samuel, 164-5
Property, private, 12-13, 15, 77, 106, 135, chapter 11 *passim*, 308
Prophesyings, the, 67-9, 80
Protestant ethic, the, 90, 117, 162, 168, 184, 291, 322, 335
Protestantism, Protestants, Part II *passim*, 120-2, 134, 168, 270-1, 304, 309, 338
Prynne, William, 79, 285
Purchas, Samuel, 281
Puritanism, Puritans, 6, 14, 17, chapters 3 and 4 *passim*, 52-3, chapter 6 *passim*, 90, 92-3, 100, 102, 106, 122-3, 127, 142, 177, 195, 200, 227, 233, 272-4, 280, 290-1, 298, chapter 14 *passim*, 321, 334, 338
Purnell, Robert, 240, 295, 326
Putney Debates, the, 174
Pym, John, 24, 126, 138
Pynchon, William, 103

Quakers, the, 7-8, 43-5, 47, chapter 7 *passim*, 120, 134, 147, 151, 161, 165, 194-8, 220, 228-9, 231, 233-4, 237, 243, 253, 256, 258-9, 263-4, 272, 282, 285, 311-13, 317, 325-8, 333, 335

Rainborough, Colonel Thomas, 322
Ralegh, Sir Walter, 46, 74, 99, 131, 134, 173
Ramsey, Essex, 93
Randall, Giles, 150-1, 194-6, 251
Ransom, John Crowe, 269-70, 287
Ranters, the, chapter 7 *passim*, 120, 134, 142, 147, 151-2, 156, 160, 170-2, 194-6, 198-9, 219, 221, 226, 233, 243, 256, 263, 276, 281, 311, 329-30, 335
Ravis, Christian, 284
Ray, John, 315
Reading, 97
Reay, Barry, 229
Reeve, John, 47, 131, 169, 183, 197, 234, 244, chapter 12 *passim*, 276, 328, 331
Reevonianism, 265
Reformation, the, 14, 19-22, 25-6, 37, 41, 47, 53, 63-5, 68, 76, 103, 107, 126, 133, 236, 271, 302, 304
Restoration of 1660, the, 8, 16, 43-4, 58-9, 91, 132, 174, 224, 234, 253, 286, 313, 334-5
Revolution, the American, 115, 329, 336
Revolution, the English, 12, 19-20, 46, 75, 78, 90, 109, 129, 132, 138, 177-8, 265, 310, chapter 15 *passim*
Revolution, the French, 129, 233, 248, 287, 332, 336
Revolution of 1688, the, 337-8
Revolution, the Industrial, 338
Reyner, William, 275
Rhode Island, 107
Rich, Penelope, Lady, 60, 75
Rich, Robert, Lord, 75
Richelieu, Armand Jean du Plessis de, Cardinal, 32, 177
Rivers, Countess of, 94
Robespierre, Maximilien, 108
Robin Hood Society, the, 109
Robins, John, 171, 281, 331
Robinson, John, 308
Rochester, John Wilmot, Earl of, 16, 131, 262, 333
Rogers, John, of Gloucestershire, 96

Rogers, John, Fifth Monarchist, 272, 283, 295, 327
Rogers, Thomas, 104, 164
Rolfe, John, 29, 279
Roman Empire, Rome, 31-2, 41, 63, 196, 273, 275, 282-3, 328
Root and Branch Petition, the (1640), 79
Rousseau, Jean Jacques, 222, 235
Royal Society, the, 131-2, 134, 285, 287, 334
Royalists, the, 217, 224, 233, 325, 337
Rudyerd, Sir Benjamin, 15, 22, 56
Rumbold, William, 108
Russell, Conrad, 34
Rutherford, Samuel, 150, 163, 166-7, 170, 194-5, 276
Rye, Kent, 92

Sabbath, the, Sabbatarianism, 30, 124 129-30, 192, 212, 291, 314
Sacheverell, Henry, 134, 302, 317
Sadler, John, 201, 295, 299
Saint-Evremond, Charles de, 134
St. George's Hill, Surrey, 95, 100, 185, 203, 221, 227, 230
St. John's College, Cambridge, 132
Salisbury, 97
Salmon, Joseph, 152, 195-7, 239, 261, 326
Saltmarsh, John, 99, 102, 105, 128, 151, 154, 168-9, 176, 178, 181, 195-6, 198-9, 238
Sanderson, William, 42
Sandys, Edwin, Archbishop of York, 53
Sandys, George, 281
Savoy Declaration, the (1658), 6, 286, 312
Saxony, 38
Saye and Sele, Richard Fiennes, Lord, 54
Scargill, Daniel, 132
Scotland, Scots, 20, 30-2, 43, 55, 57, 61, 63, 70, 74, 82, 97-8, 108, 125, 150, 193, 275, 278, 282, 302, 304, 309, 325, 327, 336-7
Second Coming, the, chapter 11 *passim*, 277, 279-80, 292, 303, 326-8
Sectarianism, sects, 5, 7, 21, 43, 74, 78, 90, 101, 132, 134-6, chapter 14 *passim*
Sedbergh, Yorkshire, 96
Sedgwick, John, 150-1, 164, 170

Sedgwick, William, 240, 259, 275, 326-7
Selden, John, 13, 15, 17, 284
Seneca, L. Annaeus, 262
Separatism, separatists, 43, 303, 305, 307-8, 310
Servetus, Michael, 122, 199
Settlement Act (1662), 314
Settlement, Act of, 1701, 59
Sevi, Sabbatai, 281, 287
Shakespeare, William, 45, 322
Sheldon, Gilbert, Archbishop of Canterbury, 59
Shelford, Robert, 271
Shepard, Thomas, 93, 98, 102, 120, 163, 170, 175, 275, 295
Ship Money, 94-5
Shoe Lane, London, 166
Shuter, Christopher, 96
Sibbes, Richard, 125, 143, 195, 274
Simpson, John, 151
Slingsby, Sir Henry, 28, 58
Smith, Adam, 333
Smith, George, 199
Smith, Henry, 28
Smith, John, 182, 261
Smyrna, 281
Smyth, John, 123
Soboul, Albert, 233
Socinianism, Socinianists, 109, 128, 132-3
Societies for the Reformation of Manners, 48, 132
Somerset, 97, 105
Somerset, Edward Seymour, Duke of, Lord Protector, 63, 83
Sonship of all believers, the, 189-90, 203-4, chapter 11 *passim*
South, Robert, 16, 262
Southwick, Wiltshire, 152
Spain, Spaniards, 28, 30-2, 74, 77, 93, 148, 278-9, 283-4, 316, 323, 327, 336-7, 339
Sparke, Michael, 302
Speed, Adolphus, 119
Spelman, Sir Henry, 300
Spinoza, Benedict, 46, 287
Spittlehouse, John, 120, 240, 295
Sports, Books of, (1618 and 1633), 80
Squire, Adam, Master of Balliol College, 159
Stalin, Josef, 262
Stanton-by-Highworth, Wiltshire, 151
Star Chamber, 164, 333

Sterry, Peter, 129, 240, 272, 283
Story-Wilkinson separation, the, 96, 264
Strafford, Sir Thomas Wentworth, Earl of, 138, 174
Strangeways, Sir John, 57
Strasburg, 30, 271
Straw, Jack, 100
Strong, William, 284, 295
Stubbe, Henry, 104
Stubbe, Philip, 29
Suffolk, 164
Surinam, 286
Surrey, 103, 192, 239, 249
Sussex, 91-2
Sweden, 32
Swift, Henry, 315
Swift, Jonathan, 133-4
Switzerland, 31, 126
Sykes, Norman, 315
Sylvester, Joshua, 324
Symonds, Thomas, 170
Syria, 280

Tany, Thomas ("Theaureaujohn"), 257, 275, 281
Taunton, 28
Tawney, R.H., 140, 321
Taylor, Jeremy, later Bishop of Down and Connor, 38-9, 46, 58
Taylor, John, 92, 269
Taylor, Thomas, 15, 18
Tenterden, Kent, 92
"Theaureaujohn", see Tany, Thomas
Thirsk, Joan, 91
Thirty Years War, the, 127, 143, 183, 309
Thomas, William, 11
Thomson, J.A.F., 89
Thorowgood, Thomas, 279-80, 296
Thorpe, William, 99
Thurloe, John, 284, 298
Tidworth, Wiltshire, 160, 182
Tillinghast, John, 272, 283, 293, 295, 326
Tillotson, John, Archbishop of Canterbury, 314, 334
Tithes, 23, 44, 46, 73, 90, 101, 135, 197, 223, 233, 248, 306-7, 311, 314, 321, 334
Toland, John, 161, 234
Tombes, John, 9, 316
Tomkinson, Thomas, 263, 265, 276
Toppe, James, 275

Tories, 47-8, 59, 107, 301, 317
Towne, Robert, 149, 151, 165, 170
Traherne, Thomas, 272, 333
Trapnell, Anna, 326
Trapp, John, 175
Traske, John, 40, 99, 164, 174
Traske, Mrs., wife of the above, 164
Trendall, John, 103
Trevor-Roper, Hugh, 81
Triers, the, 7, 316
Trotsky, Lev, 262
Turkey, Turkish empire, Turks, 148, 168, 271, 273-5, 277, 280-3, 286
Turner, Thomas, 255, 257
Twisse, William, 149, 166
Tyler, Wat, 91, 100
Tyndale, William, 25, 27, 39, 96, 100-1, 303
Tyranipocrit Discovered (1649), 128, 167-8, 181, 195, 200, 231

Udall, John, 79, 280
Ukraine, the, 284, 297
Unitarianism, 134
United Irishmen, 108
Universalism, 106, 128, chapters 9 and 11 *passim*
Usher, R.G., 76, 79-80, 84
Ussher, James, Archbishop of Armagh, 276
U.S.S.R., the, 22, 249, 262

Vane, Sir Henry, 128, 197, 200
Vaughan, Henry, 277
Venice, Venetian ambassador, 94, 105, 280
Venner, Thomas, Venner's rising (1661), 97
Vintners' Company, London, 141
Violet, Thomas, Alderman of London, 330
Virginia, 278
Vox Plebix (1646), 176

W., J., 285
Wales, Welsh borders, 68, 318
Walker, D.P., 333
Wall, Moses, 276, 284
Waller, Edmund, 57
Walsingham, Sir Francis, 68, 71, 73, 306
Walton, Izaak, 12
Walwyn, William, 42, 44, 90-1, 100, 102, 126, 136, 145, 147, 149, 166-9,

176, 178, 180-1, 194, 197, 200, 231, 307, 337

Wariston, Sir Archibald Johnston of, 282, 340

Warner, John, Bishop of Rochester, 57

Warren, Albertus, 179

Warr, John, 196, 231, 249

Warwick, Robert Rich, Earl of, 94

Warwickshire, 97

Washbourne, Thomas, 148, 158

Watts, Michael R., 96-7

Weald, the, 32, 91-3

Webbe, Thomas, 152-3, 195-6

Weber, Max, 321

Webster, John, 96, 333-4

Wellingborough, Northamptonshire, 206

Wentworth, Peter, 66

Wentworth, Sir Thomas, see Strafford, Earl of

Wesley, John, Wesleyanism, 23, 108, 134, 136, 318

West Indies, the, 107, 141, 283-4, 286

Westbrook, — , tailor, 164

Western Design, Cromwell's (1655), 279, 284, 286

Westminster, 196

Westminster Assembly of Divines, the, 6, 149, 155, 166, 276, 311, 313, 325

Whalley, Major-General Edward, 285

Wharton, Goodwin, 201, 342

Wheelwright, John, 130, 171-2, 274

Whigs, 16, 107-8, 201, 341-2

Whiston, William, 280

Whitby, Synod of, 19

White, Helen, 12

White, Thomas, 98

Whitelocke, Bulstrode, 141-2

Whitfield, Henry, 280

Whitgift, John, Archbishop of Canterbury, 11, 31, 41-2, 54, chapter 6 *passim*, 120, 303-4, 311

Wickham Market, Suffolk, 164

Wigginton, Giles, 96

Wightman, Edward, 103-4

Wildman, John, 135, 140, 174, 252

Wilkins, John, later Bishop of Chester, 46, 315

Willet, Andrew, 272

William III, King of England, 59, 108, 323

Williams, Daniel, 154, 161

Williams, Griffith, Bishop of Ossory, 284

Williams, John, Bishop of Lincoln and Archbishop of York, 81

Williams, Roger, 183, 284, 307

Williamson, Joseph, 316

Wilson, Rowland, 141-2

Wilson, Sir Thomas, 38

Wiltshire, 97, 103, 105, 141-2, 151-3, 156, 160, 166, 176, 182

Winslow, Edward, 179, 184

Winstanley, Gerrard, 16, 44-5, 90-1, 95, 102, 105, 108, 119-20, 128, 153-4, 156, 163, 174, 183, chapter 11 *passim*, 255, 261, 277, 307, 312, 323, 328-31, 338-9

Winthrop, John, 86, 125, 163, 168, 170-2, 175, 324, 328

Wisbech, 103

Witchcraft, witches, 93, 98, 333

Wither, George, 29, 92, 195-6, 200, 285, 298

Woodchurch, Kent, 92

Women, 118, 235, 322. See also Divorce, Marriage, Polygamy

Women preachers, 101, 197

Worcester Association, the, 130

Worcester Battle of (1651), 223

Worcestershire, 100, 108

Wrighter, Clement, 46, 104-5, 198, 211, 330

Wyatt, Sir Thomas, 11, 92

Wyclif, John, Wycliffites, 73, 91, 101, 104, 271

Yarmouth, 7

Yelverton, Sir Henry, 294

York House Conference (1626), 80

Yorkshire, 96, 98, 102, 106, 149, 165, 168, 194, 270, 315

Zakai, Avihu, 71

Ziff, Larzer, 177

Zohar, the, 281

Zürich, 30

Zwingli, Ulrich, 30